THE
LIGHT
of ASIA

THE
LIGHT
of ASIA

the

poem that defined

THE BUDDHA

JAIRAM RAMESH

PENGUIN

VIKING

An imprint of Penguin Random House

VIKING

USA | Canada | UK | Ireland | Australia
New Zealand | India | South Africa | China

Viking is part of the Penguin Random House group of companies
whose addresses can be found at global.penguinrandomhouse.com

Published by Penguin Random House India Pvt. Ltd
4th Floor, Capital Tower 1, MG Road,
Gurugram 122 002, Haryana, India

Penguin
Random House
India

First published in Viking by Penguin Random House India 2021

10 9 8 7 6 5 4 3

ISBN 9780670094837

Typeset in Adobe Caslon Pro by Manipal Technologies Limited, Manipal
Printed at Thomson Press India Ltd, New Delhi

www.penguin.co.in

This is for Aniruddha, a poetry buff who kept me company during the Covid-19 lockdown

Contents

TO MY BIOGRAPHER

TRACE me through my snow,
Track me through my mire,
You shall never know
Half that you desire!

Praise me, or asperse,
Deck me or deride,
In my veil of verse
Safe from you I hide.

—Sir Edwin Arnold, author of *The Light of Asia*,
writing in 1893; the photograph is from the same year.

Foreword

I understand that the poem The Light of Asia by Sir Edwin Arnold on the life and teachings of Buddha, contributed greatly to the international community's knowledge of Lord Buddha and his philosophy when it was first published in the late 19th century. It is also encouraging to learn that the poem played an important role in India's cultural awakening and in its social transformation in the twentieth century.

The international fascination about the Buddha and his teachings continue to this day. A clear example of this is the very keen interest shown by the scientific community to the Buddhist perspective that I have witnessed in my more than three decades of dialogue with scientists. I understand that Sir Edwin has spoken about the close intellectual bond between Buddhism and science in his public talks.

Given this situation, this book by former Union Minister and policy analyst Jairam Ramesh throws light on the impact of Sir Edwin Arnold's book on Indian society will be particularly welcomed. Whether or not the poem was a faithful rendering of the Buddha and his philosophy, it seems to have, as mentioned by the author. Struck a chord in the lives of prominent Indian leaders like Mahatma Gandhi, Jawaharlal Nehru and Babasaheb Ambedkar.

It is also interesting to note than Sir Edwin played a role in the international attention to the sacred Buddhist site of Bodh Gaya.

I believe, what Sir Edwin's poems showed was that the message of the Buddha is timeless, eternal and relevant. I am sure the readers will find this reflected in Mr. Ramesh's book, too.

His Holiness The Dalai Lama
3 October 2020

Note on Names of Places

I have retained the names of places as they were used during Sir Edwin Arnold's time.

Name in Book	*Present Name*
Poona	Pune
Bombay	Mumbai
Calcutta	Kolkata
Madras	Chennai
Simla	Shimla
Baroda	Vadodara
Cawnpore	Kanpur
Pondicherry	Puducherry
Bangalore	Bengaluru
Mysore	Mysuru
Mahabalipuram	Mamallapuram
Burma	Myanmar
Rangoon	Yangon
Ceylon	Sri Lanka
Siam	Thailand
Persia	Iran

Sir Edwin Arnold used Buddha-Gya. Others like Dharmapala used Buddha Gaya and some adopted Buddha-Gaya. I have retained these names depending on who used them. All of these names refer to the present Bodh Gaya.

Arnold keeps referring to the 'Mutiny of 1857' although it is now considered as India's First War of Independence. It has also been called a 'Sepoy Revolt', a 'Sepoy Uprising' and the 'Great Indian Rebellion. I have retained Arnold's phraseology.

A First Word

I

This biography is of an epic poem written in blank verse[1] and first published in London in July 1879.

On its release, it immediately took England by storm, and soon thereafter America and Europe too were stirred by it. The epidemic of exuberance for it would spread to other parts of the world and last a few decades.

The book captivated an Indian monk who remains an iconic personality—Swami Vivekananda. At about the same time, it deeply moved a young man in Colombo who has become famous in history as Anagarika Dharmapala. It caught the attention of an aspiring Indian lawyer in London in 1889. This man later became immortal as Mahatma Gandhi. A few years hence it impacted a teenager in Allahabad who would, in 1947, become the first Prime Minister of India—Jawaharlal Nehru. Two copies of the book adorned the bookshelves of B.R. Ambedkar, the prime architect of the Indian constitution. It informed the work of men who were active in the movement for social justice, especially in south India in the early part of the twentieth century.

The book had a marked influence on at least eleven literary personalities from across the world. Five of them were Nobel Laureates: Rudyard Kipling in 1907, Rabindranath Tagore in 1913, W.B. Yeats in 1923, Ivan Bunin in 1933 and T.S. Eliot in 1948. The other six are legendary figures: Herman Melville, Leo Tolstoy, Lafcadio Hearn, D.H. Lawrence, John Masefield and Jose Luis

Borges. It opened new frontiers for Joseph Campbell later to become one of the world's leading authorities on comparative mythology.

The world of science and industry was not immune to its reach either. At the turn of the nineteenth century, it shaped the life of a young science student in Madras who would, in 1930, become India's first Nobel Laureate in Physics—C.V. Raman. The Russian chemist and inventor of the periodic table Dmitri Mendeleev and the Scottish-American industrialist-philanthropist Andrew Carnegie had a special affinity to it. An extremely controversial figure of the British military but a hero during his time—Herbert Kitchener—would carry this book along with him wherever he went.[2] It figures prominently in the private library of Alfred Nobel, the Swedish businessman who later endowed the Nobel Prizes.

In 1925, it was to serve as the basis for one of India's first silent films, made by a German-Indian team. This was released internationally to some acclaim. In 1945 it figured in a Hollywood classic, *The Picture of Dorian Gray*. In 1957, a very ill Raymond Chandler, the British-American detective storywriter, received a letter from his long-time secretary advising him to take solace in reading this book.

The book was translated into thirteen European, eight North and South East Asian and fourteen South Asian languages. A number of plays, dance dramas and operas were adapted from it in different countries. In the last fifty years, it has continued to evoke academic interest and has become the subject of doctoral dissertations and scholarly publications in the UK, Canada, USA and Germany. The most recent of these came out in February 2020 and dealt with its influence on James Joyce.

The book is *The Light of Asia*, a narrative of the life and message of the Buddha. Sir Edwin Arnold is its author. Its publication was a milestone in the nineteenth century rediscovery of the Buddha. It occupies an important place in the historiography of modern Buddhism.

I set out to understand how and why the book came to be written, and how and why its influence grew in country after country but more particularly in the sub-continent which gave rise to the Buddha over two and half millennia ago.

II

I first read *The Light of Asia* in my mid-teens. It has remained with me for over half a century. Two recent events rekindled my memories of the poem and its author.

First, while going through the correspondence of Jawaharlal Nehru, I discovered a letter to him dated 21 February 1955 from his British counterpart. Winston Churchill wrote:

> *I hope you will think of the phrase 'The Light of Asia'.* It seems to me that you might be able to do what no other human being could in giving India the lead, at least in the realm of thought, throughout Asia, with the freedom and dignity of the individual as the ideal rather than the Communist Party drill book. (italics mine)

Churchill was writing to a man imprisoned by the British in nine different spells between 1921 and 1945 for a total of almost ten years. The longest period Nehru spent in jail was between August 1942 and June 1945 when Churchill was prime minister. That is what makes this letter quite remarkable. But this was not all. Four months later, on 30 June 1955, Churchill again to wrote to Nehru:

> I hope you will forgive the lapse of time in replying to your letter of April 8. Events following upon my resignation, and the General Election here, have delayed my correspondence greatly.
>
> I was much touched by what you said. One of the most agreeable memories of my last years in office is our association. At our conferences [of Commonwealth Premiers] your contribution was a leading and constructive one, and I always admired your ardent wish for peace and the absence of bitterness in your consideration of the antagonisms that had in the past divided us. Yours is indeed a heavy burden and responsibility, shaping the

destiny of your many millions of countrymen and playing your outstanding part in world affairs. I wish you well in your task. *Remember 'The Light of Asia!'* (italics mine)

Only two bibliophilic prime ministers could have had a correspondence in the last decade of their lives recalling a book both had read when they were young. In fact, when Nehru was undergoing the second round of his imprisonment by the British in Lucknow jail, he wrote to his father on 13 July 1922:[3]

I have received your kind letter . . . You need not worry at all about my health. I am looking after it carefully . . . I have received the books sent by you. I have now got the following:

1. Memoirs of Babar
2. Sarkar's Shivaji
3. Bernier's Travels
4. Vincent Smith's Akbar
5. Manucci's Storia do Mogor—4 vols
6. Bryce's Holy Roman Empire
7. Poems of Keats
8. Poems of Shelley
9. Tennyson's Idylls of the King
10. Arnold's Light of Asia
11. Havell's Aryan Rule in India (this came separately)
12. Pater's Renaissance (received yesterday)

I had asked for many other books which are in Anand Bhavan [the Nehru family residence in Allahabad] . . .

And when his daughter was convalescing from pleurisy in Leysin in Switzerland, Nehru would on 22 February 1940 send 'Arnold's two little books: *The Light of Asia* and *The Song Celestial*' to keep her company.

Second, contemporary Indian politics has been impacted hugely by the dispute over the birthplace of Lord Rama the mythological hero of the epic *Ramayana*. For over four and a half centuries, a mosque stood at the site purported to be his birthplace in the town of Ayodhya. That mosque was demolished by rampaging mobs on 6 December 1992. After a protracted legal battle, Hindu organisations got possession of the site in November 2019. A temple is now under construction there.

Between 1886 and 1953, there was a somewhat similar dispute over the ownership of a temple at Bodh Gaya where Siddhartha Gautama received enlightenment and became the Buddha. With his visit to this holy site in 1886, Sir Edwin Arnold lit the spark for a long battle between a Hindu sect that had been in control of the temple since the seventeenth century and the Sri Lankan monk Anagarika Dharmapala, the founder of the Mahabodhi Society. With Sir Edwin's backing, Dharmapala launched the struggle to recover Buddhist control over Bodh Gaya from Hindu ownership. The dispute was finally resolved only in 1953—but peacefully.

Edwin Arnold was a quintessential Victorian in every way. A remarkable polyglot, he was conversant in Greek, Latin, Arabic, Turkish, French, German, Japanese, Hebrew, Persian, Sanskrit and Marathi. For about forty years he was a leader writer for London's newspaper the *Daily Telegraph*. He was a firm believer in the civilizing mission of the British Empire, but he was also at the same time an ardent Indophile. He spent two-and-a-half years in India between late-1857 and mid-1860 as the first Principal of what became the famed Deccan College in Poona. His views on education for the 'natives' were progressive by the standards of those times. He returned to India and Ceylon for a hundred days in late 1885 and left a vivid account of this trip which even today makes for riveting reading. He wrote a large number of books which were mostly translations of Persian, Arabic and Sanskrit classics.

Sir Edwin was fascinated with Hinduism, Buddhism and Islam, although he also wrote *The Light of the World*—a panegyric to Jesus Christ. His translation of the Bhagavad Gita called *The Song Celestial* first introduced Mahatma Gandhi to this classic who would keep referring to it in his correspondence till the end of his life. None of Arnold's works, however, attained the fame and longevity of *The Light of Asia*. Gandhi and Arnold were both active in London's Vegetarian Society and the two seemed to have grown fond of each other.

But for all his many-sided accomplishments Arnold has attracted only one serious biographer so far, and that was way back in 1957. I, therefore, set out to throw fresh light on who Sir Edwin Arnold was, how his life unfolded, how his relationship with India evolved and why he came to write *The Light of Asia*, which proved to be a work of such seminal importance, an enduring milestone in the world's rediscovery of an ancient philosophy and faith.

There was, to be sure, more to Edwin Arnold than his India connection. He was, for instance, an important player in Henry Morton Stanley's first Congo expedition during 1874–76 and even had a mountain and a river named after him there. He was the first to advocate a 'Cape to Cairo' rail link that epitomized British colonial interests in Africa. From 1890 his life centred mostly on Japan and his third wife was Japanese, who outlived him by almost six decades in London. In the annals of British engagement with Japan, his was an extremely influential voice. Queen Victoria was very fond of him and had she had her way he would have become Britain's Poet Laureate in 1892 at the death of Lord Tennyson.

Sir Edwin Arnold had four sons. One tried to become a coffee planter in Ceylon, but having failed, became a science fiction writer. Another explored the Yucatan in Mexico, wrote about that excavation and then worked as an editor in Burma, where he took on the British establishment. Subsequently, he moved to India, became a tutor to the Bhopal royal family and wrote two well-regarded books himself on the Hindu epics—the *Ramayana* and the *Mahabharata*. My story ends with the discovery of Edwin Arnold's great grandchildren, who live in India, Thailand, England and Australia.

Notes

1. Blank verse has been defined as 'poetry written with regular metrical but unrhymed lines'. Most English poetry since the sixteenth century is in blank verse.
2. Kitchener was the first to introduce concentration camps during the Boer war in South Africa at the beginning of the twentieth century.
3. *Selected Works of Jawaharlal Nehru*, First Series, Volume 1, S. Gopal (General Editor), Jawaharlal Nehru Memorial Fund, B.R. Publishing Corporation, New Delhi, 1972

SECTION I

1

1832–1857: The Pre-Poona Edwin Arnold

Arnold came from the landed gentry that had had no earlier links with India. He was born on 24 June 1832 in Gravesend, an ancient town some 45 kms from London.[1] In the nineteenth century, Arnold's grandfather and brother had both been mayors, the brother for quite some time. Today, Sikhs constitute about 20 percent of the town's population of around 75,000 and since 1997 there have been three Sikh mayors. Inevitably, the town, which is in Kent county, has an impressive gurdwara. The town has another Indian connection—but American Indian. It has a statue of Pocahontas, the Native American princess who married an English settler and died in Gravesend in 1617.

After five years in a school founded by King Henry VIII in the early sixteenth century at Rochester, Arnold spent a year at King's College in London. Arnold's closest friend there was the Bombay-born Frederic William Farrar. Farrar would later write *The Life of Christ*, which was one of the publishing sensations of 1874, like *The Light of Asia* would be five years later. Farrar wanted Arnold, then the editor of the *Daily Telegraph*, to review his book. But Arnold declined do so in a letter on 2 July 1874 that shed light on his religious thinking just before he wrote *The Light of Asia*.[2]

> . . . I can only say that if I am to state my reasons for believing that Christianity must disappear as all faiths—qua faiths—have disappeared and are disappearing, it must be against some champion whose lofty and noble purpose does not constantly disarm my convictions. It would take a long conversation to justify this feeling and to tell you how thoroughly I share your faith in

the divine humanity of Christ—while I look for many and many
Christs to be.

A few years later, when he was Dean of Canterbury, Farrar was to
write of his friend's best-known work:

> Buddhism, as it appears not in "The Light of Asia", but in the
> original "Life of Gautama", is but a philosophy of despair, which
> knows no immortality, no conscience and no God.

After King's College, Arnold attended Oxford University, where he
studied the classics. By a coincidence, he occupied the same room
at University College that were once the abode of the legendary
Percy Bysshe Shelley in the first decade of the nineteenth century.
Arnold was not a brilliant student but exhibited his poetic prowess
by winning the coveted Newdigate Prize. This award was founded
in 1806 for the best poetic composition by an Oxford undergraduate.
In 1839 it was won on a third attempt by John Ruskin, whose book
Unto This Last had a profound influence on Mahatma Gandhi.

One entry for the 1839 Newdigate should be of particular
interest. It was called *Salsette and Elephanta* and was written by
Arthur Henry Clough. The poem itself, consisting of '264 lines cast
in heroic couplets and divided into twenty-six stanzas', was made
public only in 1967 and was subject to scholarly analysis two years
later.[3] Clough was considered as one of the finest young minds of the
early Victorian era but never lived up to his promise. However, he
figures prominently in intellectual histories of that age that continue
to pour out.

The Elephanta island off the west coast of Bombay is now world-
famous for its magnificent Shiva temple, or what Clough referred
to as a 'Temple of the God Seeva'. The Temple at Salsette island
dedicated to the Buddha is relatively lesser known but is equally
grand. However, unlike what Clough portrayed in verse, Hindu and
Buddhist monuments cohabit in both places. Clough made use of
six books for writing his poem, only one of which could be classified

as a scholarly work. This was Friedrich von Schlegel's *Essai sur La Langue et La Philosophie des Indiens* that was translated from the original German into French in 1837. Schlegel is considered one of the pioneers of German Indology.

I bring Clough into this narrative since he represents an early generation of Victorians that was becoming aware of the Buddha and his philosophy. Arnold, of course, would take the Buddha to new heights of public glory but that was still four decades away. Five years after failing to win the Newdigate Prize, Clough, now on a fellowship at Oriel College at Oxford, began to express the most extreme form of religious doubt, the last person from whom this was expected. In 2013, Simon Heffer in his masterly *High Minds: The Victorians and the Birth of Modern Britain* drew attention to Clough's apostasy thus:[4]

> He doubted the power of the Deity; he doubted the special force of Christianity: 'Is Xianity really so much better than Mahometanism, Buddhism . . . or the old Heathen philosophy?' he asked Hawkins, the Provost of Oriel . . .

In 1843, the Newdigate Prize was won by Matthew Arnold for his poem on Oliver Cromwell. Matthew Arnold was a close friend of Clough but no relation of Edwin Arnold. Matthew Arnold too would become a religious doubter and go on to have a great literary career as a poet, critic and commentator.[5] People like Arnold (Matthew, that is) and Clough made the environment ripe for the type of reception *The Light of Asia* was to receive years later.

Edwin Arnold won the Newdigate Prize in 1852 for his *The Feast of Belshazzar*, which was recited at Oxford's Sheldonian Theatre on 23 June that year. Edward Smith-Stanley, the fourteenth Earl of Darby, had just taken over as prime minister but more importantly perhaps was being installed as Chancellor of Oxford that day when Arnold was in full flow. Darby, by all accounts, was very impressed, as was his Cabinet colleague and a future prime minister himself who was in the audience—Benjamin Disraeli.

Arnold's Newdigate Prize poem itself is taken from the fifth chapter of the *Book of Daniel*, a second century BCE 'biblical apocalypse'. Daniel, a learned Jew exiled to Babylon, was called in by King Belshazzar to read something that was showing up on the wall while a raucous feast was going on. Daniel interpreted it as the hand of God warning Belshazzar that his days were numbered for his blasphemy in drinking from the vessels looted by his father after sacking the Jewish Temple in Jerusalem. The father Nebuchadnezzar subsequently was contrite and developed humility, unlike his arrogant son. Daniel interpreted God's writing as a message to Belshazzar, that the Babylonian king would soon be destroyed by the Persians. The feast has been the subject of many paintings, of which Rembrandt's in 1635 is the most famous. The feast is also the origin of the phrase 'read the writing on the wall'.

The Newdigate Prize is still awarded today. From the point of view of this book there are two other points of interest relating to it—one direct and the other little less so.

First, in 1887 the topic for the contest was itself the Buddha—a remarkable testimony to the impact that *The Light of Asia* had had. The prize went to Sidney Arthur Alexander for his *The Legend of Sakya Muni*. Sakyamuni is, of course, another name of the Buddha. Alexander acknowledged his debt to Arnold and went to become a noted theological writer and poet. For many years he was canon and treasurer of St. Paul's Cathedral and played a crucial role in its preservation. He passed away in 1948.

Second, in 1831 the subject for the Newdigate Prize was announced as 'The Suttee'. One undergraduate, who would go on to become the Liberal Prime Minister of the United Kingdom four times and whose foreign and colonial policies would be attacked strongly by Arnold, had prepared a draft poem for submission. He may not, however, have actually submitted it. This draft was discovered in the papers of William Ewart Gladstone in the early 1970s by the historian Sarvepalli Gopal.[6] The poem is of interest to this book only because Gladstone's views on 'suttee' coincided with those of Arnold—opposed to each other mostly, the two found common cause in virtually glorifying suttee while accepting the fact that it had been declared illegal in 1829 by the British Governor-General in India, Lord William Bentinck. I will have more to say of Arnold's views on suttee later.

Arnold's very first anthology, *Poems: Narrative and Lyrical*, was published just a year after he had won the Newdigate Prize. It dealt with a variety of themes and included *The Feast of Belshazzar*. It evoked mixed reviews, but the important point was that it got noticed. He took a master's degree from Oxford, got married, had a son and taught in a grammar school in Birmingham which still exists. In 1856, his second collection, *Griselda: A Tragedy and Other Poems*, materialised. But this fell flat and was all but ignored though it contained one particular poem in praise of a lady who was then the rage of England. The poem would, however, get noticed many years later.

In October 1895, while opening the St Thomas' Medical School in London, Arnold declared that 'India will absorb any amount of feminine ability and courage' and appealed to the men assembled at the opening to 'encourage and help women who studied medicine to fit them for a field of work in India which native prejudices debarred male doctors from entering'. He 'recalled from unprinted oblivion' verses of his own dedicated to Florence Nightingale and written at the time of the Crimean War in late 1854. At that time, Edwin Arnold was an unknown and Florence Nightingale was well on her way to becoming a legend. This is perhaps the only explanation for why this poem never got any attention—there were many other bigger names euphoric about her. But by 1885, Arnold's public standing was at its peak and he may have thought it the right moment to reveal a youthful undertaking. From 1860 onwards, for almost thirty years, Florence Nightingale was to concern herself passionately with public health and sanitation in India. For his part, Arnold would be a great champion of the nursing profession and for greatly expanding the community of nurses in India.

It was sometime in early 1857 that the India Office in London made Arnold a firm offer of the principalship of the Poona

College. This institution had been created in June 1851 by bringing together the existing Sanskrit College and the English School, both established and run by the Bombay Presidency. The Poona College was modelled along the lines of the famed Elphinstone College in Bombay that had been functioning since 1836. In 1868, the Poona College would take on the name by which it was to become famous in Indian educational history—Deccan College.

A history of the Deccan College has this to say about the motivation of the British to create the Poona College:[7]

> . . . The change of name from Poona Sanskrit College to Poona College was significant. It was no longer a Hindu Institution, specifically meant for Brahmins and the study of Sanskrit.

This was a profound change. Other than the three languages (English, Marathi and Sanskrit), the Poona College imparted instruction in law, literature, logic, mathematics and the natural sciences.

How did a twenty-five-year-old Oxford graduate teaching English in the ancient King Edward VI School in Birmingham manage to get this position in Poona? Like many positions in India then, this may well have been secured through some influence.[8] The man who pulled strings in the India Office in London on behalf of Arnold was his wife's brother-in-law General John Lester, about whom, alas, nothing much else is known other than that he had been in the army in Bombay.[9] That he was somebody important to Arnold is further evidenced by the fact that Arnold's eldest son born on 14 May 1857 in England was named Edwin Lester Linden Arnold. This Edwin Lester would soon travel with his parents to Poona.

The only archival material relating to Arnold's appointment that I have been able to locate is a report prepared by Edward Irvine Howard, the Director of Public Instruction, Poona on 9 September 1858 and sent to W. Hart, Secretary to Government, General Department in Bombay, in which it is written:

Sir:-I have the honour to forward, for the information of the Right Honorable the Governor Council, the report of the examiners for senior scholarships in the Elphinstone and Poona colleges . . .

In May 1857, Mr. V. Green, of Merton College, Oxford, was appointed, on my recommendation, to act for Mr. Draper, the professor of English literature in the Poona College, who had gone to Europe on sick leave; and in December 1857, Mr. Edwin Arnold, M.A., formerly a master in the Birmingham Grammar School, was, on my recommendation, appointed Principal of the Poona College. The remarkable improvement already effected in all the departments of that institution speaks much for the vigour of Mr. Arnold's management, and the cordial co-operation of his colleagues, Mr. Green and Mr. McDougall . . .

It is entirely possible that the Oxford connection helped Arnold, for Howard too was an alumnus of that university. Arnold had definitely applied for the job and it had taken some nine months to come through.

In December 1857, while the Indian Mutiny was still on, the Arnolds would set up house in Poona. The Mutiny that had started seven months earlier from Meerut had already impacted Edwin Arnold deeply. His close friend from school days Frederick Cairns Hubbard, who was teaching at the Agra College, had been killed five months earlier. That Hubbard meant much to Arnold is obvious from a poem that the latter wrote in Birmingham in 1855 when Hubbard was working in a missionary school in Calicut. Thirty-three years later, now a celebrity in London, Arnold added the following lines to his 1855 composition to his buddy:

Ah, lightly writ was that loving verse
  In the old time Fred!
That page was a leaf I let fall on thy hearse
  A flower to the Dead!
By Jumna, thou sleepest, forgotten of men . . .

Hubbard came from a family of missionaries. His mother also perished in Agra. One of his brothers, Alfred Roots Hubbard, was killed in Delhi on the very first day of the mutiny. A third survived because he had yet to embark on his voyage to India. In December 1858, Arnold would name his second born Harold Cairns in memory of his closest friend.[10]

Arnold's heartfelt ode to his childhood friend was contained in his *Poems: Some National and Non-Oriental* that would be published in 1888. This volume also contains a full-throated ode to General Henry Havelock, who recaptured Cawnpore and led the first relief campaign for the recapture of the Lucknow Residency. Havelock finally succumbed to dysentery in Lucknow in November 1857, a few days before the Arnold family reached Poona. Arnold's encomium is called *Havelock in Trafalgar Square* and must have been written when his statue was unveiled in the heart of London in 1861. It still stands.

But in all fairness to Arnold, I must also say that while he penned *Havelock in Trafalgar Square,* he would extoll a British bête noire of 1857. He wrote the preface to *The Rani of Jhansi* or *The Widowed Queen: A Play* by Alexander Rogers that was published in early 1895. Rogers was both a scholar and a civil servant in India. Arnold applauded the martyred queen who is still recalled and eulogized in India thus:

> I have read with a pleasure and interest, which I think many will share, this striking presentment of a famous episode of the great Indian Mutiny, in the form of an English drama . . . Its heroine is the most remarkable and great-hearted woman, the Rani of Jhansi, who in the time of the Mutiny played the part of an Indian Boadicea. Mahratta by birth and of the royal and warlike line of Sivaji, she was every inch a Queen; but having a real or fancied complaint against the British Raj on account of her deceased husband's debts, which we compelled her to pay from her palace allowances, the high-spirited lady flung her angry heart and passionate nature into the scale against us . . . I too was in

India in those troubled days . . . and I have often heard Sir Hugh Rose—in later days known as Lord Strathnairn—talk about the brave and beautiful Princess who gave his column so much hard work through those fierce and fiery battles in the north-west . . . The massacre of Europeans, which the proud Princess of Jhansi allowed—nay! I am afraid I must say commanded—at her capital city in the Jokan Bagh stains unhappily with indelible shame a name otherwise illustrious; but the author has shown, with true art, how irresistible were the emotions that swayed her, and how bitter was the conflict of passions on both sides . . .

Sometime in the first few days of December 1857, Edwin Arnold, his wife and infant son reached Poona. The Mutiny had not been quelled completely. The recapture of Lucknow was to take place only on 16 March 1858 and Jhansi would be taken by the British eighteen days later. The Proclamation by Queen Victoria announcing that the Crown was now assuming complete authority over India was to be made on 1 November 1858. Poona itself was not in ferment either in 1857 or 1858. The only indirect connection it had with the uprising was that Nana Saheb, one of its most heroic figures, was the adopted son of the exiled Peshwa Baji Rao II. It was the defeat of Baji Rao II at the Battle of Khadki on 5 November 1817 that firmly established British hegemony in that part of western India. The defeat also triggered a chain of events resulting, among other things, in the creation of the Poona Sanskrit College in 1821, the third college to be started in India in the colonial era after Presidency College in Calcutta (1817) and Serampore College by the Danes a year later.

The man responsible for establishing the Poona College was Mountstuart Elphinstone, widely considered among the more enlightened British administrators in India. Elphinstone was first Commissioner of the Deccan and later Lieutenant Governor of the Bombay Presidency. Arnold and he would never meet but Elphinstone's nephew John Elphinstone, who would also be Lieutenant Governor, would be impressed with what Arnold would accomplish in Poona and compliment him publicly.

Notes

1. 1832 was a watershed year in nineteenth-century British history, the year of the Reform Bill that doubled the size of the electorate from 6 per cent to 12 per cent.
2. Farrar (1904)
3. Greenberger (1969)
4. Heffer (2013)
5. In 1853, Matthew Arnold would write an epic poem *Sohrab and Rustum*, drawn from Persian literature—his only foray into 'Oriental' themes. His most famous work was *Culture and Anarchy*, a collection of essays published a decade before *The Light of Asia*. His poem *Dover Beach* that expresses 'a crisis of faith in face of a rising tide of scientific discovery' has been much studied. Jawaharlal Nehru would use the final lines from it while writing to his daughter from Dehra Dun jail on 9 August 1933:

   > For the world which seems
   > To lie before us, a land of dreams,
   > So various, so beautiful, so new,
   > Hath really neither joy, nor love, nor light,
   > Nor certitude, nor peace, nor help for pain;
   > And we are here, as on a darkling plain
   > Swept with confused alarms of struggle and flight,
   > Where ignorant armies clash by night.

6. Raghavan (2013)
7. Sharma, Dhongde and Mate (1990)
8. Wright (1957)
9. The General's son J.F.G. Lester was Acting Superintendent of Police at Godra, then in the Bombay Presidency and now in Gujarat, when he was fatally shot by his wife in July 1895. Mrs Lester's defence was that her husband was brutal to her. Godra (later designated Godhra) would, in February 2002, become (in)famous in Indian history as the place where railway coaches were set on fire, which would then trigger horrendous communal riots in many parts of Gujarat.
10. In his *India Revisited* that would be published in 1886, Arnold would write of his friendship with Hubbard and how the two of them had made plans for Hubbard to join Deccan College after Arnold had taken over there. He also wrote of visiting the Agra Cemetery where Hubbard had been buried. Sadly, that cemetery no longer exists.

2

1857–1860: Edwin Arnold in Poona

Arnold took over from Thomas Candy as the second Principal of the Poona College on 7 December 1857. Candy had been educated at Oxford in Indian languages and was working as a translator in the East India Company. He had come out to India in 1822 to join the army but given his literary bent of mind switched occupations and became an educational officer. Along with his twin brother George, he helped James Molesworth compile the first Marathi–English dictionary that was published in 1831. George Candy became a missionary and returned to England but Thomas Candy stayed back and continued to make major contributions, first by bringing out a Marathi–English dictionary, then an English–Marathi one and finally seven textbooks for schools that were to be used for another half a century. His contribution to the 'lexicography, orthography and stylistics' of the Marathi language is invaluable. He died in Mahabaleshwar, a hill station near Poona, in 1877.

Arnold was succeeding a man who was fluent in the local language and who was a legend of sorts for the local population. But clearly his own linguistic skills were of an extraordinary order, for within a short time Arnold not only became conversant in Marathi but also acquired knowledge of Sanskrit. From Arnold's later accounts,[1] it is evident that the man most responsible for educating him in both languages was Krishna Shastri Chiplunkar. Chiplunkar, who would have been thirty-three when he first met Arnold, was a versatile scholar who had educated himself very well in English as well. A social activist and author, he has become famous as the father of Vishnu Shastri Chiplunkar, who is widely acknowledged to be the 'poet of Maharashtra's nationalist revival' with focus on

Vishnu Shastri Chiplunkar, whose father tutored Arnold in
Sanskrit and Marathi in Poona during 1858 and 1859.
Bal Gangadhar Tilak was one of the protégés of the younger
Chiplunkar. (Source: Wikipedia)

the preservation of Hindu traditions. But he is also reputed to have
stated that 'the roots of our language lay as much in Persian and
Arabic as in Sanskrit'.

Vishnu Shastri Chiplunkar was more of a radical in this regard
than his father, who, while critical of missionary activity, did not
challenge British rule. Vishnu Shastri Chiplunkar mentored a
young Bal Gangadhar Tilak, who would later emerge as a stalwart
of India's freedom movement.[2] Another of his colleagues who
Arnold would remember fondly was somebody he referred to as
just 'Kero Punt'. This must surely have been Kerupant Lakshman
Chattre, who taught mathematics at the Poona College and from
whom Tilak too learnt mathematics and astronomy. To Arnold,
Chiplunkar and Chattre had 'minds as receptive as could be found
in Oxford or Cambridge'.

Arnold would also later[3] reminisce that:

Among my students, too, were brilliant young men, who might have distinguished themselves in the front rank of our universities. I especially recall three Parsee brothers, the Pudumjis, all of whom—Dorabji, Sorabji and Nowroji—have since become leading men in the Presidency. There was also my own especial favourite among the Brahmans, Baba Gokhale, who died too young for his great capacities to bear fruit. In conducting the studies of such peoples I learned more than I could teach . . .

Baba Gokhale was one of the early learners of English in Poona and ran a private school that was giving the missionary schools a run for their money. Gokhale had a fine reputation and Bal Gangadhar Tilak had attended his school for some time. The 'Pudumji brothers' were the sons of Khan Bahadur Pudumjee Pestonjee, who was a mail contractor in the Bombay Presidency and the Deccan when the railways and telegraph were unknown. He had been rewarded by the British for his services to them during the 1857 Mutiny. The sons were amongst India's earliest entrepreneurs, launching a paper mill, a cotton mill, an ice factory and a bank. The paper manufacturing facility still exists, although under a different management. The Pudumjees were also great philanthropists and their name is associated with a number of public facilities in Poona that are still very visible.

While Arnold was in Poona, the social reform movement of Jyotirao Phule that stressed education for children belonging to non-Brahmin communities was already under way. Phule had started such schools and in September 1853 had placed them under the control of the 'Society for Promoting the Education of Mahars and Mangs'. These schools faced much opposition from the conservative Brahmin community of Poona but found generous support from the Britishers themselves. Arnold would certainly have known about Phule's pioneering venture but the only written evidence of their contact that I have been able to gather on this is the following:[4]

The public examination of the Mahar and Mang schools was held at Babuji Munagee's Coal Factory opposite the Queen's Hostel near the City Hospital on Tuesday, the 2ⁿᵈ February 1858, in the evening at half past four. A large number of European and Indian gentlemen assembled. C.M. Harrison, judge of Poona, presided. Among the gentlemen assembled were Edwin Arnold, Principal of Poona College, Mrs Arnold . . . and other officials.

It is unclear from this account whether Arnold met Phule on that occasion or not. Even so, he must have definitely been aware of the Mahar and Mang schools to which both Chiplunkar and Chattre made monthly contributions—niggardly though, in the estimation of Phule's biographer.[5] Phule was, however, well known to Arnold's predecessor and he believed that the Poona College was an institution that churned out Brahmin teachers who gave secret advice to the non-Brahmin castes not to send their children to school.[6]

In addition to Chiplunkar, Arnold learned Sanskrit from a German scholar Martin Haug from Leipzig, who had joined the Poona College in 1859. Haug, who is considered as one of the founders of Iranian studies and an expert on Zoroastrian philosophy and doctrines, died young in 1876. He was a great influence on one of his students R.G. Bhandarkar, who became one of India's greatest Sanskrit scholars. The Bhandarkar Oriental Research Institute in Poona is named in his honour.

There is nothing in the written records to indicate that Arnold visited Buddhist monuments around Poona. But he would write about them three decades later in his *India Revisited*. By the time he first came to the city in December 1858, Ajanta and Ellora had been rediscovered but they were over 300 km away. Salsette had been written about in 1839 by Arthur Clough at Oxford but this too, by the standards of those times, was at quite a distance. But within a radius of 60 km were the rock-cut caves of Karla, Bheja, Bedsa and Kondane. It is certain that he would have been aware of them. What he has written about, however, is his passion for riding, hunting, shooting, drinking, eating betel-nut and 'watching the endless movements of the Nautchnees [dancing girls] and listening to their songs'.[7]

Arnold's first effort at a translation meant clearly for college use was called *Hitopadesa With Murathi and English Vocabulary*. Chiplunkar and Haug would most certainly have helped him immeasurably in this initiative. But he nurtured other interests as well. He became fond of the forests and developed a liking for botany. He introduced and actively encouraged the teaching of science subjects and himself became an amateur astronomer of sorts. A brilliant comet had been observed in June of that year in the Florence Laboratory by Giovanni Donati. By August 1858, it had become visible to the naked eye and Arnold would write about it to the editor of the *Poona Observer* twice, the second time on 12 October 1858.

The 'Nautchnees' whose dances Arnold saw in Poona. This is from Arnold (1886)

By the closing months of 1859, Arnold had pretty much decided to move back to England. A combination of factors was responsible for cutting short his tenure. The Arnolds had lost their second son born in Poona in December 1858 to cholera in a matter of just eight months. His wife was keeping indifferent health and a third child was on the way. So back to England it was by the summer of 1860.

In September of that year, Arnold would publish a remarkable monograph some forty pages in length called *Education in India: A Letter from the Ex-Principal of an Indian Government College to his*

Appointed Successor. The successor was William Allen Russell, who, however, stayed for just two years before being replaced by William Wordsworth, the poet's grandson. The monograph is a fascinating peep into Arnold's mind after he had spent two years in Poona surrounded by Brahmins, Europeans and Parsis almost all the time. He strikes several themes.

First, he takes up British rule in India and writes:

> I suppose every thoughtful man reflected sometimes on the future destinies of India. Wedded to the Empire now, for better or worse; the one anomaly in a consistent Imperial system . . . It is certain that we cannot always retain India, and equally certain that our business is to deal with her as honest tenants, who will render back their house in fair order to the Great Landlord . . .

What would happen if and when a 'weary' England walked away as it faced a decline and fall as the Roman Empire? Arnold replied to his own question:

> . . . If India, no longer nursed, can in such a day stand alone, we shall have done our duty; if she relapses into Hindoo regimes and traditions, or merges helplessly into the undistinguished mass of Russian rule, we shall not have done it, whatever our efforts; but shall bear the blame of extinguishing the torch of civilization . . . Of course we cannot impress our civilization on the natives unless they permit us to remain with them . . . We are clearly a transitory race in India, though we may make our influence permanent.

For Arnold, education held the key to India's rejuvenation, but his reasoning is curious to say the least:

> Nature herself forbids the amalgamation which between races less akin has been possible and powerful. The northern constitution endures rather than resists the unusual climatic influence of India— and it is commonly believed there that the power of reproduction

ceases with the third generation of mixed blood, while a moral degeneration seems to accompany the physical one. I think all these considerations taking away the prospect of improvement by intercourse, increase the importance and widen the province of education in India. To bring back to her the embodied gains of the West in science and philosophy—to submit them in their simplicity to the emancipated Hindoo intellect—and to leave their assimilation to its aroused acquisitiveness, this seems the legitimate field of Indian education.

Arnold's fascination with Indian civilization becomes apparent when he tells Russell:

. . . For myself I profess a real reverence of the antique wisdom to which the West owes so much; and which, ill-understood or corrupted by priestly additions is still, as it reaches us very respectable. I am persuaded that one should enter on Indian education with such a spirit.

He does acknowledge that Brahmins have maintained a monopoly on education and advises Russell that 'it would be wiser to raise the race of scholars from the general population than so perpetuate the distinctions of caste'. But considering that he had been in Poona for over two years at a time when there was intense debate in the city over spreading education to non-Brahmin communities, Arnold is extremely tepid on this subject.

But as if to redeem himself, Arnold ends his long missive thus touching upon a theme that continued to have relevance in India over the next century and more:

I hasten, in concluding, to touch upon one fundamental point, which although not under your control, will derive a great aid and impulse from your advocacy. I mean Female Education; you think, as I know, with the Laureate that

"the mother makes us most'

and you will find it painful to recognize the fact, that her formative share in the Indian student is mainly confined to the physical production of him . . .

In Poona itself there are four private female schools *started and supported by the natives,* and containing in 1858, as many as 205 girls . . . The Poona schools have declined latterly from want of energetic Government support, and from the prejudices which still place educated girls at such a discount in the marriage market . . . I had proposed before leaving, that scholarships should be established for the best pupils, as the Brahman would perhaps accept the drawback of a cultivated understanding in a wife if compensated for by the possession of a monthly stipend, to be continued for a year or two after marriage . . . Certainly, whatever you can do to advance Female Education in India, aiming at the very possible issues of good and modest mothers, and contended and decent homes, will be a stone in the foundation of the future happiness of the country, and by so much bring it nearer . . . (italics mine)

Arnold was disdainful of the Christian missionaries active in Poona. Two organisations were particularly active—the American Marathi Mission and the Free Church of Scotland. The former brought out *Dyanodaya* that has been called 'the most important Marathi missionary periodical in western India'.[8] Among the most hyperactive missionaries was the Scot John Murray Mitchell, who had for a few months officiated as Principal of the Poona College in 1856, when Thomas Candy had gone on leave back to England. Mitchell had, by his own account, been hesitant about this assignment because he felt it would interfere with his missionary work.

But he was persuaded to accept by the powers-that-be who saw nothing wrong in this dual role. The only concession Mitchell was able to extract was that he would not be called principal but be designated as 'Visitor' and further that his appointment would not be mentioned in the Government Gazette. This, Mitchell believed, would show the position he occupied was both 'exceptional and temporary'.[9] Arnold was critical of both the style and substance of the missionary organisations. He believed that they had little or no understanding of local wisdom, culture and traditions. He does not think that Christianity was in any way superior to Hinduism, at least the Hinduism that he was exposed to daily through his Brahmin interlocutors.

A little-known feature of conversions was that initially some Brahmins themselves switched faiths, although many of them became liminal figures in the Hindu–Christian encounter. The baptism of Narayan Sheshadri in Bombay in September 1843, along with the attempted one of his brother Shripat, was the first conversion that would create a big controversy in the region. Nilakantha Goreh from an orthodox Chitpavan Brahmin family in Banaras converted to Christianity in 1848.[10] Baba Padmanji, originally from Belgaum,[11] who had converted in 1854, came to live in Poona just as Arnold was leaving. He was to be later 'hailed as the pioneer of Marathi literature' but his role in popularizing Christian literature was equally important.[12] There would be other 'high profile' Brahmin conversions in the 1880s—the cases of Narayan Waman Tilak and Pandita Ramabai, who were from Poona, have been written about and studied.[13] Govind Narayan Kane was another Chitpavan Brahmin convert to Christianity, who would translate *The Light of Asia* into Marathi in 1894.

Arnold tells Russell that the mission of the 'evangelicals' is to enforce the 'doctrinal, or rather the dogmatical part of Christianity'.

That man would be a hopeful one who, carefully regarding the mental diathesis of the Hindoos, the stages of their religious history, and their present spiritual needs, should predict that the people of India will ever be capable of receiving the unmodified dogmata as extant now in the mouths of the Missionaries . . . dogmatical Christianity, intelligible if at all to its esoteric professors, is a weary thing to the over-dogmatized Asiatic. True morality has its own divine credentials and power of persuasion; Justice bears a brow which all the world knows at sight, and the voice of divine Love is intelligible and welcome to every ear. These the unthinking dogmatist neglects for the assertion of miraculous evidence which the Hindoo parallels adroitly from his own

Poorans, or for doctrines to whose real sublimity he can claim for his own ancestral faith an earlier title.

Arnold asked the question: How can the missionaries propagate the infallibility and supremacy of the Bible in Poona when it was being called into question back in England itself? As an example, he quoted the Rev. John MacNaught vicar of St. Chrysostom's at Liverpool, who, in a letter to the Editor of the *Westminster Review* in April 1860, had said he believed that the Bible was inspired but not without error. Arnold held the Immaculate Conception as 'an instance of a dogma at which the Papal doctors have, after much vacillation arrived just as the Papal authority is passing into disregard'. He thought that 'the cultivated native knows these things and resents the insult which ignores his knowledge' and that 'it is to the cultivated (or cultivable) native that Education must appeal'. He then said something which shows that he had been reading literature on Buddhism:

A curious fact, and one that suggests a discrimination which might go far to meet these objections, is recorded of the Japanese Buddhists of the sixteenth century who 'received the inscrutable doctrine of the Trinity without difficulty, and welcomed the doctrine of a scheme of salvation; but demurred to, and rejected as inconsistent, the dogma of eternal condemnation'. My mind recurs to that marvelous cathedral of Paganism, the cave temple of Elephanta. We had crossed in Lord Elphinstone's barge making our way over the splendid piazza of the wide blue harbour to the palm-tree porticoes of the island shrine. Our table was spread under the eyes of the sculptured Trinity, whose colossal and majestic brows seemed bent on us with the same unchanging expression that had beamed on Buddhist, Jain and Brahman, before our little day. Gazing on that divinely-conceived Tri-unity, I felt how noble might be the role of the large-hearted Missionary who, with St. Paul's example before him, should know how to declare to a great people the name of their "Unknown God".

The fifth-century CE 'Tri-Unity' that Arnold saw at Elephanta Island in 1858 or 1859. According to Dr C. Sivaramamurti, a leading scholar of Indian art, this is a 'vivid representation of Siva the auspicious, shown in the central face, Bhairava the terrible with the hissing snake, frightening moustache in the face to the right, the charming feminine face . . . to the left, indicating Siva, Bhairava and the feminine part of Ardhanrisvara.' This is from Sivaramamurti (1975)

Arnold's reference to 'Japanese Buddhists of the sixteenth century' is significant. There has been much recent scholarship of the Japanese discovery of Christianity and the European discovery of Japanese Buddhism that took place side-by-side in the mid-sixteenth century and that involved an 'identical set of protagonists', mainly St. Francis Xavier and his fellow Jesuit missionaries.[14] But Arnold was writing in 1860, much before the twentieth-century literature on the Jesuits in Japan would get published. So, what was he meaning and what may have been his source?

The former question is easier to answer. His observations on Japanese Buddhism relate to the Mahayana doctrine of the *trikaya*, The Three Bodies of the Buddha and their purported equivalence to the Christian Trinity. The Christian trinity of course is very well known—Father, Son and Holy Spirit. The Mahayana trikaya is relatively lesser known and refers to *Dharmakaya, Sambhohgakaya* and *Nirmanakaya*. The first is the most exalted of all, an invisible body, but now transformed into a kind of eternal principle of enlightenment in which all Buddhas of the past, present and future partake, and from which all forms of Buddha flow. The second is the enjoyment body, a magnificent physical form that did not show up on earth but only in special realms reserved for the instruction of advanced bodhisattvas. The third is the body that physically appeared in India, was visible to people, achieved enlightenment under the Bodhi tree and taught the four noble truths.[15]

Paul Carus was to write about this extensively but his influential *The Gospel of the Buddha* would appear only in 1894. Books on St. Francis Xavier in Japan would appear years after Arnold's death. My informed guess is that Arnold had read the first publicly accessible report on Japanese religion in the West that was originally published in French in 1552. This was by Guillaume Postel, 'one of the most important Biblical scholars of the sixteenth century'[16] and a polyglot and polymath. Postel translated a report prepared in Latin by a Jesuit missionary Nicolo Lancilloto and called it *Des Merveilles du Monde (The Wonders of the World)*. It is impossible, however, to figure out how and where Arnold had read Postel.

One possibility is that Arnold came to Postel via Francis Bacon, the British philosopher-statesman of the late sixteenth and early seventeenth centuries, who had written much about the French scholar mesmerized by the fact that was reputed to have lived till the age of 120. There was also the important collection of Bernard Picart, published in English in nine volumes between 1723 and 1743 as *The Ceremonies and Religious Customs of the Various Nations of the Known World*. A third possibility is that Arnold would have been familiar with Eugene Burnouf's *Introduction à L'histoire du Bouddhisme Indien or Introduction to the History of Indian Buddhism* that would first appear in Paris in 1844. Burnouf is considered by many to be the 'founding father of modern Buddhist studies'.

During the time Arnold was in Poona most missionary activity in western India focused on upper-caste elites. From the early 1860s onwards, faced with little success, this activity concentrated on proselytization among the non-Brahmin castes in what has been called 'mass vernacular evangelism'.[17] What Arnold would have made of this missionary engagement with the populist and devotional aspects of Hinduism more in line with the Maratha region's strong local bhakti tradition is difficult to say—possibly a strong textual man, he would have found it at odds with the more intellectual and cerebral model of Hindu spirituality that he was so taken up with.[18]

Arnold's monograph meant for his successor also contains a vivid description of the Poona College itself. The institution was housed in the ancient wood palace of the Peshwas called Vishrambagh in the heart of the city. It had all the grandeur of a building constructed by and for royalty, replete with images of Hindu Gods and Goddesses. Arnold tells Russell:

> These dark and narrow stairs (trodden many a time by princes and princesses of the Murathi dynasty—more than once by the Machiavel of the Deccan, Nana Farnavees) conduct you to the upper apartments; and this is your lecture room. The first College class salutes you there with natural and graceful obeisance of the East—exact it, and repay it; a well accepted and administered salaam is mighty with the Orientals . . .

After Arnold's departure in early 1860, the Poona College would move out of its regal surroundings. In 1864, the foundation stone for a building at a new site would be laid and the name changed to Deccan College to signal that it would serve not just the city. The Deccan College was an early example of what today is called a 'public–private partnership'. The Bombay Government provided the land and shared the expenditure for the new buildings with the Parsi merchant–philanthropist of Bombay, Sir Jamsetjee Jeejebhoy. Jeejeebhoy had built a fortune in cotton and the opium trade and was the first Indian to be knighted and made a baronet.

Deccan College in its new location circa 1870. (Source: Royal Collection Trust, London)

The Deccan College in the form that existed during Arnold's time would continue till 1934 with E.A. Wodehouse, the brother of the famous British humourist-author, as principal for its last three years. The British moved to close it down in the early 1930s. However, the College's alumni mounted a huge, campaign with many public personalities also joining, and as a result the Deccan College resumed functioning from August 1939. But henceforth it was to be a post-graduate teaching and research body. It continues to be one of India's leading institutions in ancient history and archaeology.

Many decades later, in 1892, Arnold would reminisce about his Poona years to a largely American audience:[19]

> I myself had the never-to-be-regretted and never-to-be-forgotten honour of serving the Honourable East India Company in its Educational Department, and was present at the table of the Governor of Bombay, Lord Elphinstone, on the memorable night when, at Kirkee, in the Deccan, he read aloud to a brilliant company of administrators, public officials, and military and financial

officers collected round him, the proclamation transferring British India from the company to the crown [November 1st 1858] . . . It was the demise of a veritable and mighty potentate at which we assisted; the passing away of an association of empire-making traders, greater than the proud burghers of the Hague, than the Hanseatic Leaguers . . . I was in India during that Great mutiny of 1857 and of course, saw and heard things which I prefer now to forget . . . The mutiny was, however, not Indian, but Mohammedan in origin and essence, and only by the scandal of the "greased cartridges" through the pampered spirit of the high-caste Hindu soldiers did the Muslims get the Hindus to act for the for once, albeit if successful, they would have instantly set to work to cut each others' throats.

Arnold's fears about Hindus and Muslims, alas, did not prove unfounded although his countrymen were to play no mean part in keeping the two religious communities divided.

Notes

1. Arnold (1896)
2. Wolpert (1962)
3. Arnold (1896)
4. Keer (1960). The first biography was in 1927.
5. Keer (1960)
6. O'Hanlon (1985)
7. Arnold (1896)
8. O'Hanlon (1985). *Dyanodaya* was started as a weekly from Ahmednagar in 1842, became a bi-monthly between 1845 and 1873 and a weekly thereafter from Bombay.
9. Mitchell (1899)
10. Keune (2004)
11. Padmanji was not a Brahmin though and belonged to the 'Kasar' caste, which today falls in the OBC (Other Backward Classes) category in Maharashtra.
12. Dandekar (2019)
13. Kosambi (1992)

14. App (1997, 1998). I thank Richard Jaffe for drawing my attention to App's remarkable work on this subject.
15. These descriptions are from Lopez (2013).
16. Lopez (2013). Postel was also a key figure in the transmission of scientific texts in Arabic to sixteenth century Europe that had a profound impact on Copernican astronomy particularly. This role of Postel is discussed in Saliba (2007).
17. Constable (2007) writes so in the context of Scottish Presbyterian missionaries particularly.
18. I owe this and the previous thought to Professor Rosalind O'Hanlon, email communication 21 May 2020.
19. Arnold (1892)

3

1860–1876: Edwin Arnold Back in London: Empire Author, Imperial Journalist, Oriental Poet

By the summer of 1860 Arnold was back in London. It was an England already in the throes of a profound economic and social transformation triggered by the Industrial Revolution. It was also an England committed to the manifest destiny of the British Empire but anguished by the 1857 Mutiny in India. It was an England shaken by the publication of Charles Darwin's *The Origin of the Species* in 1859.[1] It was an era when the orthodoxy of the Bible was under challenge from science—the first bugle having been sounded by the publication of Charles Lyell's *Principles of Geology* during 1830–33.

For a brief while, Arnold entertained the thought of returning to India but by September 1861 found himself as a leader writer of the *Daily Telegraph* that had been launched six years earlier. By 1876 it would advertise itself as the 'largest selling newspaper in the world', quite radical in its domestic politics but solidly conservative in regard to holding on to and advancing the Empire. Arnold would be the editor between 1873 and 1899. It was of this publication that Karl Marx would famously remark:[2]

> By means of a hidden and artificial sewer system all the lavatories
> of London spew their physical filth into the Thames. By means of
> the systematic pushing of the goose quill the world capital spews
> out all the social filth into the great-papered central sewer called
> the *Daily Telegraph*.

One person who would write for the *Daily Telegraph* from India in 1897 was Winston Churchill. The fifteen articles he sent back from the sub-continent would form the basis of his first book *The Story of the Malakand Field Force*. This was about the British military campaign in the North West Frontier Province on the border with Afghanistan.

Two books published in the late nineteenth century have given accounts of Arnold's career as a journalist. The first appeared in 1882 when Arnold was at his zenith. It was by Joseph Hatton, who was editor of the *Sunday Times* between 1874 and 1881.[3] Hatton recalled:

> Although in many respects Oriental in tastes, Edwin Arnold may be regarded as a typical Englishman. He has never allowed his literary labours to overcome his love for the outdoor life. A master of field sports, he has a thorough knowledge of horses, dogs and guns, and is particularly fond of yachting. The first editorial he ever wrote in *The Telegraph* was on the British Empire in the East. Since that time, he has written upward of six thousand leading articles. During the two years and a half of the Eastern Question which is stained with the blood of the great war between Russia and Turkey, Mr. Arnold wrote between four and five hundred consecutive articles—leaders that were looked for with interest and anxiety by all classes of people . . . Mr. Arnold . . . has never been photographed and his biography has never been written.

The second was by George Augustus Sala, one of the most intrepid journalists in London of those times. He had this to say in his memoirs that were published in 1895:

> It was shortly after the death of the Prince Consort [December 1861] that I became aware of the presence of a new leading article writer in the columns of the *Daily Telegraph* . . . I was most forcibly impressed by the style of the new leader-writer; replete as it was with refined scholarship, with eloquent diction and with an Oriental exuberance of epithets. Some of the leaders giving expression to the universal feeling of sympathy for, and

condolence with Her Majesty, in her bitter bereavement—struck me as being among the most pathetic utterances in poetic prose that I have ever read. But it was the Eastern aroma of these articles which most attracted my attention and excited my admiration. It occurred to me one day to ask Edward Lawson [the proprietor-editor] who the gentleman might be who wrote so sumptuously about the Nilotic butterfly and the sacred rivers and temples of burning Ind [India]? He told me that the writer was a gentleman newly arrived from India . . . I have never ceased to entertain the sincerest appreciation of the genius, both as a poet and a prose writer, of Sir Edwin Arnold.

By mid-1861, Arnold's first serious work on an Indian theme would appear. This was *The Book of Good Counsels: From the Sanskrit of the Hitopadesa*, on which he had begun working in Poona itself.[4] This would receive favourable reviews including in the *Athenaeum* of 31 August 1861. It would say:

For English readers who have never heard of the 'Hitopadesa' and to whom the fact of a learned work translated from the Sanskrit would convey the notion of something slow, involved in style, stately and ceremonious in language, altogether a dull, dignified and unattractive book,—for the benefit of this impatient class of readers, and for their conversion from this heresy, Mr. Edwin Arnold has undertaken and executed a new translation [that] is well executed and put into a manageable form.

There had been five previous translations of the *Hitopadesa* going back to the late eighteenth century and to the redoubtable Sir William Jones, the founder of the Asiatic Society in Calcutta. This was because it had come 'to be traditionally accepted as a suitable text for beginners in Sanskrit, rather as Caesar was for Latin'.[5] Arnold acknowledged his debt to previous works but his own one was to make a special impact. *The Book of Good Counsels* was dedicated to his wife and the preface contained the kernel of his approach to and appreciation of India and its civilizational heritage. Calling Sanskrit the 'perfect language', he went on:

> The hope of Hindostan lies in its intelligent interest of England. Whatever avails to dissipate misconceptions between them, and to enlarge their intimacy, is a gain to both People; and to this end the present volume aspires, in an humble degree, to contribute. . . . A residence in India, and closed intercourse with the Hindoos, has given the Author a lively desire to subserve their advancement. No one listens now to the precipitate ignorance which would set aside as "heathenish" the high civilization of this great race; but justice is not yet done to their past development and present capacities . . . . . .

The very next year Arnold produced the first of his two-volume account of Lord Dalhousie's Viceroyalty in India during 1848–56. The second volume appeared in 1865. This would be his only foray into political history and would be the earliest such work on the tenure of this controversial Viceroy. As long as Dalhousie was in India, he was a hero in England. He was feted on his return to London and even greater things were expected of him. But the Mutiny of 1857 sullied his reputation in Britain, and he died a broken man in 1860. He is still a name in India though—a hill station north of Simla founded by him continues to bear the name Dalhousie. A road in the heart of New Delhi where the Government of India functions bore his name till 2016.

Arnold's first volume was on the annexation and the administration of Punjab. By and large, Arnold eulogized Dalhousie for the leadership he provided and for giving maximum support to people like Sir John Lawrence, to whom the volume is dedicated and who himself was to become Viceroy in 1864. It is in the second volume dedicated to his recently deceased wife that Arnold faults the Viceroy, who he otherwise admires for his modernizing zeal and ushering India into the age of the railway, telegraph and large irrigation works. Arnold sees nothing wrong in the annexation of

Oudh. His criticism is of the manner in which the Viceroy dealt with the succession issue in the princely states of Nagpur, Satara and Jhansi that in his view struck at the root of 'Hindoo' religion and law. He is ambivalent about Dalhousie's annexation of Lower Burma, saying that the ends were fine, but the methods were questionable. The Viceroy's dealings with the Nizam of Hyderabad are also held to be less-than-desirable.

There is much in Arnold's assessments of Dalhousie that will strike a chord with Indian nationalist historians. There is also much that will delight those who believe that the British did good in India. On the whole, it is balanced and sober. He ended by saying:

> One merit the writer does claim—that of the liveliest interest in the welfare of the people of India, and the deepest sense of British duty towards them—an interest confirmed, and a sense of duty quickened by pleasant days spent in Indian cities and fields.

In 2015, the noted British author Ferdinand Mount's blistering account of the way the East India Company had dealt with the princely states would appear.[6] In it he was to observe:

> We would be wrong to imagine that criticism of Dalhousie has been confined to Indian nationalist historians and anti-colonial campaigners of the twentieth century. Quite a few Directors of the Court [of the East India Company] had misgivings . . . So did Sir Edwin Arnold author of *The Light of Asia* and later editor of the *Daily Telegraph* who included a scorching analysis of the Nizam's hounding in his two-volume polemic [on Dalhousie]. . .

Mount was exaggerating a bit. Arnold's was no 'polemic' on Dalhousie's rule, but it was no hagiography either.

Arnold's summing up of Dalhousie would be used by critics of Mahatma Gandhi in the early 1920s, almost six decades after the two volumes were published. Excoriating Gandhi, the *Times of India* would write on 24 June 1921:

Mr. Gandhi's [non-cooperation] campaign is being extended, for he has now taken to non-cooperation with Clio, the Muse of History. In his paper, he writes: "I must dare to say, that the Mogul and the Maratha Government were better than the British, in that the nation as a whole was not emasculated or so impoverished as it is today. We were not the Pariahs of the Mogul or the Maratha Empire. We are Pariahs of the British Empire . . ." The opposition to British rule is perhaps the foundation for this theory of history, for he naturally wishes that no good should be thought of a man like Lord Dalhousie who attempted not only the unification of territory but also the unification of the Indian races. "We are making" wrote Sir Edwin Arnold in summing the results of Dalhousie's rule "a people in India where hitherto there have been a hundred tribes but no people".

For Arnold, the 1860s and much of the early 1870s would be consumed mainly by the *Daily Telegraph* and family life. In July 1868 he would also marry a second time. This marriage would prove crucial to the success of *The Light of Asia* in America eleven years later. His new wife Fanny Channing was the daughter of William Ellery Channing, who was a Unitarian minister, Christian socialist and a leading light of the Boston-based Transcendental Club. Members of this Club played a big role in popularizing *The Light of Asia* in 1879 and thereafter.

By the early 1870s, Arnold was known as an author and poet and as someone keenly interested in and knowledgeable about India. But it was his influence through the columns of the *Daily Telegraph* that gave him a key place in British society. This is reflected in the letter the legendary philosopher John Stuart Mill wrote to him on 22 April 1872:[7]

From your knowledge of Indian affairs, you have probably paid some attention to the case of the Bombay Bank. It has always seemed to me that although the Bombay Gov[ernment] was only a shareholder in the back, yet as high officers of the Gov[ernment] were officially members of the Board of Directors which did all

the mischief, & as the Gov[ernment] itself neglected the duty
of supervision but when repeatedly warned, even by the Gov
[ernment] at Calcutta, persisted in disregarding the warnings &
even withheld from the Calcutta Gov[ernment] the information
it demanded at a time when the disaster might still have been
prevented from being complete; the Bombay Gov[ernment] is
bound in morality and honour to indemnify partially if not wholly
the shareholders, who undoubtedly risked their money in reliance
with the supervision exercised by the Government through the
official directors. The case will shortly be brought before the H.
of C. [High Court of Calcutta] & a word from you from the
Telegraph on the subject would be of great importance.

The more things change, the more they appear to be the same. Mill
was referring to a financial scandal that had rocked Bombay in the mid-
1860s. The Bank of Bombay had been set up in 1840 with the Bombay
Government and local businessmen and merchants as shareholders.
Bombay experienced a boom during the American Civil War of 1861-
65 when textile mills in the UK began buying their cotton from the
Bombay Presidency. When the Civil War ended, this boom lost its
steam suddenly and the Bombay stock market collapsed. The joint-stock
Bank of Bombay which had lent merrily in the boom years now found
itself with a portfolio of borrowers who had been bankrupted. Worse,
it transpired that the Bank of Bombay had lent substantial sums of
money to companies owned directly or indirectly by some of the private
businessmen and traders who were themselves either shareholders or
directors of the Bank. It also turned out that the Bank of Bombay,
which had sixteen directors at the time of the crash, of which six were
nominees of the Bombay Government, had been speculating heavily in
the shares of the companies that had folded.[8]
A month later on 13 May 1872 Mill wrote again to Arnold:

Your "answer" in the Telegraph was so excellent that no other was
needed; it was rather I who should have written sooner to thank
you for it. If anything could have helped the injured shareholders

your article would have done so, it must have materially contributed to the impression made by their case, an impression which leaves some opening for future efforts . . .

This reply from Mill is important for another reason as well. John Tyndall, a physicist, is famous today for his pioneering contributions to our understanding of 'the greenhouse effect' caused by the build-up of atmospheric carbon dioxide that leads to global warming and climate change. Tyndall was also a religious agnostic and believed in a clear demarcation between faith and rationality. He spoke on 4 May 1872 at the Royal Academy and Arnold commented on Tyndall's remarks a few days later in the *Daily Telegraph*, which he had passed along to Mill:

> Never again can men think and believe as they once did. The march of science and of thought has left behind institutions which are dead without knowing it, and burdens of the human mind, which seem still borne only because the ache of the place where they pressed is still felt . . . But men must have something to believe, something to explain to them the beauty of Nature as well as her order and truth—something to restore to them in the new world opening outside the old-fashioned universe their faith in a Source of all that beauty and in a Centre of all that love and worship, the endless insatiable hope and aspiration which will not be satisfied with 'force and matter'. The cry of humanity today to the men of science is 'Give us back something to believe' in return for that which has been taken away. Science ought not to respond with a cold refusal to care for anything but facts. Emotions, affections, aspirations, as Professor Tyndall himself said are "part and parcel" of human nature; that there must be a religion—there must be a morality and a creed—to satisfy such desires.

Mill had continued his letter of 13 May 1872 by saying:

> The article certainly does express a very general and natural "longing" among those who have outgrown the old forms of

religious belief. I myself have more sympathy with the aspiration, than hope to see it gratified, to the extent of any positive belief respecting the unseen world; but I am convinced that the cultivation of an imaginative hope is quite compatible with a reserve as to positive belief & that whatever helps to keep before the mind the ideal of a perfect Being is of unspeakable value to human nature. Only it is essential to prevent a perversion of the moral faculty,

Cecil Rhodes caricatured in Punch *magazine for pushing through Arnold's Cape to Cairo connectivity idea. (Source: Wikipedia)*

that this perfect Being, if regarded as the Creator of the world we live in, should not be thought to be omnipotent.

Science was on the march. Religious doubt was deepening. Christian dogma was under assault. Here was Arnold writing that faith and reason, spirituality and rationality have to go together. Seven years later Arnold would announce to the world a formula for bridging these two worlds—the life of Buddha and his preachings.

Arnold was a 'soft' imperialist for sure, a steadfast believer in Britain's manifest destiny. Nothing illustrates this better than his call made in 1874 for a 'Cape to Cairo' link involving both rail and water transport to cut through the continent of Africa. This would be taken up later by Cecil Rhodes and be the subject of a famous cartoon in the satirical *Punch* magazine on 10 December 1892.

Arnold would also play a key role in mounting and co-financing the Anglo-American expedition of Henry Morton Stanley between 1874 and 1877 to determine the source of the Congo river and solve the African continent's last great geographical mystery.[9] One of Stanley's biographers has written that it was Stanley's meeting with Arnold in London that clinched the expedition.[10] A year before *The Light of Asia* came out Stanley had published his two-volume *Through the Dark Continent* with this dedication:[11]

Dedicated to:

Mr. James Gordon Bennett
Proprietor of the New York Herald

Mr. J.M. Levy and Mr. Edward L. Lawson
Proprietors of the Daily Telegraph

AND IN CONSEQUENCE OF THE GREAT AND CONSTANT INTEREST MANIFESTED BY HIM IN THE SUCCESS OF THE UNDERTAKING I MUST BE PERMITTED TO ADD THE NAME OF

Mr. Edwin Arnold, C.S.I & F.R. G.S.

Arnold was not just placing the journalistic and financial muscle of the *Daily Telegraph* behind this venture, but he was also a Fellow of the Royal Geographical Society. He had brought that influential body around to support Stanley. The Society was none-too-supportive of Stanley for a complex set of reasons, some of which that had to do with the very 'low' social background of Stanley, who had been born illegitimate in Wales and who had then run away to America and was therefore considered 'not British enough' by the grandees of the Society. Stanley would later name a northern tributary of the Congo river and a mountain in what is now Uganda after Arnold. One of the most unsavoury characters in a later expedition of Stanley's in 1888—James Sligo Jameson, heir to an Irish whiskey empire, who arranged to witness a staged cannibal event involving a ten-year-old slave girl—would always travel with *The Light of Asia*.[12]

In the late 1880s, Stanley would meet his would-be wife Dorothy Tennant courtesy Arnold.[13] And Arnold's very last poetic work in 1901, *The Voyages of Ithobal*, which recounts a legendary African epic, was a contemporary tribute to Stanley, who would outlive him by just two months. In a letter to Arnold, Stanley congratulated him thus:

> What most appeals to my imagination on hearing this news is that sightless as you are, & so awfully afflicted, you should have been

Mount Edwin Arnold (left) and the fall of the River Edwin Arnold, both in Africa as shown in Henry Morton Stanley's Through the Dark Continent *(1878). They have since been renamed of course.*

able to hold the image of the scene where your bold navigator
recounts the marvels he has beheld . . . I personally shall never,
never forget the conditions under which the poem has been
produced, not the pictures of the blind poet, straining his faded
eyes to see the long ago times, the hero's exploits, and his antique
ship, the marvels of the unknown sea & land . . . If your readers
could but have seen you as I saw you at work upon it, could but
be aware that behind all this warm rapture of the poet there lay so
many awful distresses of mind & of body. Their hearts I am sure
would be unspeakably full of that sympathy you deserve.

Brian Murray, from whose work on Stanley I have extracted this,[14]
has written that 'Ithobal may not have been a great poem, but Stanley
was determined to view its composition as a feat of epic endurance.
In this emotional letter, he casts Arnold in a great tradition of the
blind epicists: from Homer to Milton'.

Stanley's was not the only journey of discovery that Arnold
facilitated. In January 1873, George Smith embarked on what was
to become known as the Assyrian expedition to search for other
fragments of the ancient Babylonian epic Gilgamesh that would
help corroborate events mentioned in the Bible. The expedition
was funded by the Daily Telegraph at Arnold's instance and Smith
departed 'after receiving much advice and assistance from my friend
Mr Edwin Arnold, himself an old Eastern traveller'. In November
1873 there would be a second expedition, this time funded by
Smith's employer the British Museum, and in 1875, Smith would
write about his excavations and findings at Nineveh, then part of
the Ottoman Empire and in today's Iraq. The Museum would pay
public tribute to Arnold for triggering the expedition when things
had looked none too good.

The year 1875 would firmly establish Arnold's reputation as an
Orientalist poet not just in England but also, for the first time, in
India as well. The last quarter of that year would see the publication
of his translation of the Gitagovinda, a late twelfth-century CE
sensuous poem of divine love in Sanskrit by the Bengali poet

Jayadeva. Arnold's book was called *The Indian Song of Songs*, with other Oriental poems and was dedicated thus:

To My Many Hindoo Friends
In Token of Affectionate Recollection

In his preface, Arnold acknowledges the 'labours and expert guidance' of Christian Lassen, a Norwegian–German scholar who was the Professor of Old Indian Languages and Literature at the University of Bonn. Lassen had himself produced an extremely influential Sanskrit text annotation, textual interpretation and a Latin translation of the *Gitagovinda* in 1836. Arnold offers his own new translation as a step forward to a 'closer acquaintance of England and India—an object always dear to the present writer'.

Arnold's long association with the London-based publishing house Trubner & Co. also began in 1875. A brief description of Nicholas Trubner, 'known for years in the London book trade as the prince of oriental publishers',[15] will not be out of place here considering the role he would play in popularizing Arnold's books in England and elsewhere, including India. Trubner, born in 1817, was German and had studied languages in Heidelberg before coming to London in 1843. He was a pupil of Theodor Goldstucker, the Sanskritist who had moved from Berlin to London in late 1848. It is, however, not entirely clear whether Trubner became his student in Germany or in London. Apart from *The Light of Asia*, Trubner is best known for launching *Trubner's Oriental Series* that began in 1878 with *Essays on the Sacred Language, Writings and Religion of the Parsis* by Martin Haug, Arnold's colleague at the Poona College. Trubner died in 1884 and in the words of one his fellow-publishers who became a big brand himself, William Heinemann:[16]

Nicholas Trubner was the friend and adviser of all who were engaged in the study of Oriental literature. His firm during this period has been the intermediary between Europe and the East. His agents are scattered all over the globe, and they send from the remotest part

*Nicholas Trubner, the London-based publisher
and himself an Indologist who did much to
popularize books on Indian themes in the period
prior to the mid-1880s. (Source: New York Public
Library)*

the literary productions of every people of the world to London.
Here they are catalogued and carefully described, and Trubner's
Record makes them widely known among librarians and scholars.

Trubner & Co. would become part of Kegan Paul, Trench, Trubner
& Co. Ltd but the Trubner Oriental Series was to continue till
1930. In all over a hundred books would be published in this series
and many became classics. As part of this series, the two-volume
Economic History of India by Romesh Chandra Dutt that came out
in 1902 and 1904 became essential reading for nationalists agitating
against British rule in India and would be quoted by Mahatma
Gandhi in his book *Hind Swaraj*. Some years earlier, in 1894, Dutt's
Lays of Ancient India had appeared, in which he had remarked:

Max Muller has translated the ancient Upanishads and the
Buddhist work Dhammapada into English prose; and the genius

of Sir Edwin Arnold has made thousands of readers in Europe and America familiar with the wealth of Indian thought and imagery, and the beauty of Buddhist precepts and doctrines.

One of the 'other Oriental poems' in the 1875 *Gitagovinda* volume of Arnold's was called *The Rajpoot Wife*. The story was straightforward. It tells the tale of 'Ranee Neila', the wife of 'Soorj Dehu, Lord of the Rajputs of Nourpoer', who avenges the killing of her husband by 'Abdoul Shureef Khan', a Muslim invader. Neila pierces a dagger into Khan's heart after dancing in front of him and his army, described as being 'aflame with lawless wine' and 'wagging their goatish chins'. She then kills herself because, as she tells her brothers-in-law:

For where a Rajpoot dieth, the Rajpoot widow burns.

This poem merits attention because it would form the basis of a Hindi play *Nildevi* by the noted author Bhartendu Harishchandra in 1881. Harishchandra has often been called the father of modern Hindi literature as well as theatre. Arnold's poem is indubitably a glorification of sati, for Neila burnt herself willingly and with pride with her husband on the funeral pyre. Sati was an act of supreme self-assertion on her part. But Arnold seemed to have no overt political agenda with his poem. He would also write one in praise of King Saladin, who led the Muslim armies against the Christian crusaders in the Levant in the later twelfth century.

On the other hand, Harishchandra certainly had a political design that was one of collective Hindu resistance to Muslim rule, a confrontation between alien and treacherous Muslims on the one hand and brave and righteous Hindus on the other. It was a one-sided and blinkered view of the past. But it would be inappropriate to look at Harishchandra with today's lens, for he also 'exhibited solidarity with Muslim rule or even the original religious impulse wherein Islam originated'.[17] There was both a 'progressive' and 'regressive' element embedded in his endeavours. A believer in the self-purification of Hindu society, Harishchandra lived and wrote mostly out of Banaras and *Nildevi* was a runaway success there and in other places in the Hindi heartland like Agra, Kanpur, Allahabad, Ballia and Dumrao.[18]

For a man who believed in modernity, Arnold's attitude to 'suttee', which was abolished by law in 1829, was somewhat curious to say the least. In 1860, he had told his successor at Poona that there were many 'Hindoo customs as an enlarged moral sense has shown to be no longer in the harmony of things' and had gone on:[19]

Many of them have happily disappeared, and many will yet disappear
before the allied force of truth and reason, best exercised by an appreciative

Commemorative stamp issued by the Government of India in honour of Bharatendu Harishchandra in 1976. His play Nildevi *of 1881 was based on Arnold's poem* The Rajpoot Wife.

*reformer. Suttee, and the refusal of a second marriage to the widow, has not
only much to recommend them as customs of a European people, but arose
more or less directly from sentiments that challenge admiration. What was
good in them has long ago been overlaid by priestly greed of power, money
and show; and India is well-rid of a rite which, however, with all its
faults was at least full of the "love stronger than death;" and the like of
which wins the eloquence of Livy, in the death of the heroic Sophonisba.
No narrow heart dictated these shlokes of the Sanskrit Hitopadesa,*

> *"When the faithful[20] wife, embracing tenderly her husband dead,
> "Mounts the blazing pile beside him, as it were the bridal bed;
> "Though his sins were twenty thousand, twenty thousand times "o'er-told,
> "She shall bring his soul to splendour[21] for her love so large and "bold."*

Even in his second volume on Dalhousie, Arnold wrote quite a bit
about the 'redeeming traits of this rite', that is, of 'suttee'. Admitting
that it may well have been 'barbaric and superstitious if you will',
he also termed it 'sublime' when 'women with ordinary affections,
ordinary habits of life' were 'suddenly lifted to a sublimity of
passion—to the death—by an influence they were unable to repress
or control'.

As far as the translation of the *Gitagovinda* is concerned, Arnold's
was certainly not the first. Sir William Jones had done so in 1792.
Subsequently, it had been translated into German in 1802 and 1837
and Latin in 1836. But with this book Arnold made a name for
himself in England and in India as well. It found elaborate mention
in the *Calcutta Review*, a widely read quarterly that had been founded
in 1844. A few months after *The Indian Song of Songs* was published
it carried a very favourable review. After complimenting Trubner 'on
the variety and excellence of his Oriental publications', the reviewer
went on:[22]

Mr. Edwin Arnold's charming rendering of Jayadeva's luscious
pastoral though slighter in bulk and lighter in subject than most
of the volumes before us demands our first attention . . . We

have no hesitation in saying that we have seldom read any poetry, translated or glowing, so glowing with the warmest and tenderest passion, and at the same times so perfectly refined and graceful, as this most delightful little pastoral . . . The Indian Education Service which has already given such distinguished names as those of Sir Alexander Grant and Professor Cowell to English prose literature, may well be proud of having produced a poet of the order to which Mr. Arnold belongs. We believe that the Indian Song of Songs will be more highly appreciated as it becomes better known; and confidently predict for the author no ignoble place in the roll of the poets of the present century.

The reviewer would also take note of the other four 'Oriental poems' in the book, draw pointed attention to *The Rajpoot Wife* by quoting some of its lines but admitting that the other three were not inferior to it in any way. Just three years later the reviewer who confidently predicted for Edwin Arnold 'no ignoble place in the roll of poets of the present century' would be more than proved right. Edwin Arnold would become a global celebrity with his *The Light of Asia*.

Before writing *The Light of Asia* Arnold would, of course, have encountered the Buddha while translating *Gitagovinda*. The introduction to the poem has the 'Hymn to Vishnu', where Jayadeva extolls each of the ten incarnations of Vishnu. Arnold translates the description of the ninth avatar thus:

> *Merciful-hearted! when thou camest as Boodh—*
> *Albeit 'twas written in the Scriptures so—*
> *Thou bad'st our altars be no more imbrued*
> *With blood of victims: Keshav bending low*
> *We praise thee.*

A less florid and more intelligible translation is this:[23]

> *Moved by deep compassion, you condemn the Vedic way*
> *That ordains animal slaughter in rites of sacrifice.*

You take form as the enlightened Buddha, Krishna.
Triumph, Hari, Lord of the World!

Jayadeva was writing his poem in the twelfth century and this 'contains one of the earliest lists of incarnations' of Vishnu.[24] By then the Buddha had been appropriated by the Brahmins as part of a deliberate strategy to 'assimilate heterodox elements into the Vaishnavite fold'.[25] The reference to the Buddha in the *Gitagovinda* has been said to represent 'a defeat of the Buddha because this tribute comes from a very theistic tradition and Buddha had always denied the existence of God'.[26] But at the same time Kalki, the tenth avatar of Vishnu and the incarnation yet to come, may well have been inspired by Buddhism, 'which taught the coming of Maitrerya Buddha long before the Vaisnavites devised the Kalkin'.[27] The earliest inscription mentioning the Buddha as an avatar appears in the Adivaraha cave at Mahabalipuram on the coast of Tamil Nadu, dedicated to the boar incarnation of Vishnu.[28] This is in Sanskrit and has been dated to the eighth century CE.[29] But not all Brahmins were complimentary to the Buddha. Tulsidas, author of *Ramcharitmanas*, which has contributed so heavily to the development of a Hindu identity, especially in north India, wrote in the mid-sixteenth century:[30]

The glory of the Vedas is incomparable. Condemning them the incarnation Buddha himself earned condemnation.

As far as the Buddha is concerned, Arnold's Brahmin interlocutors in Poona would definitely have been of Jayadeva's view but I suspect that some of them may also have had sympathy with what Tulsidas had declared.

On 8 February 1876, the British Parliament saw Queen Victoria 'being seated on the Throne adorned with Her Crown and Regal Ornaments' and heard the Lord Chancellor deliver her customary annual address. It was a speech that lasted a mere six minutes but had this momentous announcement:

I am deeply thankful for the uninterrupted health which my dear Son, the Prince of Wales, has enjoyed during his journey through India. The hearty affection with which he has been received by my Indian subjects of all classes and races assures me that they are happy under my rule, and loyal to my throne. At the time that the direct Government of my Indian Empire was transferred to the Crown, no formal addition was made to the style and titles of the Sovereign. I have deemed the present a fitting opportunity for supplying this omission, and a Bill upon the subject will be presented to you.

The Prince of Wales would be in India for eight months beginning October 1875. In November 1875 he would visit the paternal home of Arnold's favourite students, the Pudumjees, who hosted the heir apparent with great pomp in Poona. The Queen's announcement was least expected, and it was the doing of just one man. Prime Minister Benjamin Disraeli had slipped in this paragraph at the last moment. He shared a very warm relationship with his Sovereign. He was also somebody Arnold knew since 1854 and who Arnold had supported for his foreign policy on the grounds that he was the one person who understood Britain's imperial destiny.

On 1 January 1877, Queen Victoria was officially proclaimed as Empress of India, nineteen years after India had come under the British Crown. Along with this announcement came the news that she had conferred Arnold with a royal honour. The Order of the Star of India had first been instituted in June 1861 to reward 'conspicuous merit and loyalty' and five years later it had come to be awarded in three classes: Knight Grand Commander of the Star of India (GCSI), Knight Commander of the Star of India (KCSI) and Companion of the Star of India (CSI). Arnold became a CSI but was still *Mr* Edwin Arnold.

A few months later he would demonstrate his formidable linguistic skills by publishing *A Simple Transliteral Grammar of the Turkish Language*, explaining his motivation for doing so thus:

This book is merely a compilation formed by the author in his own study of Turkish and offered to other beginners as an aid towards acquaintance with that language, in the present singular dearth of Turkish grammars and instruction books. The Eastern Problem has re-arisen in any absorbing manner to give new interest to a tongue spoken over so vast and important an Empire . . .

The difficulty of representing the Turkish letters could not have been quite overcome without fuller details; but further study must supply precision, and in the present unassuming sketch the author aims at no credit except that of simplicity, and to render a small service in the great matter of "Justice to Islam".

This book coming at a time when Arnold was using the columns of the *Daily Telegraph* to advocate strong British support for Turkey in her disputes with Russia[31] brought him recognition from the Sultan of Turkey—the Third Class of the Imperial Order of the Medjidie in 1876. One factor that was always at the back of Arnold's mind was the possibility of Russia getting stronger and threatening British interests in India. The fact that Muslim opinion in India would be favourable to any backing of the Sultan of Turkey could also have dictated his stance of muscular British intervention that had prompted the noted British Liberal politician Henry Labouchere to call him the 'Prince of Jingoes'.[32]

The 1870s were a period when the British discovery of *Indian* Buddhism was proceeding apace. I stress *Indian* Buddhism because the discovery of Buddhism in other parts of Asia like Japan and China had begun in the mid-sixteenth century by Jesuit priests and had been taken forward, particularly in France.[33] This journey had started some half a century earlier and its story has been told very well in four books.[34] I will, therefore, instead focus on the *immediate* backdrop to *The Light of Asia*.

In 1871 there appeared in London an epic poem by Richard Phillips called *The Story of Gautama Buddha and His Creed*. The poem had thirteen cantos and a total of 618 verses, each eight lines in length. In his preface, Phillips wrote that 'the founder of a religion, which after more than 2000 years, is still professed by 455,000,000 of human beings, is ignored, misrepresented and foolishly despised'. He went on:

> The Great Ascetic deserves to be better known. Both the attractive beauty of his life, and the tremendous influence of his creed, demand for him more attention than either thoughtful persons or even our wise men have hitherto accorded him.

Phillips concluded his preface by confessing that his epic poem was no 'attempt at an undue exaltation of the Buddha, between whom and Christ there is in many particulars so striking a resemblance; nor an indiscriminate laudation of that system which is so like Christianity in its ethics, but so unlike to it in its doctrines'. The entire poem published by Longman, Green and Co. but soon forgotten is now available easily on the internet. It finds mention in the best reference work on articles and books published in the nineteen and twentieth centuries on Buddhism (till 1961), which contains over fifteen thousand entries.[35] The poem has been studied by noted scholars.[36] But Phillips himself is a mysterious figure of whom nothing is known other than the fact that he wrote two other poems, *Dreamland and Other Poems* in 1873 and *Scripture Riddles in Verse* five years later, and that he belonged to Leamington in Warwickshire in the UK.

In 1876 the prestigious *Encyclopaedia Britannica* had, for the first time, an elaborate entry under 'Buddhism'. It was written by 'T.W.R.D'. These were the initials of Thomas William Rhys Davids. Davids had been a civil servant in Ceylon and had developed a fondness for and fluency in Pali while in that British island colony.[37] A barrister on his return to London, he had already become an authoritative voice on Buddhism. In his *Encyclopaedia Britannica* entry, Davids summarized the sources of the then available information on the life of the Buddha:

1. *The Manual of Buddhism* published in 1860 by the Rev. R. Spence Hardy, adapted from various *Sinhalese* sources;

2. The translation into English (published by Bishop Bigandet in Rangoon in 1858 under the title *Legend of the Burmese Buddha*) of the translation into Burmese of a Pali work called by Bigandet *Mallalingara-Wouttoo*, of unknown author and date;

3. The original Pali text of the Jataka commentary, written in Ceylon in the 5th century A.D., edited in 1875 by Mr. Fusboll of Copenhagen (this is our best authority);

4. Mr. Beal's recently published translation into English (under the title (*The Romantic Legend of Sakya Buddha*) of a translation into Chinese, made in the 6th century A.D., of a Sanskrit Re work, called *Abhinishkramana Sutra*;

5. A Sanskrit work called the *Lalita Vistara*, undoubtedly very old, but of unknown author or date, the text of which has appeared in the *Bibliotheca Indica* in Calcutta, and a translation through the Tibetan into French by M. Foucoux in Paris (1848).[38]

Rhys Davids pointed out that the first three books 'represent the views of the southern Buddhists whose sacred books are in Pali, while the last two books 'represent the views of the northern Buddhists whose sacred books are in Sanskrit'. He believed that the first three were more reliable and complete while those based on Sanskrit sources were 'inflated to a great length by absurd and miraculous legends'. The southern Buddhists were those associated with the *Theravada* tradition prevalent in Ceylon, Burma, Siam and Cambodia, while the northern Buddhists were those associated with the *Mahayana* tradition in small parts of India, Tibet, Japan and China.

James Fergusson's *History of Indian and Eastern Architecture* was also published in 1876. It has been described as a 'masterpiece' and as 'the first chronologically and geographically comprehensive history of Indian art, albeit confined to architecture'. Fergusson was essentially a businessman who came out to India in his late teens to work as a trader in his family's mercantile house in Calcutta. He developed a keen interest in ancient Indian architecture and antiquities and from 1855 onward had been publishing his findings. The 1876 volume was the culmination of some two decades of his work in this area. His main conclusion was subsequently to be discredited, but at that time it became the accepted view and helped deepen interest in Buddhism. Fergusson put forward the 'somewhat amazing proposition that the religion of the Vaishnavas and that of the Jains were indistinguishable at that time, and that this was also true of their temples, which he saw as derived from Buddhist temples'. Fergusson also proclaimed that 'Sivite' temples too were 'originally appropriated to the worship of the Buddha'.[39]

A year later, that is in 1877, Rhys Davids followed up with his *Buddhism: Being a Sketch of the Life and Teachings of Gautama, the Buddha*. This book was published by the Society for Promoting Christian Language under its Non-Christian Religious Systems series. At about the same time a book called *Hinduism* would also come out as part of this series authored by Monier Williams, who in 1860 had beaten Max Mueller to become the second Boden Professor of Sanskrit at Oxford.[40]

The year 1877 is significant for yet another book—but this time not by a scholar like Max Mueller or Rhys Davids or Monier Williams but by someone totally different, a maverick who had led a peripatetically chequered life. Her public impact would exceed that of the respected academics though she appeared to be neither. This was Helena Petrovna Blavatsky or Madame Blavatsky or HPB, as she would come to be known. In 1875, Blavatsky, originally from Russia, had joined hands with an equally charismatic American called Colonel Henry Steel Olcott in New York to establish the Theosophical Society. This society, founded in a belief in the unity of all religions, would move its headquarters to Madras in 1882 and play a key role in popularizing *The Light of Asia* all over the world—and it continues to do so even now.

Blavatsky's book published in September 1877 was called *Isis Unveiled: A Master-Key to the Mysteries of Ancient and Modern Science and Theology*.[41] Blavatsky would court great controversy later and be dubbed a fraud as well but in 1877 her book, in which she explained

The commemorative stamp issued by the Sri Lankan Government to mark the birth centenary of T.W. Rhys Davids, a legendary name in Pali and Buddhist studies, in 1981.

Sir Monier Monier-Williams, Boden Professor of Sanskrit at Oxford. Born in Bombay, he was respected hugely by Arnold. He was, however, a critic of the Buddha and of Buddhism. (Source: Wikipedia)

that 'pre-Vedic Brahmanism and Buddhism are the double sources from which all religions sprang' and that 'Nirvana is the ocean to which all tend', created a stir.[42] Blavatsky wrote the manuscript and Olcott edited it. They were convinced that Buddhism and Hinduism championed religious tolerance while Christianity, especially in in its Catholic form, denounced it. The book was both hailed both as 'one of the most remarkable productions of the century' but also as a 'large dish of hash'. But one fate it did not suffer—it certainly was not ignored, and it continued to get written about and has never lost its appeal. Blavatsky died on 8 May 1891 in London and, according to the terms of her will, a reading from *The Light of Asia* was carried out on that day at Adyar. That tradition has continued unbroken since 1892.[43]

Finally, Max Mueller's immensely popular Hibbert Lectures, delivered at the Westminster Abbey in London in April 1878, invite mention. Max Mueller was Professor of Comparative Philology at Oxford and had already acquired a formidable reputation going beyond the confines of academia after moving to England from Germany in 1850. The year 1874 would see the publication of the sixth and final volume of Mueller's magnum opus—the translation of the *Rig Veda*. When differences arose between him and Oxford, Mueller resigned, and Arnold wrote a fulsome tribute to him in the *Daily Telegraph* of 8 December 1875 hailing his path-breaking contributions in the field of comparative philology in general and Sanskrit sacred texts in particular. This had evidently pleased the Oxford don, for Arnold wrote to him on 14 December 1875:

My dear Professor:

I did not write but dictated the article which I am glad to find has given you pleasure and that it expressed less perfectly than was intended the deep concern felt by me, in common with many old Oxford men, at your approaching departure from the University. Had editorial duties permitted it, my own pen should have made

*Stamp issued by the Government of India in 1974 to mark
the 150th birth anniversary of Max Mueller. He was much
loved by Queen Victoria for his supposed resemblance to her
husband.[44] He was a man deeply admired by Arnold.*

the public still better acquainted with the debt due to you from all
those who love scholarship illuminated and inspired by a faithful
liberalism . . .

As it turned out, Max Mueller stayed back.[45] His Hibbert lectures
*On the Origin and Growth of Religion as Illustrated by the Religions
of India* were delivered to packed audiences. Six years earlier, he
had delivered a series of lectures at Kiel in Germany, which was
published as *Lectures on the Science of Religion.* This contained a paper
on Buddhist nihilism and a translation of the Buddhist holy text
Dhammapada. But the London lectures were far more impactful,
and they were delivered in the city that mattered most at that time.

By the mid-1870s Arnold had established himself in London not only as a widely read scribe but as a man deeply interested in and knowledgeable about India. It was no wonder that he would get asked to speak on India or write about it. One such invitation came from Philip Stewart Robinson, who had been born in India and had lived there and who was now a journalist in London. Robinson's offbeat *In My Indian Garden* appeared in 1878 with a preface from Arnold. Robinson was a keen naturalist and sharp observer of India's biodiversity, reflected in his book, which still makes for delightful reading. Arnold commended it because 'it conveyed so just a sense of the vivid vitality of the Indian scenes and creatures and so much sympathy for the Asiatic side of our empire down to its simplest everyday objects'. Robinson would later write more on Indian birds, animals and trees and was an early exponent of humorous Anglo-Indian literature.

The man, the milieu and the moment would all come together in 1879 and *The Light of Asia* would blaze forth. It is to this I now turn.

Notes

1.   There would be another book that would be published in 1859 but only with its greatly revised second edition nine years later would it become a classic and have a frenzied impact that would deepen public interest in literature with 'Eastern' themes. This was Edward Fitzgerald's *Rubaiyat of Omar Khayyam*. Its fourth edition would come out in 1879, the same year as *The Light of Asia*.
2.   Wilson (1999)
3.   Hatton (1882)
4.   His Poona manuscript. 'Hitopadesa, being the Sanskrit text, with a vocabulary in Sanskrit, English and Marathi', prepared for students at the Deccan College, was printed in the Education Society's Press, Bombay in 1859. Arnold's *Hitopadesa* has been analysed in great detail in Killingley (2018).
5.   Killingley (2018)
6.   Mount (2015)
7.   The Mill letters are from Mineka and Lindley (eds) (1972). Six years earlier, in January 1866, Mill had angrily refused Arnold's invitation to

write for the *Daily Telegraph* because of the stand taken by the paper on the 'Jamaica question', on which Mill said, 'not only every principle I have, but the honour and character of England for generations to come, are at stake, but in the condign punishment of atrocities of which by their own not confession, but boast, the Jamaica authorities have been guilty; and while the question is pending, select as my official organ on another subject, a paper with which, in a matter of such transcendent importance, I am at open war'. Edwin Arnold had evidently *supported* the British Governor Edward John Eyre, who had crushed the 1865 insurrection at Morant Bay and punished its leaders. This Jamaica issue had divided the intellectual classes in Victorian England: Thomas Carlyle, Joshn Ruskin, Charles Dickens and Lord Tennyson came out in Eyre's support, while Mill, Charles Darwin and Thomas Huxley were critical of his actions and supported those locals who had rebelled. The 31 January 1866 letter of Mill to Edwin Arnold is in Filipiuk, Laine and Robson (1991).

8.   A good discussion of this episode is in Lahiri Choudhury (2010).

9.   Butcher (2008)

10. Newman (2004)

11. Stanley (1878)

12. MacLaren (1998)

13. There is epistolary evidence to suggest that in the early 1880s Arnold was, for a while, himself besotted with Dorothy Tennant. But by 1885 his ardour seems to have abated. From mid-1885 she was taken up with Stanley but three years later was bewitched by Sir Alfred Lyall, who had been an administrator in British India and a poet himself. Lyall reciprocated her feelings but advised her to settle down with Stanley. Ultimately, Dorothy Tennant married Stanley in July 1890. An account of these relationships is in Jeal (2007). Dorothy's mother Gertrude Tennant conducted England's most influential salon in the heart of political London, in which Arnold was a regular. A fine account of Gertrude's life is in Waller (2009). It was at Gertrude Tennant's house in May 1884 that Arnold first met Col. Henry Steel Olcott, who would take over as President of the Theosophical Society seven years later in 1891. But even before they had met, the Theosophical Society had been championing *The Light of Asia* vigorously all over the world. Another son-in-law of Gertrude Tennant was Frederick William Henry Myers, who founded the Society for Psychical Research in 1882. Arnold was closely associated with Myers and the Society.

14. Murray (2017)

15. Howsam (1998)

16. Howsam (1998)
17. Dalmia (2006)
18. Hansen (1989)
19. Arnold (1860)
20. In 1886, Arnold would use the word 'Hindoo' instead of the word 'faithful' in Arnold (1886).
21. Similarly, Arnold would use the word 'Swarga' (heaven) instead of the word 'splendour' in Arnold (1886).
22. *Calcutta Review* (1876)
23. Miller (1977)
24. Basham (1954)
25. Ibid. But Gombrich (1997) gives another point of view drawing from the Puranas. He writes: 'Some said that in taking this form Vishnu's aim was to mislead the gullible and weed out those who were not true Vaisnavas . . .' In response to another question of mine Gombrich had this to say via email on 30 March 2020: 'It is probably more than 60 years since I so much as opened *The Light of Asia*, and I very much doubt that I ever read it all through. I am aware that it used to be well known in India; presumably it owes its popularity to the fact that it is one of the few books by the British rulers which treats an Indian figure with respect . . . When Arnold wrote *The Light of Asia*, there was very little information about the Buddha available beyond some myths circulating . . .'
26. Arjunwadkar (1986)
27. Basham (1954)
28. Ray (2019)
29. In this context, it is pertinent to recall what Diana Eck wrote: 'We should note, however, that even before it came to signal divine descents of Vishnu, the term avatara was likely first used by Buddhists, to describe the descent of those who, like Siddhartha, took birth on earth to become fully awakened Buddhas'. Eck (2012). Thapar (2002) also puts forward the thesis that 'the idea of incarnations is a reminder of the theory of previous births of the Buddha and the bodhisattvas'.
30. I thank Puroshottam Agarwal for drawing my attention to this verse from Tulsidas' *Dohavali*.
31. In the Crimean War of October 1853–February 1856, Britain and France had sided with Turkey in its war with Russia.
32. Wright (1957)
33. Apps (2010)
34. Almond (1988), Allen (2002), Franklin (2008) and Allen (2016). All four, however, are heavily Anglo-centric accounts.

35. Hanayama (1961)
36. Almond (1988), Franklin (2008) and Tucker (2008) are three examples.
37. The definitive biography of Rhys Davids in Wickremeratne (1984).
38. Although Rhys Davids did not attribute any authorship to *Lalitavistara* *(Detailed Narration of the Sport of the Buddha)*, Kenneth Ch'en in his magisterial account of Buddhism in China mentions a Chinese catalogue of the early sixth century CE which attributed the authorship to Dharmaraksha, who was 'one of the most important monks and translators during the formative years of Chinese Buddhism'. Ch'en writes that Dharmaraksha lived in Tun-Huang in the late third century CE, was of Yueh-Shih ancestry, and was born in China and proficient in a number of Central Asiatic and Indian languages. Ch'en (1964)
39. I owe these observations on Fergusson to Tratakov (1997).
40. Monier Williams became Monier Monier-Williams after he was knighted in 1887, and that is the name by which he is remembered.
41. Isis is the Egyptian Goddess who represents the mysteries of nature.
42. Prothero (1996) is the best biography of Olcott in his Asian avatar.
43. Madame Blavatsky's multi-faceted life has been described well in Cranston (1993).
44. One of the best biographies of Max Mueller is by Nirad Chaudhuri, called *Scholar Extraordinary: Life of Friedrich Max Mueller* (Chatto and Windus; London 1974)
45. A.N. Wilson, *Charles Darwin: Victorian Mythmaker*, John Murray, London, 2017

SECTION II

4

1879: *The Light of Asia*

In February 1879, one of the earliest books on India's Buddhist heritage would come out. This was by Alexander Cunningham, the founder Director-General of the Archaeological Survey of India. Of this work with a long title, called

THE STUPA OF BHARHUT

A BUDDHIST MONUMENT ORNAMENTED WITH NUMEROUS SCULPTURES

ILLUSTRATIVE OF

BUDDHIST LEGEND AND HISTORY

IN THE

THIRD CENTURY BC

Max Mueller would say:

> In the sculptures and inscriptions of Bharhut we shall have in future a real landmark in the religious and literary history of India and many theories hitherto held by Sanskrit scholars will have to be modified accordingly.

The Bharhut excavations took place in the early 1870s and many of its fabulous finds are now at the Indian Museum in Kolkata. Cunningham re-enters this narrative a little later.

*Alexander Cunningham, the father of Indian archaeology and
a key figure in the rediscovery of Buddhism in India in the
nineteenth century. Arnold would consult him for his Buddha
Gya campaign to establish Buddhist control over the Mahabodhi
Temple there. (Source: Archaeological Survey of India)*

Afghanistan had dominated the political discourse in England
ever since the Second Anglo-Afghan war had begun in November
1878. The Treaty of Gandamak had been signed on 26 May 1879
as the Amir of Afghanistan had sued for peace. At about the
same time, Max Mueller launched his famed 'Sacred Books of
the East' series, with his translation of the Upanishads being the
very first volume.[1]

So far, Arnold had written a two-volume study of Dalhousie
as Viceroy. He had published translations of two very well-known
Indian literary classics. In addition, he had brought out a number
of original poems on Indian themes. But in 1879 he would hit
the jackpot as it were and bring out the blockbuster that would
reverberate across the world. The Buddha was very much in the

air, what with Rhys Davids, Max Mueller himself and Madame Blavatsky having generated up great interest in him. It was natural for a man of Arnold's background and inclinations to be drawn into writing something on this theme.

The Light of Asia came with a formidable dedication. It was 'dutifully inscribed' to:

The SOVEREIGN, GRAND MASTER AND COMPANIONS
OF
THE MOST EXALTED STAR OF INDIA

The Most Exalted Star of India had been instituted in 1861 following the Mutiny to occasionally recognize merit but more importantly to reward loyalty among the Indian subjects to the British crown. The Sovereign in the dedication was clearly Queen Victoria herself, while the Grand Master was the Viceroy Lord Lytton. The Companions, of whom Arnold was one himself, comprised largely of Indian royals and a few others. The title page reads thus:

The LIGHT OF ASIA
Or
THE GREAT RENUNCIATION
(MAHABHINISHKRAMANA)

BEING

THE LIFE AND TEACHING OF GAUTAMA
PRINCE OF INDIA AND FOUNDER OF BUDDHISM

(AS TOLD IN VERSE BY AN INDIAN BUDDHIST)

So, from the beginning, it is clear that Arnold has adopted a novel technique: the life, character and philosophy of Prince Gautama of India, the founder of Buddhism, are being depicted 'by the medium of an imaginary Buddhist votary'. He does this because, as he says:

to appreciate the spirit of Asiatic thoughts, they should be regarded from the Oriental point of view; and neither the miracles which consecrate this record nor the philosophy which it embodies, could have been otherwise so naturally produced.

Clearly, the two-year stint in Poona had left an indelible imprint on Arnold. In his preface he says that he wants to elucidate on Nirvana, Dharma, Karma and other chief features of Buddhism (like the doctrine of Transmigration), saying that it was his firm conviction that a 'third of mankind would never have been brought to believe in blank abstractions, or in Nothingness as the issue and crown of Being'. He was taking the orthodox Christian critics head-on.

Apart from quoting Jules Barthelemy St. Hilaire's adulatory comments on the Buddha, the only source Arnold acknowledges specifically for his poem is 'the imperfect Buddhistic citations much as they stand in Spence Hardy's work'. St. Hilaire was a French philosopher and politician whose *Le Bouddha et sa Religion* was first published in 1860.[2] Arnold writes:

> Even M. Barthelemy St. Hilaire, totally misjudging, as he does, many points of Buddhism, is well cited by Professor Max Muller as saying of Prince Siddhartha: His life was utterly stainless . . . His constant heroism equalled his conviction; and although the doctrine that he propounded is false, the personal examples that he gave are irreproachable. He is the perfect model of all the virtues that he preached; his abnegation, his charity, his unalterable gentleness never failed for a single instant . . . In silence he prepared his doctrine during six years of retreat and meditation; he propagated it solely by the power of the word and of persuasion during more than half a century, and when he died in the arms of his disciples it was with the serenity of a sage, who was certain that he had found the truth.

Spence Hardy was an early British Methodist missionary who had spent more than ten years in Ceylon between 1825–65 before his demise in April 1868. Hardy's *A Manual of Buddhism in its Modern Development* was derived from Sinhalese manuscripts and his own observations while in Ceylon. It had first appeared in 1853 although Rhys Davids ascribed it to 1860 in the *Encyclopedia Britannica*, as mentioned earlier. His final work, *Christianity and Buddhism Compared*, would be published in 1874. Hardy was a devout and practising Christian, a steadfast believer in the supremacy of Christianity, unlike Arnold, who as a twenty-one-year-old undergraduate at Oxford and even before going out to India had written:[3]

Not by one portal, or one path alone
God's holy messages to men are known . . .

Scholars have grappled with the issue of Arnold's sources, forgetting his eclectic reading and the knowledge he would have picked up in India. In 1954, A.L. Basham in his highly-regarded *The Wonder that was India* mentioned in passing that *The Light of Asia* was based on the *Lalitavistara*.[4] In 1960, this would be another verdict:[5]

The principal source for The Light of Asia, then, is Professor Beal's translation of the Abhinishkramana Sutra. This combined with lesser borrowings from Spence Hardy and Arnold's first hand experience of Buddhism and of Indian life constitutes the material of the poem.

And in 1972 there would be yet another conclusion:[6]

Arnold had read many books on Buddhism which were available in 1879, but his poem is basically derived from four sources: The Romantic Legend of Sakya-Buddha, translated by Samuel Beal from the Chinese version of the Abhinishkramana Sutra; R. Spence Hardy's A Manual of Buddhism in its Modern Development, a lengthy survey of the Theravada Buddhism of Ceylon by a long-time Wesleyan missionary; Buddhaghosha's Parables and, in the same volume, F. Max Mueller's translation of the Dhammapada, a collection of Buddhist proverbial wisdom; and T.W. Rhys Davids' Buddhism, probably the best general book on the subject written in English before the twentieth century. Of these Beal's work is the most important, for it is the biography on which the poem's narrative is mainly based.

So, who was this Samuel Beal? He was very much a man of the Anglican Church who had served with the British Navy in China in the mid-nineteenth century and had come to be proficient in Chinese. He emerged as the most prodigious translator of Chinese works on Buddhism in England in the latter half of the nineteenth century. Beal's *The Romantic Legend of Sakya Buddha* was published by Trubner and Co. in 1875. As Beal himself explained in the introduction:

> This work is a translation of the Chinese version of the 'Abhinishkramana Sutra', done in that language by Djnanakuta, a Buddhist priest from North India who resided in China during the Tsui dynasty, i.e., about the end of the sixth century, A.D.

Beal also acknowledges that the India Office facilitated him greatly—first by granting him access to the Chinese text that was in its archives and then by giving him a temporary job to complete the translation. Beal points out that the original Sanskrit text may well have been in circulation in India 'prior to 69 or 70 AD', some four centuries after the death of the Buddha. He also reveals something that would not have been apparent after reading the 1876 *Encyclopedia Britannica* entry on Buddhism: that the *Abhinishkramana Sutra* is also called *Lalitavistara* by a different group of Buddhists. So, Basham may not have been wrong after all and he does have one supporter. Writing in 1988, Philip Almond, an Australian scholar,[7] has said that Arnold based his *The Light of Asia* on Philippe Edouard Foucaux's French translation of the *Lalitavistara*. Foucaux was Europe's leading Tibetologist in the latter half of the nineteenth century.[8]

The sources for *The Light of Asia* were revisited after a long gap in 2008 by a noted American scholar who would write that while Arnold would have read Rev. P. Bigandet's *The Life or Legend of Gautama* (1858) derived from Burmese sources[9] and Spence Hardy's *A Manual of Buddhism* (1860) derived from Sinhalese sources, it is unlikely that he would have related to them because neither was sympathetic to the Buddha or Buddhism. Instead, the American academic Jeffrey Franklin writes:[10]

> In 1871, Henry Alabaster published his still influential work, *The Wheel of the Law: Buddhism Illustrated from Siamese Sources*; it includes a sympathetic retelling of the life of the Buddha and an articulate defence of Buddhism addressed specifically to Western readers . . . Two of the most important other sources for Arnold were Samuel Beal's *The Romantic Legend of Sakya Buddha* (1875) and T.W. Rhys Davids' widely-read *Buddhism: Being A Sketch of the Life and Teachings of Gautama, the Buddha* (1877) . . .

Henry Alabaster first worked for the British in Siam during the reign of King Rama IV before becoming the key aide to King Rama V for about fifteen years till his death in 1888. His is a name still remembered in Thailand. Towards the very end of this narrative his name will crop up again.

The Light of Asia was in 'eight books of blank verse, with some five or six hundred lines in each'. Arnold did not give any descriptive title to each of the books and refers to them simply in chronological order.

Book the First deals with the birth, boyhood and childhood of Siddartha[11] and contains 436 lines.

Book the Second concerns his teenage years leading up to his marriage to Yasodhara and has 515 lines.

Book the Third is about the luxurious life he leads as a husband and father but also with his growing doubts after seeing an old man, a sick man, a corpse and a wandering ascetic. It has 601 lines.

Book the Fourth deals with his Great Renunciation and the beginning of his search for the cure to the ills of human existence. This is covered in 568 lines.

Book the Fifth elaborates on his self-mortification in the company of wandering ascetics and has 560 lines.

Book the Sixth explains his disenchantment with self-mortification as a solution, his partaking of Sujata's gift of milk to end his starvation and his attainment of Buddhahood under the Bodhi tree. Not surprisingly, it is the longest and has 780 lines.

Book the Seventh deals with his father's grief, his wife's anguish and his son's bewilderment at his absence, his homecoming and their recognition of what he had accomplished. It has 520 lines.

Book the Eighth is the easiest to read, with 611 lines, and goes over the establishment of the order of the monks and expositions of the Buddha's teachings and doctrines. It is probably the most powerful section of the entire poem.

In all, there are 5300 lines and 41,000 words in *The Light of Asia*.[12] The poem starts off thus:

The Scripture of the Saviour of the World,
Lord Buddha—Prince Siddhartha styled on earth—
In Earth and Heavens and Hells Incomparable,
All-honoured, Wisest, Best, most Pitiful;
The Teacher of Nirvana and the Law.
Thus came he to be born again for men.

Book the Eighth is clearly the crux of *The Light of Asia*. It contains stirring descriptions of the Buddha's philosophy and his teachings, his exposition of the Four Noble Truths and the Eightfold Path, his Five Rules for good behaviour and explanation of the doctrines of Karma and Nirvana. More than anything else in the poem, the closing of Book the Eighth perhaps caught the public imagination the most:

Here endeth what I write
Who love the Master for his love of us.

A little knowing, little have I told
Touching the Teacher and the Ways of Peace.
Forty-five rains thereafter showed he those
In many lands and many tongues, and gave
Our Asia light, that still is beautiful,
Conquering the word with spirit of strong grace;
All of which is written in the holy Books,
And where he passed and what proud Emperors
Carved his sweet words upon the rocks and caves:
The Buddha died, the great Tathagato,
Even as a man 'mongst men, fulfilling all:
And how a thousand crores since then
Have tred the Path which leads where he went
Unto NIRVANA where the Silence lives

-----------o----------

AH! BLESSED LORD! OH, HIGH DELIVERER!
FORGIVE THIS FEEBLE SCRIPT, WHICH DOTH THEE
     WRONG,
MEASURING WITH LITTLE WIT THY LOFTY LOVE.
AH! LOVER! BROTHER! GUIDE! LAMP OF THE LAW!
I TAKE MY REFUGE IN THY NAME AND THEE!
I TAKE MY REFUGE IN THY LAW OF GOOD!
I TAKE MY REFUGE IN THY ORDER! *OM!*
THE DEW IS ON THE LOTUS! —RISE, GREAT SUN!
AND LIFT MY LEAF AND MIX ME WITH THE WAVE.
OM MANI PADME HUM, THE SUNRISE COMES!
THE DEWDROP SLIPS INTO THE SHINING SEA!

The very first edition was presented to the public in mid-July 1879:

as a modest octavo volume bound in yellow cloth, with the name
of Trubner and Company on the spine. The title page was made
up of no less than seven different fonts of type and the ugly

plates of this first printing remained the identifying mark of all authorized editions, both English and American, for the next fifty years.[13]

However, this edition had no illustrations whatsoever. In spite of this, it proved to be a runaway success. What happened to the original manuscript of *The Light of Asia*? Its fate would not be known till 1920, when the autobiography of one of America's greatest industrial magnates was published. Andrew Carnegie had passed away the previous year and his widow decided to publish the memoirs left behind by him, in which at one place he would recall:[14]

"The Light of Asia" by Edwin Arnold came out at this time and gave me greater delight than any similar poetical work I had recently read. I had just been in India and the book took me there again. My appreciation of it reached the author's ears and later having made his acquaintance in London, he presented me with the original manuscript of the book. It is one of my most precious treasures.

Hailing from Scotland, Carnegie was amongst the most ruthless businessmen in America but also amongst its most philanthropic. He considered himself the 'moral philosopher of industrial capitalism'.[15] Arnold had written to him on 6 July 1883.

Dear Mr. Carnegie:

. . . Of thousands in America whose generous words of praise and appreciation have so richly rewarded my labour in "The Light of Asia", none has shown a friendlier feeling for the work than yourself. Accept therefore as a 'keepsake' the MS of the poem written with my own hand, from which it was printed. Some day perhaps, it will have the value with those to come, which it has, I know, today in your kind eyes.

This 230-page manuscript now lies in the Carnegie collection at the Library of Congress in Washington DC. Interestingly, Arnold's original title for the poem was *The Gospel of Asia*. He changed it to *The Light of Asia*.

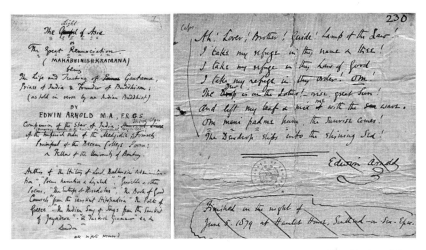

The title page and last page of the original handwritten manuscript of The Light of Asia *now at the Library of Congress, Washington DC.*

Reviews of *The Light of Asia* started appearing as soon as it was published. It was as if it had been eagerly expected and had finally arrived. On 1 August 1879 *The Daily Review* wrote:

> . . . But, without sharing the admiration which have given Mr. Arnold much of his literary skill, we must all the more testify to the grace and beauty of the poem. It is in truth "an Idyll of the King" with Gautama instead of Arthur for its hero and Nirvana instead of the Christian ideal and the Holy Grail as its aim . . . We marvel that one whose days are without leisure should have kept up his Oriental studies and have found the calm of spirit and the time to write such verse . . . Here is the best that can be said for Buddhism by its most enthusiastic votaries. It is all so sad to him who knows Christ the Divine Son of the Personal Father—yet to stimulating to the true Christian to proclaim the glad tidings of great joy which are to all people.

Eight days later *The Athenaeum*, while praising Arnold for elucidations of the much-misunderstood ideas of *karma* and *nirvana*, drew attention to the influence of John Keats and Alfred Tennyson on the structure and style of *The Light of Asia*. It was critical but at the same time said 'it is not merely on account of its subject that this poem deserves attention; it is full of poetical merit, and its descriptions are often exceedingly beautiful'.

On 19 August 1879 the *Pall Mall Gazette* wrote about it in some detail, saying that 'its real merit is that it is true to Indian feeling, and bears the marks of long and profitable study of the philosophy and legends of Buddha' and ended thus:

> The most difficult part of Mr. Arnold's task was of course to present the distinctive doctrines of Buddha. Out of the tangled and forbidding technicalities of Buddhistic theology he had to sift a system which would not seem unintelligible to Western minds, and yet would faithfully represent the terminology and teaching of Gautama. It appears to us that he has succeeded well. As a poem his work is more than respectable; as presenting a philosophical and religious condensation of Buddhism, and a picture of its Founder, it deserves popularity.

The Observer of 31 August 1879 complimented Arnold for a 'remarkable poem' and for enriching 'our literature by a fine poem abounding with vivid and faithful descriptions of Indian scenes' and for conveying 'the lofty character of the founder of Buddhism and of the purport of his doctrines'. Quoting at length from the poem it pointed that the 'author had modified some of the views generally accepted with regard to Buddhism' but that the 'author's wide knowledge of India and genuine interest in his subject enhance the value of his researches, and entitle his opinions with respect, whilst his powers of description carry the reader with them'.

Almost all major publications in the UK had reviewed the poem within a few weeks of its publication. The initial reaction to *The Light of Asia* had been excellent. But it was, truth be told, unexpected even by those considered to be experts on Buddhism. Rhys Davids himself, for instance, began his review of the book[16] by saying:

> Mr. Arnold has maintained with great dramatic consistency the role of his Buddhist enthusiast; and has caught with commendable accuracy and sympathy the spirit of the ancient faith . . .

And after acknowledging that:

> . . . critical acumen and historical accuracy would have been inconsistent with the character who is supposed to tell the tale . . .

went on to add:

> A poetical version of a tale the main incidents of which are so familiar must lose all interest depending on mystery of plot; and the strangeness and distance of the scene and of the time demand of the reader some intellectual effort. It is scarcely possible that an author who has to struggle against such disadvantages can expect his work to appeal to the popular taste.

The greatest British scholar of Buddhism during the later half of the nineteenth century was to be very soon proved spectacularly wrong. The stunning success of *The Light of Asia* would cause bewilderment and some heartburn too amongst those who had spent years on the subject without having achieved the public admiration and commercial success that Arnold would soon do. Decades later it would be said that the immediate interest in Buddhism that *The Light of Asia* aroused did much to promote the sale of Rhys Davids' own *Buddhism* that had been published just the previous year.[17]

The poem would get an even greater boost by the reception it would receive across the Atlantic. This American response would further enhance the poem's value in the UK and soon Europe too would be in its thrall. But before we get to the American review, I must mention one review in India that would prove hugely influential in popularizing *The Light of Asia* in India and Europe. Three reviews that appeared in India were noteworthy. *The Pioneer* was then one of India's leading newspapers, published out of Allahabad. Rudyard Kipling would have much to do with it many years later. Its editor was Alfred Percy Sinnett, who was an early theosophist and would remain so till the end of his life in 1921. The review called *The Light of Asia* the greatest poem since Lord Byron's *Childe Harold's Pilgrimage* that had appeared in four parts between 1812 and 1818. On 13 September 1879, the *Times of India* reproduced the review of the *Pall Mall Gazette.*

But it was the review in the inaugural issue of the *Theosophist* that would prove most impactful. The *Theosophist,* launched from Bombay, declared itself to be 'A Monthly Journal Devoted to Oriental Philosophy, Art, Literature and Occultism; Embracing Mesmerism, Spiritualism and Other Secret Sciences'. It was a publication of the Theosophical Society that called itself 'a Republic of Conscience', that claimed to derive inspiration from the 'unremitting labour' of Orientalists' and that felt 'equal respect and veneration for Vedic, Buddhist, Zoroastrian and other old religions of the world; and a like brotherly feeling towards its Hindu, Sinhalese, Parsi, Jain, Hebrew and Christian members as individual students of "self", of nature, and of the divine in nature'.

The very first issue of the *Theosophist* in October 1879 had a signed article by Madame Blavatsky called 'Persian Zoroastrianism and Russian Vandalism'. It had an 'exclusive' excerpt from the autobiography of Dayanand Saraswati, the social reformer who had founded the Arya Samaj in April 1875 and who was then close to the Theosophical Society but would break with it later. There were also articles on yoga and ancient Aryan trigonometry, apart from a long piece on the aims, objectives and approach to life of the theosophists themselves. Placed in between all this was the unsigned review of *The Light of Asia.* It has been believed that Madame Blavatsky had written it. It could have been Henry Olcott too for that matter. But my view is that it was somebody else, a scholar in Bombay whose identity we will never know.

The *Theosophist* called Arnold's latest work 'a timely work in poetical form and one whose subject—perfect though the outward clothing be—is sure to provoke discussion and bitter criticisms'. It went on:

> . . . we regard the poem as a really remarkable specimen of literary talent, replete with philosophical thought and religious feeling . . .
> The Miltonic verse of the poem is rich, simple and yet powerful . . .

It quotes from the poem extensively, observing that 'Buddhism from its beginning has changed the moral aspect of not only India but nearly all of Asia' and that 'Mr Arnold's views are those of most of the Orientalists of today, who have at last arrived at the conclusion that Nirvana—whatever it may mean philologically–philosophically and logically is anything but *annihilation*'.

In America, very soon after the poem had appeared, the *New York Daily Tribune* had, on 12 August 1879, called it a 'poem equally striking for its novelty of conception, its vigor of execution and the exquisite beauty of its descriptive passages'. But this is not what led *The Light of Asia* to gain acceptance there. Amos Bronson Alcott was an American philosopher and writer of the nineteenth century, a leading figure of what was known as the Transcendental Club, a group of like-minded men (and a few women) in and around Boston who believed in the essential unity of all religions. Three of the biggest names of this movement were Ralph Waldo Emerson, Henry David Thoreau and Walt Whitman. Sometime in mid-August 1879, Alcott would receive a letter from his friend William Henry Channing, who happened to be Arnold's father-in-law. Channing sent a copy of *The Light of Asia* to Alcott suggesting, 'Poem and Poet should be widely known and heartily welcomed by the nation that providentially serves as a mediator between Europe and Asia, to unite the East and West, the Ancient and the Modern Ages, in unity'.

Alcott received *The Light of Asia* in Boston on 19 August 1879, less than a month after it had first made its debut in London. From Alcott it passed on to Oliver Wendell Holmes, another prominent member of the Transcendental Club, a great polymath and, among other things, the author of the phrase 'Boston Brahmin', which applied to him very well. Holmes would not just review *The Light of Asia* but write a mini thesis on it, running into twenty-seven pages in the *International Review*, a monthly published from New York. Holmes would also be responsible for the early 1880 US edition of the book out of Boston, those being the times when British works were not protected by copyright in the United States. Very soon, *The Light of Asia* would take America, coming out of a prolonged sixty-five-month period of economic contraction, by storm. It has been described as the book that introduced the Buddha and Buddhism to America at a time when that country was in the midst of what has been called 'the gilded age'—a period of unprecedented wealth creation and fabulous individual fortunes. It was almost as if *The Light of Asia* was offering a moral compass in these tumultuous times.[18]

Holmes called the poem a work of great beauty and went on to extoll it:

> It tells a story of intense interest, which never flags for a moment; its descriptions are drawn by the hand of a master with the eye of a poet and the familiarity of an expert with the objects described; its tone is so lofty that there is nothing with which to compare it but the New Testament; it is full of variety, now picturesque, now pathetic, now rising into the noblest realms of thought and aspiration; it finds language penetrating, fluent, elevated, impassioned, musical always, to clothe its varied thoughts and sentiments . . . The reader of the poem we have been looking over together has before him one of the world's greatest ideal characters, in a narrative embodying some of the most striking legends of the story-telling East, all woven together in the richest and most effective phrases of an affluent English vocabulary . . .

Holmes' account of *The Light of Asia* would contribute heavily to Arnold's great reputation in the USA.

Oliver Wendell Holmes Sr, who brought The Light of Asia *to the notice of America in late 1879. His son bearing the same name would later become one of America's most respected jurists while serving on the US Supreme Court. (Source: Wikipedia)*

Five months after *The Light of Asia* first came out, Arnold received this letter dated 5 December 1879 from Bangkok:

Sir—My father devoted much time to the study and defence of his religion, and although I, being called to the throne while young, had no time to become a scholar like him, I too have interested myself in the study of sacred books . . . I thank you for the copy of your poem, "The Light of Asia" presented to me through my Minister in London. . . . I can say that your poem "The Light of Asia" is the most eloquent defence of Buddhism that has yet appeared . . .

To mark my good opinion of your good feeling towards Eastern peoples and my appreciation of your high ability and the service you have done to all Buddhists by this defence of their religion, I have much satisfaction in appointing you an officer of our most exalted order of the White Elephant . . .

I am yours faithfully
(Manu Regia) CHULALONKORN, King

The diploma is embossed on parchment in black, red and gold and reads thus:

Somdelch Phra Paramindr Maha Chulalonkorn, Phra Chula Chom Klao, King of Siam, fifth sovereign of the present dynasty, which founded and established its rule at Katana Kosindr Mahindr Ayuddhya, Bangkok, the capital city of Siam, both northern and southern and its dependencies, the suzereign of the Laos and Malays and Koreans, & c., &c.,—To all and singular to whom these presents shall come. Know ye, we deem it right and fitting that Edwin Arnold, Esquire, author of 'The Light of Asia', should be appointed an officer of the most exalted order of the White Elephant, to his honour thenceforth. May the power which is most highest in the universe keep and guard him, and grant him happiness and prosperity! Given at our palace Parama Raja Maholarm, on Tuesday the 11th waning of the lunar month Migusira, the first month from the cold season of the year Toh Ekasok, 1241 of the Siamese era, corresponding to the European date 9th of December, 1879, of the Christian era, being the 4046th day or 12th year of our reign.

"(Manu Regia) CHULALONKORN, R.S"

This award may well have been the King's way of projecting Siam's 'soft power' derived from its ancient Buddhist heritage that was under attack by Christian missionaries. His father had founded a new sect called Thammayut, which was a modernised version of the traditional Buddhism in Siam, and Chulalonkorn's recognition of *The Light of Asia* could also have been a way of giving greater legitimacy to his father's legacy.

King Chulalonkorn of Siam, who was captivated by The Light of Asia *when it first appeared in 1879. He became a great admirer of Arnold. (Source: Wikipedia)*

As soon as he got the letter from the King of Siam, Arnold set off on 8 December 1879 with members of his family for a four-month voyage upon the Nile. As for King Chulalonkorn, in early July 1896 he would visit the vast Borodudur temple complex in Java and take away reliefs and statues to Bangkok. In 1904 the King would publish his translation into Thai of thirty *Jatakas* from Pali. This would be a milestone in recent Siamese history.[19]

I have spoken about how different scholars have tried to locate the sources of *The Light of Asia*. Some have pointed to the influence of English translations of Pali texts or the influence of French translations of Sanskrit texts. Let us not forget that Arnold was an extraordinarily well-read man, a man who had spent over two years in an atmosphere of intense Sanskrit learning in India. He would also have had a sense of the oral traditions of the life of the Buddha such as they existed in mid-nineteenth-century western India. Before *The Light of Asia*, he had translated the *Gitagovinda*, which depicted the Buddha as the ninth incarnation of Vishnu. And I cannot believe that as a student of Sanskrit poetry Arnold would not have been familiar with Ashvaghosha's *Buddhacarita*, an epic of great stylistic flourish composed in Sanskrit sometime in the first century CE.

So it was that in 1879 *The Light of Asia* came to be. One Indian who would later be hailed as 'Father of the Nation' was ten years old then. Another Indian who was to be his designated political heir would be born ten years later. *The Light of Asia* was published exactly midway between the births of Mohandas Karamchand Gandhi and Jawaharlal Nehru. The year 1879 was also when one of India's most gifted English poets Sarojini Naidu was born. In 1896 she would hail Arnold and Alfred Austin as 'rare geniuses and true poets'.[20] In 1905, her anthology *The Golden Threshold*[21] would be published in London, in which the very last poem was called 'To a Buddha seated on a Lotus'. This would be included in the voluminous *The Oxford Book of English Mystical Verse* (1917)[22] that also had selections from Book the Eighth of *The Light of Asia*. Sarojini Naidu would be the only Indian in the collection—strangely, Rabindranath Tagore, who had by then won the Nobel Prize for Literature, does not figure in it.

In September 1882 Arnold would write the preface to his *Pearls of the Faith*, a poem extolling the ninety-nine names of Allah. He had just completed a hugely successful visit to America and so this book would come out in early 1883 with a dedication to:

The Many Friends in America
(known and unknown)

of

The Author
of "The Light of Asia"

In the preface to the *Pearls of the Faith*, Arnold would explain:

I have thus at length finished the Oriental Trilogy which I designed. In my "Indian Song of Songs" I sought to transfer to English poetry subtle and lovely Sanskrit idyll of the Hindu theology. In my "Light of Asia" I related the story and displayed the gentle and far-reaching doctrines of that great Hindoo prince who founded Buddhism. I have tried to present here, in the simple, familiar and credulous, but earnest spirit and manner of Islam—and from its own points of view—some of the thoughts and beliefs of the followers of the famous Prophet of Arabia.

This is the most straight-forward explanation of why *The Light of Asia* came to be written. It is interesting that Arnold takes *Gitagovinda* as the "Hindoo" pick for his trilogy and regards Islam as very much an "Indian" religion. Two years later his *The Song Celestial or Bhagavad Gita* would be published, which would make him even more of a name among the educated Hindu communities. This book, like *The Light of Asia*, would immortalize him but Arnold did not consider it part of his trilogy.

Another reason for *The Light of Asia* would be revealed many years later in 1942 by Arnold's son.[23] By then Julian Arnold was running seventy-nine and had written a book of recollections of famous people he had met over the decades. According to him, his father wrote *The Light of Asia* to unwind and to get his mind off politics and to 'uncurl his brain' when he came home after writing thundering editorials and articles on what the British should be doing on the confrontation between Russia and Turkey. Julian Arnold recalled:

It would be difficult to select literary tasks more dissimilar than the cares of a wartime editor, and the writing, in epic form, of a clear and wondrously colourful exposition of the metaphysics of Buddha. Like a mountain torrent he forcefully aided to sweep from his country's course all impediments—then changing to the mood of a poet, passed to levels where thought formed pools in the deep calm of which the eternal hills were mirrored. Too pent with intellectual energies to desire rest, he deliberately chose a counter-balance to his daily work so different in its nature that it served as a relaxation.

Julian Arnold went on to also provide his remembrance of how his father wrote his immortal poem:[24]

> Nor was the method of writing *The Light of Asia* less remarkable than the time chosen for its inception. He would jot down, in train or carriage or wheresoever he happened to be, a few lines as they came to him, using any scrap of paper at hand, such as margins of newspapers he had been reading, or the insides of envelopes, or the back of his menu card at dinner . . . At home, in the evenings, he would write long passages, undisturbed by the conversation around him.
>
> Those fragmentary writings he assembled into a book which he called his "brick pile", and after he had revised, expanded and polished its contents, he copied the whole into another book. That final manuscript passed on to his publishers as the harmonious and connected poem we know as *The Light of Asia*.

Notes

1. Of the forty-nine translations of sacred books to be published as part of this series, twenty belonged to Hindu, eleven to Buddhist, nine to Zoroastrian, five to Chinese, two to Islamic and two to Jain traditions. The very last volume in 1894 was E.B. Cowell's translation of the famous biography of the Buddha by Ashvaghosha in Sanskrit. The fiftieth and final book would be an index volume and that would come out in 1910.

2. It was also rumoured that he was the illegitimate son of Napoleon I. Arnold quotes from the original French but I have used the English translation provided in Peiris (1970).

3. It is only some years later that Arnold would undoubtedly become aware of a similar sentiment in the Rg Veda: *Ekam Sat, Viprah Bahuda Vadanti:* Truth is One, the Learned call it by different names.

4. Basham (1954). Basham describes *The Light of Asia* as 'a lengthy poem on the Buddha's life which enjoyed much popularity at the end of the last century, and is still readable, though its style has somewhat dated'.

5. Sastry (1960)
6. Clausen (1972)
7. Almond (1988)
8. *Lalitavistara*, translated as 'The Play in Full', was orginally in Sanskrit and is usually dated to the third century CE. Apart from its significance as a description of Gautama Buddha's life, its value lies in the fact that 'it was written at a time when most societies had difficulty handling numbers beyond 1000'. *Lalitavistara* not only has no problem with gigantic numbers, but 'seems to revel in giving them names' (10^{421} is the highest number quoted and given a name).
9. It was Bigandet who first wrote: "It is not surprising that we should have to acknowledge the fact that the voyages of two Chinese travellers, undertaken in the fifth and seventh century of our era, have done more to elucidate the history and geography of Buddhism in India, than all that has hitherto been found in the Sanskrit and Pali books of India and the neighbouring countries". Bigandet was, of course, referring to Faxian and Xuanzang. To this must be added a third traveller—Yijing—also in the seventh century, whose account became available in English only in 1896.
10. Franklin (2008)
11. In the entire poem Arnold uses the name Siddartha to refer to the Buddha in his pre-enlightenment years. In his talks and other writings he would also use the name Gautama.
12. The description of each of the eight books of *The Light of Asia* follows Peiris (1970) very closely.
13. Wright (1957)
14. Carnegie (1920)
15. Nasaw (2007)
16. *Academy*, vol 16, no. 379 N.S. (1879), pp 98-99
17. Humphreys (1956)
18. This is also almost the same period that has been called 'The Age of Decadence' in the UK by Simon Heffer in Heffer (2017).
19. Jory (2002)
20. She wrote on 13 January 1896 as a teenage undergraduate at Cambridge to her beau: 'Take that lovely singer Edwin Arnold and that graceful writer, the laureate of the English, Alfred Austin—who says we have no rare geniuses and true poets in these days'. I am thankful to Makarand Paranjape for drawing my attention to this. The full letter is in Paranjape (1996).
21. Naidu (1905)

22. *The Oxford Book of English Mystical Verse*, chosen by D.H.S. Nicholson and A.H.E. Lee, Oxford University Press, 1917. It would be regularly reprinted by that Press till 1962. It would be reprinted by The Apocryphile Press in May 2012.

23. Arnold (1942)

24. Much earlier writing in *the Theosophic Messenger* in July 1911 under the name of J.B. Lindon, Julian Arnold would recall that portions of *The Light of Asia* were composed in the summer of 1878 at an ancient mansion with a lot of history attached to it at Glengyle in the highlands of Scotland. Lindon remembered his father often sitting and writing under an old oak which stretched its protecting branches over the house, which he called his 'Bodhi-tree'. Today, Glengyle is known for the whisky it produces.

5

1880–1885: Basking in the Glory of *The Light of Asia*

Cashing in on the burgeoning popularity of *The Light of Asia*, Arnold brought out *Indian Poetry* in 1881. It contained his already published translations of the *Gitagovinda* and the *Hitopadesa* and other poems like *The Rajpoot Wife*. He added a few more poems on 'Hindoo' and Islamic themes. But more importantly *Indian Poetry* contained translations from the Sanskrit from the 'two books of the *Iliad* of India', namely the *Mahabharata*. Two years later came *Indian Idylls*, dedicated to his father-in-law William Henry Channing, whose gentle nudge had helped *The Light of Asia* to become a sensation in America. *Indian Idylls* contained more translations from the *Mahabharata*, and Arnold explained what lay behind the new offering:

> Sometime ago, I wrote and published in a paper entitled "The Iliad and the Odyssey of India", the following passages: "There exist two colossal, two unparalleled epic poems in the sacred language of India—the *Mahabharata* and the *Ramayana*—which were not known to Europe, even by name, till Sir William Jones announced their existence; and one of which (the larger) since his time has been made public only by fragments, by mere specimens, bearing to those vast treasures of Sanskrit literature such small proportion as cabinet samples of ore have to the riches of a silver mine. Yet these most remarkable poems contain almost all the history of succeeding and countless millions of Hindoo people . . .
>
> I believe that certain portions of the mighty Poem which here appear, and many other episodes, to be of greater antiquity than those ascribed to the *Mahabharata* generally . . . The Sanskrit verse (ofttimes as musical and highly-wrought as Homer's own Greek),

bears testimony, I think—by evidence too long and recondite for citation here—to an origin anterior to writing, anterior to Puranic theology, anterior to Homer, perhaps even to Moses himself.

Both *Indian Poetry* and *Indian Idylls* were received well. By then Arnold had become an exceedingly recognizable figure and these books found a market outside England as well. Many years later, on 1 August 1911, the future Mahatma was to write from his Tolstoy Farm near Johannesburg to his nephew Chagganlal Gandhi, who was then at the future Mahatma's Phoenix Farm in Natal:[1]

> I read *Indian Idylls* (Edwin Arnold's) to the boys. It has excellent translations of attractive poems from the *Mahabharata*. Amongst them I read "The Enchanted Lake" and found it to be superb. What is the Sanskrit title? Please let me know if you or anyone there knows it. I have been thinking that we should have a free translation made into Gujarati verse and publish it. All the Pandavas go to a lake in the hope of finding water. But in their impatience, they drink from the lake without answering questions [put to them] by the Yaksha, the guardian spirit of the lake, and fall down unconscious. Yudhishthira goes last and drinks water after giving the answers. All his answers relate to [nature of] obligation but they are very ingenious . . .

The boys being referred to by Gandhi in this letter were twenty-five in number and included his three younger sons, the youngest of whom was eleven.

I have already mentioned Arnold's *Pearls of the Faith* that appeared in early 1883. It was a collection of poems set around the ninety-nine names of Allah. He used George Sale's translation of the Koran that had been published in 1734, which was 'one of the chief sources from which English readers gain their first knowledge of the Bible of Islam'. *Pearls of the Faith* received mixed reviews but one of the poems in it continues to get included in compendiums of late nineteenth-century Victorian poetry. This was his composition

on the sixtieth name of Allah, *Al-Mu'hid* or The Restorer. It would
be reprinted as a stand-alone poem with the title *After Death in
Arabia*, although Arnold himself would refer to it as *He who died at
Azan* since that is how the poem began:

> *He who died at Azan sends*
> *This to comfort all his friends*

The Light of Asia would have a stunning impact in Ceylon. For the
devout Buddhists of that country Arnold was and continues to be a
revered figure. A 'Light of Asia' annual oratory contest for school
children has been taking place every year for long in Colombo. Yet
when Queen Elizabeth II visited Sri Lanka in October 1981, she
was presented with a somewhat unusual gift from a lady who came
from a leading Sri Lankan business and political family. That gift
lies in the Royal Collection Trust in London and the entry for it
reads thus:

Pearls of the Faith: or Islam's Rosary, being the ninety-nine
beautiful names of Allah (Asma-El-Husna); with comments in
verse from various oriental sources by Sir Edwin Arnold, 1883

Description

2nd ed. 8vo.

Provenance

Presented to Queen Elizabeth II by Noorul Ameena Macun
Markar during her State Visit to Sri Lanka 21st-25th October 1981

Mrs Markar passed away many years ago and her grandson is unable
to recollect any family lore on why she made this present to the
Queen of England. But that she did is quite remarkable and shows
the longevity of Arnold's 'Muslim' poem.[2] The Sultan of Turkey

would honour Arnold a second time in 1886 for this poem—this time it would be the Second Class of the Imperial Order of Osmanli.

1883 would also see the publication of an American edition of *Poetical Works of Edwin Arnold: Containing the Light of Asia, The Indian Song of Songs, Pearls of the Faith*. This was the trilogy that Arnold had himself had conceived. This edition would be read by a very famous American writer, who would annotate it as well. This was Herman Melville, most known for his *Moby Dick*. His recent biographer has written:[3]

> Whether he attempted any of the meditative practices he read about is doubtful, but in *The Light of Asia* he discovered in more than one place the most prevalent of Buddhist mantras used in meditation: "Om, mani padme, hum" . . . Three of the volumes of Honore de Balzac that Melville read late in his life contain lengthy introductions by George Frederic Parsons that deal principally with Balzac's interest in Eastern religion, especially Buddhism. Running through all three of these introductions is Parsons's conviction that Balzac's thought is grounded in Buddhism. He frequently quotes Edwin Arnold admiringly . . .

In 1884, Arnold would write the foreword to the first English translation of Bankim Chandra Chatterjee's novel *Bisha Briksha*. The translation was called *The Poison Tree* and was by Miriam Knight. Arnold would hail Chatterjee, the author of India's national song *Vande Mataram*, as a man of 'superior intellectual acquisitions, who ranks unquestionably as the first living writer in his Presidency [Bengal]'. He described *Bisha Briksha* as belonging to 'the modern days in India, and to the new ideas that are spreading—not always quite happily—among the families of the land'. He went on to say:

> . . . Bengal has produced a writer of true genius, whose vivacious invention, dramatic force, and purity of aim, promise well for the new age of Indian vernacular literature.

That which appears to me most striking and valuable in the book is the faithful view it gives of the gentleness and devotion of the average Hindu wife. Western people are wont to think that because marriages are arranged at an early age in India, and without the betrothed pair having the slightest share in the marital choice, that wedded love of a sincere sort must be out of the question and conjugal happiness very rare. The contrary is notably the case . . .

Miriam Singleton Knight was the most prolific translator of Bankim Chandra Chatterjee's works in England in the late nineteenth century and did much to have his name established there.

Trubner and Co. issued the first illustrated edition of *The Light of Asia* in late 1884 in time for Christmas that year. The edition was billed as 'an appropriate Christmas gift'. It sold out instantly and in early 1885 another illustrated edition was in the market with this 'Notice' from the publisher:

The illustrations are taken, for the most part, from photographs of Buddhist sculptures and frescoes found in ancient ruins of India, averaging 2000 years old, many of them being identified by eminent archaeological authorities, both in India and at home, as actually illustrating scenes in the Life of Gautama Buddha the founder of Buddhism and the hero of Mr. Arnold's poem.

The character of the illustrations will be fully appreciated only by those who have thoroughly entered into the spirit of the poem, and who therefore know how to interpret them philosophically and artistically. Nevertheless, these engravings cannot fail it is believed to interest the general public as revealing an antique school of art unfamiliar indeed, yet for the most part full of spirit and beauty.

The 1879 edition of *The Light of Asia* was, of course, historic. But these later 1884 and early 1885 ones were no less so. These editions brought together, perhaps for the first time, around fifty illustrations from the life of the Buddha in a systematic and chronological manner. Three people were responsible for this achievement: Sir

George Birdwood, who was then working in the India Office and who would have a life-long connection with India in diverse fields after having been born in Belgaum there six months after Arnold; James Fergusson, an important figure in the nineteenth-century discovery of ancient India by the British; and a Miss Manning, who was the literary executor of her aunt Charlotte Speir, who, as Mrs Manning, had written the well-received two-volume *Ancient and Medieval India* (1869). The illustrated 1885 edition provoked this letter to Arnold from Sir Henry Ponsonby, Queen Victoria's top aide:

Buckingham Palace
March 31 1885

Sir,

I understand from Lady Ely that you think I have been remiss in laying your books transmitted through my hands to The Queen. If you mean that I have delayed their delivery I must confess that in one or two instances I have kept them for 12 or perhaps 24 hours for I keenly appreciate their worth though I fear that I regard them too much from the occidental point of view.

I have however always placed them before The Queen except a copy of the Light of Asia illustrated—which came addressed to me without any other inscription so that I do not know who forwarded it or whether it was intended for Her Majesty or not—I have in the mean while placed this volume in the Royal library.

The Vegetarian Society had been founded in September 1847 at Ramsgate, a seaside town some 150 kms southeast of London. It would attract a number of personalities who have since become famous. One such person in whose life there has been a revival of interest in recent times was Anna Kingsford. While addressing the Society in London on 12 January 1885 the firebrand anti-vivisectionist and women's rights campaigner would tell her audience:

The cover image of the 1885 illustrated edition of The Light of Asia *depicting (from below) the four principal events in the life of the Buddha: birth, meditation, preaching and death, taken from a fifth-century* CE *bas-relief found at Sarnath by Alexander Cunningham in 1835–36 and given to the Asiatic Society of Bengal in Calcutta. Subsequently it was handed over to the Indian Museum in that city. (Source: Indian Museum)*

... There have been a great many illustrious names connected with vegetarianism: men of the calibre of Gautama Buddha, whose life has been given to the world in that beautiful poem, *The Light of Asia*, which is now issued as cheap as possible—at one shilling. You should read that work and teachings of Edwin Arnold, and if that does not convert you to Vegetarianism, nothing will; it is full of the most beautiful language and most pathetic sentiment possible to imagine. You will find that a book to smile over, and a book to weep over. It is the sort of literature I should like to see widely disseminated in London.

Kingsford was active in the Theosophical Society as well. She would become a one-woman army for propagating *The Light of Asia* and a few months later on 2 August 1885 she wrote to her friend Lady Caithness:

... I have been trying to persuade Lady Archibald Campbell to produce next year, as a pastoral play, in Coombe Wood, the story of Buddha, founded on Edwin Arnold's magnificent poem, *The Light of Asia*. You know this has long been a dream of mine to educate people by means of the stage, by reproducing in tableaux or spectacular drama the lives and teaching of the world's holiest and noblest. *The Light of Asia* lends itself peculiarly to such an idea. The verse melodious and dramatic, the situations are excellent, and the scenery, being mostly forest and jungle, quite easy to manage ......

Kingsford died relatively young in February 1888. Had she lived she would almost certainly have met up with a young Indian student who would get converted to vegetarianism while in London after reading Henry Salt's *A Plea for Vegetarianism* that had been published in 1886.[4] Henry Salt and common salt would play a profoundly important role in Gandhi's life.

Notes

1. Gandhi's Phoenix Farm in Natal was inspired by the Englishman John Ruskin while his Tolstoy Farm in the Transvaal was inspired by the Russian Leo Tolstoy. Ruskin hated everything about India but yet Gandhi derived much from him.

2. In April 1884, *The Girl's Own Paper*, a weekly British publication catering to girls and young women, would publish 'The Rose and the Dewdrop' with words from Arnold's *Pearls of Faith* set to music by Clara Angela Macirone, the pianist and composer. The publication had been started in 1880 and would continue in one form or another till 1956.

3. Dillingham (1996)

4. Slate (2019) writes that the word 'vegetarian' entered the English language in the 1840s and that Henry Salt, who was born in India, was the intellectual godfather of the British vegetarian movement.

6

1881–1895: Attacks on *The Light of Asia*

It would only be a matter of time before the missionary community would hit back at Arnold. It started in America because of the tremendous response *The Light of Asia* had received there. In 1881, a forty-page monograph called *Christ or Buddha* was published in Salem, Massachusetts. It was a review of *The Light of Asia* by G.T. Flanders, a theologian. Flanders accepted that the poem had had a wide circulation and had shaken the confidence of 'many intelligent and thoughtful persons' in the biography of Christ. Although Arnold had not discredited Christ in any way, Flanders believed that the Englishman had a diabolical design to bring disrepute to Christianity and show Christ in relatively poor light. Flanders called *The Light of Asia* 'an extraordinary book' but for that very reason it was also dangerous and had to be countered. He ended by saying:

> The whole case as it stands today is before the reader; and in the light of the facts we have recited, the modern pretensions set up for Buddhism are seen to be a monstrous fraud. And yet there is danger that uninformed and unsuspecting people will be sung by the dulcet and eloquent strains of "The Light of Asia" into conclusions detrimental to Christianity . . . Let the historical facts, especially with respect to Buddha and Jesus, be brought into the clearest possible light; and, for one, we have no fear of the result.

Three years later an ever more vicious attack on *The Light of Asia* would be mounted in William Cleaver Wilkinson's *Edwin Arnold as Poetiser and as Paganiser*. Wilkinson was a Baptist preacher, professor of theology and a literary figure as well. He was between jobs at the Rochester Theological Seminary and the University of Rochester in America when his attack on Arnold appeared. He was clearly worried that *The Light of Asia* was acquiring an influence on the American mind 'quite out of proportion to any significance attaching to the poem by virtue of its own intrinsic character'. He explained his motivation thus:

> The publication of Mr. Arnold's work happened to coincide in time with a singular development, both in America and Europe, of popular curiosity and interest concerning ethnic religions, especially concerning Buddhism. "The Light of Asia" was well adapted to hit this transient whim of Occidental taste . . . Mr. Arnold has, no doubt, whether by merit or by fortune, been, beyond any other writer, the means of widening the American audience prepared to entertain with favour the pretensions of Buddha and his teachings. The effect is very observable. There has entered the general mind, an unconfessed, a half conscious, but a most shrewdly penetrative, misgiving that, perhaps, after all, Christianity has not of right quite the exclusive claim that it was previously supposed to possess, upon the attention and reverence of mankind . . . My critique, while superficially of Mr. Arnold, becomes fundamentally of Mr. Arnold's subject not less . . .

After over 175 pages of literary and theological criticisms, Wilkinson comes to the conclusion that 'whether as literature, then, or exposition of Buddhist doctrine and life, the "Light of Asia" must be pronounced unworthy to survive'. He ends with a bitter invective on Arnold's previous works:

> As to the other pagan poems of Mr. Arnold, his "Pearls of the Faith", his "Indian Idylls," and his "Iliad of India," it is quite enough to say of these productions that they had from the first their only chance of immortality in parasitic attachment to the fortunes of the "Light of Asia". In due time, principal and parasite,

they with the false religions of which they treat, will go to the limbo of things abortive, one and all of them confounded and forgotten together.

Samuel Henry Kellogg had been a Canadian Presbyterian missionary in India. He had written a *Grammar of the Hindi Language* in 1875 and was at the Western Theological Seminary near Pittsburgh in the USA when his *The Light of Asia and The Light of the World* appeared in 1885. He would be less polemical but equally unyielding in the superiority of his faith over Buddhism. He called Christ *The Light of the World* and started off with a chapter called 'Buddhism and Modern Unbelief' in which he said:

> The interest that has been taken of late in Buddhism by a large number of intelligent people in various Christian countries is one of the most peculiar and suggestive religious phenomena of our day. In the United States, interest had prevailed for a considerable time among a somewhat restricted number of persons who have known or thought that they knew something about Buddhism; but since 1879, through the publication of Mr. Edwin Arnold's *The Light of Asia*, the popularity of the subject has in a very marked degree increased. Many who would have been repelled by any formal, drily philosophical treatise upon Buddhism, have been attracted to it by the undoubted charm of Mr. Arnold's verse. The issue of cheap editions of the poem, selling for only a few cents has helped in the same direction . . .

Kellogg would return to India and continue his proselytizing. He died in Landour, which is part of Mussoorie, in 1899 and the Presbyterian Church there was later named Kellogg Church in his memory. It still exists and serves a non-denominational congregation with services taking place in Hindi.[1]

Wilkinson and Kellogg were American missionaries. But Sir Monier Monier-Williams was the Boden Professor of Sanskrit at Oxford, Arnold's alma mater and one of the glittering names of

British Indology. He had had an intimate connection to India ever since his birth in Bombay in November 1819. Arnold respected him and, in fact, five months before *The Light of Asia* had first appeared Arnold had written to him:

My dear Sir:

. . . As I am writing to so high an authority on Indian topics I shall venture to ask you a question upon a point which greatly engages me. I have in hand and considerably advanced, a poetic work on Buddha. My studies of the great theme have convinced me that no adequate or even logical statement exists of the veritable doctrines of Gautama although I feel sure that he taught an esoteric as well as an exoteric creed. The central difficulty seems, how to reconcile the transcendental nature of his philosophical teaching, with the practical realism of his morality: and the question which I shall like to put to a really enlightened Buddhist priest would be this: How can you harmonise Gautama's declaration that all phenomenal existence is "Maya" (illusory) with the value set by him upon preserving life, pursuing charity, foregoing self? The doctrine of Buddhism denies the importance of those social and civil relations which its ethics affirm more nobly than in almost any other culture. How can crime be forbidden where criminal or victim have no real individual existence? Would it be too much to ask you to give me your ideas briefly upon this obvious contradiction in all extant descriptions of so profoundly influential and important a faith?

Sadly, Monier-William's reply to this question of Arnold is not available. Later scholarship would, however, give an answer: The Buddha 'declared that he had made no distinction between esoteric and exoteric teaching, but had preached the full doctrine to them [his disciples]'.[2] When *The Light of Asia* was published, Arnold wrote to the Oxford don again on 15 July 1879:

My dear Sir:

Will you accept the accompanying copy of new poem on Buddhism "The Light of Asia". I cannot be more deeply conscious of its demerits than when I address the book to you but you will at least recognize in it another proof of my interest in India.

And five months after *The Light of Asia* had come out, Arnold would inform Monier-Williams on 31 October 1879:

My dear Sir:

My "Light of Asia" has had an expected and extraordinary reception, testimony to the increased interest felt by the public in Indian matters.

Monier-Williams was a driving force behind the establishment of the Indian Institute at Oxford. On 28 April 1883 he would write to Arnold:

Dear Mr. Arnold,

I enclose a ticket for the ceremonial of the laying of the Stone of the Indian Institute.[3] You have been so interested in the project that I trust you will be able to be present. The Vice Chancellor intends asking you for the lunch in Balliol Hall afterwards. Please come if you can . . .

Monier-Williams had been to Buddha Gaya in 1884, two years before Arnold's visit. In mid-1889 he would give a series of lectures in London that would be published as *Buddhism in its connexion with Brahamanism and Hinduism and its contrast with Christianity*. On Buddha Gaya he would say:

I was much struck by the evidence which Buddha-Gaya affords of the inter-relationship between Buddhism and Hinduism-especially that form of the latter called Vaishnavism . . .

माहेयं माध्यशाखानां ज्ञानोत्तेजनतत्परैः ।
परोपकारिभिः सद्भिः स्थापितार्योपयोगिनी ॥ १ ॥
आल्वर्टेड्डिर्दितिख्यातो युवराजो महामनाः ।
राजराजेश्वरीपुत्रखत्प्रतिष्ठां व्यधात्स्वयम् ॥ २ ॥

अङ्करामाङ्कचन्द्रेऽब्दे विशाखस्यासिते दले ।
दशम्यां बुधवारे च वास्तुविधिरभूदिह ॥ ३ ॥

ईशानुकम्पया नित्यमार्यविद्या महीयताम् ।
आर्यावर्तेङ्गलभूम्योश्च मिथो मैत्री विवर्धताम् ॥

**This Building, dedicated to Eastern sciences, was founded for the use of
Aryas (Indians and Englishmen) by excellent and benevolent men desirous
of encouraging knowledge. The High-minded Heir-Apparent, named Albert
Edward, Son of the Empress of India, himself performed the act of inaugu-
ration. The ceremony of laying the Memorial Stone took place on Wednesday, the tenth lunar day of the dark half of the month of Vaiśākha, in the
Samvat year 1939 (= Wednesday, May 2, 1883). By the favor of God may
the learning and literature of India be ever held in honour; and may the mutual friendship of India and England constantly increase!**

*The famous Sanskrit inscription in the Old Indian Institute Building at Oxford. This is from
Trautmann (1997)*

This feature had completely escaped Arnold, as we shall soon see. But
he did echo Arnold's views on its importance to the Buddhists—in
fact, he used the same analogy that would be propagated first by
Arnold. Monier-Williams acknowledged that:

In truth, Buddha-Gaya is a kind of Buddhist Jerusalem,
abounding in associations of thrilling interest not only to the
followers of the Buddha, but to all those who see in that spot the
central focus whence radiated a system which for centuries has
permeated the religious thought of the most populous regions
of Eastern Asia, and influenced the creed of the majority of the
human race.

But on the whole Monier-Williams was very critical of Buddhism and found Buddha a completely negative preacher who came across very poorly when judged against Hindu thought and philosophy. At the very end, Monier-Williams summed up his arguments thus:

> It seems a mere absurdity to have to ask in concluding these Lectures—who shall we choose as our Guide, our Hope, our Salvation, "the Light of Asia", or "the Light of the World": the Buddha or the Christ. It seems a mere mockery to put this final question to rational and thoughtful men in the nineteenth century. Which Book shall we clasp to our hearts in our last hour—the Book that tells us of the dead, the extinct, the death-giving Buddha or the Book that reveals to us the living, the eternal, the life-giving Christ.

In September 1895, the Rev. R. Collins would write a sixteen-page critique called *Buddhism and the "The Light of Asia"* that would make the rounds in intellectual circles in England. While saying that 'Sir Edwin Arnold's poetry is admirable in that it is picturesque in a high degree' and while acknowledging that 'Buddha was a reforming ascetic amongst the many ascetics of his day', Collins contended that since it declares 'no power higher than man's' it cannot 'be with justice ranked as a religion'. It was founded, according to Collins, 'upon a mere wreck of a religion'. One who agreed with Collins was the Reverend George Uglow Pope, the Anglican missionary who is considered a legend in Tamil studies. Commenting on Collins's paper in a meeting in London at that very time, Pope explained how once Buddhism was predominant in the Tamil country but gradually lost out to the 'Shivaite system' because of its many imperfections and its inability to provide people 'assurance of the existence of the soul or any conscious state of blessedness or rest after this visible phenomenon of existence has passed away'.

Notes

1. Miedama and Miedama (2014)
2. Basham (1954)
3. The building, completed in 1896, has had a chequered history and now houses the Oxford Martin School. It was financed entirely by 450 private donors in India and England (including Queen Victoria and the Prince of Wales), all organized by Monier-Williams.

7

1885 and Beyond: *The Song Celestial* and Mahatma Gandhi

Today, the Bhagavad Gita is considered by many as Hinduism's defining text. There has even been a demand to declare it as a national text. But, as Prathama Banerjee has astutely observed, way before the Bhagavad Gita became iconic, another book was far more widely known in the sub-continent and indeed in the world outside.[1] This was the *Panchatantra*, which had first been translated into Pahlavi, Old Cyriac and Arabic by the end of the eighth century CE and into Greek, Latin, Persian and Hebrew by the end of the twelfth century CE. By the end of the sixteenth century CE. Latin and English translations were available. The *Hitopadesa* which Arnold had translated in 1861 is derived primarily from the *Panchatantra*.[2]

Modern interest in the Bhagavad Gita was triggered in 1785 by the publication of Charles Wilkins' translation into English. Wilkins was an employee of the East India Company with a great interest in Sanskrit. He was encouraged in his endeavours by the Governor-General of Bengal, Warren Hastings. Wilkins' translation was to lead to German, Russian, French, Latin and Greek versions by the time Arnold came to write his. In the nineteenth century three authors had preceded Arnold in translating the Bhagavad Gita into English: J. Cockburn Thomson in 1855, John Davies in 1882 and Kashinath Trimbak Telang also in 1882. Telang was an early Indologist and a noted lawyer of Bombay when his translation appeared as Volume 8 of Max Mueller's famed *Sacred Books of the East* series. Telang would later become Vice Chancellor of Bombay University and a judge of the Bombay High Court.

The Bhagavad Gita occurs as an episode in the sixth of the eighteen books of the *Mahabharata*. In 1881 and 1883 Arnold had already translated some other books of the *Mahabharata* and it was natural that he would then take up the Bhagavad Gita. He would definitely have been familiar with it from his Poona days. There was a thirteenth century Marathi translation of the Bhagavad Gita by Sant Dyaneshwar that Chiplunkar would certainly have brought to Arnold's attention.

Arnold's translation of the Bhagavad Gita, published in early 1885, was called *The Song Celestial*. It is dedicated to India. Arnold's English rendering of the dedication does not fully capture the beauty of his own original Sanskrit composition. Even so the message comes across:

इत्यं वासुदेवस्य पार्थस्य च महात्मनः ।
संवादमिममश्रीषमद्भुतं रोमहर्षणं ॥
इति इह ज्ञानमाख्यातं गुह्याद्गुह्यतरं मया ।
तेभ्यस न मे किन्धु लद्न्यः प्रियतरो भुवि ॥

And so have I read this wonderful and spirit-thrilling speech,
By Krishna and Prince Arjuna held, discoursing with each;
So have I writ its wisdom here—its hidden mystery,
For England; O our India I as dear to me as She!

In his preface, Arnold pays tribute to Thomson and more so to Davies, and goes on to add:

> Mr. Telang also produced at Bombay a version of colloquial rhythm, eminently learned and intelligent, but not conveying the dignity or grace of the original. If I venture to offer a translation of the wonderful poem after so many superior scholars, it is a grateful recognition of the help derived from their labours and because English literature would be incomplete without possessing in popular form a poetical and philosophical work so dear to India . . .

The Song Celestial would get uniformly great reviews both in the UK and the USA. It brought the Bhagavad Gita into the public consciousness like no other translation before it had and made it non-denominational. It was acquired by public libraries and was even advertised as being 'suitable for Christmas presents'. It had 'brought the original closer to the reader, rather than bringing the reader closer to the original'. Clearly, Arnold had not just translated but had 'reinvented' the *Gita*.[3] But much more important than these reviews and responses was the fact that some four years after it was published, it would be read by a young Indian student who would later spearhead India's freedom movement. *The Song Celestial* would remain an integral part of Mahatma Gandhi's life till his very end.

Gandhi would come to London in September 1888 when he was nineteen. In 1889 (we don't know the exact date or month) he came into contact with Bertram and Archibald Keightley, 'actually uncle and nephew, wealthy theosophists whose home at 17 Landsdowne Road, Notting Hill, had been placed at Mme. Blavatsky's disposal'.[4] The Keightleys had been reading *The Song Celestial* and needed an Indian to help them with the original. Gandhi would himself recount this incident in his life thus:[5]

> Towards the end of my second year in England I came across two Theosophists, brothers, and both unmarried. They were reading Sir Edwin Arnold's translation—*The Song Celestial*—and they invited me to read the original with them. I felt ashamed as I had the divine poem neither in Samskrit nor in Gujarati. I was constrained to tell them that I had not read the *Gita*, but that I would gladly read it with them . . . I began reading the *Gita* with them. The verses in the second chapter

> *If one*
> *Ponders on objects of the sense, there springs*
> *Attraction; from attraction grows desire,*
> *Desire flames to fierce passion, passion breeds*
> *Recklessness; then the memory—all betrayed—*
> *Lets noble purpose go, and saps the mind,*
> *Till purpose, mind, and man are all undone*

made a deep impression on my mind, and they still ring in my ears. The book struck me as one of priceless worth. The impression has ever since been growing on me with the result that I regard it today as the book par excellence for the knowledge of Truth. It has afforded me invaluable help in my moments of gloom. I have read almost all the English translations of it, and I regard Sir Edwin Arnold's as the best. He has been faithful to the text, and yet it does not read like a translation.

The Keightleys made one more everlasting contribution to Gandhi's life, as reflected in his own words:[6]

The brothers also recommended *The Light of Asia* by Sir Edwin Arnold, whom I knew till then as the author of *The Song Celestial*, and I read it with even greater interest than I did the *Bhagavad Gita*. Once I had begun it, I could not leave it off . . .

Gandhi also writes of this period of his life as a time when 'my young mind tried to unify the teaching of the *Gita*, *The Light of Asia* and the Sermon on the Mount. That renunciation is the highest form of religion appealed to me greatly'.[7] As far as the Keightleys are concerned, there is no evidence that they and Gandhi stayed in touch, although Bertram Keightley was to make India his home for over four decades. He continued to be involved with the Theosophical Society and finally passed away in Kanpur in October 1944.

Towards the end of his student days in London, Gandhi actually met Arnold and got to know him. This must have been sometime between March 1891 and June 1891. In Gandhi's own words:

Vegetarianism was then a new cult in England . . . Full of a neophyte's zeal for vegetarianism, I decided to start a vegetarian club in my locality, Bayswater. I invited Sir Edwin Arnold who lived there, to be Vice President. Dr. Oldfied who was Editor of *The Vegetarian* became President. I myself became Secretary. The club went well for a while, but came to an end in the course of

Prominent members of the Theosophical Society in London 1892. Bertram Keightley is standing second from left while Archibald Keightley is standing second from right. Annie Besant is seated third from left. Standing at the very back is Col. Olcott. This is from Nethercot (1960)

a few months. For I left the locality, according to my custom of moving from place to place periodically.

Josiah Oldfied, who edited the journal of the London Vegetarian Society, and Gandhi shared rooms in Baywater, and Oldfied later wrote about this association. Sadly, Arnold himself left no account of his encounters with Gandhi. What is particularly interesting about this vegetarian club that Gandhi reminisced about was that Arnold was by then a very famous man and fifty-nine years old. He was playing second fiddle in the club to a fellow Englishman who was twenty-eight and taking instructions from an Indian who was twenty-two—of course, only on matters related to diets! Both Oldfield and Gandhi would for sure have been aware of *The Light of Asia*'s eloquent admonitions against animal sacrifice in Book the Fifth, which made Arnold their comrade-in arms.

While still our Lord went on, teaching how fair
This earth were if all living things be linked

Meeting of vegetarians at the Isle of Wight, 1890. Gandhi seated on ground extreme right and next to him (with beard) is Josiah Oldfield. Arnold is missing in this photograph being away in Japan that entire year. This is from the National Gandhi Museum, New Delhi.

In friendliness and common use of foods,
Bloodless and pure; the golden grain, bright fruits,
Sweet herbs which grow for all, the waters wan,
Sufficient drinks and meats. Which when these heard,
The might of gentleness so conquered them,
The priests themselves scattered their altar-flames
And flung away the steel of sacrifice;
And through the land next day passed a decree
Proclaimed by criers, and in this wise graved
On rock and column: "Thus the King's will is:-
There hath been slaughter for the sacrifice
And slaying for the meat, but henceforth none
Shall spill the blood of life nor taste of flesh,
Seeing that knowledge grows, and life is one,
And mercy cometh to the merciful".

Gandhi's fascination, and that is his own description, for *The Song Celestial* never ceased. Not only did he keep it beside himself all his life but he would recommend it to family, friends, colleagues and all and sundry. A few examples would reveal this enchantment of his.[8]

In late 1921 Gandhi and the poet Rabindranath Tagore had a disagreement on the former's insistence that cotton yarn spinning was a 'sacrament to be performed by all'. Tagore had objected and Gandhi had defended his position, saying that he derived his belief from the Bhagavad Gita and had given 'Edwin Arnold's rendering of the verses from his *Song Celestial* for those who do not read Sanskrit'. On 19 February 1922 he wrote to the up-and-coming star of the Indian National Congress, Jawaharlal Nehru, who was then serving the first of his nine prison sentences under British rule:

> . . . Above all, whatever you do don't you be disgusted with the spinning wheel. You and I have reason to get disgusted with ourselves for having done many things and having believed many things, but we shall never have the slightest cause for regret that we have pinned our faith to the spinning wheel or that we have spun so much good yarn per day in the name of the mother-land. You have the 'Song Celestial' with you. I cannot give you the inimitable translation of Edwin Arnold, but this is the rendering of the Sanskrit text. 'There is no waste of energy, there is no destruction in this. Even a little of this dharma saves one from many a pitfall'. 'This Dharma' in the original refers to Karma Yoga, and the Karma Yoga of our age is the spinning wheel . . .

On 1 January 1926 he exhorted Satis Chandra Das Gupta to 'read again and again *The Song Celestial* by Edwin Arnold'. On 9 December 1926 he recommended *The Song Celestial* and *The Light of Asia* as readings on Hinduism to Gordon Law in New York. Gandhi always believed that Buddhism was an integral part of Hinduism.

Between February and November 1926—over a period of nine months—Gandhi gave daily discourses on the Bhagavad Gita after his morning prayer meetings at his Sabarmati Ashram in Ahmedabad.

These were to be published later both in Gujarati and English, with the most recent edition coming out in September 2014.[9] In his introduction, Gandhi explains how he was first introduced to the Bhagavad Gita through 'Sir Edwin Arnold's excellent translation of the poem' and how 'the last nineteen stanzas of Chapter II have remained engraved on my heart' containing as they do 'the essence of dharma'. These are the very verses, incidentally, of which the historian D.D. Kosambi has written would not have been possible without Buddhism and the concept of karma propounded by the Buddha.[10]

On 6 July1936 he told Kamalnayan Bajaj, the son of one of closest associates as the young man was leaving for England, that he should read the Gita in the original every day and 'keep a copy of Edwin Arnold's *Song Celestial*'.

On 11 December 1939 he sent a message to *Kesari*, the newspaper started by Bal Gangadhar Tilak, who had himself translated the Bhagavad Gita into Marathi in 1915, but drawing a different lesson from it than Gandhi:

> . . . I have called it my spiritual dictionary for it has never failed me in distress . . . Its Sanskrit is incredibly simple. I have read many English translations, but there is nothing to equal Edwin Arnold's metrical translation which he has beautifully and aptly called *The Song Celestial*.

Ten months before he was assassinated, Gandhi told Gladys Owen, a Quaker educationist and preacher:

> . . . My confidence is a little shaken because I have begun to fear that I might not quickly reach the requisite state of detachment described in the Gita. Read if you care the last 18 verses of Chapter II of the Gita in Edwin Arnold's translation . . .

Clearly, *The Song Celestial* was special to India's 'Father of the Nation'. But Gandhi's philosopher-grandson Ramchandra Gandhi had a somewhat different take on the title that Arnold had given his translation. According to the younger Gandhi, Arnold was consciously down-sliding the Bhagavad Gita from 'Divine', which would have placed it above 'Holy' (which is what the Holy Bible is), to 'Celestial', which is about a lesser asterism. This is somewhat like the difference between canonization (Saint . . .) and beatification (Blessed . . .). By the time *The Song Celestial* came out, Arnold was under attack from Christian circles. He would be forced to write *The Light of the World* in praise of Christ six years later. So, there may be something to Ramachandra Gandhi's thought,[11] although his paternal grandfather entertained no such doubts.

The Song Celestial has a connection with one of India's greatest philosophers, who became President of the country in 1962. S. Radhakrishnan translated the Bhagavad Gita with a long 'Introductory Essay' and dedicated it to Gandhi. It was published in London just a few days before the Mahatma was killed in January 1948. In it Radhakrishnan praised Arnold saying:

> Those who do not know Sanskrit will get a fairly correct idea of the spirit of the poem from the beautiful English rendering by Sir Edwin Arnold. It is so full of ease and grace and has a flavour of its own which makes it acceptable to all but those who are scrupulous about scholarly accuracy.

But what is generally not known is that there had been a plan before the war by Henry Norman Spalding, the noted London philanthropist, to reissue *The Song Celestial,* and Radhakrishnan had agreed to provide an introduction and notes. When Radhakrishnan began the task, 'it seemed to him that it would be more worthwhile to prepare his own translation in modern prose'.[12]

In 1885 itself, a few months before *The Song Celestial* was published, Arnold's *The Secret of Death with some Collected Poems* was issued. While it was dedicated to his daughter, 'the author's only authorized American edition' issued simultaneously came with this message:

TO AMERICA

Thou new Great Britain! famous, free and bright!
West of thy west sleepeth my ancient East;
Our sunsets make thy moons: Daytime and Night
Meet in sweet morning-promise on thy breast.
Fulfill the promise, Queen of boundless lands!
Where, as thine own, an English singer ranks.
I, who found favor at thy sovereign hands,
Kiss them; and at thy feet lay these, for thanks.

Arnold had never been to America as yet but *The Light of Asia* had reaching dizzying heights of sales there. He would go across the Atlantic four years later.

The Secret of Death with some Collected Poems had a varied fare but the highlight was clearly *The Secret of Death* itself. This is from the *Katha Upanishad*, which Arnold had first read in Sanskrit along with a Brahmin priest in Poona a quarter of a century earlier. The *Katha Upanishad* teachings relate to 'the soul's successive incarnations and hope of finally merging with the Supreme Soul'. Stephen Hay has written that *The Secret of Death* is 'probably the book Gandhi recommended to his Secretary Mahadev Desai in 1918 referring to it as "Life Beyond Death"'.[13]

The Song Celestial too would run into many editions and continues to get referenced—but at times wrongly as well. July 16 1995 marked the fiftieth anniversary of the first nuclear bomb test at Alamogordo in New Mexico in America. As the plutonium bomb detonated and the mushroom cloud emerged, the scientist-director of the Manhattan Project J. Robert Oppenheimer famously quoted a few lines from Chapter XI of the Bhagavad Gita that is called "The Yoga of the Vision of the Universal Form'. Writing in *The Times of India* on the day after this anniversary, India's foremost strategic guru K. Subrahmanyam gave credit to *The Song Celestial* for Oppenheimer's quotations from the Bhagavad Gita. Arnold's translation of the verse recollected by Oppenheimer reads:

Thou seest Me as Time who kills, Time who brings
   all to doom.
The Slayer Time, Ancient of Days, come hither to
   consume;

The Sanskrit word which Arnold translates as 'Time' is *'kala'*, and indeed almost all translations do so. But one of the very few that translates *'kala'* as "Death' is that by Arthur Ryder, who taught Sanskrit to Oppenheimer at the University of California, Berkeley in the late 1920s. Oppenheimer's recollection on July 16 1945 as he saw the gigantic mushroom cloud was 'I am become Death, the shatterer of the worlds'. The most deeply studied analysis of the sources of the Bhagavad Gita quotations recollected by Oppenheimer on that fateful occasion came to the conclusion that:

> In rendering of the passage, Oppenheimer followed Ryder. This variant [Death instead of Time] was especially appropriate for describing a nuclear explosion, which could bring a great deal of Death in very little Time.[14]

The year 1885 would also see the publication of a book completely different from *The Song Celestial*. If *The Song Celestial* reflected Indian philosophy at it spiritual best, *Ananga-Ranga* translated by Richard Burton and Francis Arbuthnot epitomized Indian culture at its guiltless erotic best. Two years earlier, *Kama Sutra*, also translated by Burton and Arbuthnot, had hit the headlines. Burton and Arnold's lives and interests overlapped in so many ways that one would suppose they knew and corresponded with one another. Yet, the biographers of neither Burton nor Arnold could trace a connection.[15] But I managed to find one in the recollections of Julian Arnold—Arnold's son:[16]

> One day, after reading some pages of his translation of one of The Arabian Nights with their amazing footnotes describing Arab customs referred to in the text, I suggested to him that he might

wisely show the manuscript to my father, who happened to be in Cairo at that time [1881]. He assented but Sir Edwin, being an experienced editor as well as an Arabic scholar and conversant with both oriental customs and occidental scruples, promptly commissioned me to carry back to Burton a note advising him, "Make more decorous your anthropological footnotes. Their worth is beyond measure, but scarcely may they find place, under their present candid form, in a popular work. The digestion of the public is not sufficiently robust to assimilate literary food so strange and strong. Soften your instruction, disguise your splendid knowledge, and you will sell two hundred thousand copies of the most colourful book in the world.

But Burton did not alter a single word or phrase. Julian Arnold goes on:

In due course, the first edition appeared, enriched to the full with its curious collection or pornographical footnotes, and the sales were necessarily limited to a scholarly group of subscribers. Victorian scruples militated for a while against wider distribution. Other times, other manners and these days of tolerance [early 1940s], the verdict condones the obstinacy of Burton. Nevertheless there was a period when he regretted his rejection of the counsel given to him, as the following letter . . . admits:

December 21st 1882

My dear Arnold,

I have not followed your advice, and I regret not having done so. *Mariez vous on ne vous mariez pas* [to get married or not to get married] just explains my condition.

Had I not put in those confounded footnotes, I should have wished that I had.

However they shall disappear from the next edition. Meanwhile, the Book of the Sword [17] is getting on merrily.

Ever yours faithfully,

RICHARD F. BURTON

Eleven years older to Arnold, Burton has been called 'one of Victorian Britain's protean figures' and shared with the author of *The Light of Asia* an abiding passion for Indian and Arabic texts. Both were prolific authors as well. It is impossible to think that they would not have been in touch. But alas, the archives are empty on this score. In November 1935 when major archaeological finds were announced in the ancient city of Ujjain, the *Times of India* would get mixed up saying that Ujjain was the land of Vikramaditya, whose memory had been immortalized by Sir Edwin Arnold, while the fact is that it was Sir Richard Burton who had done so in 1870 with his *Vikram and the Vampire.* The only connection that Arnold had with Ujjain was that he had translated parts of a very famous poem by the man acknowledged to be Sanskrit's finest poet and dramatist, who lived there during the fourth-fifth century CE. In the mid-1880s, Arnold had translated that portion related to the summer season from Kalidasa's *Ritusamhara.*

Notes

1.   Banerjee (2019)
2.   One scholar wrote that 75 per cent of the *Hitopadesa's* content was derived from the *Panchatantra.* Sternbach (1960)
3.   This and the previous observations on the response to *The Song Celestial* are from Sinha (2010).
4.   Hunt (1978)
5.   *Collected Works of Mahatma Gandhi* Vol 39
6.   Ibid
7.   Ibid
8.   All these letters of Gandhi are from different volumes of the *Collected Works of Mahatma Gandhi*, the Publications Division, Ministry of Information and Broadcasting, Government of India.

9. This was by Jaico Publishing House, Mumbai.
10. Kosambi, D.D. (1962)
11. These views of Ramchandra Gandhi were related to me by his youngest brother Gopalkrishna Gandhi.
12. Gopal (1989)
13. Hay (1989)
14. Hijiya (2000)
15. Wright (1957) for Arnold and Kennedy (2005) for Burton. Kennedy highlights a fact overlooked in the encomiums for Sir Richard Burton, that two Indians—Bhugwantal Indraji and Shivaram Parshuram Bhide—were the ones who actually carried out the translations from Sanskrit manuscripts and that Burton's contribution was limited to polishing the English text. Arnold's knowledge of Sanskrit was far superior to that of Burton.
16. Arnold (1942)
17. This 'History the sword and its uses in all countries from the Earliest Times with 300 Illustrations' was to be published in London in 1884.

8

1885–1886: Edwin Arnold in India and Ceylon

After a gap of twenty-five years Arnold revisited India between November 1885 and March 1886. He had left India praised for his work at Poona College. He was coming back, along with his wife and daughter, now a celebrity in England and America, well known in Europe and well-regarded in India as well. He has left behind a detailed and delightful account of his travels in the sub-continent in *India Revisited*, which was published soon after his return to London. Actually, Arnold had been sending dispatches to the *Daily Telegraph* as his trip progressed and so the book itself was a collection of these articles plus some new ones as well.

Arnold disembarked in Bombay on 24 November 1885 and visited, in that order, Poona, Baroda, Bhavnagar, Ahmedabad, Jaipur, Alwar, Delhi, Panipat, Agra, Banaras, Patna, Bodh Gaya, Calcutta, Madras, Colombo, Kandy, Ooty and Hyderabad before departing from Bombay on 5 March 1886. He was in India for some hundred days, touched around twenty towns and cities in India and Ceylon and covered around seven thousand miles by rail, road and sea. It was hectic, packed and eventful. He was particularly impressed with the princely state of Bhavnagar and called it a 'model native principality'. While at Bhavnagar he would meet the principal of Samaldas College and be bowled over by Manilal Dwivedi's learning, saying that 'his book just published on the *Raja Yoga* ought to become widely known in Europe'. One young Gujarati who would spend six months at this College, between January and June 1888, would meet Arnold a year later in London and follow the *Raja Yoga* book while in South Africa: M.K. Gandhi, as he was known then.

Arnold spent time in Delhi visiting landmarks associated with the 1857 Mutiny. He made it a point to go to near-by Panipat to be on 'soil consecrated to the legendary history of India'. He writes of Panipat as a town dating back to the *Mahabharata* and in modern times the place where three decisive military battles took place—in 1526, 1556 and 1761. But he was upset that nobody could identify where exactly these decisive encounters happened and 'in wrath and bitter disappointment wrote the following lines on the walls of the Lursowlie Road bungalow near Panipat:

> *"From Delhi unto Panipat I came*
> *To view those fields of immemorial fame*
> *Where three times Asia was lost and won,*
> *'And "Bhagwat Gita" told to Pritha's son—*
> *But where on "Kurukshetra" that was taught*
> *None knew, nor if those famous fields were fought!*
> *Therefore, bethinking what a dream is fame,*
> *From Panipat to Delhi I came"*

From history's point of view his visit to Bodh Gaya, or Buddha-Gya as he calls it, was the most fateful. Chapter XIV of *India Revisited* is called '*Benaras and the Land of the "Light of Asia"*' and covers his trip to the major Buddhist sites of Sarnath and Buddha-Gya, apart from Rajgir. Arnold writes:

> Benaras—the Oxford and Canterbury of India—has been a city of sanctity and learning ages out of mind . . . Yet it is not Hinduism which—to my mind, at least—chiefly consecrates Benaras. The divine memory of the founder of Buddhism broods all over the country hereabouts . . . Modern Brahminism is really Buddhism in a Shastri's robe and sacred thread. Shunkuracharya and his priests expelled the brethren of the yellow robe from India, but the spirit of Sakya Muni's teaching remained unbanished; just as

> "Greece, overcome, conquered her conqueror"

Buddhism ought surely to be esteemed more interesting than the most ornate Brahminic temples, or the proudest and most mosques and palaces of the Mogul. And all the country of the Buddhist chronicles may be visited within a week . . . Bhuila which is the ancient Kapila-vastu, the place of his birth; Kasia, that of his death; Sarnath, near Benaras, which is the ancient Isipatana, where he preached; and Buddha-Gya where—upon a spot known to a rood, to a yard of ground—this lofty and tender teacher elaborated in solitude that statement of belief, which, rightly comprehended, is so full of love, of hope, of peace, and of philosophic truth.

It is at Buddha-Gya, that 'most hallowed spot where, under the Bodhi tree, the sun of Truth rose for Prince Siddartha', that Arnold feels the most depressed and anguished. He views 'the lofty temple built in tiers or stages and adorned with seated figures of Buddha' and calls it 'the great central shrine of the Gentle Faith'. Then he uses a term for it which would cause endless political controversy for the next half a century and more. He calls the shrine 'the Mecca of Buddhism'. Arnold goes on:

Inside the adytum of the temple is a seated Buddha, gilt and inscribed, before which were fluttering numberless gilded ribbons; while the granite floor was carved with votive inscriptions, and desecrated in the middle, by the Brahmans who have usurped the place, with a stone Lingam . . . Buddha is unknown and unhonoured upon his own ground by the Sivaites . . . It was strange to see these votaries of Mahadeo rolling sacrificial cakes— pindas—and repeating mantras on the spot Sakya-Muni attained so much higher religious insight . . . Painful it certainly is, to one who realizes the immense significance of this spot in the history of Asia and of humanity, to wander round the precincts of the holy tree, and to see scores and hundreds of broken sculptures lying about in the jungle or in the brick-heaps . . . . . .

I will be discussing separately the impact of Arnold's use of the 'Mecca of Buddhism' description for the temple at Buddha-Gya. For the present, it would suffice to note that Arnold, by his own admission, 'appealed to the Government of India and to all enlightened Hindu gentlemen, by a public letter, against such sad neglect of the noblest locality in all their Indian philosophic annals; and I cherish the hope of seeing the temple and its precincts—which are all Government property—placed under the guardianship of Buddhists'.

The second event of significance during Arnold's India visit took place in Calcutta a few days later, between 21 and 23 January 1886. In his own words:

> . . . Another singular pleasure was to witness a performance of the "Light of Asia" played by a native company to an audience of Calcutta citizens whose close attention to the long soliloquies and quick appreciation of all the chief incidents of the story, gave a high idea of their intelligence, and proved how metaphysical by nature these Hindu people are. The stage appliances were deficient to a point incredible for a London manager; and the *mise en scene*[1] sometimes almost laughable in simplicity. Nevertheless there was a refinement and imaginativeness in the acting, as well as an artistic sense entirely remarkable, and the female performers proved quite as good as the male . . .

Arnold had just witnessed a play at the Star Theatre Company that had been launched in 1883 by Girish Chandra Ghosh, the celebrated producer, writer and actor who is recognized as the father of modern Bengali theatre. Ghosh had translated substantial parts of *The Light of Asia* into Bengali and called it *Buddhadeb Charit*, with a dedication to Arnold himself. It was actually more than a straightforward translation. The drama was staged for the first time on 19 September 1885. A month before Arnold saw the play, Calcutta's *Hindu Patriot* had commented on 14 December 1885:[2]

> Any writer on Buddha coming after Mr. Edwin Arnold's *Light of Asia* must, in the nature of things, derive his inspiration largely from that exquisite and incomparable Idyll and we are not surprised to see

the author of Buddhadeb Charita [Girish Chandra Ghosh] claims to be no exception. But even Mr. Arnold's manner of treating the subject had to be departed from, for dramatic reasons and so cleverly has the departure been made that Mr. Arnold himself when he comes to Calcutta in the course of his present tour and sees the hero of the poem on the stage will, we venture to think, have little reason to regret the departure. . . . . . . We are glad to notice that the efforts of this popular caterer of amusement are appreciated and patronised by the public. Babu Girish Chandra Ghosh has deserved well of his co-religionists and his countrymen by his endeavours to improve the moral tone of our stage to popularise Hindoo religion and to develop the slender literary and dramatic resources of the country.

The *Hindu Patriot* of 1 February 1886 would reproduce the letter which Arnold had written to the Manager of the Star Theatre before leaving Calcutta:

> I cannot leave Calcutta . . . without expressing the singular pleasure I derived from witnessing the performance at your theatre on the Life of Buddha, founded on my poem *The Light of Asia* . . . None of the undeserved honours done to me and my work has touched me more than the play at your theatre for which please accept my thanks and convey them to your accomplished company.

Girish Chandra Ghosh was an ardent disciple of Sri Ramakrishna ever since the holy man had dropped in at the Star Theatre on 21 September 1884 to see Ghosh's *Chaitanya Lila*, a production on the fifteenth-century mystic who would inspire the Hare Krishna movement five centuries later. On 23 October 1885, about three months before Arnold was in Calcutta, Ramakrishna lay seriously ill, and what happened that day was to be later described in the authoritative *The Gospel of Sri Ramakrishna.*[3]

> It was evening. Sri Ramakrishna was seated on his bed, thinking of the Divine Mother and repeating Her hallowed name. The

devotees sat near him in silence. Laltu, Sashi, Sarat, the younger
Naren [Vivekananda], Paltu, Bhupati, Girish, and others were
present. Ramtaran of the Star Theatre had come with Girish to
entertain Sri Ramakrishna with his singing. A few minutes later
Dr. Sarkar arrived . . .

Ramtaran began to sing:

> *Behold my vina; my dearly beloved,*
> *My lute of sweetest tone;*
> *If tenderly you play on it,*
> *The strings will waken, at your touch,*
> *To rarest melodies.*
> *Tune it neither low nor high,*
> *And from it in a hundred streams*
> *The Sweetest sound will flow;*
> *But over-slack the strings are mute,*
> *And over-stretched they snap in a twain.*

Doctor (to Girish): "Is it an original song?"

GIRISH: "No, it is an adaptation from Edwin Arnold".

Ramtaran sang from the play, *The Life of Buddha*:

> *Nor in our bygone lives, how well we played our parts;*
> *Like water in a stream, we cannot stay at rest; onward we flow*
> *   for evermore.*
> *Burst thou our slumber's bars, O Thou that art awake!*
> *How long much we remain enmeshed in fruitless dreams?*
> *Are you indeed awake? Then do not longer sleep!*
> *Thick on you lies the gloom fraught with a million woes.*
> *Raise, dreamer, from your dream, and slumber not again!*
> *Shine forth O Shining One, and with Thy shafts of light*

Slay Thou the blinding dark! Our only saviour Thou!
We seek deliverance at Thy feet.

As Sri Ramakrishna listened to the song, he went into samadhi.

Ramakrishna would pass away on 16 August 1886, five months after Arnold's visit to Calcutta. A few years later he would be immortalized by a close friend of Ghosh, who would speak of *The Light of Asia* often to his audiences, particularly in America— Swami Vivekananda. If Vivekananda was the most celebrated of Ramakrishna's disciples, Girishchandra Ghosh was perhaps the most colourful one. His authoritative biography, written by a monk

Girish Chandra Ghosh, who adapted The Light of Asia *for the Bengali stage in September 1885. His play* Buddhadev Charit *would be performed to sell-out audiences for two years. The photograph is dated to the late 1880s or early 1890s. This is from Chetananda (2009)*

of the Ramakrishna Mission, that described him as 'A Bohemian Devotee of Sri Ramakrishna', would be published in 2009.[4]

In *India Revisited*, Arnold mentions meeting Sarat Chandra Das in Calcutta. Das is a little-remembered man today but in the late nineteenth century had acquired the reputation of being a fine linguist and Buddhist scholar. He was also, as it turned out much later, a British agent who had inveigled himself into a closed Tibet, spending six months there in 1879 and fourteen months in 1881. His *Journey to Lhasa: The Diary of a Spy* would come out in 1902, just before Lord Curzon got Sir Francis Younghusband to lead a British military expedition into Tibet.[5]

Arnold died on 25 March 1904, some six months before Younghusband finally reached Lhasa.[6] A few days before his death Arnold had written an article on his meeting Das in Calcutta in January 1886. It was found among his papers and published in the *Daily Telegraph* of 4 April 1904. This extensive account of history, geography and culture of Lhasa begins thus:

A British expedition is now far advanced on the road to the Buddhist metropolis. The Romans had a proverb which ran, "It is not everybody who has the luck to go to Corinth". The same might be said about the mysterious little city in the Himalayas . . . It is rare to have conversed with any traveller who has sojourned in the capital of the Dalai Lama. Curiously enough I am one of the latter category. When I was travelling through India in 1886, and staying for some time in Calcutta, there was resident there at that date a young Hindu gentleman of great accomplishments, since then very well known to geographers as Sarat Chandra Das. He had just made the arduous journey to Lhasa, and had come back alive, whereupon Lord Dufferin [the Viceroy], aware of my interest in Buddhism sent the young explorer to me that I might hear his story. Sarat Chandra Das was very intelligent, polite and communicative, and told me almost all I know about the hidden city and the road to its jealously-guarded walls and monasteries. He gave me a small figure of the Buddha . . . some religious scrolls and a copy of his travelling notebook. This last I handed over to the India Office at the time of the Sikkim expedition, for it was then almost the only existing itinerary.

The other great scholar of Buddhism who lived in Calcutta at that time was Rajendralala Mitra. Just a few months earlier Mitra had become the first Indian to be elected President of the Asiatic Society. His monumental report on 'Buddha Gaya', prepared at the instance of the British authorities in Calcutta, had been published in 1878. He would receive a letter dated 12 June 1885 from Theodore Duka, the Hungarian Orientalist:[7]

> A short time ago I had rare opportunity of seeing the Queen's Private Library in Windsor Castle and among the few books on the reading table what should I see? Your monumental work certainly the most deservedly worthy of such a place—your Buddha Gaya . . .

It would have been very surprising had Arnold and Mitra not met. Sadly, there are no records anywhere to conclusively establish that they had indeed done so. There is also no evidence that Arnold met a young man then twenty-five years old whose literary talents were blossoming and who would be heavily influenced by Buddha in many of his later poems and books—Rabindranath Tagore. However, Arnold did meet two other Tagores who were part of the extended Tagore clan—the musicologist Sourindra Mohan Tagore and his brother the philanthropist Jatindra Mohan Tagore. He also mentions meeting 'old and valued Calcutta acquaintances like Mr. Abdur Rahman, son of the Prime Minister of Bhopal'. Over three decades later Arnold's son Channing would become a tutor to the young Bhopal princes but that story will come much later.

Arnold was captivated by Ceylon and some of most beautiful passages in *India Revisited* are to be found in Chapter XVI, called 'Ceylon and the Buddhists'. He went to Galle, Panadura, Kandy and Colombo. Panadura is about 30 kms south of Colombo and Arnold

writes of meeting 'the learned Weligama Sri Sumangala' there, who
'presides over the college and Vihara'.[8] But there was more than
Buddhism to Weligama Sri Sumangala.[9] He was the author of the
first Sinhalese translation of the *Hitopadesa*, which Arnold had also
translated into English in 1861. Sumangala was not just a Pali and
Sinhalese scholar but had researched ancient Sanskrit works as well
and had produced a commentary on *Mugdhabodha,* a standard work
on Sanskrit grammar.

Sumangala and his colleagues presented Arnold with addresses
and speeches, one of which he quotes:

May you be happy!

Let this address of elders and all of us, who are the continent and
ascetic disciples of Lord Buddha, be (acceptable) to the far-famed
and distinguished Edwin Arnold, Esq., C.S.I . . .

You, meritorious and accomplished Sir, who have eclipsed the
fame of other learned men as a mountain of diamond would lustre
the mountains of other precious stones, though born in a distant
land, blessed with neither the religion of Sri Sakhya Muni of
Solar Dynasty, the Most Holy Subduer of all desires, and World-
honoured Conqueror of evil passions, nor the intercourse of His
devotees, have written in your own native language an elegant
poem on His most holy and incomparable life, a poem embracing
the close of His metempsychosical sojourn, as a noble Bodhisat
in Tusitha Heaven and the attainment of the Four Noble Truths,
great and holy; a poem agreeing to the very letter and disagreeing
in no respect with all the popular Buddhistical Scriptures, the
Canon, and the commentaries; . . .

. . . .You alone, therefore, of all the English Scholars, are
entitled to our loving praise . . .

Under similar circumstances it has been the custom of all the
Buddhas as well as of other truly great and wise ones, to gratefully
acknowledge the merits of the deserving. We too, therefore, most
meritorious Sir, tender our heartfelt thanks to you whom we

see before now in the happy company of your beloved wife and daughter . . .

We, in conclusion, have the honour, illustrious Sir, to subscribe our names, hereunto on behalf of all our superior and subordinate priests assembled here.

GOONERATANE TISSE TERUNNANSRE of Rankoth
    Wihare, Panadure.
DHARMADAKARE NAYAKA TERUNNANSE of Kapina
    Mudalindarama Welitara.
PRAWARANERUKTIKACHARIA MAHA WIBHAWI
    SUBHUTI TERUNNANSE of Pathradhatu Chaitya
    Rama Wascaduwa.
WAGISWARA GUNANANDE of Dwipaduthama
    Wihara Colombo.

Arnold then reports an extended conversation he had with Weligama Sri Sumangala on 'the deepest mysteries of Buddhism'. He asked the monk 'whether there existed anywhere *Mahatmas*, men greatly advanced in esoteric wisdom, and elevated beyond humanity by abstinence and purity, who possessed larger powers and more profound insight than any other living philosophers'. The question had been very much in the public discourse because both Madame Blavatsky and Col. Olcott were propagating the idea that such superior souls did, in fact, exist and that they had been in touch with them. The reply that Arnold got was emphatic: 'No! Such do not exist! You would seek them vainly in this island, or in Thibet, or in Siam, or in China'. Over time Blavatsky would be discredited because of her repeated claims that she was in touch with such 'Higher Masters'.

Arnold then writes of another address being presented to him 'at the Maligha Kanda College in Colombo'[10] with some thousands of Buddhists—priests and laymen—assembled:

HONOURED SIR:--We come to you, of the Buddhists of this ancient and historic island, the heartiest, the most sincere of

Weligama Sri Sumangala as he appears in Arnold's East *and* West *(1896). He originally inspired Arnold to launch the campaign for Buddhist control of the Mahabodhi Temple at Buddha-Gya.*

welcome. By your transcendent genius and under the inspiration of a noble heart you have caused the revered name and sublime doctrines of our Lord Buddha to be respected and valued by crores of people of various Western countries. You have thus won the right to our gratitude and devotion . . . Though you, more fortunate than many great authors, have been rewarded even during your present life, by seeing your labour crowned with the world's applause, yet the blossoms that time shall not wither will be wreathed by posterity in your honour, and the historian of a coming age shall write your name high up on the list of the expounders of the Tathagatho's Law. It is a misfortune to Ceylon that as yet so few of our people have a sufficient knowledge of English to enable them to read your work in the original. But the rumour is spreading throughout Asia that a wise and eloquent friend has arisen in the land beyond the seas, and is shedding a moonlight lustre over the Dhamma which has comforted our people for more than seventy generations.

Then followed addresses in Sanskrit and Pali, after which Arnold spoke of the 'lofty and compassionate doctrines of Siddartha, as well as of the necessity of studying closely the true maxims of the Teacher'. He made it a point to stress that 'appreciation of the deep wisdom embraced in some of the Buddhistic books did not in the least imply hostility to other inspired religions', an observation not without its contemporary relevance not only in that island country but elsewhere as well.

The flowery address presented to Arnold in Colombo in the presence of the patriarch Hikkaduwe Sri Sumangala rued the fact that *The Light of Asia* was available there only in English. Curiously, it would continue to be read in English in Ceylon and a Sinhalese translation would become available only in the late 1950s: *Asia eliya* by Vinnie Vitharana in 1955 and *Peradigu eliya* by D.J. Doluweera in 1959.

The Great Buddhist Tooth Temple at Kandy in Sri Lanka in February 1886 when Sir Edwin Arnold visited it. This is from Arnold (1886).

Arnold makes a strange omission in his book—he does not mention that he had run into Olcott in Colombo. Olcott had been a great admirer of *The Light of Asia* ever since it appeared. In 1880 he had himself written *The Life of the Buddha*, a slim booklet that had initially been distributed in Ceylon. It was to be formally published by the Theosophical Society in Madras for the first time in May 1912 though. In it, Olcott's admiration for *The Light of Asia* is crystal clear and he extracts a number of verses from it to demonstrate its beauty and power. At one place in the booklet, for instance, Olcott invokes lines from Book the Fourth from the poem, as Siddhartha contemplates leaving the life of luxury to blaze a whole new trail in search of meaning and truth:

> *To tread its paths with patient, stainless feet,*
> *Making its dusty bed, its loneliest wastes*
> *My dwelling, and its meanest things my mates;*
> *Clads in no prouder garb than outcasts wear,*
> *Fed with no meals save what the charitable*
> *Give of their will, sheltered by no more pomp,*
> *Than the dim cave lends or the jungle-bush.*
> *This will I do because the woeful cry*
> *Of life and all flesh living cometh up*
> *Into my ears, and all my soul is full*
> *Of pity for the sickness of this world:*
> *Which I will heal, if healing may be found*
> *By uttermost renouncing and strong strife.*

Thus masterfully does Sir Edwin Arnold depict the sentiment which provoked this Great Renunciator.

In 1881 Olcott had published *Buddhist Catechism*, which quickly became a sensation in Ceylon and still remains so. Olcott recorded his encounter with Arnold at Colombo thus:[11]

I found Mr. (now Sir) Edwin Arnold, his wife and daughter in town, and at once set to work to organize a befitting public reception to one who had laid the whole Buddhist world under deep obligations by the writing of his *Light of Asia*. But a very few Sinhalese knew this, although Sir Edwin was happily ignorant of the fact, and I had to get my intelligent Colombo Buddhist colleagues to go with me to the priests and secure their cooperation. Fortunately, the *Ceylon Observer* made a virulent attack upon for his sympathy with Buddhism, which made our task a light one . . . A copy of the proposed address was given Sir Edwin at his request and the function duly came off with complete success.

Olcott was to remain an indefatigable champion of *The Light of Asia*. Speaking to Japanese Buddhists, for instance, in 1889, he would say:[12]

> There is one book called *The Light of Asia*, a poem by Sir Edwin Arnold, of which several thousand copies have been sold, and which has done more for Buddhism than any other agency . . .

Olcott may well have been right insofar as the Colombo reception to Arnold was concerned. But what about the earlier one at Panadura? Arnold was not a complete unknown in Ceylon as Olcott seems to make out. Be that as it may, Olcott is still a living and visible presence not only in that island country but also in Madras. His definitive biography came out in 1996.[13]

There is one other contemporary account of the reception Arnold got in Ceylon. This was from the journalist George Augustus Sala, who was also there on his own for a holiday. He had run into Arnold and Olcott and wrote somewhat irreverently after a month and a half in a British newspaper:[14]

> Is not Buddha's tooth—which is not really a tooth at all, but a huge malformed piece of ivory—preserved at the temple of Kandy? The Cinghalese rose at Mr. Arnold . . . I was present at a grand religious function of welcome offered to the author of "The Light of Asia", at a Buddhist college near Colombo, at which between two and three thousand persons must have been present. Mr. Arnold stood in the centre of a raised platform under a baldaquin, a kind of sanctuary surrounded by Buddhist clerics, in yellow satin

dalmatics. They were "bossed" by a very fat hierarch—the High Priest of Adam's Peak, indeed. *Litanies* were intoned, chorales chanted and anthems halloaed in Pali and in Cinghali.

A third commentary on Arnold's visit to Ceylon was by Constance Gordon Cumming, who may well have derived it from *India Revisited*[15] though. Cumming was a prodigious traveller and writer who had spent two years in Ceylon in the 1870s. She called Arnold a 'beautiful writer', who 'in his passionate admiration for the good and the noble, depicts things not as they really are, but as he would have them to be; for truly what he called "*The Light of Asia*" has most practically proved to be only bewildering darkness'. She then went on:

> Surely such an ovation as was accorded to him by the Buddhists when he visited Ceylon in 1886 was doubtful honour for a Christian. At one Buddhist college near Colombo well-nigh three thousand Buddhist assembled to testify their gratitude to the poet who has painted their leader in colours all borrowed from the life and teaching of Him [Christ] WHO is the true LIGHT OF THE WORLD . . . The honoured guest was placed on a raised platform beneath an honorific canopy while Buddhist ecclesiastics robed in yellow satin chanted litanies and anthems in Pali and Singhalese, Sir Edwin replying in Sanskrit.

India Revisited is a very vivid description of India in the late nineteenth century and can still be read not just for pleasure but also a commentary on its towns, cities and people at that time. Arnold repeatedly expressed wonder at how the railways—the great gift of British rule—were transforming India beyond recognition. But in addition to the rapidly expanding rail network, which had reached close to ten thousand miles by the mid-1880s, Arnold would express amazement at one more contribution of the British. He would write after his stay in Bhavnagar something that has great contemporary relevance:

Trees will save India and are saving her from the fate of Central Asia, desiccated by the nakedness due to waste of wood. The forest conservancy promoted by the British Raj is one of its greatest benefits to the peninsula. India would have been a "howling wilderness" if the sway of the Moghul or the Mahratta had lasted. It is her trees which hold the precious water in the earth and give shade, moisture, life. The peepul, the asoka and the aswattha have never been half enough worshipped. Every forest officer is the priest of a true religion.

What Arnold did not say, however, is that the British Raj made use of German silvicultural expertise to promote what he called 'forest conservancy' in India. Between 1861 and 1910, the forest establishment in India was to be headed by Dietrich Brandeis, William Schlich and Berthold Ribbentrop. Brandeis, in particular, is considered the father of modern Indian forestry.[16]

Arnold bid farewell to India on 5 March 1886 on board the *S.S. Siam* in the manner he knew best:

An Adieu

INDIA, farewell! I shall not see again
   Thy shining shores, thy people of the sun
   Gentle, sift-mannered, by a kind word won
   To such quick kindness. O'er the Arab main
Our flying flag streams back; and backwards stream
   My thoughts to those fair open fields I love,
   City and village, maidan, jungle, grove,
   The temple and the rivers! Must it seem
Too great for one man's heart to say it holds
   So many Indian sisters dear,
   So many unknown brothers? that it folds
Lakhs of true friends in parting? Nay! But there
   Lingers my heart, leave-taking; and it roves
   From hut to hut whispering "he knows and loves!"

Good-bye! Good-night! Sweet may your slumbers be,
   Gunga! and Kasi! and Saraswati!

That *India Revisited* had left an enduring impact is evidenced by
the fact that in its daily column 'A Hundred Years Ago' on 26 June
1986, the *Times of India* chose to recall what had been written on
Arnold's book:

> . . . No one, either in prose or verse, has ever caught the local
> colouring so truly, or has so successfully revelled in gorgeous
> descriptions of tropical scenery and oriental sunshine as the author
> of the "Light of Asia".

But for all his enchantment with India, Arnold never said or wrote
anything of note on the growing Indian desire for self-government.
In late 1885 a number of prominent citizens of Bombay and some
others had met secretly at the residence of William Wordsworth—
the poet's grandson—who was then Principal of Elphinstone
College to lay the foundations of the Indian National Congress
that would be launched on 28 December 1885.[17] While he was in
Bombay earlier that month on 3 December 1885, Arnold had, in
fact, met with many leading lights of Bombay at the residence of
Dosabhoy Framjee. They included some of the founding figures of
the Indian National Congress like Dadabhai Naoroji, K.T. Telang
and Pherozeshah Mehta. But quite curiously Arnold makes no
mention of this in *India Revisited*.[18]

Even in the columns of the *Daily Telegraph*, while he was lyrical
on different aspects of India's diverse civilizational heritage, Arnold
never supported 'home rule' for India—and for that matter neither
for Ireland, which was then a burning issue in British politics.
Arnold was a quintessential Tory in this regard, but a Tory who
was steeped in Orientalism in the best sense of the term, with a
genuine understanding and appreciation of Indian literature, culture
and philosophy. He appears to have had no meaningful contact with
Dadabhai Naoroji, the most eloquent and visible representative

of Indian political aspirations in London for almost four decades. The only political figure of Indian origin he seems to have been in touch with was Mancherjee Bhownaggree, a Tory himself, who would become the second Indian to be elected to the British House of Commons in 1895. Bhownaggaree had intimate ties with the princely family of Bhavnagar, with whom Arnold too was close.

Notes

1. The arrangement of the scenery, props, etc. on the stage of a theatrical production
2. Das Gupta (1944)
3. *The Gospel of Sri Ramakrishna* first appeared in Bengali in five volumes (1902, 1904, 1908 1910 and 1932) as *Sri Ramakrishna Kathamrita.* It was written by Ramakrishna's foremost householder-disciple Mahendra Nath Gupta, who based it on a diary he kept on his daily interactions with the mystic between 1882 and 1886. The English translation of Gupta's account by Swami Nikhilananda was published in 1942. Margaret Woodrow Wilson co-edited the translation along with Joseph Campbell, who figures elsewhere in my narrative. She was the daughter of the US President Woodrow Wilson and had moved to the Aurobindo Ashram in Pondicherry in 1938, where she died six years later. I have used Swami Chetanananda's translation, *Ramakrishna as We saw Him,* published by the Vedanta Society of St. Louis, USA in 1990.
4. Chetanananda (2009)
5. This was reissued in 2017 with a very informative introduction by Parimal Bhattacharya. Das (2017)
6. French (1998) is a fine biography of Younghusband. Three years before his death in 1942, Younghusband would write an introduction to Frank Lee Woodward's "Some Sayings of the Buddha", which revealed his deep admiration for the Buddha. Woodward was a theosophist and Pali scholar. Younghusband's expedition and its aftermath overshadowed the publication of Ippolito Desideri's account of his visit to Tibet during between March 1716 and April 1721. Desideri, a pioneer in the study of the Tibetan language and of Tibetan Buddhism, was a Jesuit priest who would spend time in India as well. Desideri's journal, completed in 1728, would finally be published in Rome in 1904, the year of Arnold's death. It would be savaged by British critics, presumably because they did not wish to see their claims to Tibet challenged. Arnold may have

known of Desideri because the Jesuit was mentioned in early eighteenth century works of Buddhist studies and the discovery of his account was announced in the Geographical Journal as Arnold was giving the finishing touches to *The Light of Asia.*

7. Mitra (1978)

8. Panadura was the site of a famous debate in August 1873, when Buddhist monks engaged with Christian missionaries and 'won'. An account of this debate is generally believed to have profoundly influenced Colonel Henry Steel Olcott and Madame Helena Blavatsky, the founders of the theosophical movement, to take an interest in Buddhism and in Ceylon, as it was known then.

9. He is different from the more senior Hikkaduwe Sri Sumangala, another venerated Buddhist figure of Ceylon, who is the subject of Blackburn (2010).

10. Arnold was for sure referring to Vidyodaya Pirivena, which is in the Maligakanda neighbourhood of Colombo. I thank Gitanjali Surendran for pointing this out to me.

11. Olcott (2002a)

12. Olcott (2002b)

13. Prothero (1996)

14. 'Mr G. Sala in India', *Aberdeen Weekly Journal*, Monday, 29 March 1886; Issue 9712, quoted in Eiben (2016)

15. Cumming (1892)

16. This was not the only contribution of the Germans to the British Raj. In 1781, the British raised two infantry regiments in Hanover to augment their forces to fight the French and native rulers in India. One young German who was thus recruited was Carl August Schlegel. He was to be killed in Madras eight years later, but not before kindling interest in India in two of his younger brothers, who would both later pioneer German Indology—August Wilhelm Schlegel and Friederich von Schlegel. Paulin (2016) is a fine biography of August Wilhelm Schelegel.

17. Patel (2020)

18. The *Times of India* of 5 December 1885 carried a fairly long report on 'a reunion' given by Dosabhoy Framjee in honour of 'Mr. Edwin Arnold'.

9

1886 and Beyond: Edwin Arnold and the Buddha-Gya Temple Campaign He Launched

Many historians have written books and learned papers on the issue of the Mahabodhi Temple. Academic work on it continues to get published. The standard reference works are those of Dipak Barua, whose *Buddha Gaya Temple: Its History (1981)*, and Alan Trevithick, whose *The Revival of Buddhist Pilgrimage at Bodh Gaya (1811–1949)*, came out in 2006. There have been a couple of doctoral dissertations as well.[1] My concern is really with the role of Arnold that begins in 1886 and lasts for a decade or so.

In Book the Sixth of *The Light of Asia,* Arnold describes the hallowed place of Siddhartha Gautama's enlightenment:

> *The Bodhi-tree (thenceforward in all years*
> *Never to fade, and ever to be kept*
> *In homage of the world), beneath whose leaves*
> *It was ordained the Truth should come to Buddh:*
> *Which now the Master knew; wherefore he went*
> *With measured pace, steadfast, majestical,*
> *Unto the Tree of Wisdom. Oh ye Worlds!*
> *Rejoice! Our Lord wended unto the Tree!*

There is, of course, no mention in the poem of the Mahabodhi Temple in whose precincts the sacred tree is now located. The reason for this is obvious—the Temple would be built only centuries after the enlightenment. As we have seen, Arnold visited this temple in January 1886. This visit would trigger a huge controversy that would not be settled till May 1953. The historical background to the dispute that lasted almost seven decades is a long and convoluted one. But certain basics are not contested.[2]

First, ten years after his consecration, that is in around 259-8 BCE, the Mauryan ruler Ashoka visited the hallowed Bodhi tree under which the Buddha had gained enlightenment.

Second, a century or so later 'a representation at the Buddhist stupa of Bharhut in Central India depicted a throne, with the trunk of the Bodhi tree behind, surrounded by an open-pillared pavilion' and 'this throne was most probably erected by Ashoka at Bodh Gaya'.

The earliest representation (second century BCE) of the Mahabodhi sacred area is from Bharhut in Madhya Pradesh, from the massive stone railing that is now in the Indian Museum, Kolkata. It shows the throne that Ashoka is supposed to have donated and the pillar of a religious structure he built there. The Vajrasana that Ashoka is said to have donated is a symbol of the Buddha, among the many that represented him before he came to be depicted in human form. (Source: Nayanjot Lahiri)

Third, various types of structures, including some form of a temple, were built over time to honour the Buddha, with the temple having undergone reconstruction around the fifth century BCE.

This terracotta plaque, now at the Patna Museum and found at Kumrahar near Patna by D.B. Spooner in 1914, is the earliest visual we have of a temple at Buddha Gaya. It is certain that it does not depict the original Ashokan temple. As for the plaque's date, the dominant view is that it belongs to the fourth century CE. (Source: Patna Museum)

Fourth, as Buddhism began to gradually fade away (and the process was *gradual*) Hindu icons came to be worshipped too in its precincts.[3] Over the centuries, the Buddha was also worshipped there, but as a Hindu deity.

Fifth, from the thirteenth century the Mahabodhi temple became a model that was emulated in other places like Burma and Siam.

Sixth, the temple continued to draw visitors not only from India but also from Ceylon, Burma, Siam, Tibet, China and Japan.

Seventh, sometime in the last decade of the sixteenth century a wandering Sivaite sannyasi established his abode close to the ruins of the temple. In August 1727, a Mughal prince gave the Sivaites a deed to establish ownership rights in the area (although it was unclear whether the deed covered the actual temple or not). The Sivaites took control of the temple and its surroundings following the grant of the deed and from then on, both Hindus and Buddhists had access to it.

Eighth, repairs to the temple were carried out by Burmese Kings in the early nineteenth century, who continued their patronage till the time of the Third Anglo-Burmese War of November 1885, just two months prior to Arnold's visit to Buddha-Gya.

In mid-January 1886, Arnold visited the site of the sacred temple and the Bodhi-tree. What he saw anguished and angered him immensely. As he left Calcutta for Colombo, he wrote to Sir William Wilson, who was then a member of the Viceroy's Executive Council, responsible mainly for education. This letter was carried in Calcutta's *The Englishman's Overland Mail* on 26 January 1886:

> I have the honour to address you upon a subject of importance to all who are interested in the religious history of India encouraged to do so by your personal friendship and your well-known acquaintance with her records.
>
> In visiting lately the various sites in this country connected with the story of Sakya Muni, the founder of Buddhism, I came to Buddha-Gya. There can be no question of the authenticity of the spot, described as it is by the Chinese pilgrims, and identified by so many natural and artificial marks. The vicinity of the temple, and of the little Pipul-tree now standing there, is undoubtedly the same in which the great "Teacher of the Law" completed his meditations and attained to the Buddhaship . . .
>
> Everybody of enlightened mind must attach importance to such a spot, which is, nevertheless, I regret to declare, in a state of abandonment deplorable to describe and realize . . . a

vast number of sculptured and inscribed relics which have been disinterred during recent excavations and "reparations" now lie in and near the spot, neglected and perishing . . . I was shown in some miserable shed, some "selected specimens' to the extent of hundred more, heaped one upon another, in a dreadful chaos of neglect and contempt, although the first which I took bore the sacred formula of Buddhism and the second had an elephant adorning that *Dharma Chakra,* as perfect a carving as could be seen . . . Who can deny that to treat the records of a truly sacred spot is dishonourable to the age, to India, and to every one who has the power to rescue these ancient relics and does not exercise it?

I would especially through you, appeal to those Indian gentlemen who feel pride in the glorious share which their country has borne in the history of Philosophy and Religion . . . To collect all that can be found; to cleanse and to arrange them under some proper and permanent shelter; and to provide for the guardianship of these and whatever else might be discovered upon the same hallowed site, would nor be costly; but costly or not, if it not be soon effected by the native public spirit which I have ventured to invoke, or by some other agency, many an important memorial will surely pass away for ever.

This was an unexceptionable letter, a perfectly justifiable plea for governmental and public support for the preservation and protection of India's heritage. Who could argue with that? But in a few weeks Arnold would shift course radically after his visit to Panadura in Ceylon and his conversation with Weligama Sri Sumangala, which I have mentioned earlier. In that conversation, after Arnold had given a description of 'localities in the life-history of the Buddha that I had recently visited', the venerable Ceylonese monk 'expressed an ardent wish that the Buddhists might someday recover the guardianship of that sacred ground in Buddha-Gya where "the Lord" meditated so long under the Bodhi tree and finally attained his Buddhaship'. Arnold also writes that Weligama Sri Sumangala had told him that the place where Buddha had received enlightenment and also the place where he entered into Nirvana 'ought no longer to be in any hands except those of Buddhists'.

Many years later, Arnold would insist that it was *he* who had first mooted the idea of Buddhist control over Buddha-Gya. That has since become conventional wisdom repeatedly stressed even by Weligama Sri Sumangala's acolyte Anagarika Dharmapala, who is the central figure in this long and tortuous episode.[4] But that is definitely *not* what Arnold had written soon after his visit to India and Ceylon in 1886. In fact, even his dispatch from Colombo in the first week of February 1886 and published in the *Daily Telegraph* of 11 March 1886 clearly stated that it was Weligama Sri Sumangala who had suggested that Buddhists must have full control over both the place of enlightenment and of nirvana.

The experience of his visit to Buddha-Gya, where he felt the Buddha and everything associated with him, was treated with complete disdain by the Hindu priest at the temple, and his conversation with Weligama Sri Sumangala triggered something in Arnold. He would write this longish letter to Sir Arthur Gordon, Governor of Ceylon, sometime in November 1886. It was published in the supplement to the *Manchester Courier and Lancashire General Advertiser* of 20 November 1886:

> The temple and enclosure at Buddha-Gya are the most sacred spots for Buddhists in the whole world. To them this locality represents what Jerusalem is to Christians, Mecca to Muslims and Benaras to the Hindoos. But Buddha-Gya is occupied by a college of Shivaite priests, who worship Mahadeo there, and deface the shrine with emblems and rituals foreign to its nature. The shrine and the ground surrounding it remain, however, Government property and there would be little difficulty, after proper and friendly negotiations in procuring the departure of the Mahant, with his priest, and the transfer of the temple and its grounds to the guardianship of Buddhist monks from Ceylon. It is to carry out this project that I earnestly wish to win your Excellency's goodwill. I have considered it respectful and becoming to address you alone,

in the first instance, but I have consulted high authorities, and among them a General who thoroughly sympathises with the idea and declares it entirely feasible. I need not point out that if it could be accomplished as I believe, without the least vexation to the present tenants, not only would all your island would revere the Governor who had given back to Buddhism its geographical centre, but that the Buddhists of Siam, of our new province of Burma, of Tibet, of Japan, and of China, would become attracted to British civilization by this single act than by another that could be devised. I am sending a copy of this letter to Lord Dufferin and to the two chief priests in Colombo and Kandy, Sri Weligama and Sri Sumangala.

Arnold was invoking the name of a legendary figure in Indian archaeology—Alexander Cunningham, who, after his retirement from the British Army in India, had led India's first comprehensive, government-sponsored archaeological survey that had begun in December 1861. Cunningham had carried out explorations at Buddha-Gya in early 1862 and revisited the site a decade later. From 1871 till 1885 he was the Director-General of the Archaeological Survey of India, and when Arnold met him, Cunningham was in retirement in London.[5] This same letter of Arnold's with a couple of extra lines italicized by me below was reported in the *Times of India* on 28 December 1886:

> *I am venturing to suggest to you a Governmental Act, which would be historically just, which would win for you the love and gratitude of all your Buddhist population and would reflect enduring honour upon your administration.* It is this: The temple and enclosure at Buddha-Gya are, as you know, the most sacred spots for Buddhists all over the world. To them this locality represents what Jerusalem is to Christians, Mecca to Muslims and Benaras to the Hindoos. But Buddha-Gya is occupied by a college of Sivaite priests who worship Mahadev there, and deface the shrine with emblems and rituals foreign to its nature. That shrine and the ground surrounding it

remain, however Government property . . . and there would be little difficulty, after proper and friendly negotiations, in procuring the departure of the Mahant, with his priests, and the transfer of the temple and its grounds to the guardianship of Buddhist monks from Ceylon. It is to carry out this project that I earnestly wish to win your Excellency's good-will. *I apprehend that a certain sum of money might be required to facilitate of the Brahmans and to establish the Buddhist College. In my opinion, a lakh of rupees could not be expended by either Government in a more profitable manner.*

I am not entirely sure whether only one or both letters were sent. My own guess is that the italicized portions above may have been edited out from the letter published in November 1886. Arnold had set the Buddhist cat among the Hindu pigeons. Actually, he had set it among some British pigeons as well.

Arnold's letters to the Viceroy and the Governor of Ceylon must certainly have been read but there appears to have been no worthwhile action taken on them. In February 1887, Arnold had again written in the *Daily Telegraph* calling for the Government of India to arrange for 'the surrender of this unspeakably hallowed locality [the Mahabodhi Temple at Buddha-Gya] by the Mahant who now holds it'. Arnold was suggesting that the Mahant be suitably compensated financially as an incentive to get him to relocate his Hindu establishment elsewhere. He wanted the temple placed in a charge of representative Buddhist priests from Ceylon, Siam, Burma and Tibet. This would 'earn goodwill for the British among all Buddhist peoples'.[6]

The picture would, however, be transformed with the entry of the Ceylonese Buddhist monk Anagarika Dharmapala into this story in early 1891.[7] He is considered to be the key founding figure of Sinhala nationalism. Equally, for about four decades till his death in April 1933, Dharmapala was a one-man army for the recovery and revival of India's Buddhist heritage and traditions. According to a chronology of his life drawn up by recent biographer of his, it was in 1882 that:

Dharmpala reads a passage in *The Light of Asia* that convinces him to take up a life of renunciation.[8]

By his own accounts though, Dharmapala had read *India Revisited* in 1886 and had been angered by Arnold's account of the blasphemous goings-on at the Mahabodhi Temple. Three years later while convalescing in a hospital in Kyoto he would read *The Light of Asia*, finding in it 'consolation and hope'. There can be little doubt that Blavatsky and Olcott had helped introduce Arnold's books to Dharmapala since he was very much part of the Theosophical Society circle at that time.

On 22 January 1891, Dharmapala, accompanied by a Japanese priest and Pali scholar Kozen Gunaratna,[9] reached Bodh Gaya. By his repeated later recollections, seeing how the Mahabodhi Temple had become essentially a place of worship for Hindus and getting a sense that its importance for the Buddhists was being treated with utter contempt by the Hindu priest, Dharmapala vowed that the Mahabodhi temple would 'once again be a properly functioning Buddhist temple'.

Dharmapala (sitting) and Kozen Gunaratna at the Mahabodhi Temple, January 1891.

On 31 May 1891 he founded the Mahabodhi Society in Colombo. Weligama Sri Sumangala, who had met Arnold in February 1886 and first spoken of Buddhist control over Buddha-Gya, was its President, Olcott was its Director and Chief Adviser and Dharmapala its General Secretary. The managing committee had members from different parts of the world, with Arnold as one of its 'London Representatives'. In July 1891 four Ceylonese monks were sent to Buddha-Gya on behalf of the Society, which would also organize an international conference there in October 1891. But realizing that all the action needed to get Buddhist control over the temple lay in the then capital of British India, Dharmapala moved the Society to Calcutta a year later.

In July 1893, the *Journal of the Mahabodhi Society* would reproduce an article by Arnold that had appeared four months earlier in the *Daily Telegraph*. It was called 'The Temple of Maha-Bodhi'. It was, in large part, a rehash of the description he had provided seven years earlier in the same paper as well as in his book *India Revisited*. But there was one very significant change. In 1886 he had written that the idea of Buddhist control had first been suggested at Panadura in Ceylon by Weligama Sri Sumangala. Now, however, Arnold changed that position and said that during his meeting with Sumangala and others:

> I gave utterance to the suggestion that the temple and its appurtenances ought to be, and might be, by amicable arrangements with the Hindu College and by favour of the Queen's Government placed in the hands of a representative committee of Buddhist nations.

Arnold had clearly contradicted himself. Whether it was inadvertent or an attempt to enlarge the niche for himself in Buddhist history is impossible to tell. All that can be said is that Arnold's March 1893 version of what had happened at Panadura obliterating his own 1886 version of events would become the stuff of books, theses and articles—and continues to be so.

After his article on Buddha-Gya in the *Daily Telegraph*, Arnold would badger Lord Kimberley, the Secretary of State for India in the British Government. On 24 March 1893 he would send the first of his missives:

Dear Lord Kimberley:

I beg you to read the paper which I have written, in the copy of the "Daily Telegraph" forwarded herewith. It is indeed quite impossible to exaggerate the Asiatic importance of the matter of the Temple at Buddha Gya and your Lordship might cover your Administration with glory and gratitude, by half a word to the Bengal Authorities.

Four days later Kimberley replied saying that his understanding of the situation was that the Government of Bengal would not interfere but that:

. . . if any such movement is made by those who are interested in the Temple to buy out the rights of the present possessors, the authorities would assist the purchasers in making the necessary arrangements for the transfer.

Arnold saw this as a step forward and wrote back to Kimberley on 31 March 1893:

Dear Lord Kimberley:

Thank you very much for your kind letter. What you are pleased to say is as much as we could expect. But please preserve towards my Buddhists your benevolent inclination, and if opportunity given soon do give expression to it in your communications with the Viceroy. You know me as too faithful a servant of your Indian Empire to encourage anything contrary to the peace of the dear and honourable Empress.

A few weeks later on 29 April 1893 Arnold would inform Kimberley that the 'King of Siam is deeply interested in the matter [of Buddhist control over Buddha-Gya temple]' and reassure him that he [Arnold] would 'take care nothing is done to vex the Hindu occupants'.

Sometime in mid-July 1893 Arnold would write an article called 'The Temple at Maha-Bodhi' in the *Daily Telegraph*. In this he mentioned that he had gone to see Lord Cross the then Secretary of State for India and had this conversation:[10]

"Do you wish, Lord Cross," I asked, "to have 400 millions of Eastern peoples bless your name night and day, and to be forever remembered in Asia, like Alexander, or Asoka, or Akbar the Great?

"God bless my soul, yes" answered the Minister, "how is that to be done?"

Then I repeated all the above facts [the history of the Maha-Bodhi Temple and the need to have Buddhist control over it considering its association with the life of the Buddha]

Lord Cross did indeed take up Arnold's plea with the Viceroy Lord Lansdowne, who, in turn, took a pragmatic stance which ensured that the idea went nowhere—that the Calcutta Government would favour friendly negotiations so long as no religious ill-feeling was aroused and no 'pecuniary grant was asked from the Indian treasury'.

In July 1893, Dharmapala came to London on his way to Chicago to attend the World Parliament of Religions there two months hence. He was received at the docks by Arnold. They were meeting for the first time. Dharmapala was Arnold's guest. Together they called on Lord Kimberley. Dharmapala would make an impassioned plea for the transfer of the temple at Buddha-Gya to the Mahabodhi Society as the representative of the world's Buddhists. He was given a patient hearing, but the British did not want to do anything dramatic, fearful of antagonizing Hindu sentiment.

On 10 October 1893 Arnold received a letter from a Japanese admirer of his called H. Doki:

> ...I believe I shall at least spend a couple or three months in India, going round all the holy places in connection with Buddhism and studying the present aspect of the Buddhist movement there. I make it my sole objective to restore the Buddha Gaya temple to begin with. I shall be most happy if you kindly allow me an interview and disclose your noble idea ...

The meeting of Arnold, Dharmapala and Kimberley had one result: The Viceroy in Calcutta was sounded out. Kimberley wrote to Arnold on 13 November 1893 after he had heard from the Viceroy in Calcutta:

> Dear Sir Edwin Arnold:
>
> I received by the last mail an answer from Lord Landsdowne (to whom I had sent your letter to me of Aug 16) about the Buddha Gya Shrine. The Bengal Govt. have been consulted on the matter, and they are not willing to consider the question of transfer of the shrine to the Mahabodhi Society at the present time when agitations of a religious character possesses people's minds in Behar. Even when the present excitement passes away, the Govt. would probably not see its way to allowing the proposed transfer to be affected. It is stated that Buddha-Gya is regarded with reverence by the Hindus and no mere agreement for transfer between the Hindu Mahant and the Mahabodhi society would meet or cover all the considerations raised by the subject.

Arnold replied the very next day:

> Dear Lord Kimberley:
>
> I have the honour to acknowledge your Lordship's letter of the 13th Nov in which you inform me of Lord Landsdowne's reply about the Buddha Gya Temple.

I have first to thank your Lordship—for the enlightened consideration which—like your Predecessor in the India Office—you have been pleased to give to my representations upon this important subject: and, next, to recognize—as one not ignorant of Indian affairs— the strong reasons which justify Lord Landsdowne's unwillingness to further, at present, the desire of all Buddhist communities.

Under the circumstances, I conceive it my duty to acquiesce respectfully in the decision of a Government which I have had the honour to serve, and although the movement initiated for the restoration of the Temple to its rightful guardians is now too general (?) and influential to terminate without results, I shall counsel its leaders either to await a more propitious time, or to direct their future efforts towards an absolutely amicable and voluntary arrangement with the Mahant and the Hindus.

On his way back from Chicago, Dharmapala first stopped off in Japan, where in November 1893 he was presented with a 700-year-old ancient Buddha image, enshrined in a temple at Kanagawa near Yokohoma. The presentation was made by the High Priest Asahi, the head of the congregation of the Tento-kuji temple at Siba in Tokyo. It had been carved, according to one account, by 'the great General who erected the enormous and famous bronze Kamakura statue of Buddha in 1252 CE'. Dharmapala sought permission from the British government to install the Buddha image he had been given in the sanctum sanctorum of the Mahabodhi Temple. But the British prevaricated, worried about antagonizing Hindu sentiment and suspicious of Dharmapala's Japanese links. Both Arnold and Dharmapala were giving up hope, contrary to the former's public postures. Dharmapala recorded in his diary on 16 July 1894:

. . . received letter from Sir Edwin Arnold. No hopes of getting any help from Govt. Stand on our own resources. Fight it out till the last or abandon it . . .

Finally, before sunrise on 25 February 1895 Dharmapala took unilateral action and entered the temple and placed the statue in its sanctum sanctorum, which was then empty. He was about to start worship when a group of armed men, clearly followers of the Mahant, themselves barged in, grabbed the statue and dumped it elsewhere. It was to be placed in the Burmese rest-house nearby. Dharmapala then decided to file criminal charges against the Mahant and his men for trespassing into a place of worship and for damaging religious property. It is instructive to note here that Dharmapala's legal action went against all the advice he had received, including from Sumangala and Olcott, who were most probably aware that while the Buddhist right to pray in the Mahabodhi Temple was unimpeachable, their legal right to its ownership was ambiguous.

The case was first heard on 8 April 1895 by the local Magistrate D.J. Macpherson. The defendants' written statement ended thus:

We believe that neither Dharmapala nor the Maha-bodhi Society in any way represent the interests of the Buddhists: but that the whole agitation, which has for its object to oust the Mahant from the possession and control of the Maha-Bodhi Temple is being fomented and fostered by Sir Edwin Arnold and Colonel Olcott, neither of whom were Buddhists or connected with Buddhism . . .

To be fair, both Arnold and Olcott favoured 'amicable negotiations'. Olcott had actually tried to dissuade Dharmapala from filing the criminal case. But the aggressive Ceylonese, who was itching for a confrontation with the Mahant from the beginning, was obdurate and had gone ahead.

On 19 July 1895 Macpherson gave his judgment. He acquitted two of the defendants but held three of them in violation of the Indian Penal Code. They were fined and given a jail sentence of a month. On the larger issue of ownership of the Temple which Dharmapala was hoping to have settled definitively, the magistrate ruled that the 'Mahant did enjoy possessory rights of a certain kind' over the Temple and its precincts but that 'they could not have thought these rights to be of so complete a character as to connote full proprietorship or carry with it the right claimed by the Mahant to do what he liked inside the temple'. Macpherson characterized

The Japanese statue that Dharmapala tried to place in the sanctum sanctorum of the Mahabodhi Temple at Buddha Gaya in February 1895 but which was thrown out of there by the Mahant's men. It now resides in the Mahabodhi Society in Kolkata. (Source: Mahabodhi Society, Kolkata)

the proprietorship of the temple as being one of 'dual custodianship' between the Mahant and the government. The government had come into the picture because of the restoration works it had carried out at Buddha-Gya.

This was a partial victory for Dharmapala. But very soon the Mahant submitted an appeal in the district sessions court. The appeal was heard by Herbert Holmwood, who suspended the jail sentences but retained the fines. On 30 July 1895 he held that the Mahant's proprietary rights over the temple and its surroundings found expression in the government's own list of Ancient Monuments issued in 1886 but that this did not constitute a 'deed or grant'. The Mahant was still not satisfied and submitted a second appeal, this time to the Calcutta High Court. A two-judge bench delivered its verdict on 22 August 1895. It set aside both the fines and the jail sentences. More importantly, one of the judges (the British one) held that 'if the temple is not vested with the Mahant, it does not appear to be vested with anyone', while the other judge (an Indian) held that 'the question of what the exact nature and extent of the Mahant's control over the temple is, the evidence adduced in the case does not enable us to determine'.

Dharmapala had received a huge setback. Arnold commiserated with him publicly. On 18 September 1895, the 'Letters to the Editor' section in London's *The Times*, carried this item under the caption 'Ashoka's Temple'.

SIR,-The thanks of all Oriental scholars and of those who take an interest in the future of the chief Buddhist nations are due to you for your luminous and impartial summary of recent proceedings in connexion with the Mahabodhi Society and the great temple of Budh-Gaya. For the moment the effort to redeem the temple— immeasurably sacred to so many pious people—has been thwarted, and the High Court at Calcutta has issued a judgment which would make the Ottoman ashamed at the Holy Sepulchre and the Mussalman blush at Mecca. The chief loser by this regrettable decision, which upsets the finding of the local magistrate and the elaborate decree of the Supreme Court, is, I grieve to say, her Majesty's Government in India. To have declared the temple open to the decorous and governed use of the Siamese, Burmese, Cingalese, Tibetan, Chinese and Japanese pilgrims who desired to repair thither would have been worth untold moral force to England in Asia. The opportunity is for the present lost . . .

Yours obediently,
EDWIN ARNOLD

His letter to *The Times* drew a sharp and caustic response in Calcutta's *Englishman* of 16 October 1895:

> The mail has brought, amongst other items of information, the news that Sir Edwin Arnold has been unburdening himself to the editor of the Times on the subject of the recent Bodh-Gaya Temple case. We cannot confess to any surprise at Sir Edwin's indignation over the result of the dispute; for the Mahabodhi Society and its crusade for the recovery of the famous shrine owe their existence and their present notoriety almost entirely to his vivid imagination and his picturesque and facile pen . . . We have no doubt he has thoroughly impressed himself with the grandeur, and we wish we could add the utter futility of the task he has set before him. We have every sympathy with his ambition to have his name remembered for ever in Asia with the alliterative string of individuals with which he vainly sought to lure Lord Cross from the dull office routine of his daily life [page 149]. Nor can there be a doubt that from a purely sentimental point of view, there is much to be said for him and his crusade. But sentiment cannot pretend to override the rights and privileges of property . . .

Evidently, Arnold also toyed with the idea of coming back to India to negotiate a settlement with the Mahant. The *Englishman* of 23 October 1895 spoke of his 'coming visit to India'. The trip did not materialize but Arnold would mention that he had written to the Mahant (in Hindi). That letter, however, has not survived.

By early 1896 the British had had enough. They decided to remove the Japanese image of the Buddha from Buddha-Gya to the Indian Museum in Calcutta. Dharmapala protested angrily and was able to mobilize support for his position that the image should remain in Buddha-Gya itself. The *Indian Mirror*, the *Bihar Times* and the *Bengalee* advocated Dharmapala's cause and finally on 29 May 1896, the Government of Bengal informed Dharmapala that it had decided against the relocation and that the Japanese image would be permitted to remain at the Burmese Rest House. Dharmapala had won a victory—not complete no doubt but he had made a telling point. On 2 June 1896, he wrote to Arnold giving him the details of all that had transpired:

Peace and Blessing to All

My dear Sir Edwin Arnold:

The cause of Truth has triumphed at last and Buddha Gaya has been restored to the Buddhists after seven centuries of oblivion. The sacred image of the Buddha sent by the Japanese Buddhists has been our Liberator. This great image had a mission to perform; and these 3 years it was doing the work of a Harbinger. For full nine months it remained in 1894 and from July 25 1895 it became the subject of dispute and the basis of the great Temple Case which made the Mahant to spend nearly a lac of rupees, and this year it became the victim of Mr. Cotton's selfishness and now after having gone through all trials it has found a place in the Royal Monastery at Buddha Gaya. Glory to Buddha! Sir Edwin Arnold has won a place in our Holy Shrine. The Burmese Monastery is declared as Buddhist property under Govt. control, we have the right to keep priests and now we have the sacred image—and we are safe. The Mahant has been baffled in the great struggle. His wealth, his influential friends, his acute lawyers have had their day, but the future is ours . . .

The Indian Mirror, the Behar Times and the Bengalee advocated our cause and nobly defended our interests. Babu Norendra Nath Sen, a blood cousin of the late Keshub Chandra Sen is the Editor of the Indian Mirror, Honble Surendra Nath Banerjee is Editor of the Bengalee and Pandit Mahesh Narayan is Editor of the Behar Times. Babu Nanda Kishore Lall, MA is the man who set the wheel of agitation in motion . . .

The work initiated by you in 1886 has been successfully realized in 1896 and the glory of it is yours. My work has been that of a bugler. . . I hope you will visit India and make a triumphant progress in all Buddhist countries . . .

One interesting feature of Dharmapala's campaign was that newspapers run by Indians supported him whereas newspapers aligned to British interests were critical of him. The names that he mentions in this letter were all noted names of the times in Calcutta.

A couple of months later Arnold received a letter from Princess Bhanuranghi of Siam, who had written to him on 5 August 1896:

I have to thank you for a copy of your great work the "Light of Asia" . . . It has given me profound pleasure alike to learn that your historical work on our religion is achieving such an immense and well-deserved success and your agitation in respect of Buddha Gaya has borne such satisfactory results . . .

But Bhanuranghi, Dharmapala and Arnold had not reckoned with the Mahant fully. The Mahant would not take this lying down and mobilized his supporters in Calcutta—and he was a very rich Mahant, given that he owned some 30,000 acres of land. He represented to the British, who once again started a review of their review. Ultimately on 29 December 1897, Arnold wrote to the editor of the *Daily Telegraph*:

Sir,-I have great satisfaction in communicating to you the subjoined official dispatch, which has reached me from India which shows that the principle contended by the Mahabodhi Society and by myself has now been accepted by the Indian Government, in consequence of which the famous and sacred temple of Buddha-Gya is proclaimed to be a Buddhist temple open henceforth to all the Buddhist world.

What Arnold had 'subjoined' to his letter was the following:

From the Chief Secretary to the Government of Bengal, to the Secretary of the British India Association, dated Darjeeling, October 14 1897:-

I am directed to acknowledge the receipt of your letter dated January 29 1897, in which the Association prays for the removal of the Japanese image of the Buddha from the Burmese rest house in Buddh-Gaya on the ground that the presence of the image close to the Buddha Gaya Temple which they assert has been pronounced by the High Court to be a Hindu Temple is deemed objectionable by a considerable section of the Hindu community.

In reply I am to say that the representation of the Association has been fully considered by the Lieutenant Governor and the Commissioner of the Patna Division and the Collector of the Gaya district have been fully consulted but that his Honour is unable to accept the contention of the Association that the temple is a Hindu one.

The Government has throughout adopted an attitude of strict impartiality in regard to the temple and desires to maintain that attitude. While spending chiefly in the interests of the Buddhists (and also for the sake of antiquaries conservation), large sums on the restoration of the shrine and its precincts, and on keeping the rest-house in repair, it has recognized the hereditary position of the Mahant. It has, however, also appointed a Government custodian on its own part to see that the temple is not injured. Free access to the temple has always been given to the Buddhists, and the Mahant being entitled to receive any offerings made. The conditions which existed before Mr. Dharmapala brought the Japanese image to Buddh-Gaya can still be observed by both parties, unless they agree hereafter to any change by amicable arrangements and his Honour trusts that they will be observed. The Japanese image can remain in the rest house without giving rise to any disturbance, and the Mahant will, no doubt, recognize the duty of checking any disposition on the part of his men to create any trouble.

The Japanese idol would move to the headquarters of the Mahabodhi Society in Calcutta in 1910. Dharmapala would continue his campaign to get full Buddhist control over the temple at Buddh-Gaya. In 1922, the Indian National Congress would hold its annual session at Gaya and an appeal would be made to Gandhi to have the issue resolved once and for all. But Dharmapala soon despaired, recording in his diary on 7 May 1925:

> Gandhi has no knowledge of Buddhism and the only book he had read on the subject was *Light of Asia* . . .

That very day Gandhi had spoken at the Mahabodhi Society in Calcutta, where he began by recollecting:

> Nearly 40 or 38 years ago I went to England as a lad and the first religious book that was placed into my hands was the *Light of Asia*. I had read nothing of any religion in the world . . . So when I found myself in possession of the *Light of Asia*, I devoured it. . . . I closed the book with deep veneration for the expounding or teaching which has been so beautifully expressed by Sir Edwin Arnold. I read the book again when I commenced the practice of my profession in South Africa.

Two years later, Gandhi was in Colombo and on 25 November 1927 he repeated what he had said in Calcutta: 'that his first introduction to any religious study was through a single book, viz, Sir Edwin Arnold's *The Light of Asia*, which fascinated and engrossed him'. He wrote to his nephew Narandas Gandhi from Yeravda Jail in Poona on 18 May 1930 that he was then 'reading Edwin Arnold's *The Light of Asia*'. On 26 October 1932, he told his son Ramdas that he should try and understand the Gita in its original Sanskrit and that he should also read Tolstoy's essays and Thomas Kempis' *Imitation of Christ*. He added that 'you must read an account of the life of the Buddha, and *The Light of Asia*, if you can understand it'.[11]

Dharmapala's criticism of Gandhi's knowledge of Buddhism may well have been unfair but his frustration was understandable. In 1922, he had pinned hopes on Gandhi for getting control over the Mahabodhi Temple at Buddha-Gya and all that Gandhi had done was delegate that responsibility to his trusted lieutenant from Bihar, Rajendra Prasad.[12] The man who would later become independent India's first President toiled over the issue for the next quarter of a century. Meanwhile Dharmapala passed away in April 1933 but not before having Sarnath completely renovated[13] and not before expressing a wish that he would like to be reborn as a Brahmin in India!

Notes

1.   Doyle (1997) and Geary (2009) are two deserving special mention.
2.   Lahiri (2012) and Ray (2014)
3.   This has been discussed in Lahiri (2012)
4.   Guruge (1965)
5.   Singh (2004) has a detailed account of Cunningham at Buddha-Gya.
6.   The *Times of India,* 2 March 1887
7.   Dharmapala was born Don David Hewavitarane in 1864 but between 1886 and 1890 had come to be known first as Hewavitarane Dharmapala and later as Anagarika ('homeless') Dharmapala. Dharmapala was also, coincidentally, the last great 'Buddhist' ruler in any part of India. A late eighth-century ruler, he belonged to the Pala dynasty in Bengal.
8.   Kemper (2015)
9.   Shaku Kozen had become a Buddhist in Ceylon in 1890 and became known as Gunaratna Thera. Jaffe (2019) discusses his life.
10. Lord Cross was Secretary of State for India till 11 August 1892. Hence the conversation recorded by Arnold must have taken place prior to that date.
11. The 'if you can understand it' proviso had something to do with the difficulties of self-education and distance education, Ramdas being in South Africa. Gandhi had also downscaled all English learning in the home-schooling of his sons with the result that a text like *The Light of Asia* was shrouded in the darkness of inherent un-access. I owe this explanation to Gandhi's grandson Gopal Gandhi, email communication with me dated 26 May 2020.

12. This was at the Gaya session of the Indian National Congress, where a forceful plea for Buddhist control over the Mahabodhi Temple had been made by Rahul Sankrityayan, an important figure in the revival of Buddhism in India. Born into a Brahmin family in Bihar in 1893, Sankrityanan joined the Arya Samaj in 1915 and a few years later embraced Buddhism. Thereafter he became a Communist. There is no mention of *The Light of Asia* whatsoever in his works, although I would imagine he was familiar with Arnold and his exertions on the Mahabodhi Temple. It was also highly probable that Ramchandra Shukla's translation of *The Light of Asia* into Hindi would have had some impact on Sankrityayan. A recent biography of his is Chudal (2016).

13. It is interesting to note that some of the finest images of the Buddha dating back to the Gupta era (third to fifth century CE) were to be excavated in the nineteenth century CE. The Guptas were, in today's language, 'orthodox Hindus' but that did not prevent them from being great champions of Buddhist iconography.

10

1881–1900: Translations of *The Light of Asia*

In spite of all the diatribes of various missionaries, editions of *The Light of Asia* would roll out year after year in England and America. The contagion would spread to Europe, where the first translation into a European language would take place in the Netherlands in 1881. The poem would be published in Dutch as *Het Licht Van Azie: Leven En Leer Van Buddha* by Hago Uden Mayboom, who was a professor at the University of Groningen. In the late nineteenth century, there was considerable interest in Buddhism among Dutch liberal Protestants, coinciding with the emergence of the comparative study of religion at Leiden University in the 1870s. The first Leiden professor of Sanskrit Studies, Hendrik Kern, was born on the Indonesian island of Java. Some liberal Protestants, particularly those who wanted to supplement the rather rationalist liberal Protestant theology with a 'mystical' introspection, felt that their religious views had more in common with Buddhism than with orthodox Christianity.

Hajo Uden Meyboom (1842–1933) was the son of a liberal Protestant minister. His introduction to the first edition of *Het Licht Van Azië*, Meyboom states that he translated Arnold's poem into Dutch 'to arouse interest in the Buddha and his admirers' philosophy of life', legitimizing his translation by arguing that 'it is desirable to increase our knowledge of religious geniuses outside the Christian West in our age of "humanism"' . In his introduction to the second edition (1895), however, Meyboom explicitly states that 'no one will suspect me of an uncritical preference for Buddhism'. His personal interest in Buddhism might have been triggered by his father, the Dutch Reformed minister Louis Suson Pedro Meyboom

(1817–1874), who wrote a small entry on Buddhism in his 1873 *Handbook of Religious Education* (*Schets ten gebruike bij het godsdienst-onderwijs*).[1]

I have already mentioned that on 19 September 1885 Girishchandra Ghosh, the 'Bohemian Devotee of Ramakrishna' and close friend of Swami Vivekananda, had premiered his play *Buddhadeb Charit* with a manuscript version dedicated thus to Edwin Arnold:

Noble Poet!

Your world famous "Light of Asia" poem has inspired the writing of this epic poem of mine. O Sir! With folded hands I offer my gratitude, do accept it yourself.

Calcutta   In debt
Bagbazar   Girishchandra Ghosh
4 Ashwin 1292
(19 September 1885)

On 22 April 1887, Ghosh's play was formally published as a book. After Dutch, Bengali would be the second language into which *The Light of Asia* was translated. A little while later in the same year, a third translation would come out, and this would be in German in Leipzig. Arthur Pfugnst came from a well-to-do family in Frankfurt. He was a doctorate in chemistry and mathematics but at the same time had developed an extraordinary interest in Buddhism and in ancient Indian philosophy. At the young age of twenty-five he rendered *The Light of Asia* into German.[2] There would be other translations to follow in the late nineteenth and early twentieth centuries but Pfugnst was the pioneer.

He wrote many other works on both Buddhist and Hindu themes and was a great admirer of Max Mueller's *Ramakrishna: His Life and Sayings* that was published in 1898. A religious humanist and an important member of the German Society of Ethical Culture, he did much to support the first Germans who converted to Buddhism and who went to live in Ceylon and Burma. He was also the German representative of the Mahabodhi Society for many years. A Dr Arthur Pfungst Foundation was set up in Frankfurt in 1918 and is still active, mainly in the field of education.

Four years after Pfungst's translation another German version of *The Light of Asia,* this time by Konrad Wernicke, would appear, and this too would be from Leipzig. Wernicke was a classical archaeologist and philologist who, like Pfungst, would also die young. Years later, in 1923, a third German translation, this time by Albrecht Schaeffer would be published. Schaeffer has been described as 'an extremely gifted writer, bent on formal perfection, and a highly qualified master of the German language'.[3] Unlike Pfungst, who came to *The*

Arthur Pfungst, who translated The Light of Asia *into German in 1887. He was a great Indophile, enamoured of both Buddhism and Hinduism. (Source: Wikipedia)*

Light of Asia out of fascination with Buddhism, Schaeffer seems to have come to it purely on literary grounds. German translations of *The Light of Asia* would continue to be published into the 1980s and beyond. Wernicke's translation itself would be reissued in 1995.

In 1888, a Swedish translation would appear with a long title: *Asiens ljus elier den stor forsakelson, Gautamas, Buddhismens stiftares, ilf och lara: Dikt.* A well-known publisher of Stockholm, Albert Bonniers brought it out with a foreword by one of Sweden's most famous authors and mysticists, Viktor Rydberg. The Theosophical Society was virtually founded in his home at Djursholm that year, and a scholar has written that 'Central to his interests was neo-Platonism and he even showed partiality to Buddhism'.[4] A keen Theosophist was none other than King Oscar II himself.

January 1888 would see Mr Edwin Arnold become *Sir* Edwin Arnold. It was undoubtedly in recognition of his standing in British society as one of the most influential journalists, author of a spectacularly successful poem and other works that had been received very well. The 'New Year's Honour Gazette' refers to him as the 'author of "Light of Asia" and other works'. Arnold would send copies of all his works to Buckingham Palace. *The Light of Asia* had been dedicated to the Queen herself. It was customary for the recipient of the honour to attend the Court to 'kiss hands' in token of appreciation for the favour shown. When asked by his son what the Queen's hand was like, the newly anointed poet answered:

> I would not wish to appear lacking in respect, but frankly it is podgy. However, it is not the hand which one sees. That little royal hand, lifted on your own, which your lips do not actually kiss, though they bow over it in homage, is scarcely seen or felt. It is an emblem. You sense that you are raising to your lips the symbol of a thousand years of the most fruitful story in the annals of mankind—a story which tells of Alfred the Great and the Saxons, of William the Conqueror and the Normans, of Good Queen Bess and the Tudors, of Cromwell and the Bill of Rights, of Trafalgars and Waterloos, and of a race whose language is spoken over half

the world. Yet do not think this kissing of hand is an easy ordeal.
Stout hearts yield to its suggestions . . .

This is quintessential Arnold, true or not—the account comes from
his son's memoirs, published fifty-four years later, when the son
himself was almost eighty years old.[5]

In 1885, the Russian writer Leo Tolstoy began to write the
life of Buddha in Russian, but his work was not completed and
published during his lifetime. It was only in 1916, six years after
his death, that portions of what Tolstoy had written came out in
print. A scholar has concluded that Tolstoy's version of the Buddha
'closely resembles Edwin Arnold's poem *The Light of Asia*'. Tolstoy's
confidant Vladimir Chertkov had written to him on 14 April 1889:

> I am sending you my paraphrase of the preaching of the Buddha
> as given by Arnold. I interpreted the Buddha as I understood him
> from Arnold; however I feel that Arnold has not comprehended
> the depth of the Buddha. This is the reason why I would like to
> give a new reading to the Buddhist doctrine relying upon sources
> such as Beal and the like.

It is interesting that just when a sixty-one-year-old Russian legend
was discovering *The Light of Asia*, a twenty-year old Indian who
would be profoundly influenced by Tolstoy was also reading the
same book for the first time in London. I have already mentioned
Gandhi's first exposure to the book.

In 1890, the first of the Russian translations of *The Light of
Asia* would come out. This was by Aleksandra Annenskaia and
was called *Svet Azvi Poema*. Annenskaia was a children's writer
and hers was a translation in the prose form. Her book had a
foreword by one of Russia's foremost philosophers, Vladimir
Lesevich, which contributed to its success. Another contributory
factor may have been the fact that one of Arnold's sources may
well have been a biography of the Buddha 'by the Russian scholar
Issak Jacob Schmidt of St. Petersburg published in the Asiatic

Dmitri Mendeleev, the great Russian chemist and inventor of the periodic table of elements. He was deeply moved by The Light of Asia *and passed on that interest to his son. (Source: Wikipedia)*

Journal of 1825'.[6] Whatever it was, Anneskaia's translation would be continuously in print till 1917.

That very year, on 23 October 1890, the Crown Prince, later to become Czar Nicholas II, embarked on a grand journey of Egypt, India, Ceylon, Thailand, Japan and China, a journey that would last ten months. Accompanying him was, among others, Vladimir Mendeleev, who became the photographer of the tour. He was the son of Russia's great chemist Dmitri Mendeleev, who is familiar to all students of chemistry as the inventor of the periodic table that arranges elements systematically. The father had sent the son *The Light of Asia* when the imperial retinue was sojourning in India.[7]

In May 1896, Arnold would be in Moscow covering the coronation of Nicholas II as Czar and met with a number of Russians who remembered him fondly as the poet of a famous poem on the life of the Buddha. By that time poetic translations of *The Light of Asia* would also have been published in that country: I. Yurinski's in 1891 and 1895 and A.M. Fedorov's also in 1895 (to be reprinted in 1906 as well). Two other prominent Russian literary personalities on whom the influence of *The Light of Asia* has been traced[8] are Konstantin Balmont and Ivan Bunin, who would later be the first Russian writer to be awarded the Nobel Prize in Literature in 1933. Cultural networks being what they were then in Russia, the influence of *The Light of Asia* diffused into other areas like painting and music as well.

Also, in 1890, the year when Arnold visited Japan for the first time, there would appear a partial Japanese translation of *The Light of Asia—Asia no Kouki* by Nakagawa Taro. This was published in

Photograph taken by Vladimir Mendeleev at the colossal statue of the Buddha Daibatsu at the Kotokuin Temple in Kamakura, Japan. The entourage of the visiting future Czar Nicholas II of Russia is seen. Mendeleev was given The Light of Asia *to read during the trip by his father the great chemist Dmitri Mendeleev. This is from Di Ruocco (2011)*

Kyoto. The translation had begun in late 1888 itself and had the support of the Buddhist Propagation Society in Kyoto. The Society had been founded to help in the 'spread of Buddhism to other lands'. In September 1888, the Society had also launched a bimonthly English journal, inspired by Arnold, called *The Bijou of Asia*.[9] This was sixteen months *before* Arnold first set foot in Japan.

Nothing much is known about Taro except that he taught English at what would later become Ryukoku University, one of Japan's leading Buddhist institutions. There would, however, be a complete Japanese translation of *The Light of Asia* in 1908, four years after Arnold's death, whose title read in English reads *The Great Sage: The Buddha Sakyamuni*. It had a preface written in September 1908 by Takakusu Junjiro, a prolific Buddhist intellectual, that would reveal much about the 1890 translation as well:

> As a distinguished great work of the nineteenth century, *The Light of Asia*, by the bard Sir Edwin Arnold, is one of the books of poetry to receive the greatest praise worldwide. Twenty years earlier, when I was studying in Kyoto, my fellow students and I met to engage in its explication. When we had questions about ambiguous points in the biography of the Buddha, the anecdotes related by the author, and of course about the Sanskrit, which was difficult for us to understand, we asked Dr. Nanjō [Bun'yū], who was at that time teaching at [Tokyo Imperial] University, or our classmate and friend, Higashi Onjō, who was studying abroad at the Deccan College in India, with which the author [Arnold] has a deep connection, and sometimes we would send letters to the bard himself at his residence in South Kensington, London, to ask for help.
>
> Before long, the bard visited Japan, so it seemed that the time was right for a translation of *The Light of Asia*. Therefore, our former instructor, the Bachelor of Agriculture Mr. Nakagawa Tarō [dates unknown], translated sentence by sentence into Japanese. I myself took that translation to the now-deceased Master Saitō Monshō [1840-1904], a *kangaku* [a high-ranking officer of the

institution], and requested that he amend the prose. I entrusted the draft of the two chapters that resulted to the publisher Kōkyō Shoin, and set off on my own foreign study. After that, the book came out under the title *The Light of Asia* [original Japanese: *Ajia no kōki*]. I believe that the abbreviated biography of the bard which appears at the head of the book is something I wrote, but matters of old are hazy, and all like a dream.

As soon as the Russo-Japanese War started [1904], I had reason to go to England. I saw the bard lying ill in his residence, and before we could even speak about old days, he had died. He was cremated in the London suburbs. I suppose that this must have been an unusual posthumous request. His widow, Madame Tama Kurokawa, still resides in London, and took care of his posthumous writings. Now, on the occasion of our completing the complete retranslation of this book, I have recorded these former matters and substitute them for a preface.[10]

Takakasu Junjiro mentioned Higashi Onjo in his preface. Higashi Onji was a student in Deccan College Poona, most probably between 1888 and 1893, when he died in Bombay. This was the College of which Arnold had been the Principal three decades earlier. Higashi Onji wrote to a Buddhist journal in Japan in which he argued strenuously that Arnold was actually a Buddhist himself, despite having written of the personality of the Buddha as 'the highest, gentlest, holiest and most beneficent, with one exception, in the history of thought'. Higashi Onjo held that Arnold included the phrase 'with one exception' simply so as not to alienate his readership.

Notes

1. I owe all information on Mayboom to Tom-Erik Krijger, email communication 2 June 2020.
2. In 1881, Hermann Oldenberg's landmark book *Buddha, Sein Leben, sein Lehre, seine Gemeinde* had been published. This was translated a year later by William Hoey as *Buddha: His Life, His Doctrine, His Order*.
3. Schueller (1967)

4. Torma (2013)
5. Arnold (1942)
6. Peiris (1970)
7. Di Ruocco (2011)
8. Ibid.
9. I owe this information to Jaffe (2014).
10. I owe the entire preface to Micah Auerback, email communication dated 14 June 2020.

11

1889–1895: Edwin Arnold in America and Japan, *The Light of the World* and Sri Aurobindo

By 1889, *The Light of Asia* had run into numerous editions in England and America, where Arnold had become a very well-known figure even though he had never been there. His second wife having just passed away, he decided to get away from London. So it was that Arnold, along with his daughter, left for America and Japan in late-August 1889. A month after he left, a British newspaper carried this item:[1]

CONVERTED TO BUDDHISM

A REMARKABLE ceremony took place some time ago in Colombo. It was no less than the admission of a Christian gentleman from America who recently arrived in Ceylon, into the Buddhist creed. The proceedings took place in the Theosophist Hall, under the guidance of the Buddhist High Priest, assisted by eleven yellow-robed monks . . . The gentleman's name was Powell . . . A meeting was afterwards held in which Mr. Powell explained the reasons for having embraced Buddhism, and described the mental process which he had gone through before he had arrived at the convection of the truth of Buddhism. It appears that nearly forty years ago, when he was a child, he came across a book in his father's library in which was a picture; it was that of a figure "seated cross-legged on something like a flower". . . . On asking who or what picture it was, Mr. Powell says, "I was told that it was the picture of a heathen god, but his memory clung to me . . . After some time spent in cogitating on the vanity of human affairs, and the inexplicability of mundane problems, Mr. Powell appears to have sought a refuge in agnosticism, as many men have before him, but the comfortlessness and the apparent cowardice of a doctrine that says "I cannot know, so I will leave the matter alone," seemed to have disgusted him. At last a *deus ex machina* was found in Sir Edwin Arnold, whose poem "The Light of Asia" aroused in Mr. Powell the desire to take refuge in the law of Lord Buddha.

At this time Arnold's translations from the Dhammapada had also appeared in a weekly journal called *The Buddhist*. This had been launched in Colombo by Olcott's controversial colleague Charles Leadbeater, who had then been entrusted with the responsibility for popularizing both the Theosophical Society as well as Buddhism in Ceylon. Arnold had translated from Pali the first chapter of the Dhammapada. Much later, in 1950, it was to be hailed as 'being poetic, comes nearer the original than any other translation published'.[2]

And just about this time, in mid-1889 or thereabouts, the noted British journalist F.A.H. Eyles published his *Popular Poets of the Period* that continued to have a readership for long. Some sixty poets were covered. The book opens with a sonnet to Arnold by another poet WM. Cartwright Newsam and has selections from Book the Eighth of the *The Light of Asia*. The sonnet reads:

> *O mighty mind, O sweet poetic pen!*
>   *What noble thoughts your lofty strains inspire,*
>   *To glow within the soul like living fire.*
>   *Things, long unseen, undreamed by meaner men,*
> *Stand forth unveiled to Arnold's keener ken:*
>   *His graceful words express the heart's desire,*
>   *And, when his cunning hand doth touch the lyre,*
>   *All, all is harmony and sweetness then:*

His song fills every soul with pure delight,
   Rasing each grovelling thought from earth away,
   Far from the shadowy regions of the night,
Up to the radiance of celestial day,
   Where all is pure, and beautiful, and bright,
   And Heaven's unchanging light shines on for aye.

Arnold was in America for about a month and a half. He was introduced as an Oriental poet and, of course, as the author of *The Light of Asia*. In forum after forum, he spoke of the indissoluble and natural links between the British Empire and America and what an example the latter was to the rest of the world. Three moments stood out on this trip.

The first was his visit to the home of the father of the Transcendental Movement, Ralph Waldo Emerson, after whom Arnold had named one of his sons. Five years earlier, Protop Chunder Majumdar, the Brahmo Samaj leader, had remarked while addressing the Concord School of Philosophy near Boston that had played a crucial role in the success of *The Light of Asia* in America:[3]

> Amidst the bustle of American materialism Emerson seems to some of us a geographical mistake. He ought to have been born in India.

Majumdar himself, like many in the Brahmo Samaj, had been inspired a great deal by *The Light of Asia*. Arnold would describe this visit to Emerson's home as a 'pilgrimage' and write about tracing in more than one volume of Emerson's modest library the 'footsteps of his [Emerson's] serene and radiant mind, especially in the Indian translations'. Emerson had had a special affinity for the Upanishads and the Bhagavad Gita. After spending some time with Mrs Emerson, he went to Walden Pond, home of the second great Transcendentalist Henry David Thoreau, who would later have a major influence on Gandhi's thinking on civil disobedience.

Arnold would actually meet with a living giant of Transcendentalism—Walt Whitman. It is now well accepted that Whitman was greatly influenced by both Hindu and Buddhist spirituality. Arnold may well have seen in him a kindred spirit. The two spent about half an hour together, with Arnold telling Whitman the great love with which the American's poems were held in England and quoting from some of those with ease. Arnold would meet Whitman again at the latter's residence two years later, and this time the American would repeat many lines from the Englishman's works.

The second highlight of Arnold's visit was a meeting with none other than the American President Benjamin Harrison himself. Arnold would send a dispatch to the *Daily Telegraph* on it. It was pleasant and informal banter, with Anglo-American ties being the main topic of the conversation. When Harrison observed that 'if we had remained one people geographically, you would have to be governed from Washington perhaps, as we are preponderant in numbers and area', Arnold shot back 'as to that, you must put Canada and our colonies in the scale, and India'. It was all in good humour and Arnold took leave hoping that 'together England and America will someday dictate peace in the interests of universal humanity' and that 'the language of Shakespeare will become that of the globe'. Harrison too hoped that such a day would arrive.

The third episode that stood out was Arnold's presence at Harvard University. In fact, the visit to America itself had been at the invitation of Harvard's President Charles Elliot. Arnold delivered two lectures in very early October 1889, one on the *Upanishads* and the other on the *Mahabharata*. This part of his remarks at Harvard was to be quoted approvingly in the American media long after he had left. It just about sums up his approach to India:[4]

Cultivate, therefore, I venture to entreat, the philosophy and literature of India, rejecting what your strong, sober sense perceives to be useless in them, and utilizing for the repose and exaltation of your minds what they contain of noble and refining thought. Do you know that the *Mayflower*, which brought your ancestors hither, went down on her last voyage in Indian waters, which I have traversed off Masulipatnam, with a "general cargo". Raise her some day in fancy, and freight her with a new load of investigations from Massachusetts bay, where we shall find the Old World interpreted by the New World and the American scholars outdoing the best of England and Germany. If I should live to see that day, or should return from some other existence to the delightful groves of Harvard, I should feel like Robinson Crusoe, who shaking forth a few poor grains from his almost empty sack upon a generous and fertile soil, passed by thereafter to find upon the spot a splendid and fruitful harvest.

Arnold and his daughter set sail for Japan in mid-October 1889, and they were to remain in that country for almost thirteen months.[5] It would completely transform Arnold's life. He met a twenty-year-old Tama Kurokawa and tongues instantly started wagging. But he would send a telegram to his brother in September 1890 denying any truth in published statements that 'he was about to wed a Japanese lady'. The *Washington Post* of 14 November 1890 would report:

A Cruel Joke on Sir Edwin
From the New York Tribune

An absurd rumour about Sir Edwin Arnold being infatuated with a Japanese woman is denounced by the Tokio correspondent of the Boston Post as a cruel and slanderous imputation. He says: "The origin of the story is traced to a certain English editor, who in revenge for the letter of Sir Edwin to the Daily Telegraph in favour of treaty revision between England and Japan, determined to get even with him, and accomplished his purpose by a circulating a fiction.

Edwin Arnold most probably with Tama Kurakowa in Yokohoma, 1890. This is from Arnold (1891)

Arnold would give two public lectures in Tokyo that would be widely reported in the Japanese press. The first was in late November 1889, where he demonstrated through the use of his quatrains in *The Light of Asia* that Buddhism and modern science went together and that there was a close intellectual bond between the two.

If we gather up all the results of modern research and look away from the best literature to the largest discovery in physics and the latest word in biology, what is the conclusion—the high and joyous conclusion—forced upon the mind except that which renders true Buddhism so glad and hopeful? Surely it is that the Descent of man from low beginnings implies his Ascent to supreme and glorious developments ; that 'the Conservation of Matter and of Energy', a fact absolutely demonstrated, points to the kindred fact of the conservation and continuity of all Life . . . that death is probably nothing but a passage and a promotion; that the destiny

of man has been, and must be, and will be worked out by himself
under the eternal and benign laws which never vary and never
mislead, and that for every living creature the path thus lies open,
by compliance, by effort, by insight, by aspiration, by goodwill,
by right action, and loving service, to that which Buddhists term
Nirvana, and we Christians 'the peace of God that passeth all
understanding'.

Declaring that 'Buddhism, just understood, touches the hand of
modern science' and telling his audience 'if your patience permits, I
will be bold enough to read from *The Light of Asia* a few verses which
exactly express my views', Arnold would go on to read from Book
the Eighth:

> *Before beginning and without an end,*
> *As space eternal, and surety sure,*
> *Is fixed a Power Divince which moves to good,*
> *Only its laws endure.*

> *Its thread as Love and Life; Death and Pain*
> *The shuttles of its loom.*
> *It maketh and unmaketh, mending all,*
> *What it hath wrought is better than had been;*
> *Slow grows the splendid pattern that it plans*
> *Its wistful hands between.*

The second talk was in early December 1889 and was entitled
'The Range of Modern Knowledge,' in which Arnold 'ranged over
astronomy, geology and earthquakes, modern chemistry and oxydised
glycerine, literature, some verses from *The Light of Asia* about
Buddhism and science and English as the future world language'.
By then, translations of *The Light of Asia* had already begun in Kyoto
and these would be published while Arnold was in Japan.

In April 1892, Arnold would be back in Japan. He spoke on
restoring 'Buddha-Gya' to the Buddhists of the world and the

destined role of the Japanese to make this possible. He would write about this visit a year later:

> Last summer [that is in 1892] in the Japanese capital, the Buddhist High Priest, with certain of his fraternity, begged me to come to the temple at Atagoshita and speak to the brethren about the Holy Places in India and especially upon the prospects of acquiring for the Buddhist world, the guardianship of the Temple of the Tree [the Mahabodhi Temple at Buddha-Gya]. Since then the High Priest writes to me thus from Tokyo:
>
>> After your regretted departure from Japan, the Indo-Bussiki Kofuki Society has not been idle, and now I am glad to inform you that we are trying to buy a certain piece of land near each of the sacred sites according to your kind advice to us [at the sites of the birth, enlightenment, first sermon and death]. Mr. Dharmapala of the Mahabodhi Society is doing all he can to help us in India . . .

Arnold may well have been embellishing a little. Richard Jaffe has written about Kitabatake Doryu, who in November 1883 had become the first known Japanese to visit Buddha-Gya, although there had been a few others who had come to India earlier.[6] By the time Arnold gave his talk in Buddha-Gya in Tokyo in the summer of 1892, two Japanese translations of *The Light of Asia* had also already appeared. The Emperor of Japan conferred the Order of the Rising Sun on him.

At Yokohama, Arnold met Rudyard Kipling for the first and only time and encouraged him to visit the imposing statue of Buddha in the city. This resulted in Kipling's 1892 poem *The Buddha at Kamakura*.[7] But besides all this, Arnold married Tama Kurokawa in Yokohama according to Japanese rites. The thirty-seven-year age difference between them, unusual by any standards, let alone Victorian, raised many eyebrows and caused consternation in the family. It was only in October 1897 that a re-marriage would take place in London and Tama Kurokawa would officially become Lady Arnold. The *New York Journal* would comment on 3 November 1897:

It is intimated that Sir Edwin Arnold married a Japanese woman in order that he might have some one to listen to his Japanese poems. Sir Edwin is not the first man to marry an audience in order to get a hearing.

Lady Arnold would outlive her husband by almost six decades and passed away in London in 1962.

Arnold would publish three books on Japan in two years. The first was *Seas and Lands* in 1891. This was a collection of all the articles he had written for the *Daily Telegraph* during his year in Japan. The second, also in the same year, was *Japonica*, which was based on essays on Japan that he had written for an American magazine. The third, called *Adzuma or The Japanese Wife*, was a play in four acts that appeared in 1893. His intention in writing it was 'to show how the karma of previous lives must be worked out in subsequent incarnations'. There were some shades of *The Light of Asia* in it.

During the late 1890s Arnold would become active in the Japan Society in London and emerge, both through his writings and speeches, as perhaps the strongest voice for closer Anglo-Japanese ties. He sided clearly with Japan in its war with China in the mid-1890s and wrote that because it epitomized both Buddhist and Christian values, it was superior to a Confucian China. He would be condemned in the American media for both his romantic views on Japanese women and for suggesting Japanese annexation of Hawaii, which the Americans themselves coveted. In the British magazine *Punch*, he would be caricatured as 'Sir Edwin Mikarnoldo'[8] and be dubbed 'A Real Good Jap'. But as in the case of the attacks on *The Light of Asia* by Christian missionaries in the 1880s, these criticisms and lampooning did nothing to dilute his ardour for Japan one bit. He campaigned relentlessly for a formal Anglo-Japanese alliance, which was finally signed in London in January 1902.[9] A few days before he passed away Arnold would write a highly laudatory piece on Japanese Prime Minister Ito Hirobumi, hailing him as the 'Bismarck of

Japan'. Eleven days after his death, the *Daily Telegraph* would publish what it called 'one of the last writings of Arnold'—an article entitled 'Romance of Japan'.

Arnold's articles on Japan over a twelve-year period would not only make him a favourite of the Japanese but would also impact an Indian who would write an emotional message called 'To Every Japanese' in his publication on 18 July 1942:

> I must confess at the outset that though I have no ill-will against you, I intensely dislike your attack on China. From your lofty height you have descended to imperial ambition. You will fail to realize that ambition . . . Ever since I was a lad of eighteen studying in London over fifty years ago, I learnt through the writings of Sir Edwin Arnold to prize the many excellent qualities of your nation . . .

Gandhi was writing this from his Sewagram Ashram in Wardha. He was invoking Arnold to explain his admiration for the Japanese but sympathy and support for the Chinese. Arnold himself would have found it ironic for he, in all probability, may well have backed the Japanese. Twenty-two days later Gandhi would launch his Quit India Movement, the final campaign to get the British to grant independence.

Arnold would make a second visit to America between November 1891 and February 1892. By this time his *The Light of the World or The Great Consummation*, written while he was in Japan earlier in the year, would appear with an introduction by the American critic and poet Richard Henry Stoddard. It was dedicated to 'The Queen's Most Excellent Majesty' and Arnold's biographer believes that it is the most complete exposition of the poet's religious views. But there could well have been other motivations. Arnold may have wanted to answer his critics' accusations that he had become a Buddhist. He was also very keen on becoming Poet Laureate, and being famous only for his 'Oriental' poems would be a disqualification for that coveted position. A long poetic tribute to the life of Christ would, on the other hand he may have felt, work to his advantage in more ways than one.

One person who felt betrayed by his writing *The Light of The World* was the lady who had enthusiastically and exuberantly welcomed *The Light of Asia* when it was first published and whose Society had done much to propagate that work—Madame Blavatsky. She lambasted him:[10]

> Sir Edwin Arnold author of the unparalleled *The Light of Asia* has tried to make his peace with the Christian world by means of a ruse which oversteps even the large license allowed to the priests of the Muses . . . We can only sincerely regret that Sir Edwin Arnold has gone so far out of his way to spoil his honourable record; and cause both East and West to blush over such a sad spectacle . . .

A few days after this scathing piece appeared, Madame Blavatsky was dead. For over two decades this charismatic, controversial and entrepreneurial woman had had much of the world in her thrall, had taken on organised Christianity frontally and done much to revive interest in Buddhism not only in the West but also in places like Ceylon and India. Her soulmate Henry Olcott would take her work even further. Blavatsky's death anniversary—8 May—has been marked by the Theosophical Society since 1892 as 'White Lotus Day'.

Another great friend of Arnold who was disappointed with *The Light of The World* was the explorer Henry Morton Stanley, who recorded in his diary:

> After reading a few hundred lines of Edwin Arnold's new poem, 'The Light of the World', I perceived he had not hit the right chord. It is 'The Light of Asia', in a feeble, vapid style; or, to put it more correctly, it is a Buddhist trying to sing the glories of the Christian's Lord. His soul is not in his song, though there are beautiful passages in it; but it is the tone of the unbeliever. Alas

Blavatsky and Olcott in London, October 1888. Blavatsky would pass away three years later, and her death anniversary is still marked by readings from The Light of Asia *at the Theosophical Society, Adyar and other places. There is a statue of Olcott in Colombo and a school in his name in Chennai. (Source: Theosophical Society)*

for this! What a poem he could have written, had he but believed in the Saviour of the world!

Stanley must have been doubly disappointed because he was among the few who had actually read *The Light of Asia* before it first came out in July 1879 and had been impressed with Arnold's poem but had advised him that a sequel with 'the Christ as the central figure' would be an even greater success.

The Light of the World got good reviews no doubt but failed to match the appeal of *The Light of Asia*. The Poet Laureateship fell vacant on the death of Lord Tennyson in October 1892. The previous year, on 25 March, Tennyson had written to Arnold:[11]

We liked your "Light of Asia" so well that we had already possessed ourselves of your "Light of the World". The copy which you have

been so kind as to send thru' our common friend Mrs. Fitzgerald
I shall value not only for itself but as your gift.

Queen Victoria was in favour of Arnold succeeding Tennyson as
she was reportedly a fan of *The Light of Asia,* a fact mentioned in
the British press those days. Arnold was regularly mentioned as a
serious contender in both the British and American press. But he
had his detractors who did not consider him a serious poet at all.
Moreover, the Liberal Party, which was in power till June 1895,
was opposed to him for his strong Tory instincts, inclinations and
positions. There was a Conservative Prime Minister thereafter, who,
however, had little liking for the Oriental learning and wisdom that
Arnold epitomized.

Victoria held firm but finally gave in and on 1 January 1896,
Alfred Austin was appointed Tennyson's successor. It was the
longest period that Britain had gone without a Poet Laureate ever
since John Dryden was first appointed to the post in April 1668,
and that gap continues to hold that record. My own view is that
part of the explanation for this delay was Victoria wanting Arnold
as Poet Laureate, a desire not shared in the highest echelons of the
ruling establishment. Arnold was, however, a dignified loser, as the
memoirs of Austin testify:[12]

> From Sir Edwin Arnold I received the following touching
> telegram: [on December 31 1895]
>
>> Accept my heartiest congratulations with which no grudge
>> mingles, though I myself expected the appointment. I
>> rejoice at continuance of this appointment, which will be
>> worthily and patriotically borne by you.
>
> I would rather be the man who could send such a telegram in such
> circumstances, than be incapable of sending it, yet have written
> the greatest of poems.

Arnold would soon get into a controversy of sorts involving the Queen. Victoria's diamond jubilee was being celebrated in June 1897, and a few months before that Arnold had been asked by a monthly magazine to write something suitable to mark the occasion. The great admirer that he was of her, Arnold obliged but found to his 'intense surprise and boundless indignation' that several London papers on the morning of 14 September 1896 had published the poem in the midst of an advertisement, giving the impression that either Arnold or Victoria herself was endorsing these products that included toothpaste and the like. Arnold promptly shot off a letter to the press on this 'literary outrage:'[13]

> To my intense surprise and boundless indignation I find in some of the morning papers of today the reprint of a poem written by me for a monthly magazine. The poem is written in intimate connections of manner, type and place with advertisements of Bovril, patent medicines and other articles useful but not in any way connected with the august subject of the poem. It is most unnecessary for me to say that this has been done without my knowledge and for motives beyond my comprehension and I have instructed my lawyers to take immediate proceedings against the advertising agent and the magazine for which the poem was composed with a view to restraining a manner of publication which to me is in the highest degree injurious and unworthy. Meantime, while I deeply regret that such a thing should have occurred, my friends and the public generally will never for a moment imagine that I myself could authorize such a use of the composition.

Bovril was then the trademarked name for a thick and salty meat extract paste that continues to be marketed by Unilever. A war of words ensued between Arnold and the advertising agent of the magazine, but the matter died down quickly after causing much amusement. We don't know what the Queen herself thought of it.

From the Indian point of view Arnold's second visit to America was noteworthy for two reasons.

First, he would speak on rescuing 'Buddha's holy temple at Buddh-Gya from the Brahmins'. He did so, for instance, at Chicago on 21 December 1891, saying he had embarked 'on a mammoth project of interest to the world' and that if it did not 'reach maturity by next winter, as I believe it will, I shall go to India and close the negotiations necessary for its consummation. In fact, I ought to be there this minute'. He was clearly having delusions of grandeur, for he then went on to declare to the American audience:[14]

> I am going to affect the return of the holy temple of the Buddhists without friction or violence. It will be an event similar to Saladin giving up the sepulcher to the Lord without a struggle . . . I have hit upon a plan by which the Brahmins will surrender the property. This done, the temple will be put in the hands of a Buddhist committee. I have secured the necessary civic authority and, in fact, all that is wanted to effect the return to its own seat and home of a great world religion is the concluding ecclesiastical negotiations, which are already practically assured.

Second, he would stoutly defend British rule in India. A little while later he would write on this subject and his 'The Duty and Destiny of England in India' would be published in the *North American Review* of February 1892. It was a long paean of praise for what the British had accomplished in India and a recount of what they were doing to bring an ancient and glorious civilization into the age of modernity. Saying that the connection between the two peoples had begun quite accidently and not by any nefarious design on the part of the British, he concluded his essay:

> I believe myself that the people of England, who from all ranks of the home country have themselves furnished the soldiers, the officers, the administrator, and the statesmen that have built up British India, hold at heart a cherished principle, the maintenance

of that glorious Oriental empire until such time as our duty is fully and finally done to the great and wonderful land. Nothing on the political horizon as yet even begins to proclaim that the task of England is accomplished towards India and her countless peoples; and therefore nothing, in my mind, at present so much as even threatens the manifest destiny of England to pass insensibly and happily from the position of the mistress and protectress of the peninsula to that of its first friend, its sister, and its ally, in some far-off day when the time is come for India to manage her own happy destinies.

This article may have been written in America, but it reverberated soon in India. The London correspondent of *The Hindu* in mid-February 1892 sent a dispatch castigating Arnold, saying that he had always been critical of reform efforts and reformers like Lord Ripon, who had been Viceroy between 1880 and 1884 and during whose tenure the first steps to local self-government in India had been taken. The correspondent, William Digby, a staunch Liberal Party man and an outspoken critic of British rule in India, took particular umbrage at Arnold's remarks in the essay on education, calling them 'hardly the sort of thing we should have expected from a President of the Sanscrit College at Poona'. What had been taken offence to was this particular paragraph that Arnold had written in response to questions he was asked by Americans on independence or self-rule for Indians:

In the colleges and high schools, where degrees are conferred or prepared for, the custom has too much been to impart a superficial acquaintance with English literature, which is of no use to the student unless he obtains government employment, and not of very much utility even then. The Brahman, dispossessed of his old authority and influence in the land, has taken largely to this curricula of polite sciolism[15] and becomes "a fish out of water" utterly helpless and malcontent . . . This has mischievously bred a large and restless class of discontented young men, principally of high caste, who receive in the government colleges and schools a superficial instruction in the English language and literature, which turns them out conceited but unfitted for the duties of life. As they are far too numerous to be all of them received into the service, the large balance of disappointed Brahmans constitute a collection of people who agitate and raise political questions for which India is not ripe . . . These are they who agitate in the native press, in public meetings and among foolish and thoughtless circles in England itself, for representative institutions and other absurdities . . . I have myself been guilty of creating a considerable number of these intempestive spirits, since I was president for several years of the Sanskrit College at Poona . . .

This commentary on how English education was leading young Indian minds astray would invite a withering response from a young Cambridge-educated employee of the princely state of Baroda. Aurobindo Ghose, or, to give his full name, Aurobindo Ackroyd Ghose, wrote in a Bombay newspaper called *Indu Prakash* on 5 February 1894:

The force which they [The British in India] had in mind to construct was a body of grave, loyal and conservative citizens, educated but without ideas, a body created by and having a stake in the present order, and therefore attached to its continuance, a power in the land certainly, but a power for order, for permanence, not a power for disturbance and unrest. In such an enterprise they were bound to fail and they failed egregiously. Sir Edwin Arnold when he found out that it was grievous mistake to occidentalise us, forgot, no doubt, for the moment his role as the preacher and poetaster of self-abnegation, and spoke as a mundane human being, the prophet of a worldly and selfish class . . .

Aurobindo Ghose would a decade hence emerge for a brief while as India's leading revolutionary but after the 1920s would come to be known to the world as Sri Aurobindo—a mystic, philosopher, poet and author with no connection whatsoever to India's freedom movement. Later though, he would be hailed as the 'prophet of Indian nationalism'.[16] His description of Arnold as 'the preacher and poetaster of self-abnegation' was excoriating and his noted biographer offers this explanation:[17]

> I think Sir Edwin fell afoul of the extremely young Aurobindo (age 22) because he was a former Anglo-Indian - which of course at the time meant a Briton settled in India. Aurobindo had no love for such people especially if they spoke as "ordinary mundane" imperialists, as Arnold apparently did. Aurobindo had little love for European Sanskritists in general because of their patronizing attitude toward the Indian tradition (especially as compared to the Greco-Roman tradition). Also he did not at this point admire Buddhism, which he associated mainly with asceticism . . .

I should mention another very brief visit of Arnold in March 1892 on his way from America to Japan, when he stopped over in Honolulu. Hawaii is exceedingly important to the story of Buddhism in the early twentieth-century India because a wealthy Hawaiian lady would emerge as the single greatest benefactor of Dharmapala and of the Mahabodhi Society. There is no clinching evidence that Arnold and Mary Foster met in Honolulu on 7 March 1892, the day Arnold spent there meeting the Queen of Hawaii, her family and court. But Foster was very much part of the social, political and business circles Arnold hobnobbed with that day. Frank Karpiel, who has studied Mary Foster extensively, is of the opinion that 'it is more than likely that Foster and Arnold met'.[18]

Mary Foster was 'the daughter of an early English immigrant and half-Hawaiian descendant of a line of Maui chiefs'. She had married a Canadian who had settled and built a lucrative shipping business in Hawaii. He died in 1889 and both her father and her husband left Mary Foster very wealthy.

Distraught by this double tragedy perhaps, she turned to the Theosophical Society, which was evoking considerable interest in the islands, as indeed it was in other parts of the world as well. The late 1880s and early 1890s were also a period when curiosity

Mary Foster, probably in the 1890s. (Source: Wikipedia)

about the Buddha and Buddhism was becoming very evident in Hawaii, again in keeping with what was taking place in England and America.

Arnold was a great hit in Honolulu and was feted in a grand manner. As he left Honolulu he spoke to Honolulu's *Evening Bulletin* the next day:

My mission to India is a very interesting one—being to transfer from the Brahmins to the Buddhists the Great temple of Buddha Gya. This temple was founded by King Asoka 300 years before Christ. It is to the Buddhists what Jerusalem was to the Christians in the crusades or Mecca to the Mohammedans. My work must be accomplished by friendly negotiations, so I have been commissioned to this, both by the Buddhists of Asia and the Queen's Government at home. I appreciate that the surrender of this great temple will be a difficult matter and that it must be made upon a friendly basis or not at all. The statement may appear singular, but it is nevertheless true, that in India, the birthplace of Buddhism, there are hardly any Buddhists—not more than say 10,000, the Buddhists being found principally in Siam, Ceylon, China and Japan.

This is most curious and intriguing. Arnold is on his way to Japan and is 'talking of his mission to India'. It is possible that he intended to go there after his sojourn in Japan, but it is clear that his mission did not materialize. He certainly kept up his support from London but never went back to India in person.

As for Mary Foster, she would meet Dharmapala on 18 October 1893 in Honolulu when he was on his way back home after his sterling performance at Chicago's World Parliament of Religions the previous month. Unlike Arnold, Dharmapala would spend more than a week in Hawaii. From then on till her death in 1930, Mary Foster would contribute more than three hundred thousand dollars to the Maha-Bodhi Society in Calcutta for its activities to revive Buddhism in India and Ceylon. Foster and Dharmapala met only three times personally but her support to him and his campaigns was unstinted and sustained. In this context, Dharmapala's biographer the Sri Lankan scholar-politician Sarath Amunugama has an interesting observation:[19]

> It is a curious fact that many Eastern spiritualists of colonial times depended on the munificence and encouragement of affluent Western ladies for the propagation of their radical ideas. Like Dharmapala's sponsor, Upasika Mary Foster Robinson, Vivekananda's American benefactresses Henrietta Muller and Mrs Ole Bull, and [Jiddu] Krishnamurti's sponsors like Annie Besant and Emily Lutyens, helped them in finding a wider audience and saved them from privations which were characteristic of earlier religious activities.

What Amunugama says was true also of the Theosophical Society in the UK, Europe and America. A visitor to the Mahabodhi Society in Kolkata today would be greeted by a plaque showing the scale of her generosity—and this is but one example. She donated handsomely to enable Dharmapala to establish the Mulagandha Kuti Vihara in Sarnath that was opened on 11 November 1931 in the presence of a man one of whose favourite books was *The Light of Asia*. He had read it in his early teens and had asked for it when he was jailed by

the British for the first time in 1921. He would go on to become
Prime Minister of India in August 1947 and do much to ensure that
the symbols of Independent India—the national emblem depicting

All India Congress Committee
Swaraj Bhawan, Allahabad

OFFICE-BEARERS FOR 1931

President:
  VALLABHBHAI PATEL
Treasurer:
  JAMNALAL BAJAJ
General Secretaries:
  SYED MAHMUD
  JAIRAMDAS DOULATRAM
  JAWAHARLAL NEHRU

Telegrams: "CONGRESS"
Telephone: 350

Ref. C57/3286

December 23rd, 1931

To The Secretary,
Maha Bodhi Society,
Benares.

Dear Sir,

On the opening ceremony of the
Mulagandha Kuti Vihara on November
11th I had the honour to offer on
behalf of the Indian National Congress
a National Flag for the Vihara. I
have now great pleasure in sending
this flag in silver and enamel on a
silver stand encased in carved
and inlaid sandle wood casket. My
colleagues Shri Shiva Prasad Gupta and
Shri Sri Prakasa will personally take
this casket with the flag inside it.
I trust this flag will be a perpetual
reminder to you of the good will of
the Indian Nation towards the great
cause you represent.

Yours sincerely,

Jawaharlal Nehru

General Secretary

Jawaharlal Nehru's letter to Dharmapala of 23 December 1931 regarding Sarnath.
(Source: Mahabodhi Society, Kolkata)

four lions and the wheel in the national flag—would be derived from India's Buddhist heritage. His letter to Dharmapala of 23 December 1931 would recognize Dharmapala's unflagging efforts to get Indians to be proud of their Buddhist heritage. It would come at a time when the Buddha Gaya dispute was still to be settled and organisations like the Hindu Mahasabha resented Dharmapala's aggressive campaign to get control of the Mahabodhi Temple.

One of the colleagues Nehru would depute to go to Sarnath in December 1931 was Sri Prakasa. Sri Prakasa would go on to have a notable public service career. In 1964, a new illustrated edition of *The Song Celestial* would be published in New York with an introduction by him.[20] Gandhi himself would visit Sarnath on 21 January 1942, six days after declaring Nehru his 'political successor'.

Notes

1. *The Northern Whig*, Saturday, 14 September 1889
2. JInarajadasa (1950)
3. Buell (2003)
4. *Wichita Daily Eagle*, 23 January 1890
5. Blacker (2002) is an informative account of Arnold's first visit to Japan.
6. Jaffe (2019)
7. Paskins (2017)
8. A takeoff on the famous Gilbert and Sullivan comic opera of 1885 called *The Mikado*.
9. The alliance was signed on 30 January 1902 between Lord Lansdowne, the British Foreign Secretary, and Hayasho Tadasu, the Japanese diplomat and cabinet minister. Lansdowne had been Viceroy in India between 1888 and 1894, and Arnold had badgered him on the Mahabodhi Temple issue. A hill town named after him still thrives in Uttarakhand. Arnold and Tadasu had been in close touch for some years.
10. Blavatsky (1879)
11. Arnold had written 'A Day with Tennyson' in the December 1891 issue of the American magazine the *Forum* that had evidently irked the very reclusive and publicity-shy Poet Laureate no end. The piece itself is a delightful, if embellished account of the few hours the two spent together at Tennyson's home.
12. Austin (1911)

13. *Evening Telegraph*, Thursday, 24 September 1896
14. *Washington Post* and *New York Times*, 22 December 1891
15. The word 'scientist' was first used in March 1834 and was coined by the English philosopher and Anglican clergyman William Whewell. 'Scientist', Whewell reported, had been the suggestion of an 'ingenious gentleman' at a meeting of the British Association for the Advancement of Science, who had justified his free use of the suffix by invoking, among others, 'sciolist' (pretentious possessor of a smattering of knowledge, from the Latin *sciolus*). I was wondering what sciolism meant when I came across this paragraph in Riskin (2020).
16. Singh (1963)
17. Peter Heehs in email communication dated 23 April 2020
18. Karpiel (1996). I owe all information regarding Mary Foster to Frank Karpiel and his email communications to me on 25 April 2020 and 3 May 2020.
19. Amunugama (2019)
20. In 1905, a translation of the Bhagavad Gita by Annie Besant and Bhagavan Das had been published by the Theosophical Society. Bhagavan Das, Sri Prakasa's father, would be awarded India's highest civilian honour the Bharat Ratna in 1955. He has a major road in New Delhi named after him. Bhagavan Das was also great fan of *The Light of Asia*.

12

1890–1900: Translations of *The Light of Asia*, More Works and Swami Vivekananda

By 1890, *The Light of Asia* had been rendered into Dutch, Bengali, German and Russian. Arnold had now emerged as a very powerful voice for Buddhism. The poem's cultural impact, going beyond the world of books, can be gauged by this report that appeared in the *Washington Post* on 2 May 1890:

> For the second time in its history the Washington Choral Society presented Dudley Buck's "Light of Asia", the occasion attracting to Lincoln Hall an audience which entirely filled the structure. When the Society first essayed the work on May 6 1887, it had not been sung either here or abroad . . . The poem which Mr. Buck has chosen for his musical setting is one that is thoroughly familiar . . . As written by Mr. Arnold the poem is peculiarly oriental in its coloring, rich imagery and deep religious feeling . . . The chorus was more than adequate . . . The work of the orchestra [Boston Symphony Orchestra] was up to its accepted high standard.

Dudley Buck was an American composer and organist of those times. His three-part oratorio based on *The Light of Asia* was performed in different American cities as well as in London in 1889—the first American cantata produced in Great Britain.[1] In April 1889, there was also a call for the Bombay Philharmonic Society to 'try Mr. Buck's work', which was 'bound to be successful' in India.[2] But that did not materialize. Buck's work however continued to be popular for a decade.

In 1892, *The Light of Asia* was adapted for opera by a thirty-four-year-old English composer Isidore de Lara as *La Luce dell'Asia*. De Lara would later go on to make a bigger name for himself. *La Luce dell'Asia* opened in the Royal Italian Opera House in London's famed Covent Garden on 11 June 1892 with the libretto by William Beatty-Kingston, a journalist with the *Daily Telegraph* and an enthusiastic musicologist. Kingston had introduced De Lara to *The Light of Asia* at least two years earlier. On the evening of the opera's evening, he told the *Pall Mall Gazette* that 'when I read Sir Edwin Arnold's poem it impressed me very much; it seemed to give great opportunities to a musician, because it deals with the metaphysical side of Indian philosophy, and I have always thought that music is the art *par excellence* for the expression of metaphysical ideas'. The opera itself, set in four acts, evoked a very good audience response on its opening night but received mixed newspaper reviews and was not a commercial success. Beatty-Kingston was to later write his two-volume memoirs in which he would reveal Arnold's substantial knowledge of Indian music and his [Arnold's] profound conviction that to comprehend India fully, its music in its diverse forms has to be understood and appreciated.[3]

In 1892, Arnold published *Potiphar's Wife and Other Poems*. This contains Egyptian and Japanese poems, demonstrating his felicity with both Arabic and Japanese, and some other English poems extolling the British Empire. But also tucked away in the volume is a short poem:

TO MY BIOGRAPHER

TRACE me through my snow,
Track me through my mire,
You shall never know
Half that you desire!

Praise me, or asperse,
Deck me or deride,
In my veil of verse
Safe from you I hide.

Arnold was absolutely right. He is an archival biographer's nightmare. His papers, such as they are, lie in different libraries in the USA and UK, and for a man like him and his accomplishments, they don't really amount to much. Even a comprehensive listing of his poetic compositions does not exist. But what little there is lying scattered about shows a man of many talents that went beyond writing poetry, penning articles and knowing many languages—he was a fine artist too, as these sketches made by him reveal.

Sketches made by Sir Edwin Arnold in 1898 and found in his papers at Valdosta State University, USA.

In 1893, Arnold wrote the preface to Ernest Bowden's *The Imitation of Buddha*, the title clearly invoking the very famous Christian devotional text of the early fifteenth century *The Imitation of Christ* by Thomas a Kempis. Bowden had presented quotations from Buddhist literature for each day of the year. Arnold ended his preface thus:

This compassionateness of Gautama, if nothing else had been illustrated by the collection, would render it precious to possess and fruitful to employ; but many another lofty tenet of the "Light" of Asia finds illumination in some brief verse or maxim, as day after day glides by; and he who should mark the passage of the months from January to December with these simple pages must become, I think, a better man at the year's end than at the beginning . . .

Bowden's book, although not as enduring as Olcott's *Buddhist Catechism*, would nevertheless get translated into a couple of European languages and continue to evoke some interest.

The first World Parliament of Religions was held in Chicago in September 1893. It has become a milestone in India because of the extraordinary impact created there by Swami Vivekananda. Vivekananda had already been exposed to *The Light of Asia* in Calcutta some years earlier. He and Girishchandra Ghosh, who had adapted the poem for the stage in Bengali as *Buddhadev Charit* in 1885, were very close. While it is almost certain that Vivekananda had read the original English, these lines sung to the Buddha by two celestial maidens from Ghosh's adaptation were a particular favourite of his that he would sing often:[4]

We moan for rest, alas! But rest can never find;
We know not whence we come, nor where we float away.
Time and again we tread this round of smiles and tears;
In vain we pine to know whither our pathway leads,
And why we play this empty play.

We sleep, although awake, as if by a spell betwitched;
Will darkness never break into the light of dawn?
As restless as the wind, life moves unceasingly:
We know not who we are, nor whence it is we come;
We know not why we come, nor where it is we drift;
Sharp woes dart forth on every side.

How many drift about, now happy, now drowned in tears!
One moment they exist, the next they are no more.
We know not why we come, nor what our deeds have been,
Nor, in our bygone lives, how well we played our parts;
Like water in a stream, we cannot stay at rest;
Onward we flow for evermore.

Burst Thou our slumber's bars, O Thou that art awake!
How long must we remain enmeshed in fruitless dreams?
Are you indeed awake? Then do not longer sleep!
Thick on you lies the gloom fraught with a million woes.
Rise, dreamer, from your dream, and slumber not again!
Shine forth, O Shining One, and with Thy shafts of light
Slay Thou the blinding dark! Our only Saviour Thou!
We seek deliverance at Thy feet.

Vivekananda had been to Buddha Gaya in April 1886, four months after renouncing the world, and where, according to the official account of his life by the Ramakrishna Mission, he sat under the Bodhi Tree saying to himself, 'Is it possible that I breathe the air He breathed? That I touch the earth He trod?'[5]

A few months after his splendid performance in Chicago, on 13 February 1894, Vivekananda spoke on the subject of religious harmony in Detroit and declared:

> I belong to the Hindu religion. . . . We never indulge in missionary work . . . With no effort from us many forms of the Hindu religion are spreading far and wide, and these manifestations have taken the form of Christian science, theosophy and Edwin Arnold's *Light of Asia*.

A month later, on 19 March 1894, Vivekananda spoke to another audience in Detroit on 'Buddhism, the Religion of The Light of Asia' where he extolled the contributions of the Buddha. He ended up declaring that 'Buddhism was the foundation of the Catholic religion and the Catholic Church came from Buddhism'. Over the next few years, Vivekananda would champion the cause of Hinduism in general and Vedanta in particular, but he never lost his fascination for the Buddha and his teachings, even as he spoke of the reasons for the decline of Buddhism in India. At one point of time, he would go to the extent of saying

> Arnold's book, *The Light of Asia*, represents more of Vedantism than Buddhism.

Vivekananda was in London in 1896 and he received a very enthusiastic response. Records of his meeting Max Mueller are available but unfortunately there is no written evidence that he and Arnold met.

Vivekananda would speak twice on the Buddha in America in 1900. He was aware of the growing acceptance of Buddhism in that country and may well have seen it as a threat to the spread of Hindu thought. His most extensive exposition on 'Buddhistic India' was on 2 February 1900 at the Shakespeare Club in Pasadena, where he began by making a pointed reference to *The Light of Asia*. He ended by saying that Buddhism had indeed reformed India but that now 'Vedantism is conquering India from one end to another'. On 18 March 1900, he addressed a gathering in San Francisco on 'Buddha's Message to the World' and admitted that all his life he had been 'very fond of Buddha, but not of his doctrine', and added:

> . . . I have more veneration for that character than for any other . . . Throughout his life he never had a thought for himself . . . And consider his death. If he was great in life, he was also greater in death . . . Of all the teachers in the world, he was the one who taught us to be self-reliant, who freed us not only from the bondages of our false selves but from dependence on the invisible being or beings called Gods or gods . . .

And like he always did when he spoke on the Buddha, on this occasion too Vivekananda recalled *The Light of Asia*. It is clear that to him Arnold's poem was invaluable not so much as a tract on Buddhism but as a moving description of the Buddha's life. At one point of time Vivekananda had said:

> Have you not seen even a most bigoted Christian, when he reads Edwin Arnold's *Light of Asia*, stand in reverence of the Buddha, who preached no God, preached nothing but self-sacrifice?

Undoubtedly Vivekananda had caused a sensation at the World Parliament of Religions at Chicago in September 1893. But the Buddhist presence and impact at the assembly were no less significant. Dharmapala registered himself forcefully, as did the representatives of various Japanese Buddhist sects. He had travelled to Chicago with a copy of *The Light of Asia*, which, by his own admission, provided him an account of the Buddha as a human being.[6]

Vivekananda at the September 1893 World Parliament of Religions at Chicago. Dharmapala in white is next to him. (Source: Wikipedia)

In the aftermath of the Chicago conference, Charles Theodore Strauss became the 'first person ever to be initiated into Buddhism on American soil'. Emily Sigalow, who studied Strauss' life, speculated that *The Light of Asia* could have been one of the major influences on Strauss in the 1880s.[7] Another outcome of the conclave at Chicago was the publication in 1894 of *The Gospel of Buddha* by Paul Carus, an American philosopher, editor and publisher. Within months of its American release Carus' book would be translated into Japanese by D.T. Suzuki as *Budda no fukin* and would play a key role in the revival of Buddhism in Meiji Japan.[8] Carus, however, makes no mention of *The Light of Asia* in his work, in which he acknowledges the work of British and European scholars of Buddhism. Suzuki, of course, is now acknowledged as the man who introduced and spread Zen Buddhism in the West.

Arnold was not physically present in Chicago in September 1893. But on 21 September 1893 the following letter written to the Chairman of the World Parliament of Religions John Barrows was read out in the assembly:[9]

SHIRA PARK, Tokyo September 1893,--I do not believe it totally uninteresting to give here a short account of our Indo-Busseki Kofuku Society of Japan. The object of this society is to restore and re-establish the holy places of Buddhism in India, and to send out a number of Japanese priests to perform devotional exercises in each of them, and to promote the convenience of pilgrims from Japan. These holy places are Buddha Gaya where Buddha attained to the perfect enlightenment; Kapilavastu where Buddha was born; the Deer Park, where Buddha first preached; and Kusinagara where Buddha attained Nirvana . . .

When the ancient King Asoka of Magadha was converted into Buddhism, he erected a large and magnificent temple over the spot [at Buddha Gaya near the Bodhi Tree] to show his gratitude to the founder of his new religion. But, sad to say, the fierce Mohammedans invaded and laid waste the country, there being no Buddhist to guard the temple, which possession fell into the hands of a Brahmin priest, who chanced to come here and seize it.

It was early in the spring of 1891 that the Japanese priest, the Rev. Shaku Kionen, in company with Mr. H. Dharmapala of Ceylon, visited this holy ground. The great Buddha Gaya Temple was carefully repaired and restored to its former state by the British government; but they could not help being very much grieved to see it subjected to much desecration in the hands of the Brahminist Mahant, and communicated to us their earnest desire to rescue it.

With warm sympathy for them, and thinking, as Sir Edwin Arnold has said, that it is not right for Buddhists to leave the guardianship of the holy center of Buddhist religion of grace to the hand of a Brahminist priest, we organized this Indo-Bussiki Kofuku Society in Japan to accomplish the object before mentioned in cooperation with the Maha Bodhi Society, organized by H. Dharmapala and other brothers in India . . . I believe our Buddha Gaya movement will bring people of all Buddhist countries into closer connection and be instrumental in promoting the brotherhood among the people of the whole world.

S. HORIUCHI, Secretary

The previous year, in April 1892, Arnold had met with the Indo-Bussiki Kofuku Society during his visit to Japan. He and Dharmapala had clearly had a huge impact, and now in Chicago the Society was bringing to the notice of the world their efforts to liberate the 'Buddhist Mecca' from the hands of the Hindu priest.

In May 1894 the Buddha was brought on to the London stage by none other than the famed Sarah Bernhardt herself. The play was called *Izeyl*, and when it opened it was reported in the *Pall Mall Gazette* as 'having revived the interest in Buddhism which Sir Edwin Arnold's *Light of Asia* first awakened in fashionable London'. The play itself was 'pure invention—about a courtesan who followed Siddhartha into the forest to seduce him and bring him back to a life of indulgence and pleasure' but it bore 'the clear stamp of *The Light of Asia* in its inspiration'. It was taken to America and Canada as well, hitting the headlines because of the presence of Bernhardt. Bernhardt had by this time become a disciple of sorts of Swami Vivekananda.

By the early 1890s, *The Light of Asia* had become so popular in England that it even became the butt of typical British humour in the press, illustrated by these two examples:[10]

CULTURE IN THE CITY

"I understand', said the private secretary to a stockholder in a gas company, "that Sir Edwin Arnold got 4000 pounds for his "Light of Asia"".

"You don't tell me", was the reply; "what was it—gas or electricity?"

A POETICAL AUTHORITY

Peek (the grocer to his assistant): "You've rolled that oil barrel so close to the sugar that the sugar smells of petroleum."

Assistant: "Well sir, don't you know that Sir Edwin Arnold maintains that sweetness and light should go together?"

Arnold also figured in Victorian parody. Owen Seaman wrote:[11]

The bulbul hummeth like a book
  Upon the pooh-pooh tree,
And now and then he takes a look
    At you and me,
    At me and you.
      Kuchi!
      Koochoo!

And no less a man than Edward Lear—the King of Victorian nonsense literature and limericks—remarked after reading *The Light of Asia*:[12]

> If ever I meet with this Edwin Arnold, I shall go down plump on the knees. As it is, I am about to turn Buddhist as fast as possible, if not sooner.

The *Evening Telegraph and Star* commented on 30 June 1894:

> When Sir Arnold published "The Light of Asia" he did not think it necessary to state that Gautama, the Master had no longer any following in the country which witnessed its birth; but Sir Edwin's book produced a religious revival or something like it, among a certain class of semi-intelligent readers who are continually foraging for some new bit of religion with which to tickle the dull sense of their immortality into a relish for heaven.

Arnold was the subject of mirth even in the American press. The *Peoria Transcript* of 2 December 1889 had had some fun at his expense:

> According to the Minneapolis "Tribune", the Chicago Browning Club are so mad at Sir Edwin Arnold because he said Harvard College is the intellectual center of this country that they resolved to boycott his writing fluid. This is a mistake. They simply resolved to use kerosene instead of Mr. Arnold's "Light of Asia".

But he was a much sought-after figure too in British society on account of *The Light of Asia*. On 1 March 1894, for instance, Sir George Chetwynd, a racehorse owner and gambler, wrote to him:

> Will you give me the pleasure of your company for a dinner here at 8.30 on Thursday or Friday next. You will meet Lord and Lady Warwick who are anxious to hear "The Light of Asia".

And on 3 July 1895, Sir George Bowen, a noted colonial administrator and later a Member of the Privy Council, made a similar request:

> Will you kindly give me and my daughters the pleasure of your company at lunch tomorrow. We have got the eloquent and poetic Bishop of Demy and his wife who had written some fine hymns— also Palgrave the Professor of Poetry, Lady Gregory the widow of the late Sir W. Gregory—a clever woman—also Lord and Lady Colchester. So you will be with some other poets, though none of them has written anything to be compared to "The Light of Asia"!

The 1890s were to see two more translations of *The Light of Asia* into Bengali. Both the authors were from Chittagong, now part of Bangladesh but a region of the subcontinent where there has always been a living Buddhist presence. In the 1901 Census, for instance, there were slightly less than a quarter of a million Buddhists recorded in Bengal, largely in the region where Chittagong was located. This was by far the largest number anywhere in the subcontinent then (minus Ceylon of course).

There was a strong tradition of Pali scholarship in the nineteenth century in Chittagong, which is the hilly and coastal region in the southeastern end of today's Bangladesh. Much of this tradition was fostered and nurtured by the royalty of the Buddhist kingdom of Arakan, which had its capital in Akyab—these are parts of today's Myanmar that have hit the headlines on account of the massacres and displacement of the local Rohingya Muslim population. Buddhism received a big boost in Chittagong in 1887 with the visit of Henry Olcott, after which a Chittagong Buddhist Association was formed. This Association soon launched the first Indian journal aimed specifically at Buddhist audiences, published both in Bengali and English. There were close links between the Chittagong Buddhist Association and the Mahabodhi Society in Calcutta. This is the milieu in which Kabi Sarbananda Barua's translation *Jagagjyothi* appeared in 1891 and Nabinchandra Sen's

Amitabha in 1895. Both were very well-known poets who are remembered even today in Bangladesh and in West Bengal as well. Two decades earlier Sen had published his controversial epic poem *Palashir Yuddha*[13] (The Battle of Plassey). This had been put up as a play in September 1875 in Calcutta with Girishchandra Ghosh acting the part of Robert Clive! Beni Madhab Barua, one of India's greatest scholars on Buddhism, was also born in Chittagong in December 1888.

In 1894, *The Light of Asia* was translated into Marathi by Govind Narayan Kane. Kane, as I have already mentioned, was one of those Chitpavan Brahmins who had converted to Christianity in 1880, at which time he wrote a book in Marathi on Francis Bacon. He began a legal practice in Amravati in 1888, attended the Amravati session of the Indian National Congress held in December 1897 and went to London in July 1908 on its behalf. In 1900 he wrote a biography of the Prophet Mohammed, also in Marathi.

Kane's *Jagadguru Gautama Buddhache Charitra* would have a profound impact on one of India's greatest scholars of Buddhism of the twentieth century. Dharmanand Kosambi writes in his autobiography, the original of which is in Marathi:

During my stay in the Prarthana Samaj I made many new acquaintances. Among them was the late Shri Madhavrao Lolitkar whom I got to know well. I also went to his house for a meal a couple of times. There I met Shri Kashinath Raghunath Mitra who had come to Poona for a change of air. One day the subject of Buddha came up and he recommended that I read Shri Govind Narayan Kane's *Jagadguru Gautama Buddhache Charitra* [The Life of Gautama Buddha, Teacher of the World]. He did not own a copy but I acquired it through him and read it. This work is a translation of Sir Edwin Arnold's Light of Asia. The original is in verse, so the translation is not entirely reliable. But it has been written with such a feeling of love that the reader cannot help but be engrossed in it. . . I liked it so much at the time that I read some portions over and over again. It became for me an original religious text at the time. I have still not forgotten how, while reading certain portions of it, my throat would constrict and tears would stream down my face. I got into the habit of studying this book whenever I was dispirited . . .

This must have been most probably in late December 1899 or early January 1900. Kashinath Raghunath Mitra was actually Kashinath Raghunath Ajgaonkar. He knew and was fond of Bengali and hence the name Mitra stuck. He translated Bengali novels into Marathi and in 1893 had launched a monthly Marathi magazine out of Bombay called *Manoranjan,* which over the years became a grand success.

In his autobiography Kosambi also narrated a conversation he had sometime in early February 1900 with R.G. Bhandarkar the great Sanskrit scholar who had studied at Deccan College and who was one of the leading lights of a social reform organization called the Prarthana Samaj.[14]

Bhandarkar: I had thought until now you would join the Prarthana Samaj . . .

Kosambi: I agree with most of the beliefs of the Prarthana Samaj. I do not accept caste discrimination. I have long been convinced child marriage is bad. But I do not wish to join any society until I have acquired a complete knowledge of Buddhism. At least at present I believe that Buddhism alone is the true means for the advancement of mankind.

Bhandarkar: What is the basis of your opinion? What do you know about Buddhism?

Kosambi: I have read *The Life of Jagaduru Buddha* [Kane's translation]. That has made me believe that the Buddha's views and his religion as a whole will be beneficial to mankind.

Bhadarkar: Oh, I know that book by Kane! It is the translation of an English book. The English book does not express even a quarter of the original [in Sanskrit] and not a quarter of the English is expressed in the Marathi! And you have formed your opinion about Buddhism on the basis of such a book!

Kosambi: I admit I know nothing about Buddhism. But if the Marathi account—which according to you contains only one-sixteenth of the original—is so gripping, one can only imagine how good the original must be . . .

Kosambi went on to become a legendary figure in Pali and Buddhist studies before dying in the approved Buddhist/Jain

Dharmanand Kosambis who was profoundly influenced by The Light of Asia *and was India's pioneering scholar of Pali and Buddhism. This is the cover of the book on him by his granddaughter. (Source: Permanent Black)*

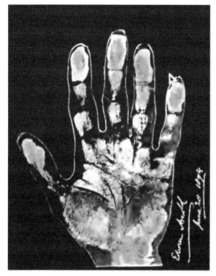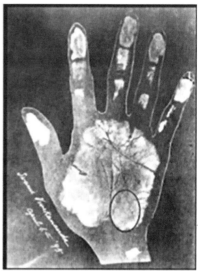

Palm reading of Edwin Arnold (left) and Vivekananda by Cheiro, 1895. (Source: Internet Archive)

manner by voluntary starvation in Gandhi's Sewagram ashram in June 1947.

Palmistry has been a perennial Indian obsession. But in the late nineteenth and early twentieth centuries, it had gripped the UK and USA as well. The most famous practitioner of the 'science of cheirognomy and cheiromancy' in the West was an Irish occult figure called William John Warner, who in later years went by the name of Count Louis Hamon but who has been known to generations of palmistry buffs simply as Cheiro. His 'Language of the Hand' first appeared in London in late 1894, in which the palms of various political and cultural personalities of the day were analysed. A few months later, a second edition hit the stands, and this included the palms along with their personal inscriptions of 'Sir Edwin Arnold' and 'The Swami Vivekananda', the former a transatlantic rage and the latter who was taking America by storm. As for Cheiro, he claimed to have been inducted into the science of palmistry by his guru who was a 'Chitpavan Brahmin from the Konkan', much like the Sanskrit gurus of Arnold in Poona in the late 1850s.

In 1895, Arnold published *Tenth Muse and Other Poems*. The significance of this volume lies in the fact that it includes translations from the Sanskrit *Mahabharata*, from a couple of Japanese poets, from the Persian poets Hafiz and Sa'di and from the Koran. This is the only anthology in which Arnold's skills in four non-English 'Oriental' languages come out strongly.

In April 1896, Arnold produced a work that has inexplicably escaped the notice of even his biographer. This was his *The Chaurapanchasika: An Indian Love-Lament Translated From the Sanskrit*. Arnold introduces the translation by recalling the discovery of the original Sanskrit manuscript in 1798 by the Norwegian–German scholar Christian Lassen in the library of the East India Company in London. Subsequently, the great German Sanskritist Peter von Bohlen would produce a Latin translation. Arnold lets us know that he 'took a transcription of the two hundred Sanskrit shlokes' to the Canary Islands while on a month's holiday there and 'made this English version of them'. He believed that the love poem was 'contemporary with Bhartrihari', which would 'date it from the commencement of the Christian era'. Actually, we now know that the author was Bilhana and that this work of his dates to the eleventh century CE.

Arnold's was the very first English translation. It was remarkable not just for the fact that he provided the original Sanskrit along with his translation, but he also included a number of his own illustrations. The illustrations were to be criticized decades later for having little relation to the translations themselves[15] but my sense is that Arnold was just having some fun. He himself made no claims to literary worth, admitting that he had written this 'little book' only to 'amuse scholars, lovers and ladies'. Quite mischievously, on 28 August 1897 he presented a copy to 'Queen Mary when Duchess of York'. She was married to the grandson of Queen Victoria, who became King George V in 1910. The poem would continue to be popular and it has been suggested that it influenced John Steinbeck, who won the Nobel Prize for Literature in 1962.[16]

A page from Arnold's handwritten, self-illustrated Chaurapanchasika showing both the original Sanskrit verse and English translation, 1896.

On 30 April 1896 Arnold wrote to his American friend Major J.B. Pond:

> I have just returned from a month's holiday in the Canary Islands . . . I am tremendously busy with politics, and also with a journey to Russia, whither I go to see the Tsar crowned . . .
>
> I wish I could see my way to once more run round with you [in America]. At present I dream of being in India all next winter about some temple business [the Mahabodhi Temple at Buddha-Gya] and appointments with that view.

Arnold never got to go to India to see his obsession come true—the transfer of the Buddha-Gya temple from Hindu to Buddhist control. Dharmapala would apprise him every now and then of his campaign in this regard but by the end of the century, Arnold had begun to grow blind. Dharmapala's diary entry for 3 September 1896 reads:

> Went to see Sir Edwin Arnold at 3 P.M. but he had not come out of his room. His wife had gone to the Theatre. I left word that I am leaving England tomorrow morning. I like Sir Edwin. He had done excellent work for Buddhism. In 1882 I read his Light of Asia and the Renunciation scene therein appealed to me intensely. After I had renounced home again his "India Revisited" which in 1886 I read incited me to visit Buddha Gaya . . . When I had thought of the blindness of Sir Edwin I remembered the Bodhisat

story when the Buddhist gave his eyes to cure a blindman. The same desire came to me to give my eyes to cure Sir Edwin [who] had done for Buddhism more than all the Buddhists together.

Just a few days earlier Annie Besant too had written to Arnold:

Dharmapala, in giving me your very kind and friendly message, mentioned that you were going to India this winter. Will you pardon my saying that if you come to Benaras we should be so very glad if you would accept our hospitality—if you do not object to our simple and Indian style of living. A note to me at the Theosophical Society, Benaras would be enough. I owe you so much gratitude for your exquisite "Light of Asia", that it would be a great pleasure to welcome you to our dear Indian home . . .

Annie Besant had much earlier reviewed *The Light of Asia* as soon as it was first published in 1879.[17] After mentioning the lines that appealed to her, she ended thus:

Mr Arnold has not written a poem, but he has given us a very pleasant book of verse. He relates the story smoothly and well, but has no glimpse—or at least he does not show that he has any glimpse—of the potential possibilities of his theme. His volume is useful, but it is not great. Yet Buddha might well inspire a Browning to unveil him to the Western world.

After Arnold's *Lotus and Jewel* appeared in 1887, she wrote:[18]

By all means let anyone who wants to do say Om. But I venture to make my protest against "poetry" of this kind, which some will regard with awe as unintelligible from the sublimity of its thought, whereas it is really unintelligible from the magniloquence of its absurdity. Very different work is this from other that Mr. Edwin Arnold has given us, and the disappointed reader has good right to complain.

Yet within just three years, as her biographer would point out, [19] 'she herself was saying 'Om' with the best of the Hindus and presumably benefitting from all the mystic advantages accruing from the proper repetition of this reverberating monosyllable'. She had joined the Theosophical Society in London in May 1889, made her maiden visit to India in November 1893 and thereafter become an Indian in every way. She would become president of the Theosophical Society in 1907 and of the Indian National Congress a decade thereafter. While Blavatsky and Olcott were taken up more with Buddhism and had, in fact, become Buddhists in May 1880 while in Colombo, Annie Besant was an unabashed champion of Hinduism.

Dharmapala would return to Chicago and on 11 October 1896 would address the Chicago Anthropological Society. He would preface his address with a rapid sketch of the life of the Buddha, 'praising Sir Edwin Arnold's "Light of Asia" as being a perfect

Annie Besant in 1897, just as she was getting into her Indian incarnation.

presentation of Buddha's search after the higher principles of living'.
He would make an appeal for Arnold's assistance on the Buddha
Gaya issue a few years later but by then the poet was completely bed-
ridden and was on his last legs.

Arnold had left Poona some four decades earlier, but Poona
had not left him. In late 1896, a plague epidemic was to ravage
western India and Poona would be very badly affected. The
Bombay Government set up a Special Plague Committee under the
chairmanship of a seasoned administrator Walter Charles Rand.
Rand had the reputation of being a strict disciplinarian and had
already antagonized orthodox Brahmin opinion in Poona by some
of his actions in near by Satara. He moved quickly and with great
authority to control the spread of the disease. British troops were
brought in to fumigate and limewash the interiors of all homes in
which plague was suspected. Anyone suspected of infection was
isolated and kept in quarantine outside the city for at least ten days.

Rand's men behaved with supreme disdain for public sentiment
and with a lack of courtesy. Rand came to his assignment suspected
by only the orthodox Brahmins but pretty soon it became apparent
that he had antagonized many other sections of Poona's society as
well. On the night of Queen Victoria's Diamond Jubilee, Rand was
assassinated by three young men who went into the pages of Indian
history as the Chapekar brothers—Damodar Hari, Balakrishna Hari
and Vasudev Hari. They were sentenced to death and executed two
years later.[20] There is a memorial to them in Poona and even today
they are venerated as heroes.

A few days after Rand's assassination, Arnold took to the
columns of the *Daily Telegraph* recalling his time in Poona almost
four decades earlier and giving his readers a tutorial on the caste
system. The original article is unavailable but a report on it in the
Edinburgh Evening News of 3 July 1897 says:

Sir Edwin Arnold who lived for many years in Poona writes in
the Daily Telegraph expressing his conviction that the present
mischief there may be attributed to a few conspirators who, acting

in many occult ways, as well as through a disgracefully malignant and seditious local press, use caste and sectarian formulae and conventions against English rule. "I would not be surprised," he adds, "to learn that those Hindu miscreants concerned have suborned Mohammedans to assist them, from ranks of many Islamites in India, who are angry just now at the eternal inequity of Christendom towards the Sultan [of Turkey] and his Empire". Caste, however, and the deep-rooted habits of Hinduism must not be spoken of as "prejudice" and "Ignorance". With the best and highest intentions, the agents of the Governments have probably grieved and alarmed the whole Mahratta public by the way in which they benevolently sought to root out the plague. I was Municipal Commissioner at Poona as well as President of the Deccan College, and when we have a bad attack of cholera in the city, we managed all sanitary matters peacefully enough by employing only Brahmin inspectors and visitors.

The Mahrattas (Sir Edwin says) are a sturdy, manly, honest race not given to dark and wicked ways. The young Brahmans, who I helped educate, perhaps do indeed oftentimes get "wind in their head" . . . They are best dealt with by a strong and calm and vigilant contempt. Assuredly the mass of Poona people in my time, which was the worst time of the Great Mutiny, were kindly, peaceful, godly and delightful to live with—and will remain so, I think, if the money-lenders do not ruin them; if Indra will only send them the good rain and the cheap grain; and if their rulers bear in mind that Hindus would rather die quickly and comfortably than live ashamed, harassed and outcasted.

By the 1890s, *The Light of Asia* had become staple reading for the educated (which meant English-speaking Indians). The book would be discussed in public forums as well. On 14 May 1897, for instance, the Triplicane Literary Society in Madras with Prof Sathianadhan of the Presidency College in the chair, would hear D. Ramanadha Aiyar of the Pachaiyappa's College on *The Light of Asia*. The next day *The Hindu* reported:

Mr. Ramanadhan, who on rising was received with cheers, began by giving a brief account of the career of Sir, so much of it as was necessary for the purposes of the meeting. He then entered into the subject proper quoting largely from the "Light of Asia" and laid before the audience the subject matter of that splendid poem, the life of Siddhartha and the tenets of the Buddhist faith so well that the whole audience was kept almost spell-bound . . .

After the lecture was over, Professor Sathianadhan rose in the midst of loud cheers and warmly congratulated himself and the audience for their good fortune in having listened to a very interesting and able lecture . . . He had read the "Light of Asia" in 1879 when he was student at Cambridge . . . The book created a profound sensation and intelligent interest and spirit of enquiry to matters Indian, both in England and America. Sir Edwin Arnold's love for India was truly great. From a literary point of view, the work was of a very high order, though Sir Edwin was but a minor poet . . . He added that it would be advisable for young men to read "The Light of Asia" and "The Light of the World" together and that he could only account for the admitted inferiority of "The Light of the World" to the "Light of Asia" by saying that in the one he was in touch with the subject, but in the other he was not . . .

A year later, the October 1898 issue of *the Theosophist* that had by then had moved its publication from Bombay to Madras contained this brief announcement:

We have received a Tamil version of "The Story of the Life of Buddha," describing the great renunciation as depicted by Sir Edwin Arnold in his "Light of Asia." It is reprinted from the Viveka Chintamani, and is a handy book written in a good and easy style, thus rendering it very useful to the Tamil knowing peoples, and the Dravidian Buddhists can by its use easily understand the history of Lord Buddha. The book is to be had from the Editor of the Viveka Chintamani Madras.

My best guess is that the author of this Tamil translation was a young A. Madhaviah, later to establish himself as a major literary figure in Madras. Here is what his definitive biographer had to say on the matter:[21]

> In 1892 (June-July), Madhavaiah wrote "Savitri Charitram" in six parts in the journal *Viveka Chintamani*. It is conceivable that he wrote his early bio of Buddha in another edition of this same journal, as he hints this in his preface to *Siddharthan* (1918, p. vii). In this work, Madhavaiah described that years earlier he had been impressed by U.V.Swaminathan's *Buddhar Charitram* and Edwin Arnold's *Light of Asia*. He also stated that he had begun a bio of Buddha, and had published portions, but was inhibited by poor health, but that he had now resumed this as he was inspired by U.V. Swaminathan and Edwin Arnold.

I will take up *Siddharthan* and another Tamil translation later.

A year later, that is in 1899, the French translation of *The Light of Asia* was published in Paris. It was called *La Lumière de l'Asie* and was by Leon Sorg. Sorg was trained in law and was the chief justice of the 'court of first instance' in the French territory of Pondicherry in the 1890s. He became an authority on law in the Tamil country (as opposed to regions like Bengal where Sanskritic traditions prevailed) and developed a deep interest in Hindu philosophy. He would later become a great admirer of Ramakrishna and Vivekananda and would translate Max Mueller's lectures on Vedanta as well into French. Sorg's French version of *The Light of Asia* would be reissued at least thrice later—first in 1921, then in 1931 and also as recently as in 2017. In 1933 another French translation by Gabriel Trarieux would appear. Trarieux was a poet and dramatist who got interested in Theosophy, particularly its occult aspects, after the First World War.

In 1888 Arnold had brought out *With Sa'di in the Garden* or the *Book of Love*, which was a translation of the third chapter of the Persian poet's *Bostan*. The Shah of Persia had decorated him that

year with the Order of the Lion and the Sun. Arnold would return to
Sa'di in 1899 with a translation of four sections of his *The Gulistan*.
Calling his translation a 'refuge from politics and body pain', Arnold
went to describe Sa'di's work in glowing culinary terms:

> It is a sort of intellectual pillaw; a literary curry; a kabab of versatile
> genius, where grave and gay, humour and wisdom, laughter and
> tears are threaded together on the skewer of wit and spiced by a
> soft worldliness and gentle stoicism that makes the dish irresistible,
> however jaded may be the mental appetite . . .

Also, in 1899 would appear Arnold's last book, *The Queen's Justice*,
dedicated to his wife. The book itself was based on a real-life
episode in rural Bengal that illustrated the manner in which British
rule dispensed justice in India. It had first been brought to public
attention in London in the 1888 by Manmohan Ghose as *The Trial
of Muluk Chand for murder of his own child. A romance of criminal
administration in Bengal.* Ghose was the first Indian barrister at
the Calcutta High Court and also, incidentally, the lawyer who
represented 'Hindu' interests in the Buddha-Gya temple case at
all stages in 1895. Arnold gave 'a new setting to bygone incidents'
saying that it called for a 'literary presentation' because it was 'a
typical and picturesque' illustration of 'the difficulties of Criminal
Administration in India' and that it had both 'forensic interest and
ethnographic colour'.

Before the century ended Arnold would come to the help of an
Indian friend of his—Kisari Mohan Ganguli—who had been the
first to translate the entire *Mahabharata* into English between 1884
and 1896. On 24 March 1899 Arthur Balfour, then the First Lord
of the Treasury in the British Cabinet, wrote to Arnold:

> The long delay which has occurred in answering your letter has
> been due to the length of time which the India Office have taken
> in answering certain enquiries I put to them in connection with
> your application: so please let the blame rest on the right shoulders.

There can be no doubt that the translation of the *Mahabharata* is a work of enormous magnitude, which must have required corresponding labour to bring it to completion. I fear, however, that this by itself supplies no ground for a Civil List Pension. I doubt whether mere translation has ever been rewarded in this way, and I feel sure it ought not to be unless the translator shows not only a competent knowledge of the two languages in which he works, but also scholarly qualities of a very special kind. Now both the Indian Government and such Sanskrit authorities I have been able confidentially to consult at home seem agreed that no such high praise can be given to Ganguli's translation, and the Indian Government, on whom the duty rests, at all events in the first instance, of dealing with such cases, have refused any assistance on this very ground. I do not see how it would be possible, under such circumstances, for me to break through the double rule that the Civil List Pensions were not primarily intended to reward translators and that it is for the Indian Government to reward Indian literary merit.

It is much against the grain that I return this unfavourable answer, but, after much reflection, I fear I have no alternative.

But Balfour—who would soon become Prime Minister—had perhaps not reckoned with the perseverance of Arnold. The poet then approached another good friend of his—the Viceroy himself. On 5 July 1899 Lord Curzon would write to him from Simla:

I have upon receipt of your memorial gone very carefully into the case of Babu Mohan Ganguli who translated the *Mahabharata*. It is not the case that the petition was rejected on financial grounds alone but because the Oriental Sanskrit authorities out here did not report upon the translation in the glowing terms adopted by the English memorialists. The Home Dept. concurred with the Finance Dept. on these grounds and Lord Elgin [Curzon's predecessor] supported their views.

I have however felt anxious to look at the matter in as generous a spirit as possible, both because it seems to me hardly fair to apply to the work of an Indian translator the tests of the higher European scholarship and because I can conceive no more fitting application of the Indian revenues than the encouragement of meritorious literary effort, particularly in connection with the old Indian classics—even if such effort be destitute of supreme literary or academic distinction.

I have, therefore, persuaded my colleagues to agree to the grant to the Babu of a pension of 600 rupees a year which in this country is considered a very high one. I trust this decision may be gratifying to yourself and to those who signed the memorial.[22]

History has been kinder to Ganguli and all scholars of the *Mahabharata* have acknowledged their debt to his painstaking and pioneering work. Ganguli would pass away in 1908, four years after Arnold's death.

Notes

1. Orr (2003)
2. The *Times of India*, 13 April 1889
3. Beatty-Kingston (1887)
4. Chetanananda (2009)
5. www.ramakrishnavivekananda.info Chapter XVIII 'The Swami Vivekananda and his attitude to Buddha', accessed 14 June 2020
6. Kemper (2015)
7. Sigalow (2018)
8. Snodgrass (1998)
9. *Chicago Daily Tribune*, 22 September 1893
10. These are from Eiben (2016).
11. Dubois (2018)
12. Whitlark (1988)
13. Chaudhuri (2008)
14. Kosambi (2010)
15. Siveshwarkar (1967)
16. Kumar (2016)
17. *The National Reformer*, 10 August 1879
18. *The National Reformer*, 4 December 1887
19. Nethercot (1960)

20. Wolpert (1962) has a finely balanced account of the Rand-Chapekar episode and of the role of Bal Gangadhar Tilak in it.
21. Sita Anantha Raman. Email communication dated 12 April 2020
22. These included Sir Arthur Arnold (Sir Edwin's brother), Sir Monier Monier-Williams, Lord Northbrook and Edward Byles Cowell, the first professor of Sanskrit at Cambridge University.

13

1900–1910: Sir Edwin Arnold's Final Years and the Continuing Appeal of *The Light of Asia*

The new century commenced with Fred Weatherly drawing upon *The Light of Asia* for his 'Nirvana' that had music by Stephen Adams. Weatherly was a versatile personality. A lawyer by education and practice, he is a forgotten man today, but during the period 1890–1925, Weatherly was one of England's most sought-after lyricists. He is estimated to have written the lyrics of at least three thousand popular songs, one of which was 'Nirvana':

> *I have come from the silent forest,*
> *My beautiful Lotos flow'r.*
> *And I stand in thy garden sighing.*
> *Thy sisters, the lotos blossoms,*
> *They ope to the moon above;*
> *Open thy window, beloved,*
> *And let me tell my love.*

> *I have knelt in the mighty temples,*
> *But the dumb gods make no sign;*
> *They cannot speak to my spirit,*
> *As thy soul speaks to mine.*
> *And the priests talk of Nirvana,*
> *And weave their mystic charms,*
> *I only know Nirvana*
> *Within thy loving arms.*

And the Lotos flow'r will perish,
The stars turn cold and gray,
The dumb gods will be shattered,
The temples old decay:
But we shall be one, beloved,
we shall be one
In the stream of life divine;
As the river flows to the ocean,
My soul shall flow to thine.

Nothing, alas, is known of how a very sick Arnold reacted to the use of the word 'Nirvana' in this manner. He would certainly not have been amused because Weatherly is actually dismissive of Buddhism. But his lyrics are, in some sense, a tribute to how widespread Arnold had made the idea of Nirvana in the public discourse of those times. It would most certainly have given Weatherley's song 'distinction in a crowded marketplace for drawing room ballads'.[1] That 'Nirvana' was a popular composition is shown by the fact that in December 1912 John McCormack, the celebrated Irish tenor, would also record it.

Arnold's eldest son Edwin Lester, who was with him as a child in Poona, was a keen naturalist trying to establish himself as an author. Arnold had, in fact, written a preface to his son's book *On the Indian Hills or Coffee-Planting in Southern India* that came out in 1893. It was an account of his experiences in Ceylon and in the Madras Presidency. The father commended 'these sketches of an adventurous life in a little-known corner of India . . . because they bring out in a simple and picturesque fashion the natural variety and woodland features of a great region whose immense resources for forestry, plantations and hunting are even now hardly comprehended by Indian authorities'. Arnold's wish would be realized sooner and in a greater manner than he would have imagined. In later years, Lester Arnold would make a name for himself as a science fiction writer.

The second son Julian would do much to keep his father's name alive in the first half of the twentieth century. He was a lawyer but ran foul of the law. After being extradited from America, he was charged and found guilty in January 1901 by a London court of embezzling a large amount of trust fund money which had been placed in his care and management. Julian Arnold would accept that the frauds he had committed 'were not pre-meditated' but 'were the outcome of the fact that he was reduced to desperation by his [financial] difficulties and lost his moral integrity'. He was sentenced to ten years in jail. He would subsequently reinvent himself in America as a businessman, poet, author and a theosophist. He would write a book of recollections on the prominent personalities that he had across being his father's son and also help Brooks Wright write the only full-length biography of Edwin Arnold that exists. Of course, there is nothing of his jail term in Wright's book. Julian Arnold would live till the ripe old age of ninety-one and pass away in 1954.

A third son, Emerson, was a highly qualified doctor and led his life in the Fiji Islands, visiting India in 1915. He too would be drawn to the Theosophical Society and would contribute an insightful article to Buddhism in England on the occasion of his father's birth centenary.

A fourth son, William Channing, was a journalist. He would write a well-received book on his travels in the Yucatan in Mexico, but this would only appear four years after his father's death. From 1910 till his death in 1938 Channing Arnold would live first in Burma and then in India. He is the subject of a separate chapter much later in this narrative. Edwin Arnold's daughter Katherine, who had travelled with him to India, America and Japan and to whom he was particularly close, had married and was leading her own life.[2]

This was the setting to a prominently displayed piece that appeared in the *Chicago Tribune* of 25 August 1901. It shows that Arnold was still news and there was still much public interest in him and in what he was up to. The new item read:

His Japanese Wife His Only Solace

Sir Edwin Arnold Old, Blind, Paralytic, and the Victim of a Degenerate Son

Sir EDWIN ARNOLD, now in his old age, blind and paralytic and grieving over the arrest of his son, is tenderly nursed and cared for by the little Japanese woman he married eleven years ago in Yokohoma.

Sir Edwin's family were shocked and grieved at this marriage. Likewise were the English friends of the author of "The Light of Asia" . . .

Sir Edwin's little Japanese bride did not promise before a great crowd of people that she took her husband for better for worse, to love, honour and obey, to cherish in sickness and in health. And yet she has done all that and more, too.

Disappointed in the son he so loved and trusted, engulfed with great disappointment and domestic griefs, stricken with blindness and disease, Sir Edwin's position would be deplorable but for the devotion of the little brown-skinned woman whom he took to be his wife in far away Japan . . .

"I am blind", said Sir Edwin the other day, in speaking of his wife, "and yet I can see. I am chained by infirmities to one spot, and yet I have feet that carry me everywhere . . .

As 1901 drew to a close, Arnold received a letter from one of his friends whose hospitality he had enjoyed in Calcutta sixteen years earlier and with whom he had lobbied for Buddhist control over the Mahabodhi Temple at Buddha Gaya. The former Viceroy Lord Dufferin wrote on 30 December 1901:

I cannot say with what concern I have learned of the terrible affliction which has overtaken you. Living as we do so secluded a life though some time ago I had seen from time to time in the papers an allusion to your having been unwell. I had no notion that you have been so severely visited. The loss of sight in the evening of one's days, when books are naturally one's principal consolation for one's growing incapacity for other amusements, is indeed a terrible privation, for which there is no adequate compensation on this side of the grave. Luckily, however, your hearing is preserved. Mine alas! is gone and my eyesight, always bad, begins to give me great anxiety . . .

Within six weeks Dufferin himself passed away.

The Light of Asia would see the first of the translations of the new century in 1902. Arnold would not have known about it, but it would be into Telugu and was called *Buddhacaritramu,* by Venkata Sastri and Tirupati Sastri. Together they called themselves Tirupati–Venkata poets[3] and were a 'powerful influence on Telugu literature in the first half of the twentieth century'. Velcheru Narayana Rao has given the background to this translation thus:

For most of their lives Venkata Sastri and Tirupati Sastri did not have stable jobs. Their major patrons were Telugu zamindars. One such zamindar was Krishna Rao [who had] read English literature. During this time, the early 1900s, Edwin Arnold's biography of the Buddha *Light of Asia* was enjoying unusual degree of popularity among English-educated Indians. If you did not appreciate *Light of Asia* you were not considered a person of good taste . . . Krishna Rao wanted the Twin Poets to translate *Light of Asia* into Telugu for him.

But why would an English-loving Brahmin zamindar want *The Light of Asia* translated into the local language? It turns out that the zamindar—Sri Rajah Kotcherlakota Ramachandra Venkata

Krishna Rao Bahadur, to give his full name—was not only a faithful ally of the British and amongst the earliest graduates in English literature in that area but also the founder of a society called the 'Andhrabhashojjeevani' for the revival of Telugu literature. Krishna Rao was the Rajah of the Polavaram Estate near Rajahmundry in today's Andhra Pradesh.

Sri Rajah Kotcherlakota Ramachandra Venkata Krishna Rao, an Andhra zamindar who commissioned the Telugu translation of The Light of Asia *in 1902. (Source: Family)*

There was a reason why *The Light of Asia* was selected as the source of the translation. For one, the patron was more comfortable with English rather than with Sanskrit. Second, translation from the English would give both the patron and the translators an opportunity to demonstrate loyalty to the British. Velcheru Narayana Rao points to the following verse from the preface of the translators themselves as illustrating the prevailing atmosphere clearly:

The three gods, Siva, Visnu and Brahma are like the Governors,
The minor gods are the lower level officials,

The great island Mandipa is like London,
And she herself is Her Majesty the Queen,
May she, the Great Goddess who rules the world,
Protect Krishna Rao with compassion.

Buddhacaritramu is put down to 1902. Clearly the preface by the Twin Poets was written well before Victoria's death, which was in January 1901. But among all the translations to Indian languages, this particular Telugu one was unique both in its background and its obsequiousness to the British. Exactly twenty years after *Buddhacaritrama* was published, *The Light of Asia* would inspire the Andhra artist Damerla Rama Rao to come out with this work:

Siddhartha Ragodaya by Damerla Rama Rao, 1922 water colour on paper. Based on The Light of Asia. *This is from Mitter (2007)*

Rama Rao died very young, in 1925, at the age of twenty-eight, but he has been hailed as a painter who triggered the Andhra artistic renaissance and was remembered in *Indian Art Through the Ages*, published by the Government of India very soon after India became independent in August 1947.[4]

The last few years of Arnold's life were marked by illness of various kinds, including loss of eyesight. By 1900 a twenty-eight-year-old Londoner, Allan Bennett, was calling himself a Buddhist after having read *The Light of Asia* a decade earlier as part of larger exploration of 'Hindu literature and Western esoteric mysticism'. That year he set sail for Ceylon to further his commitment to Buddhism and in 1901 travelled to Burma, where he renounced the work and took on the name of Ananda Metteyya, now immortalized in Buddhist historiography. He would establish 'The Buddhist Society of Great Britain and Ireland' in November 1907. But before that he launched *Buddhism: An Illustrated Quarterly Review* in September 1903. Six months before his death, Arnold wrote his very last published poem for this publication. It was called *The Golden Temple* and was in praise of the Shwedagon Pagoda in Rangoon. It started thus:

> *There came a Message from the East to me,*
> *A Message from the bank of the Rangoon River:*
> *Where the Great Temple stands aloft to see*
> *The waves dance down from Mandalay ever.*
>
> *From Peoples of the Yellow Robe it came,*
> *From Brothers of the Buddhist Doctrine, those*
> *Who, since I love them, hold my race and name*
> *Not alien, nor disdain, in cloistered close*
>
> *Or sacred shady grove, to give my song—*
> *Sung for their sake, and that my best might win*
> *Rays from the "Light of Asia-place among*
> *Their nobler scrolls, and deeper love within.*

and it ended thus:

> *Of his True Teaching take the Temple there*
> *For sign and starting point. From what point else*
> *Could weightier summons come, that men should hear*
> *With mostly grateful ears, the Four Great Truths,*

The twelve Niddanas, Dhamma and the Path?
From what diviner source or better fraught
With old authority could earth receive
Light of this fresh upsoaring of the Dawn
Of law, and Love, and Brotherhood to be
For all her children:-Light to all the World!
This was the word to utter, laid on me,
Out of the East, from bank of Rangoon River;
Where the Great Temple stands, with golden Tee
And down from Mandalay those waves dance ever.

In 1891, Arnold had written *The Light of the World* to describe the life of Christ. Whether it was sincere or strategic is hard to say. But in the closing months of his life, he wrote of the Buddha as providing 'Light to all the World'. Arnold's critics, in the 1880s particularly, had accused him of being a Buddhist. Although he never became one formally, on the strength of this very last poem it does appear that Arnold was attracted to the Buddha more than to anybody else. I should, however, mention that after his death there would be speculation that he had embraced his wife's Shinto faith.

In January 1904, while in London, Dharmapala called on him and found 'Sir Edwin Arnold a changed man; time and illness had done the work'.[5] The Japanese fleet attacked a Russian naval squadron at Port Arthur in Manchuria on 8 February 1904. Arnold wrote a flurry of pieces in the *Daily Telegraph* asking the Tsar to recognize the emergence of Japan and justifying the actions initiated by his friends in Tokyo. He would have been among the happiest when the war concluded a year later with the complete military victory of the Japanese—an event of profound political significance that would be hailed in many countries of Asia, India included, as symbolizing the defeat of a European power.

But Arnold did not live to see that day. His end came on 24 March 1904. Glowing obituaries were written in all prominent British, American and German newspapers. Two Indian newspapers of diametrically opposite political viewpoints then—the *Times of India* and *The Hindu*— joined the chorus of praise for him. The former would two months later recall this as a testimony to Arnold's nature:

> An enthusiastic scientist, Sir Henry Thompson, though personally of the kindliest nature, found it impossible to deny the advantages to surgery which were, he believed likely to accrue for vivisection. It was upon this vexed point that he was on one occasion arguing with the late Sir Edwin Arnold. "What Arnold," Sir Henry asked indignantly, "am I not to sacrifice a cat to save the life of the Archbishop of Canterbury!" "You may, my dear friend," said Sir Edwin, "but on one condition". "And what is that?" "That you may afterwards give that a burial in Westminster Abbey."

It was natural and expected for newspapers and literary magazines across the world to take note of Arnold's death and draw attention to his life, his works and to the enduring charm and appeal of *The Light of Asia*. Arnold had been a Fellow of the Royal Asiatic Society as well as of the Royal Geographical Society. Both institutions paid fulsome tributes. But to be remembered by the Aeronautical Society of Great Britain as well showed the wide canvas of his interests[6] and revealed how much of a public phenomenon he had become largely on account of his authorship of *The Light of Asia*. The notice of his death appeared in *The Aeronautical Journal* of April 1904 alongside a piece on aerial screw propellers!

The late Sir Edwin Arnold

It is with sorrow we have to announce the death of an illustrious and esteemed member of the Council of the Aeronautical Society of Great Britain. On March 24, Sir Edwin Arnold Author of "The Light of Asia" breathed his last. In the many biographical sketches of the poet that have been published, and which have so ably detailed his literary work and other pursuits, it has escaped the pen of writers that in addition to the wide range of subjects that Sir Edwin Arnold's sympathies embraced was the science of aeronautics. This fact it becomes the special duty of this journal to record . . .

In the *Daily Telegraph* of March 25 there appeared an excellent and heartfelt account of the life and labours of Sir Edwin Arnold . . . Amongst the traits of personal character mentioned in this eulogy is his "temper of imperturbable sweetness" noted in his "sunny optimism". These qualities made it possible for him to fight political battles with vigour, but not with rancour or unfriendliness of speech, so that the words of his pen seemed an expression of his own translation of the Buddhistic rule:

> *Govern the lips*
> *As they were palace doors, the King within:*
> *Tranquil and fair and courteous be all words*
> *Which from that presence win.*

Clearly the person who wrote the tribute in *The Aeronautical Journal* was very well versed with *The Light of Asia* because the piece ended with lines from Book the Eighth where Arnold is explaining the 'Eightfold Path'. The lines quoted refer to the Third element of it, relating to 'Right Discourse'.

Arnold was cremated and three of his sons and his daughter were at the funeral, which was a small and private affair, with the Japanese envoy to the UK present. Lady Arnold did not attend as she was in mourning. Wreaths were placed on behalf of the royalty of Bhavnagar, which Arnold had described as a 'model native principality' after his visit there in December 1885. His remains were later placed in the chapel of University College at Oxford, where he had studied and to which he was devoted. In January 1882, following a visit to his alma mater, he had written in *The Athenaeum:*

Mother! Mild mother! after many years—
So many that the head I bow turns gray—
Come I once more to thee, thinking to say
In what far lands, through what hard hopes and fears,
'Mid how much toil and triumph, joys and tears,
I taught thy teaching; and, withal, to lay
At thy kind feet such of my wreaths as may
Seeem the least withered. But what grown child dares
Offer thee honours, Fair and Queenly one!
Tower-crowned, and girdled with thy silver streams,
Mother of ah! so many a better son?
Let me but list thy solemn voice, which seems
Like Christ's, raising my Dead; and let me be
Back for one hour —a boy—beside thy knee.

The urn containing Arnold's ashes continues to be in the chapel of Oxford's University College, bearing this inscription:

In Memory of

Sir Edwin Arnold, M.A., K.C.I.E., C.S.I.
Sometime member of this College,
and Principal of the Deccan College,
Poona.

Born, June 10th 1832
Died, Marc 24th 1904
Whose ashes are here deposited.

Newdigate Prizeman, 1852

He found his sympathy with
Eastern religious thought
Inspiration for his great
Poetical Gifts

The urn containing Arnold's ashes, still kept in chapel of University College, Oxford University. This is the only interment of ashes to have taken place within the chapel.

Incidentally, the University College Chapel also contains a memorial to another Englishman who had founded the Asiatic Society in Calcutta in 1784 and had, amongst his numerous accomplishments, also translated the *Hitopadesa* and the *Gitagovinda* as Arnold had—Sir William Jones. Jones' 'most substantial literary work', *Sacontala: The Fatal Ring,* published in 1789, had transfixed Europe much like how the *The Light of Asia* would exactly ninety years later.[7]

It was perhaps around the time of Arnold's death that what Patrick Olivelle has called 'one of the few exciting Indiana Jones-like moments in the rather drab history of ancient Indian scholarship' took place:[8] 'the handover of the complete manuscript of the text of the *Arthashastra* written in Grantha script by a pandit from Tanjore whose name is unfortunately not known to Dr. R. Shamasastry, the chief librarian at the Mysore Government Oriental Library [in Mysore]'. It was too bad that Arnold was not around as Shamasastry went on to publish his translations in 1905, 1909 and finally as a book in 1915. The publication of the *Arthasastra* would revolutionalize our thinking of the times during which the Buddha's teachings first became what we call Buddhism.

Eight months after Arnold's death, on 4 November 1904, the *Indian Opinion,* brought out in Durban by Gandhi, carried this notice to its readers:

THE EDWIN ARNOLD MEMORIAL

We have received a copy of the circular issued by the Edwin Arnold Memorial Committee:

> The Committee think that the most fitting tribute to Sir Edwin's work would be one linking his name with his great services to Eastern literature. It was his privilege by the gift of poetry as well by his graphic and illuminating prose writings on oriental manners, customs and events, to bring to the peoples of the West in Europe and America, a fuller knowledge of the peoples of the East, thus creating a reciprocal interest and sympathy which cannot fail to contribute to the welfare and happiness of both . . . They therefore propose to endow a scholarship or scholarships, or found prizes at the University of Oxford for proficiency in Oriental literature.

The Committee include the name of the Right Honourable Lord Brassey, as Chairman, His Highness the Aga Khan, Sir M.M.

Bhownaggaree, Sir George Birdwood, the Right Honourable Joseph Chamberlain, the Viscount Hayashi, Mr. Rudyard Kipling and others. Subscriptions may be sent to Messrs Henry S. King and Co., at 65, Cornhill, London. If any of our readers would send their subscription to us, we would be pleased to acknowledge them in Indian Opinion and forward them to the Treasurers from time to time. The services of Sir Edwin to the East and West have not been sufficiently appreciated. Time alone would show the measure of those services. The Light of Asia alone has left on the Western mind an indelible impression for good. It has been said that he missed the Poet Laureateship because of the Oriental turn in his mind. We hope, therefore, that our readers, both European and Indian, will largely contribute to the Memorial Fund.

About 650 pounds would be raised by the Edwin Arnold Memorial Committee to fund a scholarship at Oxford. Gandhi himself would contribute half a pound. One of Gandhi's closest associates in South Africa in those years was the Englishman H.S.L. Polak, who was not only an ardent theosophist but had been impacted by both *The Light of Asia* and *The Song Celestial* before he had become part of Gandhi's life.[9] It is not known, however, whether he too had made a contribution to the Memorial Fund.

A contribution to the Memorial Fund also came from the Viceroy in Calcutta, Lord Curzon, with a statement that said:

> Sir Edwin was one of those whose work draws closer together the East and the West or, at any rate, those portions of the East and West whose destinies are inseparably united; and in all that he said and wrote about India he always seemed to me to combine great sympathy with imagination. It has given me pleasure to see that the proposed memorial is already being well taken up in India.

Curzon had been an admirer of Arnold. In 1902 Curzon had visited Buddha Gaya and tried his best to ensure that Arnold's vision for the Mahabodhi Temple—that of control by Buddhists—became a reality. At one stage, as a compromise, he had even suggested that the shrine be held in trust by the government. But his long and learned notings on file notwithstanding, the Mahant was powerful enough to rebuff Curzon's determined efforts.[10] A few months before his death Arnold had written a long panegyric called 'The Viceregal Rule of India'[11] in which he would provide portraits of each top British administrator going back to Robert Clive and ending up with Curzon. It was Arnold through and through—an unabashed, unapologetic and almost entirely uncritical admirer of these men.

The memorial for Arnold that both Gandhi and Curzon supported enthusiastically was to take the form of a scholarship at Oxford, intended for the study of Oriental Languages and Literature, and mainly for candidates for the Indian Civil Service 'or other Service of the Crown in Eastern Lands'. The scholarship would continue to be awarded right up until the 1980s.

Of the people who promoted the Edwin Arnold Memorial Fund, Joseph Chamberlain was a very prominent politician whose son Neville would gain much notoriety in 1938 for his appeasement of Hitler. Rudyard Kipling was well—Rudyard Kipling—who would win the Nobel Prize for Literature in 1907 after having been nominated for it by Arnold in 1903 and 1904.[12] Soon after *The Light of Asia* had first appeared in July 1879, Kipling, then in school, became 'an apostle of Buddha or Arnold for a span . . . and used to declaim very finely certain portions about "om mani padmi hum" or words to that effect'. For a while he also preached reincarnation to his schoolmates. His fondness for *The Light of Asia* had been created by his father Lockwood Kipling, who was, between 1875 and 1892, the curator of the Lahore Museum that housed Gandharan sculptures of the Buddha.[13]

R.J. Jackson has the distinction of being the first Buddhist missionary in England. Just about two years after Arnold's death, Johnson announced from the famous soapbox at London's Hyde Park that he was a practising Buddhist.[14] He was joined at these public lectures by one Colonel J.R. Pain who had served in the British Army in Burma. As they found interest growing, they opened a bookshop for the sale of Buddhist literature and also founded the first Buddhist Society in England. Jackson's interest in and devotion to Buddhism had been kindled after reading *The Light of Asia* and the Dhammapada.

During Arnold's lifetime, translations of *The Light of Asia* had appeared in Bengali, Dutch, German, Russian, Marathi and Telugu in that order. But very soon after his death new translations would begin appearing. In 1905 itself there was *Swiatlo Asji* in Polish by Wojciech Szukiewicz, who was a poet and translator as well. In later years he would become the president of the Polish Emigration Society. In 1906, the first volume of *Svetlo Asie* in Czech by Frantisek Prachar would be published, to be followed by the second volume a year later. Prachar would have another edition in 1910. Prachar is considered to be 'an eccentric character' who self-published a bunch of quite fascinating poetry, full of exotic motifs and fantastic stories. He was also into science, especially mathematics and physics.[15] The Theosophical Society would also bring out *The Light of Asia* in Bulgarian.

In 1907, Cambridge University announced the subject for the annual Le Bas Essay Prize with this forbidding title:

An Appreciation of the Chief Production of Anglo-Indian Literature in the Domain of Fiction, Poetry, Drama, Satire, and Belles-Lettres, during the Eighteenth and Nineteenth Centuries, with an Estimate of the Chief Writers in those Spheres, and a Consideration of the specially Anglo-Indian Features of the Literature.

Those days the term 'Anglo-Indian' was applied to Britishers who had worked in or on India. The prize was won by Edward Farley Oaten and the essay was published commercially in 1908 as *A Sketch of Anglo-Indian Literature*.[16] Oaten covered some hundred and a fifty authors and poets, including a few Indian ones. But, after a chapter called 'Beginnings' where he discussed William Jones and John Leydon, he singled out only two others for *exclusive* chapters each—Sir Edwin Arnold and Rudyard Kipling. Oaten saw Arnold as the legitimate successor to William Jones, who he admitted was a greater linguist and Orientalist than poet. On Arnold he wrote:

> During the last fifty years many an eye and mind have been directed upon the religion of Buddha. The researches of Max Mueller and others have interpreted to the West this Eastern faith. What these have done for the metaphysician and the student of comparative religion, Sir Edwin Arnold has done for the lover of poetry. Religion must always be poetic, and nowhere more so than in the East, and few have realized this more vividly than Sir Edwin Arnold . . . As the truest and most sympathetic interpretation of Eastern religion in the numbers of the West, The Light of Asia holds an assured place in Anglo-Indian literature, and also, we may dare to hope, a not unhonoured rank among the masterpieces of British poets.

Oaten then took up some of Arnold's other works like *The Song Celestial*, *Indian Idylls* and The *Secret of Death* and returned to *The Light of Asia* at the end, saying:

> Though the excessive sweetness of his work sometimes cloys, and it is often difficult to breathe in the Oriental atmosphere of his poems, we may reasonably hope that a certain length of life will be given to his masterpiece.

If more than a century is considered 'a certain length of life', Oaten's wish expressed three years after Arnold had passed away would be more than fulfilled, as we shall see as we go along. Oaten would have a long life, passing away in 1973 at the age of eighty-eight but not before earning for himself a niche in the history of India's freedom movement. In 1913, he went to the Presidency College in Calcutta to teach. In 1916, a young Indian student would be expelled from the College for his complicity in beating up Oaten, who he had heard had manhandled some Indian students. Many years later Oaten would recall:

Did I once suffer, Subhas, at your hands?
Your patriot heart is stilled, I would forget!
Let me recall but this, that while as yet
The Majesty that you had once challenged in your land
Was might; Icarus-like your courage planned
To mount the skies, and storm in battle set
The ramparts of High Heaven to claim the debt
Of freedom owed, on plain and rude demand.
High Heaven yielded, but in dignity

Like Icarus, you sped towards the sea
Your wings were melted from you by the sun,
The genial patriot fire, that brightly glowed
In India's mighty heart, and flamed and flowed
From her Army's thousand victories won.

The expelled student, the courageous freedom fighter who had met an untimely death in an air crash in 1945 which Oaten was lamenting was, of course, Netaji Subhas Chandra Bose.

It was not only *The Light of Asia* that would keep Arnold's name alive even after his death. A slim monograph he had written way back in 1887 called *Death—and Afterwards* had proved to be extremely popular and its fifteenth edition would be published in 1907. Arnold's thinking on death had been shaped decisively by *The Song Celestial* and, in fact, the booklet begins by recalling what Krishna famously tells Arjuna in Verse 20, Chapter II of the Bhagavad Gita:

Na Jayate, Mriyate Va Kadachin
Nayam Bhutva Bhavita Va Nubhuyah.
Ajo Nityashashvatoyam Purano
Na Hanyate Hanyamane Sharire.

Never the spirit was born, the spirit will cease to be never;
Never was time it was not; End and Beginning are dreams!

Birthless and deathless and changeless remaineth the spirit for ever;
Death hath not touched it all, dead though the house of it seems!

In 1909 there was major archaeological discovery in the Indian sub-
continent. Relics of the Buddha were found near Peshawar, which
is in today's Pakistan. These discoveries led to renewed debate on
India's ancient Buddhist heritage and inevitably *The Light of Asia*
would also be recalled. The *Times of India*, for instance, would write
on 19 September 1909:

> It is nevertheless not uncommon to read in the writings not only
> of popular writers but of serious scholars the central principle of
> Buddhism described as empty Nothingness. Against this view which
> was all but universal at the time when Sir Edwin Arnold wrote his
> magnificent poem, he entered his most earnest protest. He refused
> to accept that a third of mankind would even have been brought
> to believe in blank abstractions, or in Nothingness as the issue and
> crown of Being . . . The story of Kisagotami, whom the Master sent
> in quest for five grains of mustard-seed from a house where no one
> had ever died when she came to him praying that he would call her
> dead child to life, is familiar to readers of the "Light of Asia" . . . . . .

The story of Kisagotami is one of the most famous in all of Buddhist
literature, and Arnold captures what happens when she does what
the Buddha has asked her to do and returns empty-handed, wiser:

"My sister! thou hast found," the Master said,
"Searching for what none finds—that inner balm
I had to give thee. He thou lovedst slept
Dead on thy bosom yesterday: today
Thou know'st the whole wide world weeps with thy woe;
The grief which all hearts share grows less for one.
Lo! I would pour my blood if it could stay
Thy tears and win the secret of that cure
Which makes sweet love our anguish, and which drives

O'er flowers and pastures to the sacrifice—
As these dumb beasts are driven—men their lords,
I seek that secret: bury thy child"

The relics found at Peshawar triggered a remarkable French artist of
Russian descent who had been travelling in the sub-continent with
her mother into action. Sophia Egoroff is a completely forgotten
figure now but was very well known in Buddhist and other circles
at least in the first two decades of the twentieth century. She had
become a Buddhist perhaps around 1902 or thereabouts, written a
biography of the historical Buddha in French, painted the Buddha
for the Museum Guimet in Paris and propagated Buddhism *in Paris.*
The Museum had been established in 1889 with its very architecture
reflecting a temple with its rotunda and pinnacle. It attracted people
from all over Europe for its collection of Buddhist art drawn from
across Asia. In 1898 it had organized a Buddhist ceremony called
'In the Name of Sakyamuni Buddha and All the Buddhas' which
created an awareness of the Buddha among the public not just in
France but in other countries as well.

Egoroff's book appeared in 1907 and two years later would be
reviewed positively by one of India's foremost scholars Satis Chandra
Vidyabhushana in *The Maha-Bodhi and the United Buddhist World,*
published by Dharmapala out of Calcutta.[17] On 24 August 1909,
Egoroff wrote to the Viceroy giving a background of herself and
took him to task for transferring the relics to, of all places, Simla.
She told the Viceroy:

> Certainly from Peshawar, where the relics were found, the true
> way was to deliver the casket containing the relics to Buddhists
> of Ceylon, Sarnath, Kusinara, Buddha-Gaya and transfer them to
> Buddha-Gaya. About the new Stupa, it is necessary to begin the
> restoration without delay.

In 1910 Egoroff's book would be published in Ceylon. It had a title
that covered a full page:

BUDDHA-SAKYA-MUNI
A HISTORICAL PERSONAGE
WHO LIVED TOWARDS
BC 390-320
THE DIVINE SOCIALIST
HIS LIFE AND PREACHINGS,
HIS SALUTARY INFLUENCE
ON THE
CIVILIZATION
OF THE
WHOLE WORLD

The British finally transferred the relics to Mandalay while retaining some of them at Peshawar itself. They can still be seen in both places. For a short while, Egoroff appeared to enjoy the patronage of Dharmapala, but there was a falling out and after that nothing much was heard of her. There is no biography of this woman[18] who did much for Buddhism a few years after Madame Blavatsky, but it is apparent from a reading of her book that she was very well conversant with *The Light of Asia*. She quotes from its Book the Eighth:

> The people of Ceylon . . . are searching their enjoyment in alcohol, they are very ignorant and spoiled and many crimes and suicides are committed in this island.

> *Shun drugs, and drinks which work the wit abuse;*
> *Clear minds, clear bodies, and no Soma juice.*

Within a few years of Arnold's death, the first Italian translation of *The Light of Asia* would appear in Turin. This was by Sforza Ruspoli, who evidently belonged to a family of theosophists. The *Theosophist*, published out of Madras, would comment on Ruspoli's work in May 1909:

> An excellent translation into Italian verse of part of the eighth book of Sir Edwin Arnold's immortal *Light of Asia*. The translator,

Sforza Ruspoli, gives first an interesting introduction, in which she points out the necessity for the West of understanding the Orient, especially the Buddhist Orient, possible alone by understanding its ideals. In no better form has this eastern idealism been summarised than in that part of Arnold's book which is here presented in translation. A terse summary of the life of the Buddha, in the light of the first seven books of Sir Edwin Arnold's poem, is also given, as well as a short summary of the Samskrt terms in the translated text. Altogether a sympathetic, useful and very pleasant production.

Ruspoli's *La parola di Buddha, dalla Luce dell'Asia* would have a second edition in 1911. She would also translate Arnold's rendering of the Dhammapada. Subsequently a translation by Eugenia Calabrese Verneau would enjoy a substantial following.

It was not only *The Light of Asia* that was being remembered after Arnold passed away. In March 1910 at the Bombay Art Society's 19th Annual Exhibition, Mahadev Vishwanath Dhurandhar won top honours for a painting by an Indian artist. His theme was the following lines from the very first chapter of *The Song Celestial*:

> *Arjun, whose ensign badge*
> *Was Hanuman the monkey, spake this*
> *thing*
> *To Krishna The Divine, his charioteer:*
> *"Drive, dauntless one, to yonder open*
> *ground*
> *Betwixt the armies".*

Dhurandhar was a noted and prolific artist of that era who retired from the J.J. School of Art, the same school where Lockwood Kipling, the father of the famed novelist, had served as its first Dean. There has been a revival of interest in him in recent years, and his watercolour of 1910, inspired by *The Song Celestial*, is at the Sangli Museum.

Watercolour by M.V. Dhurandhar based on The Song Celestial, *1910 now at the Sangli Museum, made available to me by Tasneem Mehta.*

At the end of the first decade of the twentieth century, Hugh Walker's scholarly *The Literature of the Victorian Era* would appear. This is still considered a landmark reference for that period. Walker, a university educator and author of various books on English literature, summed up the contemporary view of critics on Arnold thus:

> For more than twenty years Edwin Arnold had written little poetry, and he was scarcely known outside journalistic circles before the publication of his Light of Asia in 1879. At once it lifted him into fame; but his success was at least as much due to the rare felicity and timeliness of the subject as to the merits of the poet. The theme was great, and it was new. Arnold said with truth that, a generation before, practically nothing was known in Europe about Buddhism and even when he wrote knowledge was confined to scholars. Max Mueller's translation of the Rig-Veda, completed

only five years earlier, was neither attractive nor accessible to the multitude; and the works of other scholars were similarly esoteric.

Of course, it is a trifle unfair to say, as Walker does, that Arnold's poetic output was nondescript prior to 1879. His translations of the *Gitagovinda* and the *Hitopadesa* were not to be scoffed at and have stood the test of time. But Walker's essential point, that the timing of *The Light of Asia* was crucial to its phenomenal success, is absolutely spot on.

Notes

1. Derek Scott email communication, 9 July 2020
2. All accounts of Arnold's life including Wright's biography mention Katherine as his only daughter. Yet *The Edwin Arnold Birthday Book* published in America in 1884 was edited by Katherine Lilian Arnold *and* Constance Arnold, who are identified in the title page as 'his daughters'. It has proved impossible to solve this mystery.
3. Rao (2016)
4. I owe the information on Rama Rao to Mitter (2007).
5. Kemper (2015)
6. In 1882, the greatest late Victorian writer of nautical novels William Clark Russell had dedicated one his books called *My Watch Below* to Arnold thus:

    > A true friend of the sailors; and a writer whose name I am proud to associate with a volume that owes its existence to his generous encouragement . . .

7. Georg Foster's translation of this work by Kalidasa into German in 1791 would trigger an 'Indomania' amongst German literary personalities beginning with none other than Goethe himself. As for William Jones, while he had magnificent achievements to his credit, he also got some things horribly wrong, as later scholarship would reveal. For instance, he believed that the Scandinavian god Odin was the same as Buddha and that Odin's rites were imported into India at nearly the same time.
8. Olivelle (2013)
9. Allen (2017). Polak would hand over the original copy of *The Song Celestial*, which he and Gandhi used to read together after dinner in

South Africa, to the Mahatma's son Devadas Gandhi in June 1948. I owe this information to Gopal Gandhi.

10. Curzon's actions in this regard have been discussed in Lahiri (2012).

11. *The Windsor Magazine*, 1903

12. The sole nominator of Kipling for the Nobel Prize in 1903 and 1904 was Sir Edwin Arnold.

13. Information on Kipling and Arnold is from Allen (2007). Paskins (2017) is the most comprehensive treatment of the impact of Buddhism, including that of Arnold, on Kipling, whose *Kim* has a distinct Buddhist theme.

14. Kemper (2015)

15. I owe this information to Helena Capkova's email communication, 21 June 2020.

16. Oaten (1908)

17. Vol XVII April & May 1909

18. There is a brief mention of her in Turner, Cox and Bocking (2020).

SECTION III

14

The 1910s: Translations of *The Light of Asia* in South India, Rabindranath Tagore, Channing Arnold and More

So far, *The Light of Asia* had been translated into Bengali, Tamil and Telugu in India. This decade would see it burst forth in Malayalam and Tamil. It would also be rendered into Danish. And Arnold's third son would hit the headlines in Burma while his father would himself once again be back in the news.

Sometime in 1908 or thereabouts, Channing Arnold went to Burma as editor of the *Rangoon Times*. He had had wide journalistic experience writing for both British and American papers. But he clashed with the proprietors and quit to launch another publication called *Burma Critic*. In June 1912, G.P. Andrew, then Deputy Commissioner and District Magistrate of Mergui, sued Channing Arnold for criminal libel. In April 1912, Channing Arnold had written that Andrew had conspired with the District Superintendent of Police to bury a case involving the abduction and rape of an eleven-year-old Malay girl by their friend Captain McCormick, who was an English rubber planter.

Channing Arnold was convicted and sentenced to a year's imprisonment. The case attracted a lot of attention. The fact that he was taking up cudgels against the ruling establishment won him many admirers in Burma and India. He had his supporters in England too on the grounds that the case against him gravely affected press freedom. The fact that he was the son of the author of *The Light of Asia* would almost invariably be mentioned when references were made to him. The *Muhammodun* of Madras of 21 October 1912 reflected the unanimous view in India, Burma and Ceylon:

Mr [Channing] Arnold has a two-fold claim on us. First, he is
the son of Sir Edwin Arnold, the renowned author of the *Light
of Asia*. Second, since his arrival in Burma as the editor of the
Rangoon Times, nearly four years ago, he has shown himself to be
one of those few Anglo-Indians who hold independent views and
who sympathise with the aspirations of the Indians. When his
period of contract with the *Rangoon Times* was over, he became
the part proprietor of the *Burma Critic* and it was in that capacity
that he wrote the article that became the subject matter of the
complaint.

After serving four months of his sentence in Rangoon, he was freed
by the Viceroy. On his release, Channing Arnold told a great public
reception that had been organized in his honour that he believed
in the British Raj as it was not possible to find a more humane
government anywhere else in the world but, at the same time, he also
wanted to uphold the principles of justice and fair play. Meanwhile
an appeal had also been filed in the Privy Council in London on his
behalf. The Privy Council would, however, dismiss the plea in April
1914. The Channing Arnold case is still studied by students and
scholars of British rule in Burma.[1]

Just a year before Channing Arnold's case, the British had
brought a case against U Dhammaloka for sedition. Dhammaloka,
the first Westerner to be ordained as a Buddhist in Burma, had
been vociferous in his attacks on Christian missionaries and English
officials leading loose lifestyles in Burma. He was sentenced but soon
left the country. Dhammaloka, who had converted to Buddhism,
is the subject of an enthralling book published in 2020 called *Irish
Buddhist: The Forgotten Monk Who Faced Down the British Empire.*[2]
It is more than likely—I would say certain—that Dhammaloka and
Channing Arnold would have known each other but unfortunately
no evidence of that acquaintance seems to have survived.

Dhammaloka was made famous in America especially when his
ordination was covered by Mrs Everard Cotes for the widely read
American publication *Harper's Monthly Magazine.* The conversation

between her and the new Buddhist reveals the extent to which some lines from *The Light of Asia* had entered the popular consciousness. This conversation took place in 1902. Cotes reported:[3]

> . . . I grasped at the inevitable question. "Can you tell me what nirvana is?" I asked.

> His eyes darkened again with his spiritualized Irish smile. "I don't know as I could explain it, but if I maybe could, ye wouldn't understand," he said. "One thing's certain, it don't mean annihilation."

> *"If any teach Nirvana is to cease,*
> *Say unto such they lie;*
> *If any teach Nirvana is to live,*
> *Say unto such they err."*

> I quoted, and Oo-Dhamma-Nanda [Oates referred to Dhammaloka by this name] said, "That's about it".

A Canadian journalist was recalling lines from Book the Eighth of *The Light of Asia* in Rangoon almost a quarter of a century after its publication.

In late-February 1912, a play called *Buddha* was staged at the Royal Court Theatre in London. This was produced by William Poel, the noted theatre figure best known for his presentations of Shakespeare. The play was adapted for stage by S.C. Bose. It has been speculated that he was Sarat Chandra Bose, the elder brother of Subhas Chandra Bose, and later to become a prominent figure in the Indian freedom movement himself.[4] Sarat Chandra Bose was indeed in London at that time studying law. The evidence, however, is not conclusive.[5] *Buddha* was a significant success. The driving force behind it was Kedar Nath Das Gupta, who had come to London in 1907 fleeing possible police action against him in Calcutta for having been a revolutionary there. In 1912, Das Gupta would also set up

the Indian Art and Dramatic Society, which organized an evening
dedicated to the works of Rabindranath Tagore in his presence at
the Royal Albert Hall. Tagore would win the 1913 Nobel Prize in
Literature for his collection of songs called *Gitanjali*.[6]

Tagore, the poet of Indian nationalism, was India's pre-eminent
cultural and literary personality of the twentieth century. The
influence of the Buddha on his poetry and his novels has been much
studied and written about. This influence came about in diverse
ways. His immediate family was steeped in Buddhist study. In 1859
his father Debendranath Tagore had been to Ceylon and had come
back with not just knowledge of but keen interest in the Buddha's
life and his teachings. He wrote *Sakya Muni O Nirvan Tattvai* in
1882. Satyendranath Tagore, Rabindranath's elder brother, who had
accompanied their father to Ceylon, wrote *Bauddha Dharma* in 1901.
The Brahmo Samaj, of which the Tagore family was an integral part,
had also taken up the study of the Buddha's teachings. A very early
influence regarding the Buddha on Rabindranath Tagore was that of
Rajendralala Mitra, who has figured in this narrative earlier.

In January 1922, Rabindranath Tagore would visit Bodh Gaya
and issue this statement:

> I am sure it will be admitted by all Hindus who are true to their
> own ideals, that it is an intolerable wrong to allow the temple
> raised on the spot where Lord Buddha attained his enlightenment
> to remain under the control of a rival sect which can neither have
> the intimate knowledge of or sympathy for the Buddhist religion
> and its rites of worship. I consider it to be a sacred duty for all
> individuals believing in freedom and justice this great historical
> site to the community of people who still reverently carry on that
> particular current of history in their own living faith.

Rabindranath Tagore had taken *The Light of Asia* with him when
he went to Bodh Gaya. While the imprint of the Buddha is very
distinctive in many of his works, the influence of *The Light of
Asia* specifically has been traced in the poem 'Bidaye' of *Kalpana*

Kavyagrantha.[7] It has apparently never been translated into English before and is being done so for the first time here:[8]

Let me now depart,
It's time to break the bonds.
In your blissful sleep,
You shudder in dreams of separation.
At dawn your vacant eyes,
Will search and brim with glistening tears.

It's time to break the bonds.
Though Your ruby lips and sad eyes are yet to utter,
So many words of endearment.
The bird will fly across the seas
Leaving the happy nest behind.

From across the firmament I hear the call.
It's time to break the bonds.

Tagore's stance on the Mahabodhi Temple at Buddha Gaya was completely different to the one his Japanese friend and admirer Okakura Kakuzo had taken years earlier. Okakura Kakuzo was an artist who had in 1895 'issued a call for a painting competition to represent scenes from the life of the Buddha in a new form'[9]. There was an enthusiastic response and a number of works resulted, but these were 'dogged by critics' accusations of inauthenticity'. Okakura must have decided that he had to visit India to get a better sense of 'historical authenticity' to depict the life of the Buddha. In addition, he had been persuaded by a wealthy American woman, Josephine MacLeod, to join her on her journey to Calcutta to meet Vivekananda. MacLeod had been Vivekananda's ardent admirer and benefactor since 1894. Okakura was planning to host another Chicago-like World Parliament of Religions in Japan and hence his visit to the man who had been the most charismatic presence at Chicago in 1893 was most welcome.

Okakura Kakuzo reached Calcutta in early January 1902[10] and struck an instant rapport with Vivekananda and invited him to Japan. The two were in Buddha Gaya together sometime in the last week of January 1902. Vivekananda had been there sixteen years earlier. On 7 February 1902 Vivekananda told Josephine MacLeod:

> We [Okakura and he] have safely reached Benaras . . . I am rather better here than at Buddha Gaya. There was no hitch to our friend [Okakura] being admitted to the chief temple and [allowed to] touch the Sign of Shiva and to worship. The Buddhists, it seems are always admitted . . .

A few weeks later Okakura made a second trip to Buddha Gaya with another Japanese Buddhist priest Tokuno Oda, who had come to Calcutta in April 1901 as Okakura's emissary to Vivekananda. The two Japanese went to meet the Mahant to negotiate the purchase of land close to the Mahabodhi Temple. On his return to Calcutta, Okakura wrote to the Mahant on 26 April 1902 expressing his desire to 'erect a rest house [close to the Mahabodhi Temple] for followers of Mahayana Buddhism in Japan' and his willingness to purchase land at a 'fair and reasonable price' for this purpose. He had distanced himself from the 'representatives of the Hinayana Buddhism of Ceylon, Siam or other places,' who had been agitating for total Buddhist control over the Mahabodhi Temple. Okakura gave his Calcutta address as 'c/o Swami Vivekananda, the Math, Belur, Howrah'. Obviously, Vivekananda would have been in the know about Okakura's proposal, which, as it turned out, was acceptable to the Mahant as well. A few months later, on 4 July 1902, Vivekananda passed away. It is clear that Okakura was deeply influenced by Vivekananda in his views on Buddhism and its relationship with Hinduism which were at variance with Dharmapala's. Later Okakura would become an important part of Tagore's orbit for a while.

As for Sister Nivedita, born Margaret Noble, she would visit Bodh Gaya in early October 1904. Her entourage had included twenty men and women, among whom were the scientist Jagdish Chandra Bose and his wife, Rabindranath Tagore and his son, and the historian Jadunath Sarkar. She would write to MacLeod on 15 October 1904 from Rajgir:

> We have been a party of 20 spending 4 days at Bodh-Gaya . . . and I think it has been an event in all our lives . . . In the mornings we had tea by 6 and then readings—Light of Asia—Web of Indian Life[Nivedita's own book] etc, and talks. All gathered together in the great verandeh. Our Mahant is like a King. Evenings—we went out after tea—to the Temple and Tree . . .[11]

Rabindranath Tagore was not the only member of the distinguished Tagore family on whom *The Light of Asia* would have a marked influence. His nephew Abanindranath Tagore, the first Indian artist to gain international recognition just as his uncle was earning a global name for himself, had painted *Buddha and Sujata* in 1902. Partha Mitter, the noted historian of Indian art, has written that:[12]

> *Buddha and Sujata* departed from Varma's historicism [Raja Ravi Varma, who painted mythological figures]. Abanindranath chose an actual historical figure, though the Buddha here was the saviour imagined by the Orientalist Edwin Arnold. His description of the shy maiden who brought the Buddha his first nourishment was the inspiration here.

In Book the Sixth, of *The Light of Asia*, Arnold describes that transformative moment thus:

> *So,—thinking him divine,—Sujata drew*
> *Tremblingly nigh, and kissed the earth and said,*
> *With sweet face bent, "Would that the Holy One*
> *Inhabiting this grove, Giver of Good,*
> *Merciful unto me his handmaiden,*
> *Vouchsafing now his presence, might accept*

These our poor gifts of snowy curds, fresh made,
With milk as white as new-carved ivory!"

Today, about a twenty-minute walk east from the Mahabodhi Temple
in Bodh Gaya stands Sujata Stupa or Sujata Ghar that honours
this milkmaid who ended the seven years of self-mortification of
Siddhartha Gautama paving the way for his enlightenment.

The Light of Asia would not escape the psychoanalyst's gaze even
as it continued to be read and adapted for different art forms. In
1912, Carl Gustav Jung's *Psychology of the Unconscious* first appeared
in German. Four years later its English version would be published.

Buddha and Sujata by Abanindranath Tagore, 1902, inspired by
The Light of Asia. *This is from Mitter (1994)*

Jung would use these passages from the very beginning of the poem
not once but twice. In the chapter 'Symbolism of Mother and
Rebirth', Jung would write that:

> In the poetic rendering of the history of Buddha's birth by Sir
> Edwin Arnold ("The Light of Asia" p 5) the motive of an embrace
> is also found.

and go on to quote these lines from the poem's Book the First of
Arnold's epic:

> *Queen Maya stood at noon, her days fulfilled,*
> *Under a Palsa in the Palace grounds,*
> *A stately trunk, straight as a temple-shaft,*
> *With crown of glossy leaves and fragrant blooms;*
> *And, knowing the time come—for all things knew—*
> *The conscious tree bent down its boughs to make*
> *A bower about Queen Maya's majesty,*
> *And Earth put forth a thousand sudden flowers*
> *To spread a couch, while, ready for the bath,*
> *The rock hard by gave out a limpid stream*
> *Of crystal flow. So brought she forth her child . . .*

At a later stage in the chapter on 'The Dual Mother Role' where
he is elaborating on the theme of 'fertilisation through the breath
of a spirit', Jung once again recalls 'Buddha's marvellous birth story
retold by Sir Edwin Arnold' and uses these lines from Book the First
of *The Light of Asia* to prove his point:

> *Maya the Queen, asleep beside her Lord,*
> *Dreamed a strange dream; dreamed that a star from*
> *heaven—*
> *Splendid, six-rayed, in colour rosy-pearl,*
> *Whereof the token was an Elephant*
> *Six-tusked, and white as milk of Kamadhuk—*

Shot through the void, and, shining into her,
Entered her womb upon the right . . .

Jung then draws attention to what happens during Queen Maya's conception as described by Arnold:

A tender whisper pierced. "Oh ye," it said,
"The dead that are to live, the live who die.'
Uprise, and hear, and hope! Buddha is come!"
Whereat in Limbos numberless much peace
Spread, and the world's heart throbbed, and a wind blew
With unknown freshness over lands and seas.

Jung was comparing the symbolism associated with the Buddha's birth with that of Christ's and their similarity. The symbolism was needed in both cases because 'the birth of the hero is not that of an ordinary mortal but is a rebirth from the mother-spouse'.[13]

This decade would see *The Light of Asia* in more South Indian languages. It would be translated by two literary personalities who were also social activists and reformers. Their translations informed their outlook on social justice in a caste-ridden society. In 1914, Nalapat Narayana Menon published *Paurasthyadeepam*, and just a year later Kumaran Asan's *Sree Buddha Charitam* would appear. While Nalapat Narayana Menon is given credit for bringing out the first complete translation of *The Light of Asia* in Malayalam, there had actually been a partial translation earlier but it has been overshadowed. This was by Tharavathu Ammalu Amma, who was proficient in Malayalam, Tamil, English and Sanskrit. Her prose work *Buddha Caritam*, based on *The Light of Asia*, appeared in 1912. Not being satisfied with the details of the Buddha's nirvana given by Arnold in his poem, she read other books and expanded on what *The Light of Asia* had said on this transformative event.

Even though Nalapat knew Sanskrit and was aware of biographies of the Buddha in that language, he deliberately chose *The Light of Asia* to translate. He was, by his own admission, an admirer of Arnold who had chosen to translate Indian works of philosophy and literature that showed India in a glorious light. Nalapat had been very impressed by *The Song Celestial* but since there was already a Malayalam translation of the Bhagavad Gita, he chose Arnold's life of the Buddha instead to render into his mother tongue. Nalapat wrote that *The Light of Asia* gave him the courage to confront Brahminical forces in Kerala's society.

But there is some evidence that he saw *Paurasthyadeepam* as not just a literary work but also 'as an exercise of a duty in the form of faith and surrender cast upon him on account of his being a member of the Theosophical Society'. However, Narayana Menon's influence in Kerala is more because of his translation of Victor Hugo's *Les Miserables*. His *Paavangal* is considered to have not only changed the course of Malayalam fiction in a big way but also had a profound impact on young men who were to later become spearheads of the Communist movement in what is now Kerala. One of the most prominent Marxist intellectual politicians of twentieth-century Kerala, E.M.S. Namboodripad, has acknowledged his debt to *Paavangal*.

Kumaran Asan was seventeen in 1890 when he first came into contact with Sree Narayana Guru, the greatest social reformer of Kerala. Narayana Guru was to later have a transformational impact on Mahatma Gandhi as well. Both Narayana Guru and Asan belonged to the disadvantaged Ezhava community. Thereafter Asan spent five years outside Kerala—in Bangalore, Madras and Calcutta. These were the years when he was introduced to English and Sanskrit on the one hand, and Buddhist philosophy on the other. The latter must have been in the two years he spent in Kerala. In 1903, Narayana Guru started the Shri Narayana Dharma Paripalana Yogam (SNDP), which was to become a great catalyst for social transformation of Kerala's society and which continues to be a powerful social and political force even today.

Kumaran Asan (standing right) with Sri Narayana Guru (seated centre), the founder of the great reformist organization SNDP in Kerala. (Source: Wikipedia)

Asan was the first General Secretary of the SNDP for sixteen years, and also the editor of its journal *Vivekodayam*. He started work on the translation in 1908 and published the first two cantos seven years later. The next two appeared in 1917. The fifth canto would be published posthumously in 1929 by his wife. Subsequently, the last three cantos would also be translated by a noted woman poet Muthukulam Parvathi Amma, who would be publish them under the same name, *Sree Buddha Charitam*, in 1947. Asan exercised such a pull that yet another noteworthy figure of Malayalam literature Vennikulam Gopala Kurup translated the sixth and seventh cantos to continue with Asan's work. He would publish them in 1962 as *Siddharthacaritam*.

One person on whom Asan's translation had a profound impact was Sugathakumari, a very popular poet herself and an environmental crusader. She told me that she had been reading *Buddha Charitam* since she was seven or eight, even though she has read *The Light of Asia* in the original only in parts. When I asked her how Asan's poem had impacted her life as a poet and as an activist, she responded:

> Filled my life with compassion, not only for human beings but also for birds, animals, trees, rivers. I think that compassion is behind everything in my life as an activist.

Sugathakumari passed away in December 2020. *The Light of Asia* has held a special fascination for poets in Malayalam. There would be other translations of which mention should be made of the one by 'Mahakavi' M.P. Appan, whose *Divya Dipam* appeared in 1936. It would be reprinted in 1973.

A third book influenced by *The Light of Asia* and that was linked with social reform would be published in Tamil in 1918. This was *Siddharthan* by A. Madhaviah, who, as I have mentioned earlier, had in 1898 taken a first crack at translating Arnold's poem in a Tamil magazine. *Siddharthan* was, however, a full-fledged work in prose. Madhaviah was brought up in an orthodox Tamil Brahmin family but it is clear from his 1898 effort that he was beginning to change and rebel in his late teens itself.

While having admiration for ancient Hindu philosophy and literature, he openly challenged the caste system. Believing that Sanskrit was an instrument of caste oppression and discrimination, he wrote *Siddharthan* in chaste Tamil, free from influences of Sanskrit. In his preface, Madhaviah mentions that years earlier he had been impressed by U.V. Swaminathan's *Buddhar Charitram* and Edwin Arnolds' *The Light of Asia*. His biographer calls *Siddharthan* 'a remarkable work despite a few problems'.[14] There would be another socially impactful Tamil translation of *The Light of Asia* in 1940, which I will take up later.

Two of the greatest social reformers Tamil society has seen in the late nineteenth and early twentieth centuries were Iyothee Thass and P. Lakshmi Narasu. Thass was influenced greatly by Olcott and the Theosophical Society. With Olcott's help, Thass went to Colombo and became a Buddhist in 1898, and set up the South Indian Buddhist Society in Madras. He would publish *Buddha—Light Beyond Day and Night* in 1899. Laksmi Narasu, Thass' contemporary, was a rationalist and had been in touch with the Austrian physicist Ernest Mach, who had been drawn to Buddhism. He was also a close friend of Dharmapala. In recent years there has been a substantial revival of scholarly interest in both Iyothee Thass and Lakshmi Narasu, who frontally attacked the edifice of the caste hierarchy in Tamil society.[15]

P. Lakshmi Narasu (left) & Iyothee Thass. They were two of the greatest social reformers of Madras in the early twentieth century who took inspiration from The Light of Asia. *(Source: Wikipedia)*

Arnold's work circulated much in Madras those days and was widely read. It fed into the larger public exchange of views on Buddha and his role as a social emancipator. It must have played a role in popularizing the Buddha story both for those who were part of these debates and for those to whom the figure of the Buddha was appealing. One important figure who ties Thaas, Lakshmi Narasu and Arnold together is Dharmanand Kosambi, who, as we know, had been profoundly impacted by the Marathi translation of *The*

Light of Asia in 1899. Kosambi would spend April–October 1903 in Madras meeting Thaas, Lakshmi Narasu and others virtually on a daily basis.

Thaas had started a Tamil weekly in June 1907 called *Oru Paisa Tamizhan*. On 12 November 1913, it carried a news item that translated reads thus:

> From the *West Coast Spectator*, a magazine from Malabar, we are delighted to note that Sir Edwin Arnold's verse adaptation of Bhagavan Buddha's canon, The Light of Asia is being translated into Malayalam. It is learnt that the renowned Malayalam scholar Nalapat Narayana Menon's rendering into Malayalam is to be published in a month or two. The time has come even for the Malayalam world to be enlightened by the Bhagavan's canon.

This is the same translation that I had highlighted a little earlier. There is no doubt that Thaas was more than familiar with *The Light of Asia*. But he did not go deep to unravel Arnold's take on Buddhism as much as he did with, for instance, Max Mueller's take on Buddhism. This is probably because Thass understood Arnold's commitment to see Buddhism in its own right than through the Brahminical prism as Max Mueller had done.

As far as Lakshmi Narasu is concerned, his *Essence of Buddhism* would be published in 1907 with a preface by Dharmapala. In 1948 it would have a third edition with a preface by no less a person than Dr B.R. Ambedkar himself. At the very end of his much-acclaimed book, Lakshmi Narasu writes:

> Buddhism denies as Isvara [God], and the latter cannot, therefore, be its goal and resting point. The Buddhist's goal is Buddhahood, and the essence of Buddhahood is Dharmakaya, the totality of all those laws which pervade the facts of life, and whose living recognition constitutes enlightenment . . . Dharmakaya signifies that the universe does not appear to the Buddhist as a mere mechanism, but as pulsating with life. Further, it means that

the most striking fact about the universe is its intellectual aspect
and its ethical order, specially in its higher reaches. Nay more, it
implies that the universe is one in essence and nowhere chaotic or
dualistic.

> *"Before beginning, and without end*
> *As space eternal and as surety sure,*
> *Is fixed a power divine which moves to good,*
> *Only its laws endure: (Light of Asia, Book VIII).*

Coincidentally, these were the very lines from his poem that Arnold
had quoted to his Japanese audience two decades earlier in Tokyo to
demonstrate the total compatibility between Buddhism and modern
science as it was then evolving.

Another very important figure of twentieth-century Tamil
literature was Ramaswamy Krishnamurthy, who was better known
as Kalki Krishnamurthy. He was a novelist, short-story writer,
journalist and social commentator as well. In 1976, his biography by
M.R.M. Sundaram was published, and this has continued to be in
print. In *Ponniyin Pudalvar* (*The Son of Cauvery*), Sundaram writes
of Krishnamurthy's neighbour in Thanjavur, Ayyaswami Iyer, who
became his guardian when his father died when the future author
was just nine years old. Iyer loved his books just as other people
loved their land, or property or children. According to Sundaram,
books were Iyer's assets and the treasury contained many Tamil
and English books, including 'Edwin Arnold's *The Light of Asia*.
Krishnamurthy acquired his love for reading from Iyer.

The First World War officially ended on 11 November 1918.
Five months earlier, *The Light of Asia* was staged in Hollywood[16]
thanks to the munificence of Christine Weatherhall Stevenson, a
wealthy theosophist from Philadelphia. This ran for thirty-five
performances at the Krotona Stadium in the upper gardens of the
Krotona Institute of the Theosophical Society. The renowned actor
Walter Hampden, referred to by some as the 'Dean of American
Theatre', played the role of the Buddha. Ruth St. Denis, a modern

dance innovator, choreographed and artists from the Denishawn School that she had founded also featured. One person who was moved by what she had *heard* at the Krotona Theatre but alas not seen because she was blind was Helen Keller, who later wrote that she had 'enjoyed *The Light of Asia* very much' and that she had realised 'anew that the art of being kind is the greatest thing in this sad old world'.[17]

The script itself was by Georgina Jones Walton, the daughter of a US Senator, active theosophist and very soon to become Sister Daya. She was amongst the foremost disciples of Swami Parmananda. Parmananda, in turn, had been Vivekananda's protégé and had established the Vedanta Centre in Boston in 1909. A decade later Hampden would take *The Light of Asia* to New York, but that performance would invite headlines like 'Buddha comes to Broadway' and flop. But a year later he would be on the cover of *Time* magazine for his *Cyrano de Bergerac*.

Notes

1. For example, Saha (2017)
2. Turner, Cox and Bocking (2020)
3. Cotes (1902)
4. Chambers (2012)
5. The noted historian Sugata Bose, for instance, in an email communication dated 6 September 2020, is not convinced by the evidence pointing to his grandfather S.C. Bose being the author of the 1912 play *Buddha*. The historian Bose did not find any mention of this play in S.C. Bose's letter to his mother from London. I am still ambivalent on the authorship and feel Chambers' view cannot be dismissed summarily.
6. I owe this information on Bose and Das Gupta to Chambers (2012).
7. I owe this information on the Buddha and Rabindranath Tagore to Sen (2007).
8. I owe this translation to Prof. Amrit Sen of Visva-Bharati University and information on the original Bengali to Sabuj Kali Sen.
9. Auerback (2016)
10. Most accounts place Okakura's arrival and meeting with Vivekananda on 6 January 1902. However, there is also a version according to which he may have reached Calcutta sometime in November/December 1901.

I go with the 1902 date. There is firm evidence in the *Collected Works of Swami Vivekananda* that Okakura's first contact sent an invitation (plus 300 yen or rupees) to Vivekananda in June 1901 to visit Japan.

11. I thank Reba Som for drawing my attention to this letter and for information on Okakura's visit to Buddha Gaya with Tokuno Oda.

12. Mitter (1994)

13. I have depended on Beatrice M. Hinkle's translation of *Psychology of the Unconscious* by Dr. C.G. Jung, Moffat, Yard and Company, New York 1916.

14. Anantha Raman (2005)

15. Examples are Geetha and Rajadurai (1998), Aloysius (1998), Rajangam (2018) and Ayyathurai (2011).

16. The details are from Smith (2007).

17. *The Messenger*, October 1918, page 145, Helen Keller letter to A.P. Warrington, President of the American Theosophical Society.

15

The 1920s: *The Light of Asia* in Hindi, Film and More

The King of Siam, who was so taken up with *The Light of Asia*, had passed away in October 1910. He had been succeeded by his grandson, who became King Rama VI of Siam. King Rama VI had spent a few years in England as a Crown Prince and had befriended Maynard Willoughby Colchester Wemyss. The two kept up an unusual correspondence till the King died in 1925. Over a twelve-year period, Colchester Wemyss wrote a total of 601 letters and the King replied to most of them. They covered diverse subjects—personal, political, cultural, literary and whatever else crossed their minds. One such letter from Colchester Wymss was on 27 April 1920 and reads:

Sire—

I have now read a good bit about the Tree we have exchanged letters about: the *Ficus Religiosa*. It has quite an interesting history . . .

It is indigenous to India and is regarded by Hindus and Buddhists alike with peculiar reverence. It is known under the names of Bo, Bodhi or Pipal throughout India, Burmah, Ceylon and Siam. Its native areas included Northern and Central India and it probably first received its name of Pipal (or Prepul) during the pre-historic invasion of the Brahmin shepherds from Central Asia, who thought from the shape of its leaves that it was akin to their sacred Poplar (Pipal or Prepul). It was supposed that Gautama was reclining under one of these Trees in Behar when Truth came to him on which the Buddhist faith is founded. It was therefore called Bo or Bodhi (belonging to Buddha). The most celebrated Bo Tree is the one obtained from Behar and planted at Anuradhapura in Ceylon in 288 BC. It is still alive and an object of immense devotional interest to the Buddhists of all lands.

I find that Sir Edwin Arnold refers to the Tree in "The Light of Asia".

"The Bodhi Tree (thenceforward in all years never to fade and ever to be kept in homage of the world) beneath whose leaves it was ordained the Truth should come to the Buddha".

. . . The Ceylon Bodhi Tree must be one of the oldest living trees in the world nearly 2200 years old. There are two other trees in Italy which are said to be two described by Horace, but this would be difficult to prove. I suppose the Teak attains a very great age . . .

The letters of both the King and of Colchester Wymss have been published. In this one that I have quoted, the Englishman also asks for 'a small piece of wood . . . say two feet by six inches by six inches' for the Girls' Museum at Cheltenham College in England. Alas, that piece of wood from the Holy Tree in Siam sent to Colchester Wymss no longer exists.

By the middle of 1920, Jawaharlal Nehru's father Motilal Nehru had decided to give up his lucrative legal practice and luxurious lifestyle and become a complete Gandhian in the manner of his living. This was not just because he respected Gandhi and saw him as the undisputed political and moral leader of India but also because his own son had thrown in his lot with Gandhi wholeheartedly a couple of years earlier. In the summer of 1921, Motilal Nehru would write to Gandhi from a health resort where he was recovering from asthma:[1]

The brass cooker . . . has taken the place of two kitchens . . . a solitary servant . . . that of the old retinue . . . three small bags . . . of the mule-load of provisions . . . one square meal in the middle

of the day, that of breakfast, lunch and dinner "a la Angalaise" . . .
The shikar has given place to long walks, and rifles and guns
to books, magazines and newspapers (the favourite book being
Edwin Arnold's *Song Celestial* which is undergoing its third
reading) "What a fall was there my countryman!" But really I have
never enjoyed life better.

But this would not prevent his close friends from celebrating Motilal
Nehru's birthday five years later with a 'book tea party' at his residence
in Allahabad. Each of the invitees would represent a particular book
which was their favourite. One of Motilal Nehru's daughters' would
be *Vanity Fair*; his daughter-in-law, *Arms and the Man*; his nephew,
Al Koran; his niece, *A Joy for Ever*; one of his lawyer protégés Kailash
Nath Katju, later to be home minister of India, *Sherlock Holmes*;
P.N. Sapru, the son of one of India's top legal brains, *The Light
that Failed*; Mrs P.N Sapru, *The Scarlet Letter*; the educationist of
Allahabad, Amaranatha Jha, *The Mayor of Casterbridge*; the Principal
of St. Stephens College, New Delhi, S.K. Rudra, *A Student in Arms*;
with Motilal Nehru himself representing *The Light of Asia*.[2]

The Burdwan zamindari in Bengal had been created under
Mughal rule in 1675 and continued during British rule. In 1903, the
then Maharaja Bijoy Chand Mahatab had erected a grand Curzon
Gate in the town close to Calcutta to welcome the Viceroy. The
landmark still stands there but with a name honouring its builder.
Eighteen years later, Mahatab, a patron of literature, would write
Siddhartha, which was a series of illustrated episodes from the life
of the Buddha drawn from *The Light of Asia*. It was dedicated to
Lord Ronaldshay, the Governor of the Bengal Presidency, who
was 'a very dear friend and benefactor whom Buddhism and Indian
philosophy deeply interest'. Mahatab also thanked Lady Arnold for
'permitting me to make use of a selection of the beautiful verses from
her husband's immortal work "The Light of Asia" a copy of which
has been my companion ever since I was in my teens'.

While Mahatab produced what might be called a coffee-table
volume, another book by the same name by a German author would

appear the next year. Hermann Hesse's novel *Siddhartha* was of a totally different genre and had little to do with *The Light of Asia's* hero. Originally published in German and then in English only in 1951, it was, however, a commercial success and earned undying fame. Hesse's connection with India came through his missionary grandfather, who is still a respected name in Kerala for having produced the first Malayalam–English dictionary. The nearest Hesse came to India was Ceylon, although it is often wrongly claimed that he had visited India.

Arnold's son Channing Arnold, already known in India because of the Privy Council case in Burma, added to his reputation in this decade. In 1920, he would publish in the 'Indian Classic Series', his edited version of the *Mahabharata* and a year later of the *Ramayana*. In his preface to the *Ramayana* Channing Arnold would write:

> It is with this need in view—that the Indian school-boy should be taught English as far as possible from books dealing with Indian subjects—that the present volume is placed on the market. In the great epic, the *Ramayana* and the *Mahabharata,* Hindu boys have a rich literature of their own. These famous poems are, however, in Sanskrit which to the modern Indian school-boy is very much what Latin and Greek have been for so many generations to English school-boys . . . . . . But strangely enough, until now there seems to have been no effort to place before the Indian school-boys and girls the complete story of the poems told in English. To meet this long-felt want this volume and the *Mahabharata,* uniform with it are published.

It is no wonder, therefore, to find that these two books by Channing Arnold would be used in a number of schools in India for quite some time.[3] Three decades later, Gandhi's devoted Quaker associate Marjorie Sykes would bring them back into public reckoning. Her *The Story of the Ramayana* would appear in 1951 and three years later *The Story of the Mahabharata* would be published, both described by her as 'simplifications' of Channing Arnold's original volumes.

Longmans' Indian Classics

THE

MAHABHARATA

Being the Story of the Great Epic
told in English

BY

CHANNING ARNOLD, B.A. (Oxon)

*Author of 'The Ramayana' and 'Hitopadesa'
in Longmans' Indian Classics.*

WITH A MAP

LONGMANS, GREEN & CO.
BOMBAY, CALCUTTA, MADRAS
LONDON AND NEW YORK
All Rights Reserved
1920

Channing Arnold's telling of the Mahabharata, 1920.

As Channing Arnold was making a further name for himself, the Hindi (Braj Bhasha) translation of *The Light of Asia* would be out in 1922. This was by Acharya Ramchandra Shukla and called *Buddhacharit*. This was published by the Nagari Pracharini Sabha that had been set up in Banaras in 1893 to vigourously promote the Devanagari script for Hindi.[4]

Shukla is one of the most respected names of Hindi literature. He had been drawn to the life of the Buddha from a young age.

Acharya Ramchandra Shukla, one of the giants of Hindi literature, who translated The Light of Asia *into Hindi in 1922. This photo is circa 1938.* (Source: Family)

For years he taught Hindi at the Banaras Hindu University. *Buddhacharit* is still commended for its literary value. Sudhakar Pandey, the head of the Sabha, had this to say when *Buddhacharit* was reprinted in 1985:

> Shuklaji was a scholar of Sanskrit, Pali-Prakrit, Apbhransh, English, Bengali and several other languages. His translation of Sir Edwin Arnold's *The Light of Asia*, an iconic poetic work focusing on Bhagwan Tathagat, into Brajbhasha has met with great success. The credit for publishing this work under the title *Buddhacharit* must go to this Sabha. Undoubtedly, translation of

this volume bears a great significance of its own. However, it is Shuklaji's detailed comments on Brajbhasha, Awadhi and Khadi Boli in the Preface that brings to the fore his phenomenal insight into these languages as well as his unique ability of engaging in intense study and his penetrating critical analysis. Even today, this Preface is highly valued by researchers of these languages as a document which offers itself as a sound basis for linguistic studies and intricacies of language.

Buddhacharit had a definite and lasting impact in north India but it also appears to have resonated in Nepal as well. Chittadhar Hridaya, one of the most famous of Nepalese poets, had been sentenced to five years in jail in Kathmandu in 1941 because the ruling establishment there had deemed him a subversive. While in prison he wrote his masterpiece *Sugata Saurabha,* which was to be published in 1949 in Calcutta. Hridaya had written on the Buddha in 1925, and that is what made me curious to find out whether *The Light of Asia* may have had any influence on *Sugata Saurabha.* Here is what Todd Lewis of Holy Cross College in Boston told me:[5]

I think it is virtually certain that poet Hridaya had read a Hindi translation of this text. I hadn't thought of this until I was at a conference celebrating the Toshi Numata Book Award to my and Subarna Man Tuladhar's translation of the work that was held at the University of California-Berkeley in fall, 2011. The scholar John Strong wondered what the source was of a scene in the poet's epic in which a goatherd squirted milk from the she-goat directly into Siddhartha's mouth. (A painting by fellow prisoner Chandra Man Maskey was included in the original publication, attached.) Strong knew of no known classical source with this incident, and had thought to check in *The Light of Asia.* This was a discovery for me and illustrates how the back and forth in global culture affected modern Buddhists, even in a relatively isolated country like Nepal. In the later years of his 5 years in prison when he wrote the epic,

he was allowed books that could be regarded as religious texts. I
think it is highly likely that a Hindi *Light of Asia* made its way to
him in his cell . . .

Shukla's translation would have a lasting influence on subsequent
poets who used the Buddha as their subject. Just as the Hindi
translation of *The Light of Asia* was coming out in Banaras, a musical
drama in English in five acts based on it was published in London
in 1922. It was also called *The Light of Asia* and was by a French
aristocrat called Francois De Breteuil, who lived in Paris. Breteuil had
been influenced a great deal in his thinking on Indian philosophy by
the mystic-musician Inayat Khan and his brother Maheboob Khan.
Inayat Khan had founded the Sufi Order in the West in London in
1914, later to be called the International Sufi Movement, and had
settled near Paris. In his preface, Breteuil writes:

*The image in the Nepalese poet Chittadhar Hridaya's book on the Buddha that Todd Lewis
traced back to* The Light of Asia. *(Source: Todd Lewis)*

Edwin Arnold's magnificent translations of the inspired poems of the East proved a profound revelation to the Western World. His Light of Asia . . . was both a surprise and a delight to contemporary thought, and it was in a spirit of great reverence and gratitude that I have ventured to take this masterpiece as subject-matter and, as far as possible, as text for musical drama . . .

In 2013 the British writer Andrew Rose would write about the first great love of King Edward VIII's life as Prince of Wales.[6] The lady in question would murder her husband in London in 1923 but strike a deal with the British establishment to get herself declared innocent—by agreeing not to reveal the incriminating letters the Prince had written to her in Paris. The man who had originally introduced the two to each other was the same Breteuil who would go on to write the musical drama based on *The Light of Asia*. The drama itself appeared to have been a moderate success commercially.

Till 1936, Sind was part of the Bombay Presidency, after which it became a separate province in British India. After 1947 it became part of Pakistan. Sindhi is an unusual language in India, in that it is not attached to any specific state. Jetmal Parsram Gulrajani, an ardent theosophist and follower of Annie Besant, was one of the foremost prose-writers in Sindhi in the twentieth century. In 1923, he would publish *Purab Joti*, which was an adaptation of *The Light of Asia*. This proved to be very popular. Originally, it was written in the Perso-Arabic script but after the partition of the sub-continent it was transliterated in to the Devanagari-Sindhi script and re-published as late as 1963. Much later, in 1937, the Buddha's biography in Sindhi verse was composed by Devandas Kishinani. His *Purab Sandes* that appeared in Karachi was also derived from *The Light of Asia* and was hailed for its 'vigour of narration and appeal of sensuous images'.[7]

The first feature film anywhere in the world on the Buddha was *Buddhadev* made by the pioneer of Indian cinema Dadasaheb Phalke. It was a silent black-and-white movie that was released in 1923. Nothing more is known about it. But much more is known about the Indo-German joint venture of 1925, which was called *The*

Light of Asia in English, *Die Leuchte Asiens* in German and *Prem Sanyas* in Hindi. There would be many more films in the twentieth century on the Buddha in Japan, Korea, India and Europe, of which perhaps Bernardo Bertolucci's *Little Buddha*, released in 1993, is the most famous. But the 1925 film has its own distinctive niche in the world of cinema.

The film was the brainchild of Himanshu Rai, the producer-actor who got Franz Osten to direct it. It was shot at two locations in India—near Bodh Gaya and at one of the palaces of the Maharaja of Jaipur. The script was by Niranjan Pal and was adapted from Arnold's poem. Pal was the son of the Indian revolutionary leader Bipin Chandra Pal. The film premiered in India, the UK and Europe in April 1926. On 14 April 1926, the *Times of India* carried this report:

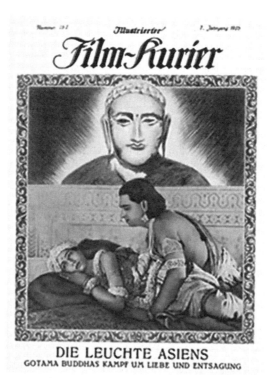

The Light of Asia *in the German film version, 1925.*
(Source: Wikipedia)

Hitherto the Light of Asia has stood to Bombay residents for tea and ham and eggs in the bleak hour before the false dawn [it was the name of a famous restaurant]. Not so now . . .

and the next day called *The Light of Asia* a 'superb film' and 'an Indian historical film of a high order', adding:

To the public of Bombay who have tired of seeing imperfect Indian films full of incongruities and anachronisms, this new picture will come as a relief in that it has attained very nearly that standard which marks western productions.

The first reference was to a very popular all-night restaurant in Bombay that has acquired iconic status, having been around for more than a century now. The film was seen in Bombay by, among others, Ruth St. Denis, who was then in the city. She praised it, saying that 'its message was of supreme human interest and that message had been most faithfully interpreted'.

That the film itself was meant primarily for Western audiences is revealed by the fact that when Gautama sees six men carrying a dead body, a popular Christian hymn 'Jesus, Still Lead On' is played.[8] However, the film was prohibited in Ceylon because of the objections of local Buddhists that it distorted Arnold's original *The Light of Asia*. It was also censored in Siam and other places. The ban in Thailand was lifted only in 1987. *Prem Sanyas* would be screened at the first International Buddhist Film Festival held during October–November 2008 and has evoked renewed interest in recent years.

Pal was to later write about the making of *The Light of Asia* in his autobiography *Such is Life*:

We launched a country-wide search [in India] for the girl to be cast as Gopa [according to some tradition Gautama's wife was called Gopa and not Yashodhara]. After having spent 10,000 rupees we had not discovered anyone, though a Goan girl had been highly recommended. We found her as much like Gopa as I am like Queen Victoria! The search ended in Calcutta where Gopa finally turned up.

Renee Smith was an Anglo-Indian girl and we came across her just when we were contemplating sending a cable to Emelka [the German production company] for German girls to play the role . . . As we were drafting the cable to be sent to Emelka, the hotel bearer said we had visitors and into the room walked a middle-aged woman with a slip of a girl, pigtails dangling down her back. Osten gasped when he was told that the girl had come in response to our advertisement. "Herr Gott Sacrament!" he whispered to me. "If the mother was a few years younger, yes, but this child?"

We were at the point of rejecting the girl when the brother-in-law, who happened to be present, suggested Renee Smith be dressed in a saree before we decided anything . . . Though we were sure it was just a waste of time, we waited for her mother to change Renee in a saree. The transformation was stunning . . . Truly the girl's whole bearing had changed with her appearance in a saree and to my mind she admirably filled Sir Edwin Arnold's classic description of Yashodhara . . .

Renee Smith was, by her own later admission, thirteen when she became Seeta Devi and London's *The Times* would say that 'the gem of the acting was the performance of Seeta Devi as princess Gopa. To see a young lady who has no trace of self-consciousness and the tricks of the film star and yet can beat the film star hollow at her own game is a rare treat.'

Sadly, while much is known of the later lives of others involved in the film, not much is known of Seeta Devi except that she acted in two other films scripted by Pal and co-produced by Rai. Rai, who played the title role, would go on to become one of the legendary figures of Indian cinema. Sarada Ukil, who played his father in the film, would become one of India's best-known artists. As for Osten, he would move to Bombay in February 1935 and direct fifteen films for Bombay Talkies, which had been set up by Himanshu Rai and his

Seeta Devi aka Renee Smith as Gautama's wife in The Light of Asia, *Indo-German silent film, 1925.*

wife the actress Devika Rani. When the Second World War broke out in September 1939, the British authorities would intern the 'German Aryan' Osten on the grounds that he was an 'undesirable enemy alien', being a member of the local Nazi party. His application for release dated 2 October 1939, backed by testimonials from Indian and British figures, to the Government of Bombay read:

> Mr. Franz Osten is 63 years of age . . . He has directed consecutive films for this company . . . He also visited India before on three occasions in 1925, 1927 and 1928 for directing THE LIGHT OF ASIA, SHIRAZ and A THROW OF DICE, the only Indian films which have been successful in the international market. THE LIGHT OF ASIA had the rare distinction of being given a command performance before their Majesties the King and Queen at the Windsor Castle [on April 26 1926]. In the production of all these three films the Government of India granted many facilities . . .

His application for release was first rejected but Franz-Osterhayr Osten was finally allowed 'to depart British India' in mid-March

1940. After Himanshu Rai's death in 1941, Devika Rani would marry the Russian Svetoslav Roerich, belonging to the famed Roerich family that had settled down in India. Svetoslav's father was Nicholas Roerich, one of whose famous paintings in 1928 was titled 'The Light of Asia'.

The year 1928 saw another painter's work on *The Light of Asia* theme. Some of Sukumar Bose's most striking wall paintings are today to be found in Rashtrapati Bhavan, which is the home-cum-office of the President of India. In February 2014, the Institute of Southeast Asian Studies, Singapore brought out *The Art of Sukumar Bose: Reflections on South and Southeast Asia*, indicative of his reach beyond India. Sometime in the 1970s, he collaborated with a noted Indian-origin dancer in Singapore, Madhavi Krishnan, for a production of *The Light of Asia*, but nothing came of that endeavour.

As *The Light of Asia* was being made into a film in India and Germany, it was also being rediscovered in Japan. In Tokyo, a week-long Lumbini Festival—named after the birthplace of the Buddha—began on 3 April 1925. It commenced with a bazaar, followed by lecture meetings, flower offerings at various places like parks, hospitals and orphanages, a flight by an aviator scattering paper lotus petals, dramas on the life of the Buddha and children carrying lanterns through the streets. The show was even more spectacular a year later. Japanese Buddhists wrote a hymn for the occasion that was to be sung not only in Japan but also across the Buddhist world— in places like Siam, Burma and Ceylon certainly but also in India. The hymn was called 'The Sunrise Comes!' and was based on the immortal last eight lines of *The Light of Asia*.

The name *The Sunrise Comes* was meant to 'invoke an image of the flag of Japan, the Rising Sun moving from East to West, an image of Japan as the "Light of Asia" restoring Buddhism to its neighbours, in the natural course of things'.[9] The Japanese would love this phrase. In March 1942, after Singapore and Java had both fallen to it in the Second World War, Japan rejected the criticism of what it called the ABCD powers (America, Britain, China and the Dutch) and proclaimed a Greater East Asia Co-Prosperity Sphere with itself as the leader, protector and 'Light of Asia'—the term chosen deliberately to imply the high ideals of the Buddha himself.

The Thais did not need to know much about the Buddha from any source other than their own lived experience as also the Jataka stories translated by the King himself. The educated elite would have had access to *The Light of Asia* in English anyway. Even so, the first Thai translation appeared in 1927, by a Lao prince from the House of Champasak by the name of Chow (Prince) Sakprasert. This translation, called *The Torch of the Continent of Asia*, was, however, not from the English but from the French version of Leon Sorg. It was not in poetic form but had been paraphrased into prose that would have allowed more lucidity to Thai Buddhist readers. The translation was made at the request of a monk named Chow Khun Phra Upali Gunupamajariya, who was also Laotian. In his preface, he suggested that Arnold had presented new information on the life of the Buddha which Thais ought to be aware of. Nidhi Eoseewong, a noted Thai academic, told me:

> The interest of the Thai elite in Sir Edwin's work was incited by new information given by the author to the Buddha's biography. This information gives credence to the historicity of the Buddha which becomes a matter of importance in the elite's response to the religious threat of Western missionaries' propagation of Christianity since the middle of the 19th century . . .

Arnold was only the second English-speaking person after Queen Victoria to be conferred with the highest royal honour in December 1879, just five months after the publication of *The Light of Asia*. The King of Siam would later also make a generous contribution to the Edwin Arnold Memorial Fund. A Thai princess by the name Daracharatsri Devakul would translate *The Light of Asia* into Thai in poetic form in 1940.

Olcott had popularized the Theosophical Society and Buddhism in Ireland during his visit there in 1889. In later years, Annie Besant being Irish herself may well have added to the appeal of the Society. Olcott's visit had been organized by one Robert Gibson, who was co-founder of Ireland's cooperative movement. Gibson was a connoisseur of butter, and when asked whether he wanted anything to read, quipped:

> Madam . . . I have the *Grocer's Gazette* and the *Light of Asia*. What more can one want?

By 1927 or thereabouts, Ireland's first Buddhist Centre was opened in Dublin by Vivian Butler Burke. She had come to Buddhism through reading *The Light of Asia*[10] and would correspond with both Tagore and Gandhi. While the poem was not translated into Irish, 'an early edition of the poem in the library of St. Patricks College at Maynooth, the headquarters of the Catholic hierarchy of bishops and a leading seminary, indicates the degree of moral panic among Catholic (and Protestant) clergy in the late nineteenth and early twentieth centuries about the popularity of *The Light of Asia*'. Arnold 'would be introduced in Ireland as author of *The Light of Asia*, and the name was given to greyhounds and racehorses—in other words, it was well-known at a more popular level'.

The 1920s also saw the beginning of the Spanish translations of *The Light of Asia*. The earliest seems to be the one published by the Theosophical Society in Barcelona in 1922. Federico Climent Terrer was a leading member of the Theosophical Society in Catalonia. Spanish interest in Blavatsky and Olcott went back to the 1880s and. Terrer's translation has been republished quite a few times, most recently in 1994. A second Spanish translation appeared five years later in Mexico, but this was in prose form. This was by Rafael Cabrera and would have dozens of editions in South America, in places like Argentina, in 1945. Cabrera was a poet who was also a diplomat. There is a memorial to him in his hometown of Puebla.

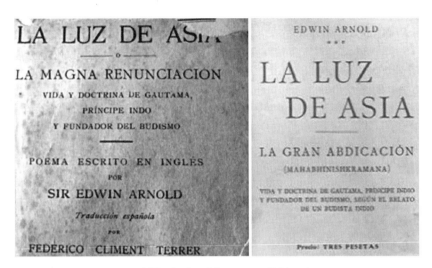

Early Spanish translations of The Light of Asia. *1922 (left) and 1928*

But even before these Spanish translations appeared, an Argentinian boy had already read *The Light of Asia* in English. In 1986, one of the greatest poets of the twentieth-century Jose Luis Borges would recall to Osvaldo Ferrari:[11]

> I was a boy and I read a poem by a fairly mediocre English poet, Sir Edwin Arnold, titled 'Light of Asia', where he recounts in fairly unremarkable verse the legend of Buddha. I remember the last lines: 'The dew is on the lotus / Rise, great sun!' and then, 'The dewdrop slips into the shining sea!' that is, the individual soul is lost in the whole. I read that poem – it was quite an effort – but those lines which I must have read around 1906 (*laughs*) have been with me ever since."

The day 9 August 1929 was catacylsmic for the Theosophical Society. That was when Jiddu Krishnamurti, heralded for two decades as the 'World Teacher', suddenly announced in the Dutch city of Oomen that he was *not* the messiah he was being proclaimed to be. Krishnamurti had been identified and picked up for future greatness on the Adyar beach in Madras by Charles Webster Leadbeater.

Thereafter Annie Besant joined the controversial Leadbeater in educating and training the Indian boy for his destined role. One of the books that had formed part of Krishnamurti's intellectual grooming was *The Light of Asia*. His authorized biographer does not make much of Krishnamurti's reading habits but recalls that sometime in September 1924, during a Theosophical Society camp at Pergine in Italy, 'he had read aloud to us *The Gospel of Buddha* told by Paul Carus and he had read *The Light of Asia*. He disclaims ever having read the Bhagavad Gita or the Gospels'.[12]

Before the decade of the 1920s was through, arguably the most controversial novel of the century was published in 1928 in Italy and a year later in France. But it would not be available elsewhere for a long time. The ban was lifted in the USA in 1959 and in the UK a year later. In India the ban still exists but it is unenforced. This book was D.H. Lawrence's *Lady Chatterley's Lover*, considered for long to be the acme of obscenity. Lawrence has spawned an academic industry and there is even a *Journal of D.H. Lawrence Studies* published annually by the D.H. Lawrence Society in the UK. Hindu and Buddhist themes are present in Lawrence's works, and one scholar has written that Lawrence's earliest contact with Buddhism came through *The Light of Asia* and 'that Lawrence absorbed Arnold's poetic exposition is clear from the early letters in which he quotes Arnold almost verbatim'.[13] This was in the 1908–1912 phase of his life, after which Lawrence began to get interested in Hinduism, yoga and theosophy.

On 26 December 1929, the *Los Angeles Times* had an announcement of an event happening that evening in the city:

COMPOSER TO BE HONORED

This evening at Mt. Washington Center, George Leibling, pianist composer, will play in honor of Swami Yogananda. Liszt's "Second Hungarian Rhapsody" will be one of the pieces. A melodramatic sketch, "The Voices of the Wind", music by Leibling, will be recited by Mrs Beulah Storrs Lewis . . .

After Vivekananda, Paramhamsa Yogananda had become the rage in America. He arrived in Boston in 1920 and very quickly established himself as a teacher of yoga and other measures of self-realisation. Leibling belonged to a celebrated musical family and had been a pupil of the famed Hungarian composer Franz Liszt. In 1900, he and Arnold had collaborated to write 'Voices of the Wind'.

A year after the First World War had started, *The Light of Asia* was recalled in London in the form of a dramatization that included detailed staging instructions, properties required, illustrated drawings for costumes and music specifically composed for the play. Quite amazingly, this dramatization would be reissued by a noted publishing firm over a century later in 2017, in a series called *Routledge Revivals* issued by the famous publisher.

SOME PHASES IN THE LIFE OF BUDDHA

TAKEN FROM

THE LIGHT OF ASIA

BY

SIR EDWIN ARNOLD

ARRANGED BY

VALERIE WYNGATE

WITH INCIDENTAL MUSIC BY	AND FOUR ILLUSTRATIONS BY
HUBERT BATH	RUPERT GODFREY LEE

Revivals. dramatization of parts of The Light of Asia.

Years later, in 1937, the Swedish composer Axel Raoul Wachtmeister would compose 'Prince Siddhartha,' an opera-oratorio in two acts and twenty scenes with the text taken mainly from *The Light of Asia*. Wachtmeister's mother had been an ardent theosophist and an intimate of Madame Blavatsky, and this must surely have had an influence on the Swedish composer's works.

Notes

1. Nanda (1963). It is somewhat curious that Jawaharlal Nehru's sister Vijaya Lakshmi Pandit, while giving a memorial lecture in London in her brother's name on June 12 1975, quoted from this very letter but mentioned not Arnold's *The Song Celestial* but *The Light of Asia*. I have gone with the Nanda version because it is corroborated by *The Collected Works of Mahatma Gandhi*, Volume 20, page 407.
2. Jha (1997). *Vanity Fair* is by William Makepeace Thackeray; *Arms and the Man* is by George Bernard Shaw; *A Joy for Ever* is by John Ruskin; *The Light that Failed* is by Rudyard Kipling; *The Scarlett Letter* is by Nathaniel Hawthorne; *The Mayor of Casterbridge* is by Thomas Hardy; and *A Student in Arms* is by Donald Hankey.
3. In May–June 1986, the noted Indian author K.R. Srinivasa Iyengar would write in *Indian Literature*, a publication of the Sahitya Akademi, New Delhi: 'For my School Certificate Course [in the Madras Presidency in the late 1920s] one of the rapid-reading texts was the condensed version of the epic by Channing Arnold'.
4. Ironically it was an Englishman, W. Ethrington, who had perhaps used the word Devanagari first in 1871 to stand for a Sanskritised Hindi, sanitized of Urdu and other 'Muslim' influences. This is discussed in Dalmia (1997).
5. Email communication, 4 May 2020
6. Rose (2015)
7. I owe much of this information to Jetley (1992).
8. Bakker (2009) has a detailed description of this film and the variations in it from Edwin Arnold's account of the life of Buddha and his teachings.
9. I owe information on the 1925 Lumbini Festival to Snodgrass (2009).
10. I owe all this information on *The Light of Asia* in Ireland to Laurence Cox, email communication 2 April 2020.
11. Borges and Ferrari (1986)
12. Lutyens (1975)
13. Doherty (1982)

16

The 1930s: Sir Edwin Arnold's Birth Centenary and More Translations of *The Light of Asia*

10 December 1930 was one the proudest days for India. On that day an Indian scientist received the Nobel Prize for Physics from the King of Sweden for his path-breaking work on the scattering of light. That evening, during the traditional banquet, C.V. Raman raised his glass full of water and, replying to the toast, spoke of the glories of ancient India and the great renunciation of the Buddha. Why he did so would become clear seventeen years later in a book of reminiscences by various personalities recalling the books that had influenced them. Raman would write:[1]

A purposeful life needs an axis to which it is firmly fixed and yet around which it can freely resolve. As I see it, the axis or hinge has been, in my own case, strangely enough, not the love of science, not even the love of Nature, but a certain abstract idealism or belief in the value of the human spirit and virtue of human endeavour and achievement. The nearest point to which I can trace the source of my idealism is my recollection of reading Edwin Arnold's great book *The Light of Asia*. I remember being powerfully moved by the story of Siddhartha's great renunciation, of his search for truth and of his final enlightenment. This was at a time when I was young enough to be impressionable, and the reading of the book fixed firmly in my mind the idea that this capacity for renunciation in the pursuit of exalted aims is the very essence of human greatness. This is not an unfamiliar idea to us in India, but it is not always

India's Nobel Laureate in Physics in 1930 C.V. Raman in conversation with Jawaharlal Nehru, India's first Prime Minister. The photograph is from the early 1950s. Both men were profoundly influenced by The Light of Asia, *with Raman acknowledging that it is one of the three books that had shaped him. (Source: Raman Research Institute)*

easy to live up to. It has always seemed to me a surprising and regrettable fact that the profound teaching of the Buddha has not left a deeper impression in the life of our country, of which he was the greatest son that ever lived.

Raman then went on to talk of Euclid's *The Elements of Euclid* and Hermann von Helmholtz's *The Sensation of Tone* as two of the great scientific books that had shaped his thinking and conduct of scientific research.[2]

The year 1932 was Arnold's birth centenary year. The London County Council had already placed its famous 'Blue Plaque' at the place where he had spent his last years. The plaque read:

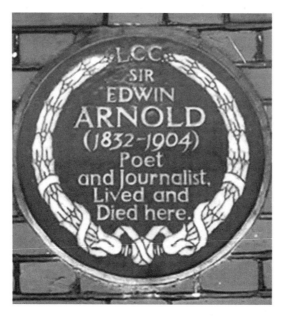

A plaque unveiled at 31 Bolton Gardens, Kensington London in 1931. Sir Edwin lived here for many years.

On 24 June 1932 newspapers in England and India marked the occasion by running articles by scholars that went over his life and career, inevitably pivoting around *The Light of Asia*. Rev. Arthur R. Slater hailed him in the *Times of India* as 'An Interpreter of Indian Thought', saying that 'the attempted analogy of the Buddha with the founder of Christian thought was resented by certain classes, but a closer knowledge of the great Indian teacher has only deepened the respect of all thinkers for his character'. The Church had clearly changed its stance since the 1880s. What is of immense value is a personal recollection *Buddhist in England* that would be offered by Arnold's youngest son in London. This was reprinted in the *Maha-Bodhi*, the monthly of the Mahabodhi Society in Calcutta as well. It is worth quoting him at length for the insights he gives into Arnold's personality:

Obliged by circumstances to remain under grey Western skies and labour for more than forty years in London on the staff of the

"Daily Telegraph", his heart remained in India and every moment of his scanty leisure was devoted to the study of her languages, religions and philosophy . . .

To anyone who, like myself, is a convinced student of Theosophy and Oriental Occultism, the phenomenon is all the more striking. For his works reveal an expert and deep knowledge of Eastern philosophy which is amazing. I hold the view very strongly myself that the explanation lies in previous Indian incarnations. My father, very patriotic and intensely British in many way, was always a semi-Oriental; in outlook, tastes, manners and thoughts, and even in appearance. I believe his brief visit to India resuscitated the sub-conscious memories of former lives spent there and that these gave him his wonderful knowledge and insight and his love for and attraction to Eastern life and philosophy . . .

His most marked characteristic, and the one I want most to emphasise because it lingers most prominently in my loving memory of him, was his gentleness . . . He was gentle, kind and courteous always to all, in manner, speech and action. He loved animals, and taught us from our earliest childhood to be kind and gentle to all living creatures . . . And although his thought and understanding were too liberal and catholic for him to conform to any one form of religion, it was this aspect of the Buddhist creed, its gentleness, that specially appealed to him and made him love it beyond all others. Again in his later years he was attracted to Japan chiefly as the "land of gentle manners", as he called it, and he rejoiced in the exquisite courtesy of the people in that great country . . .

In the "Light of Asia" he has left a jewel of grace and wisdom, which will endure for all time . . . One has only to reflect that if the Western world had been Buddhist, instead of nominally Christian, there would have been no World War, to realize how inevitable is the immortality of the poem, which so finely portrays the noble and gentle earth life and the divine doctrine of the Buddha.

On the occasion of his father's birth centenary Emerson Arnold gifted to the Buddhist Society in London the armchair on which the poet would sit in his country home in Essex while writing *The Light of Asia*. The Buddhist Society had been set up as a breakaway from the Theosophical Society in 1926 by Christmas Humphreys, a lawyer and a convert to Buddhism. The armchair still greets visitors there along with a fine portrait of Sir Edwin in the Society's library. Emerson Arnold also gifted the Society his father's collection of Buddhist art, which continues to be on display there.[3]

Jawaharlal Nehru was at this time undergoing his sixth round of imprisonment by the British. This particular spell had begun on 26 December 1931 at the Naini Central Prison in Allahabad. After two months he was shifted to the Bareilly District Jail and in June 1932 he was transferred to the Dehra Dun Jail, where he languished till August 1933. New Year's Day in 1933 saw him in a particularly reflective mood and he wrote to his daughter on that day:[4]

. . . I remember that during the last eleven years I have spent five New Years' Days in prison. And I begin to wonder how many more such days and other days I shall see in prison! But I am an "habitual" now, in the language of the prison, and that many times over, and I am used to gaol life. This letter that I am now writing is numbered 120 and this numbering began only nine months ago in Bareilly Gaol. I am amazed I have written so much already . . .

The story that my letters have contained has not been a very pleasant one. History is not pleasant . . . All manner of questions arise for which there is no straight answer; all manner of doubts come which do not easily vanish. Why should there be so much folly and misery in the world? That is the old question that troubled Prince Siddhartha 2500 years ago in this country of ours. The story is told that he asked himself this question many times before enlightenment came to him, and he became the Buddha. He asked himself, it is said:

"How can it be that Brahm
Would make a world and keep it miserable,
Since, if all powerful, he leaves it so,

He is not good, and if not powerful,
He is not God?"

Nehru was either quoting these lines from memory or, as is more likely, had *The Light of Asia* with him. This is how Book the Third of the poem ends, with the Prince telling his charioteer to head home since 'mine eyes have seen enough'. Siddhartha was, of course, referring to the four sights which had shaken him and led him to question the very meaning of life.

This was not all. Four days later Nehru wrote to Gandhi with these very lines from *The Light of Asia* still firmly embedded in his mind:[5]

My dear Bapu:

Your letter is always a tonic, and when it comes after a long interval it brings a thrill with it and its effect is all the more exhilarating . . .

I have had companions here but largely I have been left to myself, and I have grown a little contemplative, in defiance of heredity and family tradition and personal habit! . . . I have read a lot, and if wisdom could be had in books, I would be wise. But wisdom eludes me, and the big question marks confront me wherever I look. Sometimes I think of Siddhartha's old question and no answer comes:

"How can it be that Brahm
Would make a world and keep it miserable,
Since, if all powerful, he leaves it so,
He is not good, and if not powerful,
He is not God?"

Almost nine decades later a 2020 was drawing to a close, Declan Walsh's *The Nine Lives of Pakistan* appeared to considerable acclaim.[6] One of the lives he chronicles is that of Nawab Akbar Bugti, the prominent Baloch personality. Walsh writes of meeting him in Quetta in the winter of 2011:

The Nawab . . . pulled a sheet of paper from his pocket. 'A poem,' he announced, about Buddhism. He started to read.

> *"How can it be that Brahm*
> *Would make a world and keep it miserable,*
> *Since, if all powerful, he leaves it so,*
> *He is not good, and if not powerful,*
> *He is not God?"* . . .

God, indeed. In this lost corner of Pakistan, the Nawab was as close to a deity as you could get.

Arnold had never been seen as a great scholar. His recognition had come as a poet and as a leader-writer and editor. But in March 1933 he earned unusual recognition in the USA where the President of the American Oriental Society Charles Braden used the occasion of Arnold's birth centenary to pay an elaborate tribute to him. Addressing the Mid-west branch of the Society at Toledo in Ohio, Braden, a noted scholar himself, reviewed the wide gamut of Arnold's works. This was probably for the first time that an Orientalist in the academic world had called Arnold an 'Orientalist'. In 1933, that term did not carry the value-judgment that would be attached to it after Edward Said's excoriating book *Orientalism* that came out in 1978.[7] Braden's lecture contained all the essentials of Arnold's life and work. He ended thus:

Some have denied he was a real poet. Space will not permit a discussion of his merit from this angle, but this writer believes that he was. Some will deny he was an Orientalist. Sir E.D. Ross says that he narrowly escaped being one. But in closing, this writer believes that in every real sense of the word this man, who, perhaps more than any other single figure in his day, translated and interpreted clearly and sympathetically the best in the life of the Orient to the English-speaking world of the West, well deserves to be called both Poet and Orientalist.

Braden was referring to Sir Edward Denison Ross, a man who 'read in 49 languages and spoke in 30' and who was the first Director of the School of Oriental Studies at the University of London that is today known as the School of Oriental and African Studies (SOAS). Ross had written the introduction to the popular 1926 edition of *The Light of Asia*. In his long centenary tribute to Arnold in the *Observer* of 5 June 1932, Ross had written:

> Edwin Arnold, the centenary of whose birth falls on Friday, had a narrow escape from being an Orientalist. Less than two years after taking his degree at Oxford, he accepted an educational post in India and immediately became interested in Oriental languages. He was destined ultimately to become a great journalist, but the East always held him in its spell; . . . It is by the "The Light of Asia" alone that Edwin Arnold will be remembered . . . it contains many passages of compelling beauty and still remains the best description of the life of Gautama Buddha in our language.

Ironically, long before an Englishman and an American had spoken of Arnold as an Orientalist, India had already done so. A book had appeared in Madras in 1922 called *Eminent Orientalists*[8] that contained descriptions of the lives and works of twenty-five British, German, French and Indian personalities starting with Sir William Jones. One of this galaxy was Sir Edwin Arnold. This remains a very valuable single-volume collection to students and scholars and was the first to highlight the contribution of some Indians themselves to Indology.

The Theosophical Society would turn fifty in 1935. With the passing away of Annie Besant in September 1933 in Madras it would cease to be a force in Indian politics. Actually, its influence had begun to wane from December 1920 itself, with the emergence of Gandhi as the supreme, unchallenged leader. The Theosophical Society had played an important role in the Indian nationalist movement in the 1885–1918 period. It had also been hugely responsible for giving upper-caste educated Indians a great pride in their religious and cultural heritage. It had taken on the Christian establishment in Ceylon and had popularized Buddhism there. Olcott himself was tuned in more into Buddhism, while Annie Besant was more sympathetic to and supportive of Hinduism. Even so, the Society had expanded greatly and had helped propagate both Buddhist and Hindu philosophy in the UK, Europe, America, Japan and Russia as well.

On occasion of the diamond jubilee Rukmini Devi, the wife of George Arundale, who had taken over as President of the Theosophical Society from Annie Besant and a great cultural personality in her own right, choreographed *The Light of Asia*. This would become a feature at the annual conventions of the Theosophical Society. After one of them, on 22 September 1937, *The Hindu* commented:

> The Adyar players who staged twice "The Light of Asia" (dramatized from Edwin Arnold's poem) deserve to be congratulated. Life in Ancient India was reconstructed from the relics of early painting and sculpture, as the costumes and ornaments worn during the play were beautifully fashioned after the Ajanta frescoes. Some of the unforgettable episodes from the life of the great Buddha were chosen and depicted with much skill and care for aesthetic appeal . . .

Rukmini Devi would go on to become one of India's most remarkable cultural personalities. The institution that she established, called Kalakshetra, adjoins the sprawling Theosophical Society campus in Chennai. In June 1973, a Romanian couple in Bucharest would name their daughter after her. Rukmini Callimachi would much later become an award-winning reporter for the *New York Times*.

Esperanto is an international language invented in 1887 by Ludwik Lejser Zamenof, a Polish physician. It was meant to be a link language that would also promote inter-cultural understanding and fraternity. In the 1920s there was move in the League of Nations to make it a compulsory subject in the schools of the world, a move supported by India, China, Persia and eight other

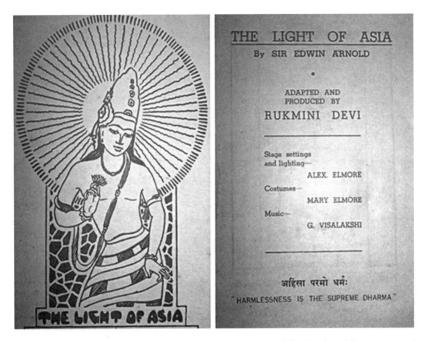

THE LIGHT OF ASIA
By SIR EDWIN ARNOLD

•

ADAPTED AND
PRODUCED BY

RUKMINI DEVI

Stage settings
and lighting—
                    ALEX. ELMORE
Costumes—
                    MARY ELMORE
Music—
                    G. VISALAKSHI

अहिंसा परमो धर्मः
"HARMLESSNESS IS THE SUPREME DHARMA"

Rukmini Devi Arundale's long-lasting dance-drama based on The Light of Asia *premiered at the Theosophical Society, Madras 1937. (Source: Theosophical Society)*

countries. India's support was largely due to the efforts of Irach Jehangir Sorabji Taraporevala, a formidable linguist who in 1939 would occupy the same position at the Deccan College in Poona that Arnold had during 1857–60. France, however, vetoed this idea. A very enthusiastic Esperantist in the 1930s was Tagore's colleague at Santiniketan, Lakshmiswar Sinha, who in the very late 1920s and early 1930s made Esperantists interested in India and vice versa. In the early decades of the twentieth century, in keeping with what was happening to it in Europe, Buddhism had become quite popular with the Esperantists. In 1925 they had set up the Budhano Ligo Esperantista in London and Riga with Geo H. Yoxon as its Secretary. Sinha's travels in Europe could well have deepened the Esperantist interest in Buddha and in 1936 *La Lumo de Azio*, an Esperanto translation of parts of *The Light of Asia* was published by the Budhano Ligo Esperantista in Heswall near London. Yoxon was its translator. Although Esperanto never really caught on as originally intended, the Internet era has led to an exponential increase in the community of Esperanto speakers and scholars.[9]

The 1930s also saw more translations of *The Light of Asia* in Indian languages: *Buddhacharit* in 1934 in Gujarati by Narsinrao Divetia and *Asia da Chanan* in Punjabi, first in 1938 by Gurbakhsh Singh and then six years later by Mohan Singh.[10] Divetia, a poet and philologist, had first met Gandhi on 15 September 1915 when he was asked by the Mahatma to translate Cardinal Newman's Christian hymn *Lead Kindly Light* into Gujarati. This happened to be one of Gandhi's favourites. Two years later, Divetia's answer appeared as *Premal Jyoti Taro Dakhavi.* He was somebody for whom Gandhi had the highest respect. Divetia has written in his autobiography of his meeting with Dharmanand Kosambi, who 'straightaway assigned me to write a song on the occasion of Buddha Jayanti'.[11] This meeting took place on 5 May 1924 in Bombay. Two years later, on 28 April 1926, Divetia records his seeing the film version of *The Light of Asia* also in Bombay and calls it a 'classic' although it departed from Arnold's book.

Divetia was profoundly influenced by English poetry, especially that of Wordsworth, Shelley and Tennyson, and this is reflected in the first four volumes of his poems. *Buddhacharita* was the fifth and final volume, containing all his poems on the Buddha, including translations of some parts of *The Light of Asia* that deal with the Buddha's worldly life.

Actually, Divetia was not the first Gujarati poet to translate *The Light of Asia.* His lesser-known contemporary Jagannath Harinarayan Oza's fuller (five out of eight cantos) translation called *Siddharth Sanyas: The Renunciation of Maharishi Gautam Buddha* had been published out of Bombay in 1921—thirteen years before Divetia's work appeared. Oza had dedicated his translation to someone he described as 'an ocean of compassion like Buddha', as someone 'who has sacrificed all for the good of society' but also someone 'who has made great efforts at cow protection and through that effort shining as a great protector of Hindu Dharma'. Oza was, of course, referring to his fellow Gujarati Mahatma Gandhi. It is noteworthy that both Oza and Divetia had in their translations focused more on the *personal* rather than the *public* aspects of the Buddha's life.[12]

Gurbakhsh Singh had first read *The Light of Asia* in Iran while working there as an engineer attached to the [British] Indian army during the First World War. He was enamoured of the exposition of the Buddha's philosophy in the poem and would read from it often in gatherings while a student at Michigan in America during 1919–23. After returning to India, he started publishing a Punjabi monthly magazine called *Preet Lari*. He started translating *The Light of Asia* and these translations started appearing in the publication. There was soon a demand for putting these translations together in a book form but Gurbakhsh Singh hesitated. A vociferous critic of the caste system, he finally published his *Asia da Chanan* in 1938. Five editions of it would appear in later years and it is considered a classic of Punjabi literature. In his introduction, he writes:

> Just as Fitzgerald translated Omar Khayyam in such a way that breathed the life of the original in it and then the world fell in love with Khayyam, Edwin Arnold took Buddha to the world who won hearts. . . . This book is not like other religious scriptures the reading of which creates a 'spiritual benefit'. It is a practical institution of Love, Compassion, Justice and Brilliance. Therefore it will ever be considered a lighthouse . . . even in those times when religion will no longer be considered the highest form of practicing piety at all . . . This is one of those books that can be read over and over again giving ever new inspiration and realisations.

Gurbakhsh Singh, an unrepentant Marxist till his very end, then went on in the introduction to discuss the personality of the Buddha, the nature of Buddhism and how it was subverted by what he called Brahmanism.

Mohan Singh came out with his own translation *Asia do Chanan* in 1944. Mohan Singh is an immensely important figure in the development of modern Punjabi and has been called the father of Punjabi poetry. Initially he had been drawn to the English Romantic

Gurbakhsh Singh's Punjabi translation of The Light of Asia, *Lahore 1938.* Sir Edwin's photograph is also shown.

poets and this may well have triggered his interest in Arnold. Later, however, he got involved with the Progressive Movement and became a public voice for social equality. In his preface, Mohan Singh draws parallels between Sikhism and Buddhism, saying how both religions diluted the hegemony of the Brahmins. He also draws parallels between the Sikh gurus, most notably Guru Nanak and Guru Gobind Singh on the one side, and the Buddha on the other, saying how both challenged the caste system. He ends up thus:

> I started translating this epic poem of Edwin Arnold in 1937 when I was working in Khalsa College, Amritsar, and have been able complete it now after exactly eight years of hard work. The peace and satisfaction that I have experienced while working on this book, has been of a kind that I have not felt while composing any other poetry, and this itself has been my reward. And if the

readers of this book also experience a similar sense of peace and well-being while reading this epic poem I will feel that my labour has been of use to others.

Mohan Singh's translation, which was in verse, would be reprinted in 1949, 1952 and 1953. More than six decades later it would inspire Karam Bir Singh Sodhi—a descendant of the fourth Sikh guru Guru Ram Das—to come out with his translation of *The Light of Asia* dedicated to the Dalai Lama.

Arnold had lost out in the race to become Poet Laureate of the UK in 1896. It was a position he had devoutly wished and perhaps even lobbied for. John Masefield had become Poet Laureate in May 1930 and nine years later would bring Arnold back into the spotlight. *The Birmingham Post* carried this report on 18 March 1939:

> The Poet Laureate is a member of the Masked Theatre Club and it was through one of the performances on the small stage that he first thought of a masked ballet. On March 31 and April 1, Mr. Masefield, in cooperation with the club, will present "Life of Buddha" at the Rudolph Steiner Hall [in London] . . . At a gathering of the Masked Theatre Club, Mr. Masefield . . . read the prologue to his new work, and in a few words of preface, told of being influenced in his boyhood by the life of Buddha, as interpreted by Sir Edwin Arnold in "The Light of Asia". His youthful encounter with Arnold, the first poet he ever met, made a deep impression on him.

Notes

1. Raman (1947)
2. Another public figure profoundly impacted by Euclid some decades earlier than Raman was Abraham Lincoln. It also 'was a potent teacher' for the African-American reformer William Hamilton, who fought slavery in America in the early nineteenth century.
3. In 1973, Christmas Humphreys would write in his introduction to a new edition of Frank Lee Woodward's evergreen *Some Sayings of the*

Buddha that '*The Light of Asia* is still the best seller of Buddhism to the West'. Woodward himself is a very important figure in the efflorescence of Sinhala Buddhism in the early twentieth century. A fine study of Woodward is Powell (1999).

4. *Glimpses of World History*, Penguin 2004 edition
5. *Selected Works of Jawaharlal Nehru*, First Series, Volume 5
6. Walsh (2020)
7. Edwin Arnold does not figure in Edward Said's classic. Two other Arnolds do however—Matthew and Thomas, the scholar of Islam, not to be confused with another Thomas Arnold, Matthew's father, the central figure in Thomas Hughes novel *Tom Brown's School Days* that was published in 1857.
8. *Eminent Orientalists*, G.A. Natesan & Co, Madras 1922. Six were Indian and one was a woman—Sister Nivedita.
9. I owe all information regarding Esperanto to Probal Dasgupta, a noted linguist, now retired in Kolkata and who served as president of the Universal Esperanto Association between 2007 and 2013.
10. For some reason that I have been unable to figure out, the date of publication of Mohan Singh's translation is sometimes given as 1935. I possess a copy of the 1953 edition of his work in which it is clearly stated that the first edition was in 1944. In his preface, Mohan Singh himself writes that he started the translation sometime in 1937 and it took eight years to complete.
11. Divetia's diaries in Gujarati were published much later, in 1953. I owe the English translation to Urvish Kothari.
12. Sitanshu Yashaschandra Mehta, the President of the Gujarati Sahitya Parishad, believes that the first reference to the Buddha in Gujarati literary culture was in 1865 by Narmadashankar Dave in his celebrated *Narmagadya*. Mehta also, after I reached out to him, prepared a scholarly paper titled 'Gautama Buddha in Gujarati Literature and Translations of *The Light of Asia* by Two Gujarati Authors: A Short Note Towards a Semiotic Reading', which is in my possession.

17

The 1940s: *The Light of Asia* in Tamil & Kannada, Hollywood and More

As the decade opened, *The Light of Asia* appeared in Tamil for the third time in the century. It had first come out in 1918 authored by A. Madhaviah. Twelve years later one of the pioneers of Tamil drama-writing, Pammal Campanta Mutaliyar, published his play entitled '*Buddha or The Light of the Universe*'. He had been to Ceylon in 1908 and had come back to Madras, in his own words, a 'different man'. He hoped that his play set in five Acts would induce at least some of his readers to follow the great teachings of the Buddha.

Desigavinayagam Pillai, who was born just twelve days after *The Light of Asia* had first come out, grew up learning Malayalam and blossomed relatively late as a Tamil poet. But when he did emerge, he created a huge impact and is considered to be one of the outstanding Tamil poets in modern times, next only to Subramania Bharati and Bharatidasan. Desigavinayagam had been honoured by the Tamil Sangham with the title 'Kavimani', soon after which his *Aasia Jothi*, adapted from Arnold's poem, was published in 1941. Excerpts from *Aasia Jothi* are still included in school textbooks in the state of Tamil Nadu. An unknown side of him was that he was a scholar as well—a pioneer in using epigraphical material extensively to explore the history of Tamils in the southern region. It appears that Desigavinayagam took to *The Light of Asia* primarily on account of its literary value (he would translate Edward Fitzgerald's *The Rubaiyat of Omar Khayyam* as well) but also used creatively the message of social equality that Arnold had expressed in verse— something that resonated in Tamil society and that has given *Aasia Jothi*'s continuing appeal.

In the mid-twentieth century, Lin Yutang was a well-known writer on Chinese philosophy in the West. He had been born in China and studied in America, France and Germany. After returning to China to teach for a brief while, he came back to America in 1935. Subsequently he taught in Singapore and spent his last years in New York. In 1942, he published *The Wisdom of China and India,* which is among the very few one-volume compilations of the great works of the two civilisations. In the Indian anthology he included extracts from the Rig Veda, Upanishads, Bhagavad Gita, Ramayana, Panchatantra and the Dhammapada.

Then he did something quite unusual. He included *The Light of Asia* in its *entirety* to conclude the Indian section of his book. Lin Yutang explains the rationale for doing so thus:

In the study of Buddhism, we may take the poetic approach or the philosophic approach, through moral surrender or through intellectual belief. Sir Edwin Arnold's famous life of Buddha, *Light of Asia*, gives the best poetic approach, while the selection from the *Suriname*, which follows, gives the best philosophic approach.

There is a reason for reprinting the *Light of Asia* complete in this volume, although it was written by an Englishman. This long poem ran into sixty editions in England and eighty editions in the United States in the course of a few years when it was published about a century ago and sold hundreds of thousands of copies at a time when there were neither best-seller lists, nor the Book-of-the-Month Club. . . . Most Western readers of the elderly generation owe their impression of Buddha to this poem. This is easy to understand. While it raised Buddha to cosmic heights, it never lost the human interest of its story. This is essentially the story of St. Josephat, borrowed from the Buddhist *Lalitavistara,* who in the romance of *Barlaam and Josephat,* became a Christian prince who was touched by the sorrow of the world and renounced his palatial glories to become an ascetic. Thus, Buddha became actually canonized as a Christian saint in the sixteenth century.

In 2014 there would appear *In Search of a Christian Buddha*, which tells the absolutely fascinating story of 'how an Asian sage became a medieval saint'.[1] Saint Josephat was a 'prince who gave up his wealth and kingdom to become a Christian monk' and his was 'one of the most popular tales of the Middle Ages, translated into a dozen languages and cited by Shakespeare in *The Merchant of Venice*'. The story of this Christian prince was actually based on the life of the Buddha.

The Picture of Dorian Gray was a philosophical novel by Oscar Wilde that had been published in 1890. Fifty-five years later it was made into a Hollywood film which went by the same name. Some of the actors and actresses became acclaimed names, like George Sanders, Angela Lansbury and Peter Lawford. The story is of a handsome and wealthy young man, Dorian Gray, who is also easily manipulated. He falls in love and is engaged to a girl. But he is then persuaded to follow a more hedonistic lifestyle. The girl commits suicide. To maintain his image of youth and beauty, Gray commits a murder, forces a suicide and facilitates an accidental killing. The story is one of how beauty can lead to evil if there is no inner moral compass. After the suicide of his fiancée, his friend, who has painted a portrait of Dorian Gray in all his youth and beauty and which is the cause of much evil, meets him when Gray confesses that for a short while he felt great remorse but that feeling had passed and he has to move on. Basil, the painter, then tells him that 'this is not you speaking' and that he had been reading the wrong book. This conversation then ensues:

Dorian Gray: What would you like me to read, Basil?

Basil (gets up from where he is sitting and goes over to where Gray is standing): Since you asked me about it . . .

Gray (looking at the book given to him): Light of Asia, The story of Booda, is it?

Basil: The Story of Booda. Good man. Promise me you will read it.

Gray: I will. Promise.

Basil Hayward has just given Dorian Gray a copy of The Light of Asia. *A scene from* The Picture of Dorian Gray, *a Hollywood film, 1945.*

The book, of course, makes no difference to Dorian Gray's life.

The very next year Jawaharlal Nehru's *The Discovery of India* was published. It was written when Nehru had been imprisoned for the tenth and last time by the British between August 1942 and June 1945. Nehru had written a number of books before, but this was to become a classic in every sense of the term, and it continues to be read, cited and critiqued. In it Nehru says:

> The Buddha story attracted me even in early boyhood and I was drawn to young Siddhartha who, after many inner struggles and pain and torment, was to develop into the Buddha. Edwin Arnold's 'Light of Asia' became one of my favourite books. In later years when I travelled about a great deal in my province [today's Uttar Pradesh], I liked to visit the many places connected with the Buddha legend.

When he was thirteen or so Nehru had been introduced to *The Light of Asia* by his private tutor, the Irish-French Ferdinand T. Brooks, who was an ardent Theosophist. Nehru himself had been initiated into the Theosophical Society by none other than Annie Besant herself. When he was sent to jail for the second time in 1922, one of the books he asked for to be sent to him was *The Light of Asia*. As India's first Prime Minister he would do much to make the country aware of its Buddhist heritage. There is no doubt that Nehru was 'attracted to Buddhism through the British reception of Buddhism, in the latter half of the nineteenth century, the new academic discipline of comparative religion and that aspect of secularization that historicized religions and their leaders'. The fact that 'it had originated in India, but more that its ethics had sedimented in Indian culture, furnished him with an important instrument with which to fashion a modern India within a modern world'.[2] Unlike his contemporary Dr B.R. Ambedkar, Nehru, however, did not see Buddhism as a way of challenging and dismantling the edifice of India's horrific caste system. He saw it more in a philosophical and cultural perspective, an instrument of India's 'soft power' in the world.

In 1948 T.S. Eliot won the Nobel Prize for Literature. Scholars who would study Eliot and his many works later would find echoes of *The Light of Asia* in his *Murder in the Cathedral*, in *A Song for Simeon* and in the first draft of his magnum opus *The Waste Land*.[3] Four years before he received the Nobel Prize, Eliot himself had written:[4]

> I came across, as a boy, a poem for which I have preserved a warm affection: *The Light of Asia* by Sir Edwin Arnold. It is a long epic poem on the life of Gautama Buddha: I must have had a latent sympathy for the subject matter, for I read it through with gusto, and more than once. I have never had the curiosity to find out anything about the author but to this day it seems to me to be a good poem, and when I meet anyone else who has read and liked it, I feel drawn to that person.

Eliot had been heavily influenced by Indic traditions—both Hindu and Buddhist—which is manifested so clearly in his *Four Quartets*.[5]

By the end of the 1940s the first translations of *The Light of Asia* in Khmer had begun to appear. So, far they had been available and read in English, French and Thai. They were first serialized in the journal *Kambuja Suriya* in 1948, 1949, 1951 and 1952. Later they were to be printed as a stand-alone book by the Buddhist Institute in Pnom Penh.[6] The translation was done by two important Buddhist scholars of that era—Nhok Them and Ray Buck. They drew upon both the earliest French and Thai translations of 1899 and 1927 respectively that had been reprinted later.[7] By the end of the 1940s, there would be a couple of fresh Japanese translations as well, in addition to the ones already accomplished in 1890 and 1911. These would both be called *Asia no Hikari* and were by Tozo Shimamura in 1940 and Koshou Yamamoto in 1944.

By the 1940s *The Light of Asia* had appeared in all south Indian languages except Kannada. That gap would be filled in 1948 with the publication of a drama *Gautama Buddha* by B. Puttaswamayya that was inspired by Arnold's poem. The drama had actually been staged much earlier, way back in 1932, in which Mohammed Peer of Bellary had played the role of the Buddha in what is even today considered a 'superlative manner'. Peer would die young in 1937 but not before making a big name for himself on the Kannada stage. He continues to be recalled even today.

There would be further editions of *Gautama Buddha* and Puttaswamayya himself would in 1978 receive the Government of India's top literary award for another of his works. In 1995, there would be a lesser known second translation called *Ashiyada Belaku* by B. Leela Bhat. Bhat was a teacher and author who is better known in Kannada literature for her book on the wife of one of the greatest literary and cultural personalities of twentieth-century Karnataka, whose inter-caste marriage in the 1930s had caused a sensation in the orthodox society of which he was then part—Shivaram Karanth.

Manjeshwar Govinda Pai must surely be one of India's most remarkable literary figures of the twentieth century—if not for anything else but for the fact that he could read and write in twenty-five languages, both Indian and European. He was a prolific writer of prose and poetry in Kannada. The reason why he figures in this narrative is because Arnold may well have had some influence on him. The evidence for this is not conclusive but is suggestive. Pai wrote *Golgotha* in 1931, about the last days of Jesus. Fifteen years later he wrote *Vaisakhi*, about the last days of the Buddha. Given that Arnold too had written on both of them, it is possible that Pai could have been inspired by *The Light of Asia* and *The Light of the World*.[8]

Notes

1. Lopez and McCracken (2014)
2. Palat (2019)
3. Murray (1991)
4. Ibid.
5. Kearns (1987)
6. The gigantic Angkor Wat Temple complex in Cambodia was built in the first quarter of the twelfth century by Suryavarman II, dedicated to the Hindu god Vishnu. By the early 1180s, Buddha and Buddhism had come to prominence at Angkor Wat under Jayavarman VII. But by the middle of the thirteenth century Angkor Wat had become heavily Shivaite under Jayavarman VIII. This is an interesting parallel to Buddha Gaya. Higham (2001) has further details on the Hindu-Buddhist twists and turns at Angkor Wat.
7. I owe this information on Khmer translations to Trent Walker, email communication 4 May 2020.
8. I owe this suggestion to H.S. Shivaprakash.

18

The 1950s: Bodh Gaya Temple, Dr B.R. Ambedkar, Sir Edwin's biography and More

Andrew Carnegie had become the 'world's richest man' in 1901. Born poor in Scotland, he had migrated to America and made his fortune. He had met Sir Edwin Arnold in London on his round-the-world trip soon after *The Light of Asia* was published and Arnold had presented Carnegie with the original handwritten manuscript of the poem. In early 1880, a forty-five-year-old Carnegie started courting a twenty-three-year-old Louise Whitfield in New York, who would soon be writing to him:

My dear Mr. Carnegie:

Just a few lines before retiring to tell you how much I rejoice with you in the possession of your treasure. How much you must prize it, and yet how much more must you value the friendship that prompted such a gift from such a man! May I hope to have a glimpse of it in some time in the Fall. I always carry the copy of *The Light Of Asia* you gave me, around every place I go. I love to pick it up, even if only to read but a few lines, and it always refreshes me and does me good. I wish I had it, as you have, at my tongue's end, but I have committed a few of the loveliest bits to memory . . .

Seven years later, in 1887, the two got married. In 1950, the biography of Mrs Andrew Carnegie would appear, based very substantially on her diaries as well as on conversations with her (she had lived till 1946). This is what Burton Hendrick and Daniel Henderson unearthed:[1]

The courtship really began over a book. A writer who was then creating a big stir in the world was Sir Edwin Arnold whose The Light of Asia first published in 1879 was sweeping the world . . . Carnegie was one of the first to read and praise it. He gave the girl a copy, and together they pored over the story of Prince Siddhartha . . . This book exercised the greatest influence on bringing the two seriously together. Miss Whitfield, as she herself said, used to carry it wherever she went, and even took it, after the troubled course of true love, on her wedding trip. Her copy, with her favorite passages marked are carefully preserved among her effects.

Carnegie not only gave a copy of *The Light of Asia* to his fiancée but also inscribed it on the same wedding trip on 8 May 1887 at the Isle of Wight.

The first gift I ever gave to my wife, then the young lady Louise Whitfield, was this book. Reading and quoting it at times to her, I first discovered she had a heart and, beyond, those of others of her own age and from that day to this (seven years) I have kept o discovering new beauties of mind and character in her . . .

In 1951, a Finnish translation of *The Light of Asia* appeared. It was by a man who had horrified the great Finnish music composer Jean Sibelius when Sibelius' daughter Ruth had brought him home. On 4 April 1915, Sibelius recorded in his diary: 'Poor Ruth, who can't see beyond the end of her nose. He is a theosophist, a vegetarian and so on . . . What a terrible thought'.[2] The theosophist and vegetarian Sibelius initially despised became his son-in-law. This was Jussi Snellman, an actor and director at the National Theatre who would, at the same time as he was scandalising Sibelius, be publishing his *Aasian valo*. Snellman's is a good example of the links between *The Light of Asia* and the Theosophical Society.

Earlier I had mentioned Viktor Rydberg in the context of the 1888 translation of *The Light of Asia* into Swedish and how he had

The world's most famous couple of the late nineteenth century, whose courtship began with and was sustained by The Light of Asia. *Mr and Mrs Andrew Carnegie, Isle of Wight, May 1887. This is from Hendrick and Henderson (1950)*

been one of the original eight founders of the Theosophical Society in that country. The Society had been launched in Denmark in 1893 and Finland in 1907, in which Snellman was active. Across Europe, the Society attracted prominent (and usually well-to-do) public personalities. Total membership was not all that large; in the mid-thirties world membership did not exceed thirty thousand. But the members were writers, artists, intellectuals and philanthropists, and so in spite of often being derided as eccentric, esoteric and sometimes even fraudulent, the Theosophical Society was visible, always in the news and impactful.

The first of several doctoral dissertations on Arnold and his seminal poem titled *Sir Edwin Arnold: A Literary Biography of the*

Author of The Light of Asia was submitted at Harvard University in 1950. In his unpublished memoirs, its author Brooks Wright would later recall:

> This was a life and critical study of Sir Edwin Arnold, a mediocre Victorian poet, journalist and orientalist whom I had first read in Karachi. The research was a such a pleasure that I could have prolonged it indefinitely—I even spent a term studying Sanskrit, until Father became alarmed that I would never finish. I was obsessed with setting down every fact I could find, so that the final text ran into nine hundred typewritten pages. I doubt if even the examining committee read it. Douglas Bush seemed to be under the impression that I had written on Matthew Arnold. Instead of questioning me about the thesis, they quizzed me in great detail about the whole range of Victorian literature; it felt like the professorial equivalent of a fraternity hazing. Afterwards I reflected with relief that no one would ever give me another examination.

In 1957, Wright's dissertation would be redone as the first and only full-length published biography of Sir Edwin Arnold. I will return to it a little later in this narrative.

The second such academic thesis, called *Sir Edwin Arnold's Buddhism,* came to fruition in June 1952 at the University of Florida.[3] John Ralph Murray had been, by his own admission, 'sporadically collecting materials for a study over a period of fourteen years'. He had known Julian Arnold and made use of his unpublished manuscript on the life of the poet. Murray's was a critical appraisal of the epic poem. It dealt with the poet's life briefly and also with the background to the poem in late Victorian England. Murray fully acknowledged the appeal of *The Light of Asia* and deeply admired Arnold's personality.[4] But he also lamented the fact that the poem did not convey in any profound sense both the breadth and depth of Buddhism, that his treatment of Buddhist philosophy was sketchy and shallow, and at times improper as well. Murray was evidently a serious student of Buddhism for he evaluated the poem in great detail almost like a Buddhist himself would. That Arnold had taken liberties with 'facts' cannot be doubted. But my own view is that Murray read more into *The Light of Asia* than Arnold himself may have intended.

Nehru had organized an Inter-Asian Relations Conference in New Delhi between 23 March and 2 April 1947, even before India attained her freedom. Leaders from thirty countries participated in the conclave, which was also addressed by Gandhi.[5] On 31 March 1947 while this assembly was in session, an All-Asia Buddhist Convention was also held in the city with representatives from Ceylon, Siam, Burma and Tibet attending along with leading Indian Buddhists as well. Nehru met with a delegation of this Convention later, whose most pressing demand was that the management of the Mahabodhi Temple at Bodh Gaya should be with Buddhists. Nehru promised them 'all support for the restoration of Buddhagaya to the Buddhists'. A year later a bill was introduced in the Bihar Legislative Assembly with following 'Statement of Objects and Reasons':

> On the site of an earlier temple built by Ashoka the Great, the present Buddha Gaya temple was erected in the 1st century BC and is the most sacred place to Buddhists all over the world because here, under a Bodhi tree, Lord Buddha attained enlightenment. But the temple passed on the possession of a Sivite Hindu Mahant who obtained a Firman from the Moghul Emperor Mohammed Shah in 1927 granting him village Taradih in which the temple stands. For many centuries, the temple has been a place of worship both for Hindus and Buddhists. Diverse Commissions, such as the non-official Commission appointed by the Government of Bengal in 1903 and the Committee under the Chairmanship of Dr. Rajendra Prasad appointed by the Working Committee of the Indian National Congress in 1924, have recommended that being a body place for two of the most important religions of the world, this temple should be under joint management. The Buddha Gaya Temple Bill, 1948, provides that the temple and its management

with vest in a Committee consisting of Buddhists and Hindus appointed by the Government; the Mahant will be a member of this Committee; both Hindus and Buddhists will have equal opportunities of worshipping in the temple according to their own persuasions, without resorting to any mode of worship objected to by followers of the other religion and that the property of the Saivite Math of which the Mahanth is the Manager, will remain unaffected.

While moving the Bill, Sri Krishna Sinha, the Premier of the Bihar Province spoke of Buddha Gaya being as sacred to Buddhists as Jerusalem was to Christians and Mecca to Muslims—exactly the analogy Arnold had drawn sixty-four years earlier. The Bill was then circulated for wider public debate. On 15 February 1949 Nehru asked his Principal Private Secretary to write to the Bihar Government with the following suggestion:

It would be desirable to give a certain international character to this temple. Perhaps the Committee as such need not be bigger than it is and may consist, as suggested of four Hindus and four Buddhists. It might be possible to have a separate advisory committee with no other powers other than advice. This advisory committee would also consist of Hindus and Buddhists, and might have a larger proportion of Buddhists. Some of these Buddhists might be nominated by the Mahabodhi Society . . .

Nehru was very mindful of the role that the Mahabodhi Society had played in the restoration of a number of sites associated with the Buddha, most notably Sarnath. The Bill was passed by the Bihar Assembly on 19 June 1949 and the transfer of ownership from the Mahant to the management committee took place on 28 May 1953 with the chanting of Sanskrit hymns, Hindi prayers and Pali gathas. On a day considered most auspicious by Buddhists, the control of the Bodh Gaya Temple was transferred from the Sivaite priests to a management board comprising of an equal number of Buddhists and Hindus with the District Magistrate being its chairman. Nehru sent a message:

> I am very happy to learn that *at last* the management of the Bodh Gaya Temple, *sacred to both Buddhists and Hindus alike,* is being handed over to a new committee of management in accordance with the law passed by the Bihar legislature. This Committee will have representatives of both Buddhists and Hindus and will look after this famous place of pilgrimage and worship in accordance with the wishes of the people concerned. The matter has been pending for a long time and had given rise in the past to much litigation. That was most unfortunate. I am happy that ultimately a settlement was arrived at by consent. I hope that in future there would be full cooperation among all those concerned with the famous temple.
>
> It is especially auspicious that this act of transfer should take place on a day which is sacred to innumerable people all over the world. On this day I offer my homage to the memory and teachings of the Buddha and I earnestly trust his message of peace will guide us in our labours. [italics mine]

The President of India, Dr Rajendra Prasad, who had grappled with this controversy for over quarter of a century at Gandhi's behest, was supposed to be present but fell ill and sent a message instead. He traced the history of the agitation and highlighted the sanctity of the 'holiest of holy places' Bodh Gaya thus:

> Ashoka built the present temple here 2200 years ago. Five hundred years later, the temple was rebuilt. Historians and scholars think that it is this temple raised 1700 years ago, which we see at Bodh Gaya today.

He paid handsome tributes to Dharmapala for his relentless campaign and then went on to add:

There is no reason for any conflict between the Hindu and the Buddhist faith. History bears witness to the fact that for long both flourished in India side by side and gave solace and guidance to millions. Buddhism has now more or less disappeared from India. It does not mean Hindus forcibly banished it. The real reason is that the Hindus adopted most of the tenets of this faith and absorbed it in their own . . .

The Mahant Harihar Giri, the Sivite Mahant of the temple, read out a declaration which must have been put together with his approval:

I offer the management of temple excepting the temple of the Panch Pandavas, the *samadhis* of my ancestors, the *havana kund* and the rest house. I offer the management of the Bodh Gaya temple to the new management committee. I fervently hope that this temple respected by the whole world will prosper under the new management and will usher in an era of mutual understanding and sympathy between Hindus and Buddhists . . .

The celebrations ended with readings from *The Light of Asia*. It was most appropriate because it was Sir Edwin Arnold's visit to Buddha Gaya in January 1886 that had started it all. Every representation made to the British drew pointed attention to this fact. It had taken sixty-seven years going back to the day Arnold launched his high-voltage campaign to liberate this 'Jerusalem', this 'Mecca' for Buddhists from Hindu control and hand it back to the Buddhist community. The victory was partial. But Arnold, I think, would have been happy at the way things had turned out. The pugnacious Dharmapala, on the other hand, would certainly not have. The Mahabodhi Society which in the initial years following 1953 played a key role in the management committee is now one of the many Buddhist organizations in Bodh Gaya. The Mahabodhi Temple was declared a UNESCO World Heritage Site in 2002, introducing a whole new dynamic.[6]

I began this narrative by reproducing the two letters Churchill had written to Nehru in 1955 mentioning *The Light of Asia*. I was convinced that he was referring to Arnold's work, but I had to reckon with what Churchill's biographer Martin Gilbert had written on this episode:

> Churchill to Eden's private secretary Evelyn Shuckburgh, 18 February 1955, six weeks before Churchill retired as Prime Minister: "I have worked very hard with Nehru. I told him he should be the Light of Asia, to show all those millions how they can shine out, instead of accepting the darkness of Communism."

> —Martin Gilbert, *Winston S. Churchill*, Vol 8, 1095

I contacted Andrew Roberts, the British historian and Churchill's most recent biographer, as well as Richard Langworth, the great Churchill expert who is Senior Fellow at the Hillsdale College Churchill Project. Initially I did not show them the Churchill letters to Nehru and they supported Gilbert's version. When I showed them these letters and said that the only interpretation possible reading them is that Churchill was referring to the poem, Langworth replied first:

> I agree.

and Roberts replied quickly:

> I'm sure Churchill took it from the book he read.

Of course, given Churchill's age then, both Gilbert and I could be right—Churchill may well have said what Gilbert recorded he said and while writing to Nehru, Churchill may well have had Arnold's poem in mind. Langworth also wrote:

> It is reasonable to believe he read *The Light of Asia*—on those long hot Bangalore afternoons when, as a young subaltern, he began

to pursue his self-education. Arnold was very popular with New Agers in the west as well as the east.

And there is the fact that Churchill's father had known Arnold well, plus Churchill himself had written those articles in the *Daily Telegraph* that became his first book. In 1937, Churchill's *Great Contemporaries* had appeared, in which he recalled Curzon:

> I remember in 1903 during his Viceroyalty in India going to see the first Lady Curzon formerly Miss Leiter—*(The Leiter of Asia,* as the wags said)—one of the most beautiful, delightful women of her day when she was recovering in England from the first attack of her ultimately fatal illness. She showed me a letter from her husband in India. It was a hundred pages long! She showed me the numbers on the pages. All was written is his graceful, legible flowing hand. But a hundred pages!

A year after Churchill's letters to Nehru, *The Light of Asia* would still be in the limelight in India as the country started preparing to mark the 2500th Buddha Jayanti, marking the *mahaparinirvna* of the Buddha (according to Thervada chronology). The Buddha Jayanti celebrations themselves lasted a full year, beginning May 1956, and evoked great interest. *The Light of Asia* was back in circulation in India and elsewhere, with articles quoting some of its memorable lines and its 'majestic verses'.

A dance drama based on *The Light of Asia* choreographed by the well-known Hima Devi would be staged in Bombay and New Delhi. Schools in other places like Allahabad would have cultural performances adapted from Arnold's poem. On this occasion, the Colombo-based Lanka Bauddha Mandalaya decided to bring out a special publication to be presented to all Heads of State. This was called 'The Path of Buddhism' and had contributions by a number of noted Buddhist monks and scholars as well as by the then Prime Minister of Ceylon, Sir John Kotelawala, who wrote on

The Buddhist World Pays Homage to.....
THE LIGHT OF ASIA

Never shall yearnings
torture him, nor sins
Stain him, nor ache of
earthly joys and woes
Invade his safe, eternal
peace, nor deaths
And lives recur. He goes
Unto Nirvana. He is one
with Life
Yet lives not. He is blest,
ceasing to be.
Om, mane padme, om, the
Dewdrop slips
Into the shining sea.

—Sir Edwin Arnold's
"Light of Asia"

TWO thousand five hundred years ago, India was stirred to her depths by a spiritual ferment churned up vigorously by conflicting philosophies and clannish wars. People, buffetted by uncertainties about life and the hereafter, floundered in the dark, trying frantically to understand the mysteries of life and death.

There was no paramount power in India at that time. The country was divided into States and clans always at loggerheads. The Sakayas of Kapilavastu were the most powerful of these clans

enlightenment of a highly developed, most compassionate most loving, all knowing perfect being. He who attains this Bodhi or a fully self-enlightened One.

The Lord Buddha's chief disciples were Sariputta and Moggallana. They were his constant companions. On their death their relics were buried in a stupa at Ranchi. When General Cunningham was excavating the stupas at Ranchi, he came upon the relics, which were taken to London and kept in the Victoria Albert Museum until 1947 when they were handed over to the Maha Bodhi Society of India. The were exhibited recently in Ceylon, Burma and India.

The four Noble Truths, preached by the Lord Buddha revolve round Sorrow, or Dukkha. These Truths were made known by the Buddha in his very first sermon preached seven weeks after his Enlightenment, and they form the very core and essence of the Buddha Dhamma pervading every part and aspect of the Buddha Dhamma. This, O disciples said the Buddha, "is the noble Truth of Dukkha: birth is Dukkha, old age is Dukkha, disease is Dukkha, to be united with the unloved one is Dukkha, to be separated from the loved one is Dukkha, not to receive what one craves for is Dukkha." In brief

'The Significance of the Buddha Jayanti'. *The Light of Asia* was also included in this volume.

The Buddha Jayanti celebrations led to an unusual exchange involving the vice president, prime minister and education minister of India, three of the most erudite and well-read political figures India will ever see. It put the spotlight on *The Light of Asia* and I will let the file speak for itself:

Ministry of Education

I think the general principle should be that requests for financial assistance for works whose primary significance is their literary importance should be considered by the Sahitya Akademi, while requests relating to publication of works of philosophical, ethical, historical, scientific or general indological interest should be considered by the Ministry of Education or the National Book

Trust . . . I should further like to add that State patronage of publication of works whose primary significance is religion should be avoided as far as possible. As regards the particular case under consideration, Srimati Mahadevi Verma's request for financial assistance for publication of her translation of "Buddha Charit"[8] should be properly considered by the Buddha Jayanti Committee . . . As regards Srimati Mahadevi Verma's translation of the Rig Veda, I do not think any financial assistance by the State be given . . .

A.K. Azad [Abul Kalam Azad]
3.8.1956

Prime Minister

Prime Minister's Secretariat

The Vice President should also see this.

J. Nehru
4.8.1956

Vice President.

Vice President's Secretariat

I agree with the Minister of Education that the Sahitya Akademi should deal only with works which are of a literary quality . . . Buddha Charita is regarded as a classic in Sanskrit literature, though it deals with the life of the Buddha. Edwin Arnold's The Light of Asia is based on this work and it is treated as a work of literature and not a text of Buddhist religion. As a matter of fact, Edwin Arnold was a Unitarian Christian, who treated Buddhist, Hindu and Christian themes in his works, The Light of Asia,

The Song Celestial and the Light of the World. Only the first has become something of a literary classic . . .

S. Radhakrishnan
5.8.56

Prime Minister.

Prime Minister's Secretariat

. . . The principle laid down by the Minister of Education is a good one. But the application of it might well produce difficulties, as the Vice President has pointed out. The Sahitya Akademi should certainly deal with books possessing a literary quality. But there are so many books dealing with historical and like subjects which are of high literary quality and treated as such. They are still read for their literary quality.

I agree with the Minister of Education about our publishing religious books. Normally we should not take them up. But books like the Buddha Charita or the Rg Veda are classics of ancient India and can hardly be considered just as religious books.

J. Nehru
6.8.1956

Minister of Education

The biggest political event of 1956 and indeed amongst the biggest ever in twentieth-century Indian history was the conversion of Dr Ambedkar to Buddhism, with lakhs of his followers, on 14 October of that year. Dr Ambedkar had had a long engagement with Buddha and Buddhism and the event came as no surprise. I tried to find out whether *The Light of Asia* had ever figured in his life. That Dr Ambedkar was very familiar with Arnold's work is evident from the fact that he had two copies of it in his personal library, now at Siddharth College in Mumbai.

Two copies (marked) of The Light of Asia *in Dr Ambedkar's personal library, now at Siddhartha College, Mumbai (Source: Ananya Vajpeyi)*

But did *The Light of Asia* have any impact on Dr Ambedkar? Here is what Aakash Singh Rathore, a noted scholar, had to say on this subject when I asked him whether the poem had meant anything to the key architect of the Indian Constitution:[9]

As for direct influence it would be a stretch to say that it was in any way robust. You've mentioned that there are 2 copies of *The Light of Asia* in Ambedkar›s collection of books at Siddharth College. I believe that I remember seeing a copy in his library at Symbiosis in Pune also, which would bring the total count of his personal copies to 3! That he read the work would seem beyond dispute. But what is really the point of focus when thinking about Ambedkarite Buddhism are the points of rupture (with the Buddhisms of his day) and the points of continuity with the classical literature, and primarily the Pali canon.

So coming then to indirect influence. Arnold awoke Kosambi and Kosambi had a huge impact on Ambedkar; however, what influenced Ambedkar was not Kosambi's transmission of ideas from Kane/Arnold, but rather his break with them . . .

What Rathore was referring to was the fact that by the 1940s Dharmanand Kosambi had put forward a very radical explanation for Siddhartha's renunciation. Arnold's poem and indeed all of Buddhist tradition believes that the Prince saw four sights in quick succession—an aged man, an ill man, a corpse and a tranquil monk. The first three set him thinking on the nature of suffering and the fourth on the way to salvation. Kosambi had discovered Buddhism after reading *The Light of Asia in* 1899, and become a Buddhist monk and the first modern Indian scholar of Pali.

But in in his posthumously published play in 1949 called *Boddhisatva: Natak,* Kosambi wrote that it was not so much revulsion for the world and hope for nirvana that set Prince Siddhartha on his search for enlightenment but actually it was his violent opposition to the use of force and conflict to resolve a water dispute between the two tribes—the Sakyas, to which his father belonged, and the Koliyas, to which his mother belonged. Some serious scholars[10] have identified its influence on Dr B.R. Ambedkar's *The Buddha and his Dhamma* that was also published posthumously in 1957, a year after his death. Vasant Moon, the editor of the twenty-volume *Dr. Babasaheb Ambedkar, Writings and Speeches,* for instance, writes:[11]

. . . After analysing all the causes which resulted in Gautama's renunciation, he [Kosambi] concludes that the frequent quarrels between the Sakyas and Koliyas were responsible for his leaving home in search of finding a way for peace. Based on this theory, Prof Dharmananda wrote a play entitled 'Bodhisatwa' and published it in 1949. I had read this play in 1962 and was surprised to find identical similarity in the story of the play and the one told by Dr. Ambedkar.

It is clear that Kosambi's late-life rejection of the conventional wisdom on the motives for Prince Siddhartha's renunciation was fully shared by Dr Ambedkar.[12] There is absolutely no doubt that Dr Ambedkar challenged the mainstream historiographies of Indic civilization through a revisionist account of the social and political role of Buddha and Buddhism in India's past. *The Light of Asia* was embedded in that historiography. This set him apart from others in India who were also great admirers of Buddha, like Tagore, Gandhi and Nehru.[13]

But at the same time I should mention that two of Dr Ambedkar's greatest patrons in his student days had been moved by *The Light of Asia*. The first was Krishnarao Arjun Keluskar, who wrote *Gautam Buddhanche Charitra* in Marathi in 1897, three years after the first Marathi translation of *The Light of Asia* appeared. In his introduction, after mentioning his friend Dharmanand Kosambi, Keluskar says:

> As soon as I completed this book I sent a copy to my beloved friend Dr. Sadashivrao Vaman Kane. At that time, his condition was bad because of asthma. His cousin Govindrao read some books for him while he was unwell. Among them was my book on Gautama Buddha. After reading it, he asked Govindrao to meet me whenever he was in Bombay and tell me that my characterisation of Gautama Buddha was excellent . . . When Govindrao gave me the message I felt like weeping and many memories of the good man stood before me . . . What was special about it is that Govindrao had translated an English poem Arnold's The Light of Asia. It was done at the behest of the doctor. It was clear from his message that Govindrao's book was inferior to mine . . .

The second was Maharaja Sayajirao Gaekwad, who, as we have already seen, was a benefactor of the Mahabodhi Society in Calcutta. He had read *The Light of Asia* in his late teens. Arnold in his *India Revisited* mentions his stay in Baroda quite a bit but it is unclear whether he met Sayajirao or not. What is definite is that he left Baroda just a couple of day before Sayajirao got married. The *Times of India* of 8 December 1885 writes:

> It is a pity that Mr. Edwin Arnold, who is staying here now, will not then be present to see the reality of his lines descriptive of the throng:

> > *Gathered to watch some chattering snake-tamer*
> > *Wind around his wrist the living jewellery,*
> > *Of asp and nag, or charm the hooded death,*
> > *To angry dance with drone of beaded gourd.*

These were lines from Book the Third of *The Light of Asia* but the reporter had dropped the previous two lines which give the context:

> *The Brahmin proud, the martial Kshatriya,*
> *The humble-toiling Shudra; here a throng.*

Sometime in 1912, Sayajirao Gaekwad would stand next to a statue of the Buddha that he had just unveiled in the heart of the city which still stands. The statue, commissioned by the Maharaja in Japan, was his gift to the city to mark the silver jubilee of his rule.

Dr Ambedkar had been invited, at Gandhi's instance, by the Indian National Congress to become a member of the Constituent Assembly that had started functioning in December 1946. The Assembly had been formed to prepare a Constitution for a free India. But differences between Dr Ambedkar and leaders of the Indian National Congress persisted in the initial months. By July 1947, however, common ground had been found between the two and the Constituent Assembly moved forward. Ramachandra Guha

Maharaja Sayajirao Gaekwad after unveiling the statue of Buddha in Baroda, 1912. The black marble statue made in Japan stands in Jubilee Bagh even today. (Source: Facebook page of Our Vadodara)

has provided an explanation of how this may have happened.[14] The breakthrough seems to have been facilitated by, among others, Gandhi's trusted aide Rajkumari Amrit Kaur, with whom Dr Ambedkar was able to develop a rapport.[15] Sometime in 1947, Amrit Kaur, independent India's first Minister of Health and herself a Christian, was to write when asked about the books that had influenced her:[16]

> Edwin Arnold's "The Light of Asia" has never ceased to inspire me. I turn to it again [and again] with infinite joy. It is the great renunciation that thrills the heart, the story of which is told in such exquisite language and perfect imagery in this great poem . . .

It was not only in India and Ceylon that Arnold would be remembered in 1956. The BBC would also broadcast a talk on 'Edwin Arnold and

"The Light of Asia'" by Francis Watson that would be published in
its weekly magazine the *Listener* of 14 June 1956. Watson had spent
a few years in India in the late 1930s and 1940s and was a radio
feature writer. In later years he would write a couple of books on
Gandhi. Watson's retrospective on *The Light of Asia* may well have
been timed to be part of the 2500th birth, death and enlightenment
anniversary ceremonies of the Buddha. Watson wrote of the poem:

> It was the first popular attempt to piece together a consecutive
> account of the life and some of the teachings of the founder of
> Buddhism, from the relatively slender materials available a century
> ago. And although subsequent scholarship has picked a number of
> holes in it, it is still true to say that most of us owe our impressions
> of the Buddha to this one long poem—even if we have never read
> it. . . . Coming back to it recently, I asked myself why it was so easy
> and so pleasurable to read this long poem . . . There is abundant
> use of the local colour . . . But above all there is a superb theme:
> compassion, self-dedication, intellectual adventure, in a simple
> dramatic narrative of one man . . .

In 1957 would appear the first and only full-length biography we
have of Sir Edwin Arnold.[17] Called *Intepreter of Buddhism to the West:
Sir Edwin Arnold,* it was actually a doctoral dissertation by Brooks
Wright at Harvard University that had been expanded into a book.
Wright came from a blue-blooded family in Boston and would write
in his unpublished memoirs:

> I entered Harvard in the fall of 1939 without applying elsewhere;
> no doubt my father's position as a faculty member and alumnus
> ensured admission . . .

In 1942 he enlisted in the US Air Force. He spent ten months in
India and fourteen months in Ceylon and wrote that 'we were not
in India to protect the country; that was Britain's job. For us it
was a way station to China'. Almost all of Wright's work involved

cryptography and most of it in Calcutta and Colombo. From his account it is obvious he preferred Ceylon to India because of the weather and the natural scenery. In late 1945, Wright entered graduate school at Harvard to specialize in English literature because, as he put it, he 'avoided Renaissance and Romance literature not wishing to invite comparison with my father'. By 1950 or thereabouts he finished his course work for a doctorate degree and his memoirs continue thus:

> Once my course work was out of the way, I spent most of my times writing a doctoral dissertation. This was a life and critical study of Sir Edwin Arnold, a mediocre Victorian poet, journalist and orientalist whom I had first read in Karachi. The research was such a pleasure that I could have prolonged it indefinitely—I even spent a term studying Sanskrit, until Father became alarmed that I would never finish. I was obsessed with setting down every fact I could find, so that the final text ran into nine hundred typed pages. I doubt even if the examining committee read it; Douglas Bush [his Professor] seemed to be under the impression I had written on Matthew Arnold. Instead of questioning me about the thesis, they quizzed me about the whole range of Victorian literature.

Wright had discovered Arnold in Karachi in June 1943. But it was, by his own admission, not *The Light of Asia* he had first read but actually *The Song Celestial*. That experience, along with his experience in India and Ceylon, seems to have lingered long for it to have become the subject of his academic study. It is fairly certain that Wright would have become aware of *The Light of Asia* in the late 1940s or early 1950s when he started writing his thesis, which then became the standard (and only) reference on Arnold's entire life and career. In Wright's archives is a letter from Arnold's widow, who wrote to him from London on 26 November 1957—she was eighty-eight then.

> This is a preliminary letter only to thank you for a copy of the book which you have so successfully published: "Interpreter of Buddhism to the West: Sir Edwin Arnold".

Unfortunately, as you know, I must wait until I have this book read aloud to me before I write to you again; but in the meantime may I say how delighted I am, and how much I congratulate you on the quality of the production. I do hope it will be successful— We shall enquire for it in bookshops here.

I do not know whether you possess copies of all my husband's writings: it would be a great pleasure to me to send any of those you may not already have.

With every good wish,
Tama Arnold

Sadly, other than this, nothing more is available as far as Lady Arnold is concerned. Wright's biography was a moderate commercial success but would begin to have substantial academic value that would grow over the years, both in the field of Victorian poetry and Buddhist studies.

The title of Wright's biography, *Interpreter of Buddhism to the West: Sir Edwin Arnold*, is both misleading and limiting. Arnold was not as much an interpreter as he was a populariser. He did, of course, speak on Buddhism to various audiences in the UK, USA and Japan but by no stretch of imagination could he be called a scholar of Buddhism, which is what is implied in the word 'Interpreter'. And his footprint was not confined to the West. He ended up having an impact in the East as well, as testified by the translations of *The Light of Asia* in many Indian and other Asian languages. In 1970—and I am fast-forwarding this narrative for a moment— William Peiris would publish, under the aegis of the Buddhist Publication Society, Kandy, a very substantive monograph titled *Edwin Arnold: His Services to Buddhism*. Peiris thanked Wright for giving him permission to 'paraphrase paragraphs from his excellent book'. Peiris would add much value from the point of view of a practising Buddhist and his publication has become a very widely-quoted work. It is still in circulation.

The Indian Institute of World Culture had been established in the late 1940s on a one-acre plot in Basavanagudi, a bustling suburb of Bangalore. On the evening of 11 August 1958, a group of men and women gathered at the Institute when they got news of the demise of its founder. Passages from the Bhagavad Gita, *The Voice of the Silence*[18] and *The Light of Asia*—three devotional books that the founder had loved for decades—were read and the next morning B.P. Wadia was cremated. Wadia had been closely associated with Madame Blavatsky, Olcott and Annie Besant. He had organized India's first labour union in Madras in April 1918. Four years later he broke with Annie Besant and started propagating his own version of theosophy, close to the original Blavatsky vision. In the early 1940s, he settled down in Bangalore. A year after his death, the road on which the Institute set up by him still stands was named after him.

Wadia was not the only Parsi of that era to be mesmerized by *The Light of Asia*. K.D. Sethna was a prolific poet and philosopher who lived till the age of 106 and died in 2011. Deeply drawn to spiritualism, he had joined the Aurobindo Ashram in Pondicherry in 1927 and remained there till his death. He was an important figure in the Ashram and an interpreter of Aurobindo's thoughts and ideas. In 1949, a leading Indian publishing house reissued Arnold's *The Light of Asia* and *The Indian Song of Songs* as a one-volume set.[19] This would be reprinted from time to time, most recently in 1999. It would have a long and learned introduction titled 'Message of *The Light of Asia*' by Sethna that would deal with the significance of the Buddha, the meaning of Buddhism and their relevance for the coming era. Sethna would explain the convergence between the Buddha's philosophy and that of Vedanta preached by Vivekananda, something that Vivekananda had himself highlighted a century earlier. Sethna's parting words were:

> Today, he is no more; but his name abides, as it would doubtless abide for generations to come—through his immortal works . . . Sir Edwin Arnold, author of The Light of Asia, the Song Celestial, The Indian Song of Songs, etc.

Sethna was not the only 'disciple' of Aurobindo to be enchanted by *The Light of Asia*. Maurice Marge was one of the first French authors to write about Buddhism and what we would now call 'spirituality'. In 1928 he had written a book called *Pourquoi je suis bouddhiste (Why I am a Buddhist)* and seven years later visited Pondicherry. In his memoirs, Magre would recall that a change in his personal destiny came about through reading Arnold's epic poem, given to him by 'une amie' (a female friend). Four years before his death he would be awarded the Grand Prize in Literature by the French Academy.

The early 1950s had seen the first doctoral dissertation on *The Light of Asia* at an American university. The end of the decade would see a similar submission at an Indian university. In 1959, K.R. Mahishi would get a Ph.D. from the University of Bombay for his *Sir Edwin Arnold: Man and Writer.* Mahishi elaborated on his subject's love of India but there is not much on the influence of India itself on Arnold's creative writings, especially *The Light of Asia* and *The Song Celestial.* Access to archival material (or any material for that matter) at that time in an Indian university would have been very tough, as would the availability of travel grants. We should not judge a thesis of that period by today's standards.

The year 1959 would also see the publication of a now-famous book, *What the Buddha Taught* by the Sri Lankan scholar Walpola Sri Rahula. Rahula was an unusual personality. He had received the traditional training and education of a Buddhist monk in that island nation. He then acquired formal academic degrees from Ceylon University and worked at the University of Calcutta. Thereafter he went to the Sorbonne in Paris to study Chinese and Tibetan texts but all the time wearing the yellow robe. It was while he was in Paris that his classic work appeared. Rahula had made wide use of original Pali texts, but also included in his bibliography was an eighty-year-old epic poem. The position in the bibliography was, however, the result of the poem's author having a name beginning with the alphabet 'A'. But for *The Light of Asia* to figure in such a landmark book was indeed a reflection of its enduring appeal.

Notes

1. Hendrick and Henderson (1950)
2. Quoted in Barnett (2007)
3. Murray (1952)
4. Ibid. Murray rightly points that as compared to other Victorian greats like Thomas Babington Macaulay, John Ruskin and Matthew Arnold, Edwin Arnold was an inveterate Indophile except, of course, when it came to Indian self-rule. Ruskin's attitude towards everything about India did not, however, prevent Mahatma Gandhi from becoming one of his ardent admirers. Gandhi's Phoenix Farm in South Africa and his tract *Hind Swaraj* were both inspired by Ruskin. I thank Gopal Gandhi for these observations and for pointing out that there were two Ruskins!
5. There were twenty-six nations plus four others with observer status. A Tibetan delegation also participated despite protests from the Kuomintang delegates.
6. Pryor (2012) is a very useful discussion of developments in Bodh Gaya during 1953–2012.
7. Four days later, the *Times of India* would carry an article that pithily analysed the decline of Buddhism in India. This was by one of twentieth-century India's greatest polymaths, D.D. Kosambi, the son of Dharmanand Kosambi, who, as this narrative has shown, had become fascinated by the Buddha after reading the Marathi translation of *The Light of Asia* in 1899 and later had converted to Buddhism.
8. This is a reference to Ashvaghosha's *Buddhacarita.*, the 'most impressive biography of the Buddha dated to the first century CE or soon after'. It was in Sanskrit. Thapar (2013) writes that 'the original Buddhacarita covered the life of the Buddha, but the existing Sanskrit text stops soon after the enlightenment—the later chapters exist in a Chinese translation'.
9. Email communication 26 March 2020. Rathore is the author of *Ambedkar's Preamble* (2020).
10. Kosambi (2010) has quite an extensive discussion on this point.
11. Moon (1992). However, it should also be mentioned that in 1940 and 1941, Kosambi's more conventional two-volume biography of the Buddha in Marathi had appeared. This would be translated into thirteen Indian languages by the Sahitya Akademi on the occasion of the Buddha Jayanti celebrations in 1956. It would also be declared as the official text on Buddha's life and work when Dr Ambedkar along with his followers would embrace Buddhism in Nagpur on 14 October 1956.

12. This is explained in detail in Macy and Zelliot (1980).
13. Another scholarly challenge to the conventional wisdom on the Buddha and his life as depicted, for instance, in *The Light of Asia* would be published in 1959. This was by the Marxist philosopher Debiprasad Chattopadhyaya in his *Lokayata: A Study in Ancient Indian Materialism.*
14. Guha (2018)
15. Guha (2018) writes: 'The credit for effecting this reconciliation with Ambedkar lies largely with Amrit Kaur, through her discussions with him on the sidelines of the Constituent Assembly. She was a Christian of Sikh background, and a woman too. Ambedkar would surely have perceived Amrit Kaur in less antagonistic terms than he had those powerful upper-caste Hindu males: Gandhi, Nehru and Patel.'
16. *Books That Influenced Me,* G.A. Natesan & Co. Madras 1947. This was the same volume in which C.V. Raman also had written about the influence of *The Light of Asia* on him.
17. Wright (1957)
18. This was a book by Madame Blavatsky.
19. Jaico Publishing House, 1949 (first edition)

19

The 1960s and 1970s: Continuing Academic Studies on *The Light of Asia* and Recollections in India and Sri Lanka

Three years after Wright's biography was published, the first of the academic works building on it was completed. This was a doctoral dissertation in October 1960 by an Indian student at the University of Toronto. The subject was 'Edwin Arnold's Anglo-Indian Poetry' and the student was Hesaraghatta Narasimha Lakshminarasimha Sastri. Sastri drew upon Wright for Arnold's biographical details but had three chapters of his own analyzing *The Light of Asia*, *The Sing Celestial* and *The Indian Song of Songs* in sharp detail. Sastri's great contribution was his analysis of sources for *The Light of Asia* and his discussion on the three main impulses in Arnold's works: 'the assimilation of Indian material to Christian patterns of thought familiar to Western readers; second, his advocacy of the Indian doctrines of Karma and transmigration as solutions to the conflicting problems of science and religion in his age; and finally, his depiction of Indian life and landscape'.

The thesis itself would remain unpublished but judging from references to it in later works, it did get known in the academic community at least. After his return to India, Sastri made a name for himself at Osmania University and at the Central Institute for English in Hyderabad that had been started in 1958. It would become the Central Institute of English and Foreign Languages in 1972 and is today known as the English and Foreign Languages University, managed by the Government of India.

Pandurang Vaman Kane was one of the greatest Indological scholars of the twentieth century. In 1962, when he was eighty-two, he published his fifth and final volume of the monumental

History of Dharmasastra. It was the culmination of three decades of unparalleled scholarship. The fifth volume was in two parts and in the second was a chapter titled 'Causes of the disappearance of Buddhism from India' in which he also dwelt on why the Buddha had become popular in the first place in Indian society:

> Buddha's renunciation of his princely position, of his young wife, child and home, to become a wandering ascetic for discovering the path of humanity's deliverance from sorrow and suffering, his subsequent mortification of the body for years, his retirement into solitude for meditation, struggle with Mara and final victory, his confidence that he had discovered the path of deliverance, his constant travels from city to city and village to village for about forty-five years for preaching the great truths he had discovered, his crusade against the slaughter of innocent and dumb animals in sacrifices, his passing away full of years and in peace and contentment—this panorama of Buddha's life has a noble grandeur and irresistible human appeal.

By the time Kane was writing this, there were numerous books that had appeared on the Buddha and Buddhism. But to amplify what he was saying, he chose a book that had been published over eighty years earlier and been translated into his mother-tongue to substantiate what he was saying. He went on:

> Edwin Arnold in his preface (p XIII) to his poem 'Light of Asia' (1884) pays a very eloquent tribute to Buddha's teachings in the following words: 'this venerable religion which has in it the eternity of a universal hope, the immortality of a boundless love, an indestructible element of faith in the final good and the proudest assertion ever made of human freedom.

In January 1962 Kane was honoured with the Bharat Ratna, India's highest civilian award, which is sparingly given.

17 September 1964 marked the birth centenary of Anagarika Dharmapala. It would be celebrated in Ceylon and India as well.

On 25 October 1964 the Indian Prime Minister Lal Bahadur Shastri planted a sapling from the historic Bodhi tree at Anuradhapura[1] in New Delhi's 2500-acre Buddha Jayanti Park that had been created as part of the 2500th *mahaparinirvana* celebrations eight years earlier. The sapling had been brought by the visiting Ceylonese Premier Sirimavo Bandaranaike. Exactly a year later would appear *Return to Righteousness: A Collection of Speeches, Essays and Letters of the Anagarika Dharmapala.* This was edited by Ananda Guruge and published by the Government of Ceylon.[2]

This was the first comprehensive and systematic collection of Dharmapala's writings. There would be many more books on contemporary Buddhism in the sub-continent that would come to be published in later years in which Dharmapala would figure prominently. But Guruge's 1965 volume is still invaluable. It reveals the great admiration that Dharmapala had all his life for *The Light of Asia* and its author. I must also say here that in this collection there are repeated references to Arnold being the man who first thought of liberating the Mahabodhi Temple at Buddha Gaya from the control of Hindu priests in 1886.

This, as I have documented from primary sources earlier, is, strictly speaking, *not* accurate. The idea may have been fermenting in Arnold's mind after his experience at Buddha Gaya in February 1886, but it was Dharmapala's 'guru' of sorts Weligama Sri Sumangala who first put out the idea, which Arnold would run with and campaign for relentlessly. In fact, on 14 December 1891, Dharmapala had written to Weligama Sri Sumangala saying that 'the benefit of your being a friend of Sir Edwin Arnold is enormous'. Two other letters of Dharmapala to Weligama Sri Sumangala are of particular interest. The first is of 16 March 1892 when Dharmapala had told the senior monk–scholar:

> It is time to propagate Buddhism in India. Educated Bengalis have faith in Buddhism. Leading members of the intelligentsia of Calcutta are keen to study Buddhism. An association has been established for this purpose. But it is difficult to do this work

without monks. If you are invited by these learned people, can you come? It is a tragedy no effort is made to propagate the doctrine. It is sad not to give the gift of the doctrine to those anxious to receive it. As we must act before Sir Edwin Arnold comes to Sri Lanka, please discuss with Sumangala Nayaka Thera (ie. Ven. Hikkaduwe Sri Sumangala Mahanayaka Thera). All members of the Sangha must come together in this task.

A few months later, on 30 September 1892, Dharmapala had informed Weligama Sri Sumangala again:

I do not know why the Buddhists of Sri Lanka do not put in a greater effort even though Sir Arnold is exerting himself immensely [on Buddha Gaya]. I request you . . . to convene a meeting of monks and laymen. It is important to have the King of Thailand as the head . . . It appears that the Japanese Buddhists are very energetic. Sir Edwin Arnold has stated in Japan that he was prepared to sacrifice his life for this cause [getting Buddhist control over the Mahabodhi Temple at Buddha Gaya] . . .

We know, however, that despite his public pronouncements Arnold never came back to the sub-continent after March 1886, but we have seen earlier how much he influenced Japanese priests to take to take up the Buddha Gaya matter with a view to getting Buddhist control over the Mahabodhi Temple there.

There is one other letter of Dharmapala included in Guruge's humungous volume that merits special mention. In June 1915 riots had broken out between Buddhists and Muslims in Ceylon. Dharmapala was in Calcutta when this happened. The British government interred him there and barred him from going back to Ceylon for five years. Dharmapala then made up his mind to 'send thoughts of love to the British Bureaucrats' who were responsible for his internment. As he put it, 'instead of hatred, compassion sprang in my heart to the British people'. The first

long missive went on 7 July 1916 to Bonar Law, then Secretary
of State for the Colonies:

> In 1891 I came to India on a pilgrimage to the holy shrine at
> Buddhagaya where the Sakya Prince Siddhartha became the
> perfect all-knowing Buddha, and seeing the neglect I vowed to
> rescue it from its then desecrated condition. Since then I have
> been an exile for my faith in India . . .
>
> From 1886 to 1890 I was engaged in Ceylon as an
> educationalist and from 1891 to 1916 I was engaged in the work
> of Buddhist revival in India, returning to the Island to see my
> parents once in a couple of years. The great moral teachers of the
> world from the Lord Buddha the oldest of all . . . have been my
> examples . . . Force, aggression, assassination, murder do not come
> under the great moral law of the Lord Buddha. Truth, freedom,
> compassionateness, aestheticism are the principles of my religion
> as shown by the Sakya Prince Siddhartha, whose life has been
> beautifully described by the late Sir Edwin Arnold in his 'Light
> of Asia' and Sir Edwin in his book "East and West" calls me "my
> excellent friend" . . .

Half a century after Guruge's volume, two grand biographies of
Dharmapala were to appear, the first in 2015 by Steven Kemper,
an American anthropologist[3] and the other four years later by
Sarath Amunugama, a Sri Lankan politician-scholar.[4] Both would
call attention to the importance of *The Light of Asia* and of Arnold
himself in Dharmapala's life, especially in the 1880s and 1890s.
Dharmapala is seen as the founding father of religious nationalism
in the country of his birth but the truth is that he was perhaps the
most important figure in the revival of Buddhism in the first half
of the twentieth century as well. And it is largely through him that
Arnold's influence on Buddhism in India and other parts of Asia
would be evident. Dharmapala was a hugely conflicted man but he
was, equally hugely, a pivotal figure in the world of Buddhism for
almost half a century till his death in 1933.

Commemorative stamp issued by the Government of India to mark the 150th birth anniversary of Anagarika Dharmapala.

Dong Trung Con was one of the most respected Buddhist scholars of twentieth-century Vietnam. He had deep knowledge of both Indian and Chinese cultures and was more than conversant with Pali and Sanskrit. After almost half a century of research and writing on Buddhism, he became a monk in the early seventies. One of his well-known publications was the Vietnamese translation of *The Light of Asia* that was published in Saigon in 1965. There would be other translations in the 1990s.

By the end of the 1960s *The Light of Asia* had made its presence felt in the Indian languages in which it had been missing so far. In 1951, Mayadhar Mansinha, one of the titans of Odiya literature, who converted to Buddhism, wrote a play called *Buddha*. In his introduction, he described his personal and intellectual interest in exploring the major faiths and the reasons why he finally chose

Buddhism. He paid a tribute to Western scholars who made the treasures of Buddhism available to the world and singled out *The Light of Asia* for its major role in spreading the message of Buddhism in the West.

One of his last acts before he passed away was to secure a plot of land for the Mahabodhi Society in Bhubaneswar. In 1958, Nikunja Krishna Das drama in Odiya appeared. Das introduced it by saying *The Light of Asia* had shown him the path. *Asiar Jyoti*, a drama in Assamese, was published in 1960. This was by Ananda Chandra Barua, a distinguished name in Assamese literature. Many years later, in 1994, Barua's work would also appear as a prose biography of the Buddha.

The world marked 1969 as the birth centenary of Mahatma Gandhi, in whose life both *The Light of Asia* and more importantly *The Song Celestial* had played a very important part. This was also the year a very adventurous French woman who had made major contributions to the understanding of Buddhist traditions would pass away near Paris. Alexandra David Neel was 101 when she died, and had spent some years in Sikkim, Tibet and India as well. She had studied in London in the 1880s when *The Light of Asia* was a rage. Drawn to the Theosophical Society in London and Paris, it is inconceivable that she would not have been moved by it, though her biographer[5] says the transformative moment was when Neel saw the fabulous collection of Buddhist art at the Museum Guimet in Paris.

It was this Museum that had sent Sophia Egoroff with an introduction to the Mahabodhi Society in Calcutta in 1907 or 1908 and it was also at this museum that Egoroff's painting *Gautama Sakyamuni* renouncing the world was exhibited. In 1969 itself Suzanne Karpales, another unusual Frenchwoman who had played a crucial role in reviving Buddhism in Cambodia, passed away. Karpales had translated for Tagore when he visited Paris in the 1920s. It is possible but not definitive that she would have related to *The Light of Asia* through either her French or Indian networks. She would spend her last years in Pondicherry in the company of yet another French woman who had come there decades earlier as

Mirra Alfassa Richards and had metamorphosed as 'Mother' at the Aurobindo Ashram.

I have already mentioned William Peiris' very widely read monograph on Edwin Arnold that was published in Kandy in 1970. Two years later in May 1972 would come the fifth doctoral dissertation on *The Light of Asia*. This would be by Christopher Clausen at Queens University in Kingston, Canada. Clausen specialized in nineteenth-century British Literature and would go on to have a noted academic career in the USA. He would also write a somewhat unusual *My Life with President Kennedy*, which is about 'the experiences and attitudes of one who came of age in the first half of that now mythical decade, the 1960s'.

Clausen's thesis remains highly readable and valuable as well even today. It is not just an examination of religious attitudes in the England of the late nineteenth century which formed the backdrop to *The Light of Asia*. It is more than an evaluation of the sources, merits and ideas of the poem itself. He compares the landmark 1879 edition with the other landmark 1884 edition and brings out the variations introduced by Arnold. More importantly, he provides extensive notes to explain 'matters relating to Buddhist legend and doctrine referred to in the poem' and clarifies in English the meaning of various Sanskrit and Anglo-Indian words and passages that Arnold had left unexplained. That is why, appropriately, the thesis is called:

The Light of Asia
By Sir Edwin Arnold

An Annotated Critical Edition

Four years after Clausen's dissertation, a volume of essays called *The Biographical Process: Studies in the History and Psychology of Religion* appeared.[6] It had contributions from leading scholars covering Buddhism, Christianity, Hinduism and Islam. The very first piece, by Frank Reynolds of the University of Chicago, examined the many lives of the Buddha, particularly in the Theravada tradition. Reynolds traced Western interest in the Buddha to as early as the fourth century CE but pointed out that it was in the nineteenth century that interest in the Buddha as a figure grew rapidly through 'the publication of translations of various Indian, Burmese, Thai, Tibetan and Chinese versions of the sacred biography, through the publication of popular romanticized renderings such as the famous work of Edwin Arnold's entitled *The Light of Asia* and through the development of a body of serious philological and historical scholarship'.

1979 would mark the centenary of the very first edition of *The Light of Asia*. It was not entirely forgotten. Vishwanath S. Naravane, a professor of philosophy at the University of Poona, would write *Edwin Arnold and The Light of Asia* in a publication brought out by the Government of India.[7] Five years earlier, Naravane along with Robert McDermott had edited the well-received *The Spirit of Modern India*, an anthology of writings on Indian philosophy, religion and culture. In his centenary piece, Naravane observed:

> India has special reasons for commemorating the centenary of the publication of *The Light of Asia* and paying a tribute to its author. Edwin Arnold belonged to that select and small band of British administrators in India who not only combined literary and scholarly pursuits with their official work but also identified themselves with the feelings, ideals and aspirations and traditions of the Indian people. He was among the first western writers who tried to remove prejudices against India in the western world and presented a fair picture of the positive aspects of Indian culture.

To Naravane, Arnold's treatment of the Buddha's life and his search for the deeper meaning behind the Buddha legend had several important features, of which three needed to be remembered:

> In the first place, he brings out the close relationship between Buddhism and Hinduism, and places the Buddha firmly in the

Indian milieu . . . The Buddha's god is to fulfill, not to destroy. Secondly, in Edwin Arnold's work there is a constant emphasis on the aesthetic side of Buddha's personality. The Light of Asia contains some fine descriptions of natural beauty, and Prince Siddhartha is shown as being keenly sensitive to the sights, sounds and scents of his natural environment . . . Thirdly, in Arnold's interpretation Nirvana—the central core of Buddha's teaching—ceases to be an abstract, empty concept. In The Light of Asia, the Buddha does not speak of Nirvana in detail. He is reticent because Nirvana, the transcendental reality, is indescribable . . .

A hundred years earlier *The Light of Asia* had owed a large part of its success to the presumed similarity that Arnold had succeeded in conveying in the lives of the Buddha and of Christ. Now, he was being hailed for producing a work that had established the natural affinity between Buddhism and Hinduism. It was indeed a reflection of the changed times. Or was it really? After all, eight decades earlier Vivekananda had declared:

Arnold's book The Light of Asia, represents more of Vedantism than Buddhism.

Not surprisingly, one of the most moving tributes to Arnold three months after his death would appear in *Prabuddha Bharata*, the publication of the Ramakrishna Mission established by Vivekananda.

Notes

1. *Mahavamsa*, the ancient Sri Lankan chronicle, says that Sanghamitta, Ashoka's daughter, carried the southern branch of the holy Bodhi tree in the Mahabodhi Temple complex at Bodh Gaya to Lanka.
2. Guruge (1965)
3. Kemper (2015)
4. Amunugama (2019)
5. Middleton (1989)
6. Reynolds and Capps (1976)
7. Naravane (1980)

20

The 1980s and 1990s: Art Exhibitions, Victorian Buddhism Examined and Post-Colonial Analysis of *The Light of Asia*

Carl T. Jackson published his *The Oriental Religions and American Thought: Nineteenth Century Explorations* in 1981.[1] He had absolutely no hesitation in tracing the beginning of interest in Buddhism to *The Light of Asia*. He pointed out that the impact of the poem was so stunning that it 'seems to have opened the door to cranks' who propagated the idea that Christ himself was actually a Buddhist. But not all were cranks. The theory that the foundations of Christianity were to be found in Buddhism and that Christ had spent time in India were actually seriously debated in the last years of the nineteenth century in America, with even books being written on it.[2] Jackson added:

> It is hard to exaggerate Arnold's role in increasing American popular interest in Buddhism and Oriental thought generally. Other writers had presented Eastern conceptions with some success—James Freeman Clarke most effectively—but none approached his ability to reach a general audience. As one writer would suggest, he took Buddhism out of the study and into the parlors and workshops. In the barbershop recently, his barber had "suddenly poised his shears and comb" and "confounded" him with the question: "What do you think of *The Light of Asia*?" Any writer whose work is discussed in a barbershop must be said to have attained some popular following. Writing twenty-five years later, Benjamin Flower, editor of *The Arena*, still looked back on Arnold's Light of Asia as "one of the most remarkable

poetic successes of the century". Scholars like Max Muller had done splendid work in opening the riches of India, but their work had only reached a few; Arnold had brought those riches "to the people".

In November 1984, there opened an unusual exhibition at the Brooklyn Museum in New York, which had been previously shown in Los Angeles and Chicago. But New York is New York. One hundred seventy-nine objects on a single subject were on display, drawn from various countries that included the USA itself, France, Germany, India, Japan, Thailand, Korea, Belgium, England and Switzerland. The exhibition would run for about three months to wide acclaim and appreciation. It had been organized by Pratapaditya Pal, then a senior curator at the Los Angeles County Museum and a recognized authority on Indian art. The exhibition was entitled *The Light of Asia* and traced the look of the Buddha as imagined by sculptors and painters in India, Ceylon, Nepal, Tibet, Korea, China, Japan and elsewhere. I asked Pal about his recollections of the 1984 exhibition:[3]

> How interesting you are writing a biography of The Light of Asia in a country that seems to have forgotten the Buddha . . . Of course, I purloined the title [of the exhibition] from Arnold as I could not think of a better title . . . As far as I was concerned there was no other alternative. I think I had a copy of the poem which I bought when I was in my teens and still love to read it from time to time.

But the *New York Times* critic John Russell had commented on 2 December 1984:

> The title is taken from a poem by Sir Edwin Arnold (1832-1904). If Arnold is kindly thought of among members of my profession [journalism], it is not for the general level of his work, which could hardly be lower, but for the line in his "Tenth Muse" that characterizes newspapermen as "Press-men; Slaves of the Lamp;

Servants of Light". This particular servant of the light has always
had trouble disentangling the syntax, let alone the sense, of
Arnold's "Light of Asia" but the poem does nonetheless embody a
general perception that has never ceased to be correct. The social
and cultural traditions of Asia owe more to Buddha Sakyamuni
than to any other human being.

Russell was however in full praise of the exhibition itself.

Philip Almond's *The British Discovery of Buddhism* came out
in 1988.[4] It was the first systematic study of why the Buddha and
Buddhism came to occupy such a prominent place in nineteenth-
century public discourse in Britain. It deals with not just the process
of discovery of this faith and founder by British administrators
and scholars (with some help from other Europeans) but more
importantly of its interpretation. Almond's work located the Buddha
in what was happening in Victorian society in the fields of religion,
politics and science as well. Almond's book was, in some ways, a
successor to P.J. Marshall's *The British Discovery of Hinduism*[5] that
had appeared eighteen years earlier.

Almond would go well beyond making a passing reference
to *The Light of Asia*; he would, in fact, begin with its immortal
closing lines and attribute to it 'an enormous upsurge in awareness
of, and interest in, Buddhism in late Victorian England'—and,
thereby, in many other parts of the world under its influence,
including America and India. I should add, however, that
Almond would come under attack in 2012 by Urs App, who
showed by a meticulous study of Japanese and Jesuit sources that
Europeans had already by the mid-sixteenth century come to
regard Buddhism as a separate religion.[6] Indeed, App traces the
birth of what has come to be known as 'Orientalism' following the
publication of Edward Said's eponymous book in 1878 to Jesuit
study of Buddhist sects, doctrines and practices in sixteenth-
century Japan.

Diwan Chand Ahir was a civil servant who had retired from
a middle-level position in the Government of India in 1986.

He had first met Dr Ambedkar in New Delhi in March 1946 as an eighteen-year-old teenager and inspired by him took up the study of the Buddha and Buddhism. A few days before Dr Ambedkar's conversion to Buddhism in October 1956, Ahir also embraced that religion. Over a period of six decades, Ahir would write hundreds of books and articles in English and Hindi on the subject. His has been described as 'a ubiquitous presence' in modern Buddhist studies in India. Some of his books are invaluable reference works even though they are, strictly speaking, not scholarly in the academic sense of the term.

His *The Pioneers of Buddhist Revival in India* appeared in 1989, in which he gave life-sketches of those who those who had given a new lease of life to an old faith. Ahir's list that had thirty names including Dharmapala, Kosambi, Iyotee Thass and Dr Ambedkar. He also had a separate section on four people he called 'Friends of Buddhism—the author of *The Light of Asia*, Rabindranath Tagore, the philanthropist Jugal Kishore Birla and Jawaharlal Nehru'. In 1994, his *Buddha Gaya Through the Ages* would highlight Arnold's role in making possible Buddhist involvement in the management of the Mahabodhi Temple.

In 1991 the influence of *The Light of Asia* on the American writer Theodore Dreiser would be unearthed by Douglas Stenerson.[7] Dreiser was a novelist and journalist who 'saw humans as pawns amid material forces'. His book *Sister Carrie* of 1900 was number thirty-three in the hundred best English novels of the century ranked by Robert McCrum in the *Guardian* in 2014. Stenerson found ample evidence of *The Light of Asia*'s impact on Dreiser's short stories, sketches and poems, as well as on his work that remained unpublished but was carefully preserved in his archives. Nine substantial excerpts of the poem were written down in his scrapbooks sometime between 1900 and 1916. Stenerson estimates that Dreiser read it in the first decade of the century 'when its vogue was still strong'. Dreiser's literary use of Hindu teachings had been known in the 1970s itself but Stenerson was the first to draw attention to the role *The Light of Asia* had played in Dreiser's life.[8]

Arnold had never been to Burma, but as I have mentioned earlier, his very last poetic piece was on the Shwe Dagon Pagoda in Rangoon. His son Channing Arnold had worked there for over five years and so had the Englishman Allan Bennett, who became Ananda Metteya, having converted to Buddhism after reading *The Light of Asia*. I would guess that the poem itself would not have been unknown among the educated sections in Burma thanks to the theosophists and to the circulation of Buddha-related literature among Thailand, Burma and Ceylon. The first translation of *The Light of Asia* into Burmese would take place in 1992, by a Myanmarese writer Maung Tha Noe.[9] He had introduced modernism into Burmese literature in the 1960s and had become one of the country's most prolific literary translators, who had also translated Edward Fitzgerald and T.S. Eliot into Burmese. There would be some more editions later as well.

One prominent Burmese author and political commentator who had been enchanted by *The Light of Asia* in the middle part of the twentieth century was certainly Shwe U Daung, the creator of the very popular 'San Shan the Detective', a Burmese adaptation of the Sherlock Holmes stories.[10] These had appeared over half a century, initially in *Thuriya*, the monthly magazine of the Young Men's Buddhist Association (YMBA) in Rangoon, which like the YMBA in Colombo, enjoyed a close relationship with the Theosophical Society.

Any scholar who studies the revival of Buddhism in India in the twentieth century will have at the top of his or her bibliography the name of C.V. Agarwal. In 1993 Agarwal would publish a slim book that looked at the role of the founders of the Theosophical Society in the rediscovery of India's (and Sri Lanka's) Buddhist heritage. It still remains a useful starting point for those looking at the confluence of both the Buddhist and the Theosophical Movements in the subcontinent. He begins his examination by recalling the final lines in Book the Sixth of *The Light of Asia*, which, in turn, correspond to verses 153-154 of the *Dhammapada* that are the celebrated words uttered by the Buddha when he attained nirvana.[11]

MANY A HOUSE OF LIFE

HATH HELD ME—SEEKING EVER HIM WHO
    WROUGHT

THESE PRISONS OF THE SENSES, SORROW-
    FRAUGHT;

SORE WAS MY CEASELESS STRIFE!

BUT NOW,

THOU BUILDER OF THE TABERNACLE—THOU!

I KNOW THEE! NEVER SHALL THOU BUILD AGAIN

THESE WALLS OF PAIN,

NOR RAISE THE ROOF-TREE OF DECEITS, NOR LAY

FRESH RAFTERS FOR THE CLAY;

BROKEN THY HOUSE IS, AND THE RIDGE-POLE
    SPLIT!

DELUSION FASHIONED IT!

SAFE PASS I THENCE—DELIVERANCE TO OBTAIN.

Agarwal's book would be reprinted in 2001 and translated into German, French and Finnish as well.

The 1884–85 Trubner & Co edition of *The Light of Asia* was be the first to be published with illustrations from Buddhist sites across India. This certainly enhanced the visual appeal of the book. The tradition of having illustrations would be continued. The 1926 edition with illustrations by the artist Hamzeh Carr was a landmark. Seventy years later, another lavishly illustrated *The Light of Asia* would appear, published by the Sri Lankan monk, the Venerable Weragoda Sarada Maha Thero, who was then heading the Buddhist Meditation Centre at Singapore, a one-man institution of book publishing as it were. The numerous illustrations this time were derived very largely from relatively little-known eighteenth-century mural paintings from Buddhist temples in Sri Lanka. This would soon become a very popular publication, still very much in circulation because of the manner in which original poem was presented and explained as well.

Ascetic Siddhartha attaining enlightenment under the Bodhi tree at Buddha Gaya. Painting by Sri Lankan artists in 1996 edition of The Light of Asia *published by Buddhist Meditation Centre, Singapore*

But in the late 1980s there would be some counterattacks too, which was only to be expected, given how the Victorian era itself, epitomized by its poetry, was under intellectual assault for being the apogee of imperialism. The bugle was blown first in 1988 by Patrick Brantlinger in his *British Literature and Imperialism: 1830–1914*, in which Arnold got a very brief mention.[12] Colin Graham's was the first serious charge in *Ideologies of Epic: Nation Empire and Victorian Epic Poetry* that appeared exactly a decade after Almond's path-breaking work.[13] Graham takes three poets to make his point: not surprisingly, Lord Tennyson, Samuel Fergusson and Edwin Arnold. So far, Arnold had been written about as being a 'minor Victorian poet' but Graham elevated his importance hugely. The poems said to represent the values of the British Empire were Tennyson's *Idylls to the King,* whose first part was published in 1842 and substantially completed in 1872, Fergusson's *Congal* that also came out in 1872 and Arnold's *The Light of Asia, The Song Celestial* and *Indian Idylls.* This was a whole new critical perspective on these three poems of Arnold.

Graham held that 'in the main Arnold's work is part of the discourse of cultural dominance typical of imperialism'. He went on:

> Arnold expresses beliefs, concerns and attitudes common with the aims of prevailing British policy to the East and the rest of the empire. But Arnold's poetry, particularly in The Light of Asia, also reveals a propensity to express a notion of the East which is bound to be sympathetic in the West. Arnold takes the value of Eastern religion, the consequences of (what the West has discovered about) Eastern 'antiquity' too far for some of his Western readers. The Light of Asia gained both popularity and hatred because it dwelt upon the similarities of Christianity and Buddhism and the fact that Buddha, who can be easily made to resemble Christ, existed, historically speaking, before Christ.

Graham's acknowledges that Arnold was convinced by 'the worth of Indian culture and the value of its epics' but his mistake was in translating them 'in terms which would be recognized by his audience'. But what else he could have done then is a question not posed. Arnold was definitely an apologist for the British Empire and was deeply, deeply hostile to even Lord Ripon's idea of self-government that had been embraced by the newly formed Indian National Congress. But to argue that through his translations he was providing justification for the continuation of the British Empire is, in my view, mistaken.

The large readership of *The Light of Asia* not just in English but also in many Indian languages does not seem to have impressed Graham. To see political meanings in his translations when none exist is wrong. I do not believe that Arnold's literary output was in any way meant to consolidate British power in India or to provide an intellectual justification for its domination over the Indian people.[14] And I wonder what Graham would have made of the fact that the fiercely nationalistic Bal Gangadhar Tilak, who was sent off to prison for six years between 1908 and 1914 in Mandalay by the British, had earlier insisted that the Deccan College in Poona where he had studied retain a portrait of Sir Edwin Arnold—which still stands.

But Graham's would be a strand of thinking that would not go away. His line of attack would be repeated in 2006 by Simon Dentith[15] and four years later in 2013 by Christopher Hagerman, who would also see in much of Arnold's literary output a justification for British (benevolent of course) rule in India.[16] It is Arnold's tracing the antiquity of 'suttee' to the first century BCE Latin poet Sextus Propertius and sympathy with it that Hagerman found baffling— and on this, as I have pointed out earlier, I too found it intriguing that a man of Arnold's sensibilities would be so antediluvian in regard to suttee.[17]

Ironically, in the same year that Graham's attack was published, a new edition of *The Light of Asia* was released. Sangharakshita, born Dennis Philip Edward Lingwood, had founded the British Triratna Buddhist Community, which was known till 2010 as Friends of the Western Buddhist Order. The present UK Attorney General Suella Braverman belongs to this community. Sangharakshita had formally become a Buddhist in May 1944 and lived in the sub-continent till 1966. He had been in close touch with Dr Ambedkar since 1950 and wrote a book on Ambedkar and Buddhism that was published. In 1998 he released a new, deluxe edition of *The Light of Asia* with an introduction by him self and published out of London. In his remarks, Sangharakshita recalled:

> Those who have read the first volume of my memoirs may recollect it [The Light of Asia] was one of the very small volumes which I packed into my kit-bag when I went, or rather when I was sent [having been conscripted into the British Army] to India in 1944, and I have had a copy of it, I think, around me since that time. . . .

[There are] five reasons for which it is worth reading. First of all, it tells the story of the Buddha's life. Second, it isn't a prose treatise . . . It is an epic poem and very often poetry can move us and inspire us much more than prose can do . . . Third it gives a very vivid picture of the way in which the Buddha was brought up, left home, struggled for Enlightenment . . . There are beautiful vignettes of Indian life . . . Fourth, it is of historical importance because for many people in the West, it constituted their very first introduction to Buddhism . . . And lastly, it was written by a man who loved India and loved the Indian people . . . He is also of importance and interest in connection with the Buddha Gaya Maha Bodhi Temple.

Notes

1. Jackson (1981)
2. In 1984, Henry Thayer Niles, a lawyer in Toledo, Ohio would publish his *The Dawn and The Day*, which was a virtual plagiarization, both stylistically and textually, of *The Light of Asia*, although Niles sanitized Arnold's otherwise 'beautiful' poem on the grounds that 'no prophet ever came from a harem'. The reference was to sections in *The Light of Asia* where Gautama after leaving his wife is 'made to pass through a somewhat extensive harem. which is described with voluptuous minuteness'. To Niles, the Buddha was *The Dawn* and Christ was *The Day*. But his sequel meant to extol Christ never saw the light of day. Thanks to the Internet, *The Dawn and the Day* is now very easily accessible. Before this book, in 1881 Thayer had authored one on the regulation of railroad transportation. Arnold's biographer would dismiss him as a mere horse breeder. But there was more to Niles than horse breeding, for he demonstrates knowledge of scholarship on Buddha, including Ashvaghosha's biography in Sanskrit.
3. Email communication 30 April 2020
4. Almond (1988)
5. Marshall (1970)
6. App (2012)
7. Stenerson (1991)
8. In the mid-1890s, Dreiser had written a series of articles excoriating Carnegie Steel for its labour management practices, the same Carnegie

who was an ardent admirer of *The Light of Asia*. Rosen (2005) is Dreiser's definitive biography.

9. There may well have been an earlier edition in 1977. Opinions vary.
10. Takahashi (2017)
11. This correspondence between *The Light of Asia* and the Buddhist holy text *Dhammapada*, which has escaped attention thus far, was pointed out to me by Shailaja Sharma of the National Institute of Advanced Studies (NIAS), Bengaluru.
12. Brantlinger (1988)
13. Graham (1998)
14. A.L. Basham, in his foreword to O.P. Kejariwal's *The Asiatic Society of Bengal and the Discovery of India's Past* (Oxford University Press, New Delhi 1988), writes: When [William] Jones translated *Sakuntala* and thus introduced the Sanskrit drama to the western world, are we to believe that he consciously thought: 'I am doing this in order that my country may dominate a subject people'? Could any such motive have been in the mind of James Prinsep when he deciphered the inscriptions of Asoka? Urs App in his path-breaking book *The Birth of Orientalism* (University of Pennsylvania Press, Philadelphia 2010) writes: 'The birth of modern Orientalism was not a Caeserian section performed by colonialist doctors at the beginning of the nineteenth century when Europe's imperialist powers began to dominate large swaths of Asia. Rather it was the result of a long process that around the turn of the eighteenth century produced a paradigm change.'
15. Dentith (2006)
16. Hagerman (2013)
17. In Arnold (1886), Propertius writing is recalled thus: '*Uxorum fusis stat pia turba comia;/Et certamen habet loedi, quae viva sequatur/Conjugium; pudor est non licuisse mori./Ardent victrices, et ilammae pectora praebent,/ Imponuntque suis cra perusta viris.*' The full English translation of this section in Book Three of his *Elegies* reads thus: '*Happy the funeral practice of the eastern husbands/skins there dyed with dawn's red glow,/With last torch cast upon the husband's bier, a band/ of loyal wives appears with unkempt hair,/and they compete for death, to follow husband living:/shame on those who cannot die./In giving bare breasts to the flame the victor's glory,/lay their burnt up lips on their man./Our clan of brides is faithless: none would play the true Evadne or Penelope.*' The English translation is from Holcombe (2009). Arnold, however, also quotes the Sikh holy book thus: 'They are not Satis who perish in the flames, O Nanuk! Satis are those who live on with a broken heart'.

21

The 21st Century: Keeping *The Light of Asia* Burning Bright

Arnold's reputation as a poet in the community of poets and amongst students of poetry was never very great even during his lifetime. He was seen more as an Orientalist, while the mainstream Orientalists considered him a journalist. Over the decades his standing as a poet fell precipitously. In 2000 the *Cambridge Companion to Victorian Poetry*, which was over three hundred pages in length,[1] devoted *barely a line* to him: 'Edwin Arnold, whose *Light of Asia* was for a time widely admired after its publication in 1879.' There was mention of why he had missed being Poet Laureate (because his poem was considered too Buddhist) and how his knighthood reflected the political importance of poetry, as opposed to prose, in the Victorian era.

On 2 March 2001, the Indian Parliament passed a resolution unanimously condemning the destruction of the famed Buddha statues at Bamiyan in Afghanistan by the Taliban. This had caused international outrage and members of all Indian political parties united to express their anguish and anger. Speaking in the Upper House that day, India's top lawyer and former Union Minister Ram Jethmalani recalled his college days when he had read 'a great book written by Sir Edwin Arnold, *The Light of Asia*'. Jethmalani went on to quote from memory these lines from the poem, which he believed 'gave the essence of that great faith'.[2]

We are the voices of the wandering wind,
Which moan for rest but rest can never find;
Lo! as the wind is, so is mortal life,
A moan, a sigh, a sob, storm, a strife.

These are some of the most beautiful lines from Book The Third of *The Light of Asia* when 'the Devas sang such words as these' to the ears of a tormented Prince Siddhartha, who had seen an old man, a sick man, a corpse and a monk. This was the transformative moment in Prince Siddhartha's hitherto cloistered and pleasure-laden existence. Arnold writes that after listening to these lines, the Prince began his quest for enlightenment.

> *We are the voices of the wandering wind,*
> *Which moan for rest but rest can never find;*
> *Lo! as the wind is, so is mortal life,*
> *A moan, a sigh, a sob, storm, a strife . . .*
>
> *We are the voices of the wandering wind:*
> *Wander thou, too, O Prince, thy rest to find;*
> *Leave love for love of lovers for woe's sake*
> *Quit state for sorrow, and deliverance make . . .*

Jethmalani was to repeat the first four lines in another Parliamentary speech of his in praise of Dr Ambedkar on 1 December 2015, a speech which I heard sitting in front of him in the Upper House. He passed away four years later at the age of ninety-six, still active as a Member of Parliament and a baiter of the Treasury Benches.

The Light of Asia and its author figure quite a bit in Charles Allen's very engaging *The Buddha and His Sahibs* that was published in 2002.[3] Allen tells the story of how 'India's Lost Religion' came to be discovered, beginning in the very late eighteenth century by a band of scholarly and enterprising Englishmen with help from some Europeans.[4] It is a true story no doubt, but the book would evoke this withering comment from India's leading historian of ancient India:[5]

> A narrative which eulogises the contributions of Orientalists without reflecting upon the colonial violence within which their work unfolded is unconvincing and suspect.

Allen also almost totally ignored the contributions of Indians (as also those of scholars in Ceylon, Nepal and Tibet) that enabled Englishmen to 'discover' Buddhism in the nineteenth century. This gap would be filled two years later in *The Discovery of Ancient India* by Upinder Singh.[6] Arnold would not have become who he became without the guidance of a number of Indian scholars themselves—a debt he did acknowledge, unlike many others.

On 31 July 2002, Bhadant Arya Nagarjuna Shurei Sasai, the National President of the All-India BuddhaGaya Mahabodhi Mahavihar Action Committee based in Nagpur, would write to Mary Robinson, the UN High Commissioner for Human Rights. The Committee, which derived its inspiration from Dr Ambedkar, requested Robinson to 'direct the Government of India to hand over the management of Mahabodhi Mahavihar at Buddha Gaya to Buddhists', a demand that Arnold had first made in 1886. In fact, the long letter began with a pointed reference to him:

. . . And several inscriptions have been found during the excavation in Buddha Gaya to prove that throughout the ages, it was truly Buddha Vihara. Sir Edwin Arnold, the world famous author of the book "The Light of Asia, visited in 1885 and appealed to British Government to hand over the Mahavihar to the Buddhists. He also appealed to the Buddhist Countries to show interest in the matter of management of the Mahavihar.

The letter then went on to recount the long history of Buddha Gaya in the twentieth century which had culminated in a joint management committee of Hindus and Buddhists being established in May 1953 to manage the Mahabodhi Temple. The Hindu priests and the Buddhists had each wanted full control by themselves. In the end, each had received 50 per cent of what they had asked for. There was 'balanced dis-satisfaction'. Throughout the sixties, seventies and eighties, there was a movement by some Buddhist groups to keep the issue of full management by them alive.

This movement by Ambedkarite Buddhists predominantly to completely liberate the Mahabodhi Temple from any form of Hindu involvement gathered momentum after the demolition of the Babri Masjid at Ayodhya on 6 December 1992 (ironically the death anniversary of Dr Ambedkar). But their campaign never gained much traction, perhaps because of the multiple Buddhisms ubiquitous at Bodh Gaya.[7] That the author of *The Light of Asia* and what he wrote about Buddha-Gya continues to have a hold on the Ambedkarite Buddhist imagination can be seen by this publication brought out by a Delhi-based publisher 'dedicated to the propagation and publication of the ideal doctrine of Buddhism . . . and also committed to publish, propagate and restore the writings of and about the Bodhisatva Babasaheb Dr Ambedkar, Jotiba Phule . . . as well as other social reformers.'

A Hindi language publication of 2010 whose title translates to 'The Liberation of the Mahabodhi Temple and Sir Edwin Arnold'. Samyak Prakashan, New Delhi.

Joseph Campbell was one of the giants in the field of comparative mythology and comparative religion in the twentieth century. His most influential work was *The Hero with a Thousand Faces* that came out in 1949, where he studied the similarities of archetypal heroes in different cultures. In 2003 the centennial edition of *The Hero's Journey: Joseph Campbell on his Life and Work* was published.[8] In this Campbell himself recalled:

> In 1924 when I was around nineteen years old . . . I was on a boat trip with my family to Europe. On the return trip from Europe there were three dark young men seated on steamer chairs on the deck. I noticed that there was a young woman who knew them. I had never seen such people before because we never saw Hindus over here [America] at that time . . . It happened that one of them was Jiddu Krishnamurti and the others were his brother Nityananda and his secretary at that time Rajagopal. This was my introduction to the world of India. And the young woman who introduced me gave me Edwin Arnold's *The Light of Asia* which is the life of the Buddha from the sutras. And that was the opening up and it was like a light going on. When I went to Europe as a student of literature, philology, romance literature and then to Germany and started my Sanskrit there was all this stuff again. I really got into it in those years. But it had all started with what I had learned from that little book about the Buddha—strange, a little touch just like that and everything changes . . .

The young woman who gave Campbell *The Light of Asia* was Rosalind Williams, later to become Rosalind Rajagopal. Krishnamurti, who Campbell refers to, was of course the famous seer, then still a protégé of Annie Besant and still the shining light of the Theosophical Society. His personal liberation from the path Annie Besant had charted out for him as the messiah of the world would come five years after he ran into Campbell.

In October 2004 would appear *How We Saw It: 150 Years of the Daily Telegraph*.[9] In it Christopher Howse would look back on the man who gave that newspaper 'much of its flavour in Victoria's last four decades' and who had been its chief editor for sixteen years and later its 'travelling "commissioner" or correspondent'. Inevitably, the phenomenal success of *The Light of Asia* was highlighted but Howse also said this:

> Arnold had a practical side, as a carpenter, a traveller and yachtsman. Into old age he liked to dress in a loose dark-blue yachting suit, his pockets bulging with carpenter's tools . . . A truly unusual habit of Arnold's was to carry jewels, cut and uncut, about with him—not for the sake of their value, but for their colour. In the bazaars of Ceylon, he had bought a bagful of sapphires, garnets, rubies, emeralds and other gemstones. With his carpenter's tools he would bore a small hole in the edge of the sideboard, the back of a chair, the newel post of the stairs, and there sat a jewel. Members of the family would find a topaz in the handle of a hairbrush or a piece of purple spar in an umbrella handle . . .

In 1883 Arnold had indeed published a book of poems called *Lotus and Jewel*. It had the usual offerings that included one that would get noticed called 'In An Indian Temple'. But what was unusual in this anthology was a set of eighteen poems on various types of gemstones that went thus:

F. FIRE-OPALS
A. AMETHYSTS
N. NEPHRITE, JADE
N. NACRE AND PEARLS
Y. YACUT, TOPAZES

M. MOONSTONE
A. AQUAMARINE
R. RUBIES
I. IDOCRASE, GARNETS
A. AGATES

A. AMBER AND LAZUITE
D. DIAMONDS
E. EMERALDS
L. LIGURE, JACYNTHS
A. AN AUREUS
I. IOLITE AND IVORY
D. DAWN-STONE
E. EUCLASE AND ESSONITE

Fanny Maria Adelaide was Arnold's second wife, whom he had married in 1864 and who would pass away in 1889. She had accompanied her husband on his four-month-long journey to India and Ceylon from November 1885 to March 1886.

Five years after Howse had offered this insight into Arnold's peculiar habit, his colleague Mick Brown visited the Buddhist Society in London, where he was invited to sit in 'Sir Edwin Arnold's chair'. He went back a second time for a good reason, and this is what he later wrote:[10]

> At the Buddhist Society I took a closer look at Sir Edwin's chair [the chair on which he sat while composing *The Light of Asia*]. Here and there were nicks and abrasions you would find on a piece of furniture this age, but no jewels. And then I found it. Running my finger along the gap between the arm of the chair and the upholstered seat I came across the indentation—deliberate it seemed—just large enough to accommodate a topaz, a garnet or a sapphire. Of course, there was nothing in it. I walked into the library and gazed up at the portrait of Sir Edwin. I could swear he was smiling.

Elizabeth Harris studied the nineteenth century Buddhist–Christian encounter in nineteenth-century Ceylon and her *Theravada Buddhism and the British Encounter* appeared in 2006.[11] One of her chapters was on *The Light of Asia* because after 1879 it had become a 'touchstone' and 'all those who wrote after Arnold [on the Buddha and Buddhism] were forced either to contest or echo him'. Her point was simple: *The Light of Asia* offered the reader 'a Buddha who embodied the most loved, devotion-inspiring human qualities like compassion, modesty and sensitivity and also a romantically appealing interpretation of the Four Noble Truths, just as they were entering Western consciousness'.

She reiterates that Arnold debunked the prevailing negative meaning of Nirvana and the path he propounded in the poem was that of an activist Buddhism. One of the reasons why *The Light of Asia* had appealed to social reformers in India in the early twentieth century was because it stressed the Buddha's opposition to the caste system. But she was the only one to notice what she called 'an inconsistent note in Arnold's epic poem with this reformist agenda'— 'Siddhartha raises no objection when a woman shows a willingness to immolate herself on her husband's pyre'. Actually, it was perfectly consistent with Arnold's views on suttee that I have discussed earlier in the context of his poem of 1875 called *The Rajput Wife*.

In April 2006 the noted Indian author Amit Chaudhuri, while reviewing a book on Tagore that had been published just then, wrote:[12]

By the time Tagore was born [1861], both the first wave of Orientalist enthusiasm and the most significant phase of Orientalist scholarship were over . . . In the second half of the 19th century, the excitement waned, despite the work of Max Müller . . . In 1879, 'Oriental' poetry received a final fillip with the publication of *Light of Asia*, Edwin Arnold's life of the Buddha, told in narrative verse . . . *Light of Asia* became an immense success on both sides of the Atlantic, and was reprinted eighty times. When Matthew Arnold visited America, he found that many people confused him with Edwin. Of course, the notion of 'high seriousness' that Matthew Arnold had himself formulated would prevail, guaranteeing that his reputation would outlast the frenetic but essentially light efflorescence of the 'Oriental' poem . . .

When I read this, I argued with Chaudhuri:[13]

It is certainly true that Matthew Arnold figures very prominently in any book on the Victorian Age, Simon Heffer's being the most recent. Lionel Trilling wrote his biography in the early 1930s and Gertrude Himmerfalb in the 1960s. By contrast, Edwin Arnold does not even merit a footnote in these works. But consider this: It is Edwin Arnold who gets translated into 12 European, 7 South-East Asian and 13 South Asian languages. It is he, not Matthew that is more remembered today, not just outside the UK but also in the UK, because of the growth in the interest in Buddhism. It is Edwin Arnold who continues to be the subject of academic papers and dissertations and not Matthew. Matthew Arnold was certainly seen as a more serious intellectual but I am not sure that his reputation has outlasted that of Edwin Arnold. Even during their lifetimes, the latter was a cult figure of sorts in the USA for instance.

Chaudhuri responded about a fortnight later:[14]

I should clarify about Edwin Arnold—the first time I heard of him was from my wife in the 1990s,[15] and we took him to be an example of how popularity and sales in a writer's lifetime never provide a reliable integer of a writer's influence or durability. As you know, those who are famous in their time are almost all forgotten (a tiny percentage survive), and there are those who are obscure (like William Blake, Kafka, and Walter Benjamin) who become key figures of literary and cultural history in retrospect, and after reassessment. I have a feeling that your study . . . may well prove Edwin Arnold's lasting merit alongside his success. Mathew Arnold continues to be an important figure in literary studies—if he has been slightly sidelined, one should recall that literary studies itself has been greatly sidelined by both the market and what's often a social science approach to the arts.

The Mathew Arnold–Edwin Arnold rivalry was well known in Victorian circles. The former enjoyed a legendary reputation as a public intellectual across the Atlantic much before *The Light of Asia* became a sensation.[16] When Matthew Arnold visited America in the mid-1880s he was assumed to be the brother of Edwin Arnold which had irked him no end. When asked about his relationship with the author of *The Light of Asia*, Matthew Arnold is supposed to have replied:

> He is no relation whatever. His book, *The Light of Asia,* seems to be quite unintelligible, and not to be compared with the great work of [Jules Barthlemy] St. Hilaire, *Le Buddha.* It is like the character of Christ written by a Jew. One prefers to go to more authentic sources.[17]

But on Matthew Arnold's death in 1888, the other Arnold would pay him a very sentimental tribute in verse in the columns of the *Daily Telegraph*, the last few lines of which were:

> *. . . Thou, that didst bear by Name and deck it so*
> *That-coming thus behind-hardly I know*
> *If I shall hold it worthily, and be*
> *Meet to be mentioned in one Age with thee—*
> *Take Brother! To the Land where no strifes are,*
> *This praise thou will not need! Before the Star*
> *Is kindled for thee let my funeral torch*
> *Light thee, great Namesake! to th' Elysian Porch!*
> *Dead Poet! let a poet of thy House*
> *Lay unreproved, these bay-leaves on thy brows!*
> *We, that seemed only friends, were lovers: Now*
> *Death knows it! and Love knows! and I! and Thou!*

That *The Light of Asia* continued to have an appeal to scholars in the twenty-first century is best illustrated by Visiya Pinthongvijayakul's tracing of the influence of a Thai Buddhist literary text on it.[18] In 2005 he wrote his master's thesis called 'Sir Edwin Arnold's The Light of Asia: Wisdom of the East in the Western World' at

Chulalongkorn University in Bangkok and in a paper a year later argued that Arnold had read Henry Alabaster's English translation of *Pathomsombodhikatha* that had appeared in 1870 as *The Wheel of Law*.

One story from this relates to how the seeker of truth was encouraged to cease self-mortification as the way to enlightenment. This was the Buddha's soon-to-be 'Eureka' moment. In the Thai text Indra appeared before Siddhartha with a three-stringed lute and performed a song. The first string he sounded was too tight and it broke. The second string was too slack, and the music just died. At last, when Indra played the third string, which was moderate, the song was beautiful. After listening to the song Siddhartha decided to practice asceticism moderately. In Book the Sixth, Arnold had written:

Fair goes the dancing when the sitar's tuned;
Tune us the sitar neither low nor high,
And we will dance away the hearts of men.

The string o'erstretched breaks, and the music flies;
The string o'erslack is dumb, and music dies;
Tune us the sitar neither low nor high.

But Pinthongvijayakul gives Arnold full credit for originality and creativity in suggesting a more humanistic rather than a supernatural Buddha. In *The Light of Asia* a human musician plays the sitar rather than Indra and there are dancing girls around as well. The English poem also has the Buddha engage in a long soliloquy that 'conveyed the image of the Bodhisattva [seeker of enlightenment] as a scientist who was conducting an experiment and trying to solve his important research question: how can humans be freed from sufferings'. I wonder whether what Pinthongvijayakul says had weighed in the mind of the King of Siam when he honoured Arnold just five months after *The Light of Asia* was first published. It was the first such accolade that the poet received for this work.

Thanks entirely to Olcott and Dharmapala, the first time Vesak, the day of Buddha's birth (and death and enlightenment) became a national holiday anywhere was in Ceylon in 1884.[19] Thereafter, this auspicious day was marked and celebrated in India for the first time on 26 May 1896 in Calcutta. That well-attended function had been organised by the Mahabodhi Society with Narendra Nath Sen, editor of the widely read *Indian Mirror* presiding. Several Englishmen were also present, including Laurence Waddell, an Indian Army surgeon and amateur archaeologist who was then in the news for his theories on where Kapilavastu—the Buddha's birthplace—was located. Sen had hailed the Buddha as the ninth avatar of Vishnu. Passages from *The Light of Asia* and from Paul Carus' *The Gospel of Buddha* were read.[20]

Over a century later, in May 2004, the day would be celebrated in Hyderabad with a dance performance based on *The Light of Asia* by a troupe from Cuttack. Two years later, the President of India kicked off the year-long 2550th anniversary celebrations in the country from the site of the Buddha's death, Kushinagar. A sign of how the nature of Buddhism had changed since Dr Ambedkar's conversion was the involvement of a large number of Dalit Buddhists and campaigners for social justice and equality in these celebrations. To one such gathering in Chennai, the chief minister of the state, M. Karunanidhi, a great literary figure himself, sent a message on 1 February 2007:

> Buddha taught love and his teachings were universal and against casteism. He was the "Light of Asia" and the "Sun of Wisdom" and his teachings are simple enough to be followed by all.

Karunanidhi, the master politician that he was, added 'Sun of Wisdom' to 'Light of Asia' because the symbol of the political party he headed was the rising sun.

Nyanatiloka Thera was a Western Buddhist pioneer who received a state funeral when he died in Colombo in 1957. He was born Anton Gueth in the German town of Weisbaden in February

1878. Twenty-one years later, while studying to be a professional musician, he was deeply influenced by a talk on Buddhism given in Frankfurt by the German Theosophist Edwin Bohme. He was ordained as Buddhist monk in 1904 and spent the rest of his life in Ceylon, where he became an iconic figure. His part-autobiography was published in German in 1995 but it was only in 2008 that a full-length biography, *The Life of Nyanatiloka Thera*,[21] was published. Two figures who played a very important role in Nyanatiloka's early life were admirers of *The Light of Asia*. The first of them was Arthur Pfungst, who had done the earliest German translation of *The Light of Asia* in Leipzig in 1887 and then went on to write a biography of the Buddha. The second was Ananda Metteyya, who had become a Buddhist on account of reading *The Light of Asia* in 1890 in London.

The Theosophical Society would keep bringing out new editions of *The Light of Asia* from time to time and keep it in circulation. So would Buddhist scholars as well. Anandajoti Metta is an Englishman who took higher ordination in the Theravada tradition in Sri Lanka in 1996 and has taught in India, Thailand and Malaysia. Currently, he is resident in the International Buddhist College in Thailand and maintains websites devoted to documentaries on Buddhism, ancient Buddhist texts and Buddhist pilgrimage and historical sites. In July 2008, he republished *The Light of Asia* especially targeted at those who have English as a second language, calling it 'a rewarding read' but also with this caveat:

> Occasionally it seems that Arnold did not quite understand the Teaching which is perhaps not surprising given the time he wrote, so in this edition I have included corrective notes and pointed out these problems when they arise. They mainly appear in the last chapter where there is a section on the Teaching.

The first work in the twenty-first century that brought a new perspective on *The Light of Asia* was that of Jeffrey Franklin. His *The Lotus and the Lion: Buddhism and the British Empire* was published in 2008.[22] In some ways Franklin takes forward Almond's earlier investigations into Victorian Buddhism. Unlike Almond, Franklin has a more expansive treatment of *The Light of Asia*, saying:

> In the face of an understanding of nature as not only potentially hostile but indifferent to the survival of the human race, and a natural law regulated only by the chances of "random selection", The Light of Asia offered a positive alternative: an universe governed neither by God nor by chaos nor by randomness, but rather governed by an orderly and just law' . . . In the face of arguments by early scholars and divines that Buddhism was "a system of cold Atheism and barren Nihilism", Arnold was able to provide a much warmer and less barren counter-image. However accurate or inaccurate, his image was more influential than that of his critics, both because of the circulation of The Light of Asia and because it simply was more pleasing for late Victorian to contemplate.

Wright's biography had almost nothing to say about the impact of *The Light of Asia* in Russia. Adele Di Ruocco would fill this gap admirably in her doctoral dissertation of May 2011.[23] Di Ruocco's subject was on the influence of the Buddhist world on modern Russian culture in the half century preceding the Bolshevik Revolution. Although the growth of the Theosophical Movement in Russia had been studied, Di Ruocco would be the first to highlight the importance of *The Light of Asia* in the lives of literary personalities like Tolstoy, scientists like Mendeleev and Oriental scholars like Baikin.

Catherine Robinson would reignite interest in Edwin Arnold with two important articles.[24] The first, that appeared in September 2009, dealt with an assessment of Arnold in which inevitably *The Light of Asia* figures. The second was in November 2014, when Robinson would take off from Wright's biography and title her article *Interpreter of Hinduism to the West? Sir Edwin Arnold's (Re) presentations of Hindu Texts and their Reception*. In spite of the question mark in her article, Robinson was not far off the mark, because Arnold has certainly a claim to being one on the strength of his translations of the Bhagavad Gita, *Gita Govinda* and the *Mahabharata*.

Academic work on Arnold has not been confined to scholars in the West. In 2012, Madras University awarded a doctorate to S.T. Tamizhselvi for her research study[25] *A Comparative Study of The Light of Asia by Edwin Arnold and Asia Jyothi by Kavimani Desiga Vinayagam Pillai.* She describes Pillai's Tamil work of 1940 not so much as a mere translation of *The Light of Asia* as much as a 'transcreation'. She defines it thus:

> A work of translation is described as a transcreation when the translator gives more importance to the cultural milieu of the target language than that of the text in the original source language and makes necessary changes in his version in accordance with the taste of his audience in the target language.

In reality, by this definition, most translations are actually transcreations. But she is right to the extent that Pillai uses his own imageries, metaphors and similes and does not always follow Arnold in a literal sense. In addition, like many other Indian 'translators' before him, he had a social reform agenda in bringing *The Light of Asia* before the public—an agenda that stressed caste equality or castelessness. Pillai was very much a social activist who was a vociferous critic of the caste system. Tamizhselvi points out that he took only those parts from the epic poem which he felt were relevant for his crusade against the Brahminical stranglehold on Tamil society.

The Princeton Dictionary of Buddhism, edited by two noted scholars, appeared in 2013.[26] It had a substantive entry under 'Arnold, Edwin', saying 'although it has long been rendered obsolete, *The Light of Asia* played a seminal role in introducing the history and belief systems of Buddhism to the West'. The entry also claimed that 'despite the animosity it aroused in many Christian circles Edwin Arnold's epic poem was a favourite of Queen Victoria, who subsequently knighted him'. I asked Queen Victoria's most recent biographer Miles Taylor about this statement and his response was:[27]

> As far as I know, Queen Victoria did not refer elsewhere to the volume written by Arnold. Her journals record her meeting Buddhist visitors from Siam and Burma but nothing about her knowledge of or interest in Buddhism in India. She was given a lot of books. But she was not a great reader!

But when I dug into British newspaper archives for the period 1893–1895, when the race for the Poet Laureateship was at its most intense, I did find quite a few publications mentioning Victoria's purported fascination for *The Light of Asia*. Whether these were Arnold-inspired leaks or Buckingham Palace-inspired leaks, or just informed speculation is impossible to establish conclusively. *The Leeds Mercury* of 13 January 1890, for instance, informed its readers of . . . Sir Edwin Arnold, whose works . . . especially the "Light of Asia" are great favourites with the Queen'. Five years later, the *Evening Telegraph* would say that 'Sir Edwin has in this country at least one appreciative reader . . . Her Majesty the Queen'. So, the *Princeton Dictionary* may not have been exaggerating after all. Moreover, the Royal Collection of the British Royal Family has this information regarding the first illustrated edition of *The Light of Asia* in its collection:

Presented to Queen Victoria by Edwin Arnold, 19 May 1885

Victoria would have seen the wonderful illustrations at least!

In August 2013, Gitanjali Surendran's doctoral dissertation at Harvard University, called *The Indian Discovery of Buddhism: Buddhist Revival in India, c.1890–1956* was approved. Surendran's was perhaps the earliest such meticulously researched endeavour. She argued that middle-class Indians in the twentieth century 'reworked, rethought and reincarnated' the Buddhism that had been 'recovered' by the British in the nineteenth century. This they did for their own political, cultural and social reasons. But all through Surendran argues:

> Edwin Arnold's already famous poem *The Light of Asia* arguably found even greater fame among the literate classes of India and was translated widely into several Indian languages within decades of its publication in Britain.

Just about the time of Surendran's dissertation, *Encountering Buddhism in Twentieth Century British and American Literature* would appear.[28] In it, Lawrence Normand would write that *The Light of Asia* was the first to transform Buddhism's reception by 'presenting a moving, persuasive account of the Buddha's life and message'. Buddhism in the pre-Arnold era was seen to be a negative, life-denying and quite incomprehensible philosophy. But Arnold changed all that by his vivid poetic language and succeeded in conveying the essentials of the Buddha's teachings in a manner that evidently caught people's imagination across the globe. It was his treatment of the life of the Buddha that Normand believed gave *The Light of Asia* such deep literary and cultural influence for at least half a century.

Following this, Emily Rose Eiben's doctoral dissertation of October 2016 would investigate the representation of Buddhism in the British media and popular culture during the period 1875–95.[29] Predictably, *The Light of Asia* would occupy pride of place in her analysis. She highlights in great depth how the mass media across the British Isles made Arnold's work a sensation and how the British stage too took it very warmly. She describes in detail how Arnold managed to create and occupy a distinctive niche between the serious and the popular and how *The Light of Asia* was read not just by elites but entered the daily discourse in which common folk participated. She even managed to unearth a female columnist for a Bristol daily who 'recalled Princess Christian (Victoria's third daughter) quoting at a recent social event, some lines from *The Light of Asia*' and then added:

... this beautiful imaginative passage from the life of the Buddha, whose doctrines and influence rightly understood are of the highest, gentlest and noblest character. In Book VII we have, I think, the poetical code of a moral and exalted life, developed and inculcated in the ancient faith of Eastern nations.

Every work on Arnold had focussed on his impact on the West. It was Douglas Ober who, in his doctoral dissertation of December 2016, looked at *The Light of Asia* in its Indian context.[30] The fact that *The Light of Asia* had been translated into numerous European languages had long been known, particularly since Wright's biography was published. But Ober was the first to locate a number of translations into Indian languages. Ober's thesis complemented in many ways but also went well beyond Surendran's in exploring how Buddhism was reinvented in different parts of India during the beginning of the late nineteenth century and ending with the conversion of Dr Ambedkar and its aftermath. He highlighted the crucial role of various organisations and individuals in promoting the cause of Buddhism in India but who are all-but-forgotten in the public memory now.

Ober's was an extensively researched thesis. Sebastian Lecourt, on the other hand, produced a short essay in 2016 that revisited *The Light of Asia* and the literary and cultural impact in the first half century after its publication.[31] His focus was on colonial Ceylon, but he also dealt with how the Western world had reacted to the poem, starting with the review in London's *Spectator*, which had prophesied in 1884:

Two hundred years hence, Mr. Arnold half-forgotten at home, except by students, may, amongst the innumerable peoples who profess Buddhism, be regarded as Psalmist . . .

Lecourt drew attention to one aspect of *The Light of Asia* that accounts for its stupendous success—its ability to appeal to different audiences in different ways. In his own words,

The case of *The Light of Asia*, however, suggests that literary forms can acquire global resonance through their capacity to facilitate several contradictory reworkings. If Arnold's poem was instrumental in propagating a certain formal construction of Buddhism, this was in part because it allowed distinct audiences to interpret that form in contrasting ways.

Arnold's influence on Kipling had been known for some time. But in 2017 Susan Paskins delved into this subject deeper.[32] Although her doctoral thesis is concerned with the religious context of Kipling's *Kim*, she also looks at *The Light of Asia* at some length because it was 'the main way in which ideas about Buddhism entered the mainstream of Victorian culture'. Also important was the fact that Arnold had been a major influence on Kipling when he was at school. Underscoring the fact that Arnold had presented more a human rather than a divine Buddha, Paskins brought out various passages in *The Light of Asia* which struck a chord with Christians. The most telling of these is in Book the Fifth, after the very famous Kisagotami episode, when Gautama, not yet the Buddha, holds a lamb marked for slaughter:

> *Alas! For all my sheep which have*
> *No shepherd; wandering in the night with none*
> *To guide them; bleating blindly towards the knife*
> *Of Death, as these dumb beasts which are their kin.*

Her comparison of *The Light of Asia* with *The Life of Christ*, written by Arnold's close friend Frederic Farrar, gives her work added value. The other important point made by Paskins that had also been highlighted by Clausen way back in 1972 was that *The Light of Asia* chimed very well with Victorian concerns—in its perceived agnosticism and appeal to reason rather than ritual and in its verses that suggested that evolution, which Darwin had just then propounded, was a philosophy that had moulded the Buddha's thinking.

The Light of Asia also helped in the exploration of the Buddhist heritage of Hazaribagh district in Jharkhand in 2018. According to one tradition, Siddhartha Gautama travelled from Itkhori, now in this district, to Bodh Gaya, where he was transformed into the Buddha. By river this would be a distance of 30 kms, although the road distance is about four times that long. The researchers and heritage recoverers Benoy Behl and Bulu Imam were alerted to this 'Last Journey of the Bodhisattva' by a passage in Book the Sixth of *The Light of Asia*, which begins as follows:

> *Thou who wouldst see where dawned*
> *   the Light at last,*
> *North-westwards from the "Thousand*
> *   Gardens" go,*
> *By Gunga's Valley till thy steps be*
> *   set*
> *On the green hills where those twin*
> *   streamlets spring,*
> *Nilanjana and Mohana! follow them,*
> *Winding beneath broad-leaved mahua trees,*
> *'Mid thickets of the sansar and the bir,*
> *Till on the plain the shining sisters meet*
> *In Phalgu's bed, flowing by rocky banks*
> *To Gaya and the red Barabar Hills*
> *Hard by that river spreads a thorny waste,*
> *Urawelaya named in ancient days . . .*

The vital clues that Behl and Imam found in this verse are as follows:

1. North-westwards is the direction of Itkhori to Bodh Gaya.
2. Thousand Gardens is literally Hazaribagh.
3. Urawelaya or Uruvela is the old name of Bodh Gaya.

Using these clues, the duo discovered a treasure of Buddhist and Hindu sculptures in Bihari village, close to Itkhori. The origin of the word Itkhori itself is explained by them thus:

Tradition has it that Gautama's maternal aunt came looking for him in his period of meditation. When she could not find him, she said *Iti Khoi* which in Pali means 'I have lost him'. It is said that this then became Itikhori, a deeply revered site for Buddhists.

Who says epic poetry does not have its practical uses? But this clearly was the law of unintended consequences working. Arnold had not buried clues in his poem for India's Buddhist heritage to be found well over a century later. It just happened.

The Light of Asia had had an enormous impact in America in the 1880s and 1890s. Its central role in the shaping of American attitudes to the Buddha and Buddhism was highlighted a century later in two books:[33] the first that came out in 1981, called *How the*

Benoy Behl and Bulu Imam, who located Buddhist and Hindu sculptures near Itkhori in the Hazaribagh district of Jharkhand with clues gleaned from reading The Light of Asia, *May 2018. (Source: Benoy Behl)*

Swans Came to the Lake: A Narrative History of Buddhism In America
and the second that was published in 1992, *called The American,
Encounter with Buddhism: 1844-1912*. In 2019, Arnold would once
again command attention with the publication of '*Very Beautiful
Heathenism': The Light of Asia in Gilded Age America*,[34] which showed
how the poem on the Buddha exposed the tensions and rifts in
Protestant American religious belief in those years of staggering
prosperity. Unprecedented economic advances in the US in the last
few decades of the nineteenth century had created a spiritual crisis
and at such a time *The Light of Asia* appeared as a beacon.

On 22 July 1947, twenty-four days before India's independence,
Jawaharlal Nehru moved this resolution in the Constituent
Assembly:

> Resolved that the National Flag of India shall be horizontal tricolor
> of deep saffron (kesri), white and dark green in equal proportion.
> In the centre of the white band there shall be a Wheel in navy blue
> to represent the Chakra. The design of the Wheel shall be that of
> the Chakra (Wheel) which appears on the abacus of the Sarnath
> lion capital of Asoka.

Not surprisingly, the resolution was adopted exuberantly. Two
postage stamps giving effect to the resolution were issued on 15
August 1947.

Postage stamps issued on the day India became independent, drawing from its Buddhist heritage.

In 2014, the historian Himanshu Prabha Ray would revisit these landmarks of modern India and discuss how ancient symbols associated with the Buddha and the Buddhist faith came to be adopted by a new nation. While doing so she drew attention to Arnold's preface to *The Light of Asia*, in which he says:

> The Buddha of this poem—if, as need not be doubted, he really existed—was born on the borders of Nepaul, about 620 BC, and died about 543 BC at Kusinagara in Oudh. In point of age, therefore, most creeds are youthful compared with this venerable religion, which has in it the eternity of a universal hope, the immortality of a boundless love, an indestructible element of faith in final good, and the proudest assertion ever made of human freedom. The extravagances which disfigure the record and practice of Buddhism are to be referred to that inevitable degradation which priesthoods always inflict upon a great idea committed to their charge. The power and sublimity of Gautama's original doctrines should be estimated by their influence, not by their interpreters; not by that innocent but lazy and ceremonious church which has arisen on the foundations of the Buddhistic Brotherhood or 'Sangha'.

Ray reiterates the basic point that the charm of *The Light of Asia* stemmed from the fact that it concerned itself with the life of the Buddha and his 'pristine' teachings. She is in little doubt of the impact it had on educated Indian elites, who formed the nucleus of the freedom movement. Undoubtedly, Arnold, never a votary of immediate freedom for India from British rule, would at least have approved of these two choices made by India's Constituent Assembly that drew upon the fledgling nation's ancient and deep Buddhist heritage. Two and a half years later, as Ray goes on to add, paintings by a team led by Nandalal Bose, a pupil of Abanindranath Tagore, would adorn India's Constitution that was adopted on 26 January 1950—among the scenes depicted were the Buddha's first sermon at Sarnath, Ashoka spreading the Buddhist Dhamma and the famous monastic-cum-educational complex at Nalanda.

Among the most recent academic works which have studied *The Light of Asia* is one by Erin Garrow,[35] whose subject is the celebrated Irish author James Joyce. Joyce derives his hold on the public imagination from *Ulysses,* which appeared in 1922, although his 1916 work *A Portrait of the Artist as a Young Man* and *Finnegans Wake* of 1939 are also very well-known. Actually, way back in 1961, a brief four-page article had appeared in the *Indian Journal of English Studies,* titled 'Sir Edwin Arnold's Role in the Artistic Development of James Joyce'.[36] The author B.P. Misra, who had done his doctorate at Trinity College, Dublin, followed it up two years later with a booklet.[37] Neither the article nor the booklet seemed to have had any significant impact and the latter has become rare. Garrow unearthed Misra's work and expanded on it hugely.

Garrow argues that sometime before 1896 Joyce had owned and read *The Light of Asia* and that this was a decisive influence on him in two of his essays written when he was around fifteen or sixteen. Subsequently there would be other influences on the young Joyce—most notably Richard Wagner and Henrik Ibsen—but *The Light of Asia* had already been firmly implanted in his consciousness. In mid-1901 he also read Olcott's *Buddhist Catechism,* which would further shape his thinking on Buddhism, which in turn would be reflected in his unpublished and published works.

As important as Garrow's work on the influence of *The Light of Asia* on the young James Joyce is, another point he makes is worth recounting. Samuel Beal's *Romantic Legend of Sakya Buddha* had been published in 1875 and it was one of Arnold's sources. Beal had included sexually explicit material in his work, but Arnold toned this down considerably, mindful of the public morals campaign of England's National Vigilance Association. Garrow accepts that Arnold never suggests that Gautama was either 'polyamourous or polygamous' but claims he leaves much to the reader's imagination in these lines from Book the Second:

But, innermost,
Beyond the richness of those hundred halls,

A secret chamber lurked, where skill had spent
All lovely fantasies to lull the mind.
The entrance of it was a cloistered square—
Roofed by the sky, and in the midst a tank—
Of milky marble built, and laid with slabs
Of milk-white marble . . . . .
And night and day served there a chosen band
Of nautch girls, cup-bearers, and cymballers,
Delicate, dark-browed ministers of love,
Who fanned the sleeping eyes of the happy Prince,
And when he waked, led back his thoughts to bliss
With music whispering through the blooms, and charm
Of amourous songs and dreamy dances, linked
By chime of ankle-bells and wave of arms
And silver vina-strings; while essences
Of musk and champak, and the blue haze spread
From burning spices, soothed his soul again
To drowse by sweet Yashodhara; and thus
Siddhartha lived forgetting.

To argue that the erotic passages in Book the Second, Book the Third and Book the Fourth were responsible for *The Light of Asia's* commercial success is far-fetched. That there are titillating sections in the poem is incontrovertible. In my view, only the film version in 1925 made some use of these sections but *The Light of Asia* had already become a sensation by then. Just as *The Light of Asia* departs from 'textual Buddhism', I would argue that it has nothing to do with 'sexual Buddhism' either. Arnold makes liberal use of words like 'lips', 'breasts' and 'kiss' in the poem but Garrow grossly exaggerates this dimension of Arnold's poem.

The newest addition to the rediscovery of *The Light of Asia* is the work of Anthony Goedhals, a South African scholar of religion. Lafcadio Hearn was born in Greece to a Greek mother and Irish father. He later made a name for himself as a newspaperman in the American cities of Cincinnati and New Orleans before landing up in Japan in 1890. He became Koizumi Yakumo in 1896, converted to Buddhism and died six months after Arnold. He was a noted author of the time whose writings provided a window to the West on Japanese society in the last decade of the nineteenth century, when Japan was still an exotic mystery to the outside world. Goedhals' deep analysis of the 'Neo-Buddhist' works of Hearn, published in early 2020, establishes the influence of *The Light of Asia* on him[38] long before he and Arnold became enchanted with Japan. Hearn had first read *The Light of Asia* in October 1879 and reviewed it for a New Orleans publication, calling it 'magnificent'. Four years later, he wrote to his friend W.D. O'Connor:

> Have you seen the exquisite new edition of Arnold's "Light of Asia". It has enchanted me—perfumed my mind as with the incense of strangely new and beautiful worship . . .

Goedhals traces the influence of *The Light of Asia* on Hearn through its themes, firstly, of atheism and individual responsibility, and secondly, of causation, karma, reincarnation and interrelationship of all phenomena. Hearn was influenced by some other poems of Arnold's as well, most notably *The Secret of Death*, a translation of a part of the *Katha Upanishad* that had appeared in 1885. Hearn and Arnold eventually established contact with each other—two kindred spirits, both mesmerised by Buddhism and by Japan.

Given that it had captivated so many educated Indians in the first half of the twentieth century, I wondered how Mohammed Iqbal had reacted to *The Light of Asia*, if at all. Mohammed Ali Jinnah was not a great reader of books, but Iqbal certainly was. However, I could find no connection whatsoever. In December 2019, I reached out to a Pakistani scholar Tariq Rahman, who promptly replied that he had discussed Arnold in one of his books on Muslim thought and referred me to it. I was quite excited till I discovered that Rahman was referring to T.W. Arnold, a great name in Islamic studies and someone who had taught at Lahore and Aligarh. Iqbal was one of his admirers. But the next best thing that I found in Iqbal was these powerful lines on the Buddha from his tribute to Guru Nanak in his *Bang-e Dara*:

> *The nation could not care less about Gautama's message—*
> *It did not know the price of its unique pearl!*
> *Poor wretches! They never heard the voice of truth:*
> *A tree does not know how sweet its fruit is.*
> *What he revealed was the secret of existence,*
> *But India was proud of its fancies;*
> *It was not an assembly-hall to be lit up by the lamp of truth;*
> *The rain of mercy fell, but the land was barren.*
> *Alas, for the shudra India is a house of sorrow,*
> *This land is blind to the sufferings of man.*
> *The Brahmin is still drunk with the wine of pride,*
> *In the assembly-halls of foreigners burns Gautama's lamp.*
> *But, ages later, the house of idols was lit up again–*
> *Azar's house was lit up by Abraham!*
> *Again from the Punjab the call of monotheism arose:*
> *A perfect man roused India from slumber.*

There are other noted poets in Urdu like Brij Narain Chakbast, Firaq Gorakhpuri and Ali Sardar Jafri in whose works the Buddha figures quite prominently. The Urdu prose writer Qurrat-ul Ain Hyder too makes creative use of the Buddha's life and philosophy. But as far as *The Light of Asia* itself is concerned, there has been only one Urdu translation named *Nirwan*, which was by the author Farooq Junoon of Allahabad, in 1959.[39] And over the past few years, Poonam Girdhani has revived the medieval Persian art form called *dastangoi* (storytelling). In June 2019 she premiered *Dastan-e-Irfaan-e-Buddh*, the story of the life and times of Gautam Buddha, in New Delhi, and in early 2020 staged it in Hyderabad. Her script is derived from a variety of sources, including Ramchandra Shukla's 1922 translation of *The Light of Asia* called *Buddhacharit*. Had the Covid-19 crisis not intervened, the play would have been taken to other places as well.

The twentieth century also expanded the list of languages into which *The Light of Asia* got translated. The list now includes Korean in 2006, Bhojpuri in 2013 and Chinese in 2015. The Chinese translation, which is part of Project Gutenberg on www.weibo.com[40] and available only online, has this promotional note:

> Light of Asia has a great influence on Buddhism in Europe and America . . . The book tells the story of the Buddha's life. The King of Thailand presented the white elephant medal to Arnold in recognition of his contribution to Buddhism. In addition the Ceylonese Dharmapala was deeply moved by the reading of the book and formed the Mahabodhi Association to carry out the cause of the revival of Buddhism.

The Chinese e-book translation of The Light of Asia *2015*

Zhang Kun has written a beautiful preface even though it has proved
impossible to establish his identity and whereabouts:[41]

> In early 2014, I made two wishes. The first was to go to Gang
> Rinpoche (Mount Kailash). The second was to translate Sir Edwin
> Arnold's work "Light of Asia". I am convinced that these two things
> are of great significance to me, so I very much hope that I can
> fulfill what I want. In my heart, the greatest commonality between
> Gang Rinpoche and "Light of Asia" is their great significance to
> Buddhism. Gang Rinpoche, as a natural landscape, is the mountain
> of God in the minds of countless Buddhist believers; and "Light
> of Asia" as a literary work is the earliest book that introduces
> Buddhism to the Western world. It is like the light of morning.
> The Light of Asia" has a beautiful style, and the language of the
> poems is like a spring on a hot summer day . . .
>
> The eight volumes of the "Light of Asia" narrate the life of
> the Buddha in the language of poetry. When I read it from the
> beginning, I was surprised by the beauty of its language. After
> reading through it, I feel the skill of the author Edwin Arnold's
> language. The characterization of details is meticulous, and his
> control of the character's emotions is even more intimate. During
> the translation process, pictures often appeared in my mind, and
> every detail was very vivid. In addition, the book is filled with
> warm human feelings. In addition to the noble Buddha being
> described, there are countless moving, affectionate scenes that
> make me cry. My feeling towards this book is not exactly to "fall
> in love at first sight", it is love at first sight. The original English
> version of "The Light of Asia" inspired my strong desire to create.
> My hope is to translate it into Chinese with my pen so more
> people can appreciate its beauty like I did.

There was also a new Spanish translation in 2008,[42] two Italian
ones in 2013 and 2018 and a new Portuguese translation[43] in 2017.
So, as I finish this narrative, *The Light of Asia* is now available in
twelve European, thirteen South Asian, four South-East Asian and

three North-East Asian languages—apart from Esperanto! Quite an
accomplishment by any standard, a testimony to the original English
poem no doubt but more to the everlasting interest in the life of the
Buddha.

Indonesia has the largest Muslim population in the world.
It is also home of the magnificent Borobudur Buddhist temple
complex, dating back to the eighth century CE. On 18 April 1908,
four years after Arnold's death, a group of theosophists—comprising
Europeans, Javanese and Chinese—climbed up to the very top of the
world's largest Buddhist stupa. The site was then under restoration
by the Dutch authorities. The Dutch scholar Marieke Bloembergen
would revisit this event in 2017 and write:[44]

> Walking along its galleries the visitors marvelled at the reliefs
> depicting the life of the Buddha. Their guide for the occasion
> consisted of the works of French and Dutch scholars, as well as
> Edwin Arnold's epic on the enlightenment of Gautama Buddha,
> *The Light of Asia* . . .

To the theosophists for whom *The Light of Asia* was an iconic
text, Borobudur represented the unity of all religions, whereas
Tagore, who visited the temple in 1927, saw it as a symbol of a
greater Indic world anchored in both Buddhism and Hinduism.
Many years earlier, on 28 September 1895, the music composer
Alberto Friedenthal had also visited Borobudur and had noted in
the guest book that he had 'climbed down from Nirvana' immersed
in the teachings of the noble Siddhartha Gautama. Two scholars
of Indonesian cultural heritage have speculated that Friedenthal's
interest in the Buddha may well have been triggered by either
reading *The Light of Asia or reading about it*.[45]

Arnold himself continues to be remembered in different ways in
different countries. On 10 June 2020, in its 'This Day' series, www.
irrawaddy.com, run from Yangon, had a long piece on him with the
title 'The Day The Poet who Introduced the West to Buddhism was
Born'. And, of course, White Lotus Day is marked every year on 8
May, the day of Madame Blavatsky's death, by the Theosophical

Society in Madras with readings from *The Light of Asia*. In Sri Lanka a tradition begun in 1925 by the Young Men's Buddhist Association still continues. An annual 'Light of Asia' elocution contest is held to 'develop oratory skills in English and inculcate Buddhist ethics and values among the younger generation'. The contest is now open to boys and girls of all religions, who are required not only to recite passages from the poem but also explain their meaning in two to three minutes. A non-profit Light of Asia Foundation, deriving its name from the poem, has been set up in Colombo to advance Buddhist values.

COLOMBO Y.M.B.A.
"THE LIGHT OF ASIA"
CONTEST - 2020

Applications are invited for "The Light of Asia" Contest - 2020. This is an island-wide Contest for the Boys and Girls between 09 and 21 years of age and is intended to encourage the youth to learn the art of public-speaking, acquire proficiency in the English Language and appreciate the teachings of the Buddha as presented in Sir Edwin Arnold's Classic "Light of Asia". The Contest will be held in the months of May, June and July 2020. Preliminarily rounds will be conducted in Colombo, Kandy, Kurunegala and Galle. The selection of overall winner and the award ceremony will be held in the month of September 2020.

The closing date for applications will be 11th March 2020.

Applications may be obtained from this office at the address given below or can be downloaded from the YMBA Website shown below. Duly filled applications should be sent back to the address given below :

Hony. Secretary for Literary Activities (English)
Colombo Young Men's Buddhist Association
70, D.S. Senanayake Mawatha,
Borella, Colombo 08.

Website - www.colomboymba.org
E-mail - ymbacolombo@sltnet.lk
Tel - 011-2698083 / 2695786

The Annual 'Light of Asia' elocution contest for school children held in Sri Lanka every year since 1925.

It is not just in Sri Lankan schools that *The Light of Asia* is being kept alive. The poem was part of the syllabus for English Poetry in Class XI in government schools in some states in India till as recently as 2018. The website www.upboardsolutions.com[46] posed twenty-two questions in English and Hindi and also provided answers in both languages to guide students and help them prepare for the examination. One question with its suggested answer reads as follows:

Question 16

Attempt a critical appreciation of the poem
Or
Why do you like the poem "The Light of Asia"?

Answer:

1. Introduction: The Light of Asia is epic on the life of Lord Buddha. The book is divided into eight cantos. The poet has described the life and teachings of Lord Buddha. The eighth canto of this book gives the message of Lord Buddha.
2. Language and Style: The poem is written in blank verse which is most suited for epic poetry. The style of the poem is interesting and charming. The language of the poem is not very simple but it is dignified. The poet has used here and there some Hindi words also which give grace to the poem.
3. Theme: The theme of the poem is very noble. It is the life of a great Prince who sacrifices his own luxuries for the cause of mankind. He looks the realities of world life with his own eyes, He is moved by pitiable sights. He resolves to relieve mankind from these sufferings.
4. Description: When we read the poem we feel as if all incidents are taking place before our own eyes. The

description of the palace, city, conversation between Prince and King [father], Prince and Channa [charioteer], Prince and his wife, etc. are also real and interesting.

5. Lessons which we learn: From the poem we learn that all the pleasures of life are vain and temporary. They end in misery. We should love all the mankind. These are the reasons why I like this poem 'The Light of Asia".

And it is not just for *The Light of Asia* that Arnold is still recalled in India. What he had said after visiting the Taj Mahal in Agra in January 1886 continues to be quoted in official publicity and marketing material:

Not a piece of architecture, as other buildings are, but the proud passion of an emperor's love wrought in living stones.

Not to be outdone, the tourist brochures on the Hawa Mahal in Jaipur recall what Arnold had written in the same month after seeing it:

. . . a vision of daring and dainty loveliness, nine storeys of daring and dainty overhanging balconies and latticed windows, soaring with tier after tier of fanciful architecture in a pyramidal form, a very mountain of airy and audacious beauty, through the thousand pierced screens and gilded arches of which the Indian air blows cool over the flat roofs of the very highest houses. Aladdin's magician could have called into existence no more marvellous abode . . .

And in keeping with Arnold's ecumenicalism, a website put up by a devout Hindu extolling the most popular elephant-God Ganesha quotes from Book the Second of *The Light of Asia:*

And on the middle porch God Ganesha,
With disc and book—to bring wisdom and wealth—
Propitious safe, wreathing his sidelong trunk.

The 1885 Illustrated Edition had this illustration to go along with these lines:

From the 1885 Illustrated Edition of The Light of Asia, *Book the Second.*

It is not just for what he said about the Taj Mahal or about the Buddha or about the Bhagavad Gita that Arnold is remembered every now and then. Sometime in 1894 or thereabouts, he wrote an article titled 'A Flight of Locusts' in the *Daily Telegraph* when a sensation had been caused by the discovery of locusts and locust-eggs in the House of Commons. Arnold recalled his visit to Palestine some years earlier and wrote:

[I saw there] one of the great sights of the natural world which may be described a thousand times without much impressing the mind, but, once witnessed, leaves an indelible recollection and a feeling almost of awe at those united infinitesimal forces of the lower animal world which would overcome evolution itself and banish man from his own planet, if it were not for the wise equilibrium that the cosmic process has established by slaying as well as creating . . . The ants alone, if they had a free antenna, would soon occupy the whole earth. The earth-worms, as Darwin showed us, have by manufacturing arable soil, done more for the cultivation of the globe than all the farmers and the agriculturalists that ever lived and have come to own it. Such facts as the mischief caused by the introduction of sparrows into America and of rabbits into Australia show that it is perilous to interfere with the arrangements of nature. I remember being justly rebuked by Sir John Lubbock for having offered to bring him back some white ants from India. "No, no!" my wise friend said; "I would not be the man to introduce the white ant into Great Britain for all in the cellars of the Bank England!"

Arnold's writing on white ants would be used by Rohan Deb Roy of the University of Reading in his unusual history of the ubiquitous white ants in the imperialist era in India, when they were seen as a threat to the British Empire because they were voracious destroyers of wood and paper, the key materials of the colonial state.[47]

Just before the world was turned upside down by the Covid-19 pandemic, the British Library mounted an exhibition on Buddhism. It began on 25 October 2019 and ran till 23 February 2020. The Library's large collection of Buddhist art objects, books, illustrated manuscripts and rare artifacts was on public display as a collective entity for the first time. There were over one hundred and twenty exhibits that brought together the story of the Buddha and of the practice of Buddhism from across the world.

The Indian origin of Buddhism was mentioned surprisingly briefly in the exhibition—a fact that did not escape some observers.[48] This may well be because of the virtual disappearance of the faith from the Indian scene. Accompanying this unusual exhibition were thirteen blog posts by various scholars which in themselves were learned treatises. The eleventh, by Jana Igunma, called *The Light of Asia: Western Encounters with Buddhism*, dealt almost wholly with the poem in its various incarnations, while the penultimate one, by Annabel Gallop, called *How translated texts, paintings and songs brought Buddhism to the western world*, also recalled *The Light of Asia* and its literary and artistic impacts.

It is somewhat ironic that when *The Light of Asia* was first published in July 1879, the Tibetan variant of Buddhism was 'already being considered as a degeneration from the highly philosophical truths of the older books [of Buddhism]'.[49] The last two lines of *The Light of Asia*, in fact, invoke the most ubiquitous mantra of Tibetan Buddhism and have become its most quoted:

OM MANI PADME HUM, THE SUNRISE COMES!
THE DEWDROP SLIPS INTO THE SHINING SEA!

Given the fact that over the past decades, it is Tibetan Buddhism that has caught the Western world's imagination, it was inevitable that I try and trace the place of *The Light of Asia* in it. The author of the wonderful *The Holy Land Reborn: Pilgrimage & the Tibetan Reinvention of Buddhist India* Toni Huber had this to say:[50]

> . . . If any Tibetan before the mid-20th century would have been interested in, or exposed to "The Light of Asia" then I think the works of the modern intellectual named Amdo Gendun Chophel would be the best place to start looking. The reason is because he was closely connected to the Mahabodhi Society in Calcutta . . .

I could, however, find no evidence that *The Light of Asia* registered with Chophel, although Arnold would certainly have been a name he would have related to, at least in the context of Buddha Gaya.

How may Arnold have come to the title of his epic poem that has gone into the history books? Without wishing to take away anything from his own fertile imagination and vast learning, could it be that these lines of Shelley in Act III of Scene III in *Prometheus Unbound* had something to do with the title *The Light of Asia?* This thought crossed my mind only when I saw a reference to them in Arnold's own work:

Asia! Thou Light of Life!
Shadow of Beauty unbeheld.

Even so, the grandson of the man who so admired Arnold and in whose life *The Song Celestial* played such an important part has a different take on the title of Arnold's epic on the life of the Buddha:[51]

> Light *of* Asia narrows the band-width of the Tathagata. It constellates him with the Star of the East which the Magi (all from the east) were guided by on their westward journey to Bethlehem. Light *from* Asia too would manacle the Buddha to a GPS.
> He was Light.[52]

That he came to be considered as the light appears somewhat ironic in view of what the Buddha, according to some versions, told his favourite disciple before dying:

Be then O' Ananda your own Lamp.

Notes

1. Bristow (2000)
2. These lines also formed the basis for the 17 January 1979 episode of the CBS Radio Mystery Theater titled *The Wandering Wind*. Coincidentally, this was the centenary year of the publication of *The Light of Asia*. The award-winning CBS Radio Mystery Theater series produced in New York ran daily between 1974 and 1980. It has been revived in recent years thanks to YouTube. *The Wandering Wind* is a forty-four-minute dramatization.
3. Allen (2002)
4. That Buddhism had been forgotten or erased from Indian memory before Allen's heroes materialized is in itself a debatable proposition. From about the eighth century, the Buddha gets represented as the ninth incarnation of Vishnu both in texts and in temple architecture. Sixteenth-

century Persian texts like the *Ain-i-Akbari* and seventeenth-century texts like the *Dabistan-i-Mazahib* discuss the Buddhist faith as practised in India. Bodh Gaya itself continued to draw pilgrims from India and elsewhere till as late as in the eighteenth century.

5. Lahiri (2002)
6. Singh (2004). Lahiri (2015) gives the example of Bhagwanlal Indraji, whose contributions to discovering Ashokan edicts in Maharashtra and Rajasthan have been much less recognized than those of his British counterparts because the bulk of his early writings was in Gujarati.
7. This has been analysed very well in Geary (2014).
8. Campbell (2003)
9. Howse (2004)
10. Brown (2009)
11. Harris (2206)
12. Chaudhuri (2006)
13. Email communication 7 May 2020
14. Email communication 13 May 2020
15. Rosinka Chaudhuri's 1999 doctoral dissertation at Oxford was titled 'Orientalist Themes and English Verse in Nineteenth Century India' and dealt with Sir Edwin Arnold briefly.
16. It was Matthew Arnold who memorably described Oxford University as a home 'of lost causes, and forsaken beliefs, and unpopular names, and impossible loyalties'.
17. Quoted in Whitlark (1981). In the same article Whitlark explored Matthew Arnold's long-standing interest in the life and teachings of the Buddha, something that has not been written about much. Matthew Arnold's knowledge of the Buddha was derived from French sources and went back to the late 1840s.
18. Pinthongvijayakul (2006)
19. The exact day and date in May varies from year to year.
20. I owe this information to Hwansoo Kim, who provided me with a copy of *The Academy* Vol 50, 18 July 1896-No. 1263, page 50, which carried a report of that ceremony.
21. Hecker and Nanatusita (2008)
22. Franklin (2008)
23. Di Ruocco (2011)
24. Robinson (2010) and Robinson (2014)
25. Tamizhselvi (2012)
26. Buswell and Lopez (2013)
27. Email communication 29 March 2020

28. Normand and Winch (2013)
29. Eiben (2016)
30. Ober (2016)
31. Lecourt (2017)
32. Paskins (2017)
33. Swan (1981) and Tweed (1992)
34. Henning (2019)
35. Garrow (2020)
36. Misra (1961)
37. Misra (1963)
38. Goedhals (2020)
39. Haidar (2007) is a very good overview of the influence of Buddhism in Urdu literature.
40. Available at www.site.douban.com/119632/
41. Besides Zhang Kun, a second translator Chen Xiaoyun is also listed.
42. In addition to ones in 1982 and 1994.
43. The first Portuguese translation was actually in 1978 out of Brazil, followed by another one in 2011, also from that country. Both were linked with the Theosophical Society.
44. Bloembergen (2017)
45. Bloembergen and Eickhoff (2020)
46. Board Solutions posted on the website on 27 September 2018
47. Deb Roy (2020)
48. Andrew Robinson in www.lancet.com Vol 395 11 January 2020
49. Bishop (1989)
50. Email communication 12 April 2020
51. Gopal Gandhi, email communication 19 June 2020. In 1934, Caroline Rhys Davids, the wife of T.W.Rhys Davids and a Pali scholar herself, had said "'Light of Asia' is not a happy title save perhaps for the publisher; it goes too far for most Christians; it does not go far enough for most Buddhists; it is not for either correct if by Light of, we mean that which lights up Asia, since this is obviously uncharitable to Islam and Parseeism, and ignores the entire north of that continent.'
52. In 731 CE, the Chinese Emperor had ordered that a *Compendium of the Doctrines and Styles of Teaching of Mani, the Buddha of Light* be composed. This was during the time when Manichaeism, named after its founder the third-century Persian prophet who saw himself in the line of Zoroaster, Buddha and Jesus, was widely followed in many parts of Asia and Europe as well. The Indian origins of Manichaeism are discussed well in Sedlar (1980).

SECTION IV

22

A Curious Case of Sir Edwin Arnold and the
Lall-Vakh Translations in Kashmir

In 2002, there appeared in New Delhi a slim thirty-five-page monograph with a long and forbidding title:

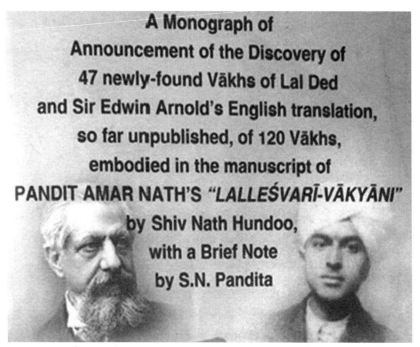

A Monograph of Announcement of the Discovery of 47 newly-found Vākhs of Lal Ded and Sir Edwin Arnold's English translation, so far unpublished, of 120 Vākhs, embodied in the manuscript of PANDIT AMAR NATH'S "LALLEŚVARĪ-VĀKYĀNI" by Shiv Nath Hundoo, with a Brief Note by S.N. Pandita

The sensational monograph published in New Delhi in 2002.

I had never heard of it; neither would have most. Had it not come up in a search of 'Sir Edwin Arnold' in the catalogue of the British Library, I would have missed this story. It is difficult to believe but it is worth telling.

Lallesvari was a fourteenth-century saint and princess revered even today by Hindus and Muslims in the Kashmir Valley. Her verse-sayings are called *Lalla-Vakhs*, the earliest compilation of which has come down to us from the early part of the eighteenth century. In 1876, the German Indologist Georg Buhler had deposited his collection of the Lalla-Vakhs, gathered by him in Kashmir the previous year, at the Deccan College in Poona. This is important, for it provides a connection to Arnold. In 1920, George Grierson, a noted British administrator in India, published *Lalla-Vakyavani*, comprising the original sixty of the early eighteenth century plus an additional forty-nine he had himself discovered and had recorded.

In May 2002, Shiv Nath Hundoo was rummaging through the papers, books and other records of his father Suna Bhatta Shastri, a great Sanskrit scholar of Kashmir. Hundoo stumbled upon a manuscript, *Lallesvari-Vakyani*, a work by his elder brother Amar Nath Hundoo, who was a brilliant Sanskrit student and who had commenced this work in early 1934 and completed it in a year. Sadly, he died very young, in February 1938.

Now here is the sensational part. In his late brother's manuscript, Shiv Nath Hundoo also found, in his own words:

> Sir Edwin Arnold's English translation, so far unpublished, of as many as 120 vakhs, of which the first sixty are those that have come down to us from Rajanaka Bhaskara [the early eighteenth-century collection] while the additional sixty vakhs appear to be those collected by Arnold from elsewhere.

Shiv Nath Hundoo also writes that the evidence points to Edwin Arnold having done the translations after receiving the knighthood [that is January 1888]. But he makes two errors of fact. He writes that Arnold must have been in Bombay in 1888–89 and later in Srinagar as well. In Bombay, Hundoo's surmise is that Arnold would have been provided with access to the Buhler collection at Poona, and in Srinagar he believes Arnold left behind his translations, which his late brother had managed to obtain.

That there is an annotation in Amar Nath Hundoo's manuscript saying 'Sir Edwin Arnold's translation' is indisputable. What is also beyond doubt is that Arnold was in Poona for a few days in November 1885. But what is also incontrovertible is that Arnold himself makes no mention of these translations anywhere, nor does his biographer. This is indeed mysterious. How did Arnold access the Buhler collection?

I tracked down S.N. Pandita, who had written a brief note in this monograph at the request of Shiv Nath Hundoo. Pandita, who lives near New Delhi, had looked into Amar Nath Hundoo's manuscript and confirmed that it contains the English translations by Sir Edwin Arnold, acknowledged in writing by Amar Nath Hundoo himself. There is one possibility. Could it be that Arnold had done the translations before he was knighted? Could he have done them during his visit to India in 1885–86? But then if indeed he had, why did he not write about them in *India Revisited* and how had Amar Nath Hundoo accessed Arnold's translations in Srinagar in the mid-1930s?

One of the most famous detectives ever was created by a man who was an early admirer of the Theosophical Movement and who would definitely have read *The Light of Asia* when it first came out. 'Arnold and the Lallesvari-vakyani' is a fit case for Sherlock Holmes. The Buddha makes his presence felt in many of Conan Doyle's stories.[1]

Notes

1.   Van Stenis (2019)

23

Coda: The Discovery of Edwin Arnold's Great Grandchildren in Bhopal and Elsewhere

While trying to unearth material on Sir Edwin Arnold at the National Archives in New Delhi, I quite accidentally stumbled up on a file named 'Fortnightly Report on the Political Situation in India for the month of September 1937'. This contained a letter from C.W. Gwynne, Chief Secretary of the United Provinces in Lucknow, to J.A. Thorne, Secretary to the Government of India, Home Department in Simla. Gwynne reported on the weather, land revenue collections, prices and the state of public health in the United Provinces in the first fortnight of September 1937 before coming to the crime situation. He wrote:

> Serious crime presents no particular features and has on the whole been light. Two cases, however, are worth reporting. One, from the Agra Division . . . The other case was from the Fyzabad Division. In Sultanpur district an attack was made on an aged Englishman who has retired there—a Mr. Arnold, a son of Sir Edwin Arnold, the author of "Light of Asia". He is a man of 68 years of age, who lives in a small bungalow at Pakri with a Muhammedan wife and two children. He receives a pension of Rs 300 a month from Bhopal. There had been a long-standing dispute regarding some jungle land of which Mr. Arnold holds a lease. The decisions of the court have always been in his favour. On August 29 he arranged to have some jungle cut and was given police assistance. In spite of this, one Parmanand, a young Brahmin, is said to have evaded the police and to have assaulted Mr. Arnold and one of his servants with a spear. The servant

died last morning and information has just been received that Mr.
Arnold also succumbed to his injuries.

This was quite a find. Channing Arnold's stay in Burma is well-
documented because of the Privy Council case that I have highlighted
earlier. I have also drawn attention to the two books he published in
1920 and 1921 on the *Ramayana* and the *Mahabharata*, establishing
himself as a scholar-of-sorts on Indian literature. But subsequently
the trail on him was cold till I discovered this information on him in
the National Archives.

Channing Arnold's killing had been reported quite prominently
in the Indian and British media—the reason being, clearly, that he
was the son of the author of *The Light of Asia*. The *Times of India* of
17 September 1937 described in some detail how he had died:

European Dies of Wounds
Attacked with Spear on U.P. Farm

LUCKNOW, September 16.

Mr. Channing Arnold, son of Sir Edwin Arnold, the author of "The
Light of Asia" died in hospital on Sunday [September 12 1937] of
wounds inflicted by an Indian who attacked him with a spear. Mr.
Arnold was attacked on his farm on August 30th . . . Mr. Arnold
owned a number of farms in Oudh . . . On August 30th while he
was supervising the cutting down of some trees on his property, a
dispute is stated to have arisen with an Indian who attacked him with
a spear . . . He has been buried in the farm where he was attacked.

On the same day, London's *The Times* carried quite a detailed obituary
recalling the significance of his Privy Council case and saying that as
a 'rebel against convention' Channing Arnold had 'something of his
father's charm and imaginative gifts, without his sanity of judgment'.
A few months later, on 28 February 1938, the *Times of India* carried
another report:

Channing Arnold Murder

DEATH SENTENCE CONFIRMED

LUCKNOW, February 25.

Mr. Justice Hamilton and Mr. Justice Yorke of the Oudh Chief
Court confirmed today the sentences of death and transportation
for life passed by the Sessions Judge of Fyzabad on Parmanand
and Ramdulare respectively for having murdered Mr. Channing
Arnold, son of the late Sir Edwin Arnold (author of *The Light of
Asia*), and Mohammed Wasiullah on August 30 last. The evidence
showed that Mr. Arnold had purchased 65 *bighas* of land from
the Raja of Hasanpur in the village of Pakree, Sultanpur District.
Parmanand claimed certain rights in the land but they were not
proved. As he was having trouble with Parmanand, Mr. Arnold
informed the police before cutting the *dhak* jungle standing on the
land. While doing so, Mr. Arnold and three others of his party
were suddenly attacked by Parmanand, who was armed with a
spear, Ramdulare, armed with a lathi.

But in none of these reports was there any mention of what
Channing Arnold had been doing in India. The reference to his
receiving a pension from Bhopal in Gwynne's letter to Thorne led
me to conclude that Channing Arnold may have been employed by
the royal family there. And sure enough, that indeed turned out to
be the case.

The very mention of Bhopal brings to mind the world's most
catastrophic industrial disaster that took place at Union Carbide's
chemical plant there in December 1984. But Bhopal is also
known for its quite remarkable quartet of Begums, who presided
over the Bhopal princely state between 1819 and 1926. The state
itself had been founded by an Afghan adventurer in 1709. The
last of the formidable women rulers was Sultan Jahan Begum,
who had taken over in 1901. Restoration of the magnificent

Buddhist complex at Sanchi that dates back to the third century BCE had begun in the reign of her mother Shahjehan Begum. But it was during Sultan Jahan Begum's rule and with her active involvement that John Marshall carried forward and completed the restoration around 1919.[1]

Sultan Jahan Begum had three sons: Nasrullah Khan the heir apparent, Obaidullah Khan and Hamidullah Khan. Nasrullah Khan in turn had two sons—Habibullah Khan, born in 1903, and Rafiqullah Khan, born in 1905. It appears that Hamidullah Khan had always been the favourite of his mother and had been given the benefit of a university education outside Bhopal—the first in his family. In March 1924, Obaidullah Khan died suddenly of cancer of the liver and less than six months later the heir apparent also passed away of diabetes. Sultan Jahan Begum then decided to name her youngest son the heir apparent. But this required British approval.

In May 1925, Lord Reading, the Viceroy in Calcutta, ruled in favour of her grandson Habibullah Khan as the heir-apparent, but as a sop to Sultan Jahan Begum, broke with tradition and referred the matter to London for a final verdict. To ensure she got her way, the Bhopal ruler positioned herself in London from late September 1925 onwards. After a dramatic meeting with King George V, she was finally informed in March 1926 that the British government had over ruled the Viceroy and backed her decision to name her son as heir apparent. Two months later, while still in London savouring her victory, she announced her abdication. Hamidullah Khan's becoming Nawab of Bhopal in June 1926 meant his eldest brother's sons—Habibullah Khan and Rafiqullah Khan—were out in the cold.

Where does Channing Arnold figure in this convoluted tale? It turns out that he had been recruited by the Bhopal royal family sometime around 1915 or 1916 to be a tutor to Habibullah Khan and Rafiqullah Khan. He had tangled with the British establishment in Rangoon and had become quite a celebrity. This, however, had not prevented Sultan Jahan Begum, a staunch loyalist of the Raj, from employing him. How and why this happened remains a mystery.

Along with tutoring both the boys of the royal house, Channing
Arnold also taught a number of girls from the noble families of
Bhopal to ensure that they became well-groomed suitors for his
two wards. 'Arnold Sahab,' as the old noble families called him, was
clearly a prominent figure in princely Bhopal. He was particularly
close to Rafiqullah Khan, after whom he named his son, Rafiq
Arnold. It was during his time in Bhopal that Channing Arnold
published his three books for use in Indian schools, which I have
mentioned earlier: the *Hitopadesa* and the *Mahabharata* in 1920 and
the *Ramayana* in 1921.

Channing Arnold and Rafiqullah Khan were not in Bhopal on
26 June 1926 when the coronation of Hamidullah Khan took place.
There are some letters from Arnold to one of his friends in India
that definitively establish their presence in London at that time. On
10 June 1926, for instance, from aboard the *SS Mooltan*, Channing
Arnold writes to Ranjit Khan in Bhopal:

> . . . .We are now off the coast of Italy and are arriving at Marseilles
> (France) tomorrow morning at 11 o'clock . . . Rafiq Mian, Kadir
> and I are very well.

Seven days later Channing Arnold would give an update on his
movements from Paris:

> . . . We arrived here, the French capital city, safely and all well on
> Saturday last. This morning we are leaving at 12.30 by airship for
> London. Kadir goes by train and steamboat with the luggage . . . I
> telegraphed to my brother who replied that he was astonished and
> delighted to learn that I was coming . . .

It is most probable that Channing Arnold was making one final
effort with the British Government to protect the future interests of
his wards—if not actually annul the coronation itself.

After Hamidullah Khan took over as Nawab of Bhopal, a new
dispute arose: who will be declared as *his* heir apparent? Sultan

Jahan Begum wanted his eldest daughter to be formally declared Hamidullah Khan's successor as soon as possible. In November 1927, Rafiqullah Khan would make representations to the British Government arguing that his brother or he be appointed the heir apparent to Hamidullah Khan. This he justified on the basis of Islamic law as well on the grounds that his father had been staunchly loyal to the British. These representations were undoubtedly the handiwork of Channing Arnold. But the new Viceroy Lord Irwin as well as the authorities in London declined to intervene. Exactly a year later, Hamidullah Khan named his eldest daughter Abida Sultaan, who was then fifteen years old, as his heir apparent.[2]

A distraught Habibullah Khan, who had been introduced to the visiting Prince of Wales in 1922 as the heir apparent to the heir apparent,[3] departed for Poona, gambled away his wealth, married an enterprising Parsi woman and died there of tuberculosis in June 1930, very shortly after the demise of his grandmother. Rafiqullah Khan, afflicted with epilepsy from a very young age and suffering from extreme mood swings that would make him violent, was admitted to a mental hospital in Ranchi in April 1947 and was officially declared a 'lunatic'. He would pass away in 1952.

Channing Arnold's position in the new Nawab's establishment had now become completely untenable and it is almost certain that the Dowager Sultan Jahan asked him to leave Bhopal sometime in late 1927. Through his Bhopal connections, he was, however, able to buy property in Sultanpur in the then United Provinces and settle down there. He married a much younger Zohra according to Muslim law, becoming, in William Dalrymple's words, a twentieth-century 'White Mughal'. They had two children: Rafiq, born in 1929, and Sajjida, born in 1931. After his killing, the distraught family returned to Bhopal to be looked after by Rafiqullah Khan.

Tragedy struck a second time soon, when Zohra, a long-time patient of tuberculosis, too passed away in 1940. Rafiq Arnold continued to stay in Bhopal, leading a life of minor nobility, and would pass away in January 1995. His sister Sajjida Arnold was adopted by the Indian Christian Mission and became Grace Arnold. In the very

Grace Turner at the grave of her father Channing Arnold very near Sultanpur in Uttar Pradesh in May 2009. (Source: Mohammed Michael Arnold)

late 1940s she worked at a centre for destitute and orphaned children in north India called the Good Shepherd Agricultural Mission, got married there in 1952 to Oliver Turner (whose father was a British pastor who had three children by a Sinhalese woman), had children and moved around in India a bit, and finally emigrated to England in October 1980.

In early 2020, at the age of eighty-nine, she published an account of her life in which she recalled her visit to Channing Arnold's grave in Sultanpur eleven years earlier.[4]

She has four children, all born in India: a son named Alwyn Turner, now settled in Thailand, a son John Turner in Australia and two daughters, Sharon Turner and Marina Turner, in London. Alwyn and I established contact. Rafiq Arnold had three daughters and two sons, who all live in Bhopal, as does their mother Kaneez Fatima Arnold. The youngest son is Mohammed Michael Arnold,

Mohammed Michael Arnold, youngest of the nine great grandchildren of Sir Edwin Arnold and a resident of Bhopal. (Source: Mohammed Michael Arnold)

with whom I was able to connect and talk of his family. His siblings have equally wonderfully syncretic names: Firoz Arnold, Nahid Arnold Ali, Farzana Arnold Siddiqui and Fozia Arnold Raza. The sprawling Sultanpur property of Channing Arnold in which he lived and in which he lies buried is now under illegal occupation.

This is a fitting end to this book—the discovery of Sir Edwin Arnold's nine great grandchildren with their sub-continental connections[5] embracing different religions. The Instinctive Imperialist who sang the praises of the Viceroy and the Inveterate Indophile who gave the world *The Light of Asia* and *The Song Celestial,* among other works, would undoubtedly have been pleased.[6]

Notes

1. Lahiri (2012)
2. Sultaan (2009) is an informative account of her life. Her son Shahryar Khan was one of Pakistan's best-known diplomats and cricket administrators. Her nephew was Mansur Ali Khan Pataudi, the legendary Indian cricketer.
3. This is mentioned in Fitze (1956).
4. Turner (2020). Grace Turner writes that she had been told in her childhood by the missionaries who had adopted her that her mother Zohra belonged to Bhopal and was actually a Hindu princess called Rani from Rajputana (today's Rajasthan), who converted to Islam to marry Channing Arnold. Turner goes on to say that Ranjit Khan, to whom Channing Arnold had written from England in 1926, may well have been Zohra's father. On the other hand, Mohammed Michael Arnold told me that his grandmother Zohra belonged to Sultanpur and had no royal connections. I have found it impossible to establish which version is authentic.
5. There may well be others whom I have been unable to trace down. Arnold's eldest son Edwin Lester certainly had a daughter named Dorothy, who became Dorothy Colville, but after that the trail is cold. Julian too had a son, on whom no information is available. Two other children of Edwin Arnold—Katherine and Emerson—were, according to whatever information I have been able gather, childless. There is reference to a granddaughter of Sir Edwin in the *Long Eaton Advertiser* of 5 August 1960, where, in a column titled 'A Poet's Diary', Teresa Hooley writes:

   > Another letter is from Kenneth Hare, the Cotswold poet, asking me if I will review a book of poems for the granddaughter of the late Sir Edwin Arnold the famous author of "The Light of Asia". Greatly flattered. I have said (not without again crossing my fingers) that I shall be delighted to do so . . .

   But who this granddaughter is has been impossible to verify. It cannot be Grace Turner, who was then very much in India. It could have been Dorothy Colville.
6. In recent years, Princeton University Press has brought out twenty-four biographies of religious books—their lives and their history. These include *The Lotus Sutra* by Donald S. Lopez Jr. and The Bhagavad Gita by Richard H. Davis. *The Light of Asia* is not a religious book in this

sense although it is about the founder of what became a religion even if the Buddha had not intended it to be so. What Adam Kirsh wrote in the *New Yorker* of 19 November 2019 is worth recalling: 'After all, the Buddha did not become the Buddha by following the Buddha—he forged his own unique path'.

24

A Final Word

So, this has been a biography of a book.[1] The book, in the form of an epic romantic poem, did much to shape the ideas of people across the world regarding the life of the Buddha. There was a mania for it for years after its publication. Its author was no great scholar but achieved in verse what no scholarly work was able to. Its impact on the Western world, at least till the end of the first quarter of the twentieth century, has been recognized and written about. Far less understood and appreciated is its enduring appeal outside the UK and the USA, especially in the Indian subcontinent. This appeal worked in different ways—through the influence it would have on prominent public personalities, through translations into numerous languages and through its use in diverse art forms. It inspired social reformers and also led to Buddhists having an equal say in managing the site of the Buddha's enlightenment, which they had not had for many centuries past.

Embedded in this biography of a book has been the life of the remarkable personality who wrote it. T.S. Eliot wrote that he was enchanted by *The Light of Asia* but that he was not bothered to know anything about its author. I am no Eliot, but I was as much interested in the man behind the poem as in the poem itself. I believe the two cannot be seen independently of each other. The personality and background of Sir Edwin Arnold profoundly informed *The Light of Asia*. He saw himself as a poet first and poet last, even if his contemporaries didn't agree with his self-view. In 1893, he translated Sappho's famous seventh-century BCE Greek poem 'To One Who Loved Not Poetry' thus:

Thou liest dead, and there will be no memory left behind
Of thee or thine in all the earth, for never didst thou bind
The roses of Pierian streams upon thy brow; thy doom
Is now to flit with unknown ghosts in cold and nameless gloom.

Sir Edwin Arnold was a man of his times, firmly anchored in late Victorian society, a quintessential British imperialist[2] but deeply in love with other cultures, most notably Indian and, towards the end of his kaleidoscopic life, Japanese as well. Not a scholar, strictly speaking, he contributed hugely to *popularizing* the classics of Indian philosophy and literature at a time when they were little known. The enduring fascination that Mahatma Gandhi had for his translation of the Bhagavad Gita is sufficient for Sir Edwin Arnold to occupy a distinctive niche in not only Indian but also world history. If you add to this the prodigious influence *The Light of Asia* had, then it would be fair to say he was a poet who helped interpret not one but two faiths—an achievement that is quite extraordinary by any yardstick. Incidentally, there is one thing that connects *The Song Celestial* with *The Light of Asia*, and that is the sacredness of the pipal tree. This is the tree under which the Buddha meditated and attained enlightenment. This is also the tree whose divinity is extolled in the opening six verses of the Bhagavad Gita.[3]

The Light of Asia came at a time when organized religion was in retreat in Victorian society and was under attack across the Atlantic as well. It came exactly ten years after the word 'agnostic' was first coined.[4] To use the title of Thomas Hardy's extraordinary poem,[5] Arnold placed Buddha in the public consciousness at a time when 'God's Funeral' was taking place.[6] *The Light of Asia's* message, that the Buddha said he was no God and preached a 'religion of humanity', free of dogma and based on reasoning and self-discovery, resonated loudly. Because it was such a spectacular success in the UK and America, educated elites elsewhere too took to it enthusiastically.

The Light of Asia did not involve painstaking academic investigation. But clearly it met a demand, fed a hunger, filled a need and fulfilled an aspiration. It had something for everybody. It appealed to the Christian non-missionary world because of the close parallels in it between the lives of the Buddha and of Christ.[7] It made Buddhists feel proud because it portrayed the founder of their faith in a glorious manner. The King of Siam, for example, could use it to counter the growing influence of English and French missionaries in his kingdom. Upper-caste Hindus in India did not see it as a potent threat because of the extensive use of Brahminical themes in the poem, as for example, these lines:

With eyes bent down before the Sage who said,
"Child, write this scripture," speaking slow the verse
"Gayatri" named which only High-born hear:-

  Om, tatsavirurvarenyam
  Bhargo devasya dhimahi
  Dhiyo yon a parachodayat[8]

"Acharya, I write", meekly replied
The Prince . . .

And it had enough ammunition for those Hindus wanting to confront the tyranny of the caste system because of the way it depicted the Buddha confronting Brahminical practices in Book the Sixth of *The Light of Asia*, which has these powerful lines preaching equality and fraternity:

And once, at such a time, the o'erwrought Prince
Fell to the earth in deadly swoon, all spent,
Even as one slain, who hath no longer breath
Nor any stir of blood; so wan he was,
So motionless. But there came that way
A shepherd-boy, who saw Siddartha lie . . .
Also he poured upon the Master's lips
Drops of warm milk, pressed from his she-goat's

bag,
Lest, being low caste, he, by touching wrong one
So high and holy seeming.
And the boy worshipped, deeming him some
*   God;*
But our Lord gaining breath, arose and asked
Milk in the shepherd's lota. "Ah, my Lord,
I cannot give thee," quoth the lad; "thou seest
I am a Sudra, and my touch defiles!"
Then the World-honoured spake: "Pity and
*   need*
Make all flesh kin. There is no caste in blood,
Which runneth of one hue, nor caste in tears,
Which trickle salt with all; neither comes man
To birth with tilka-mark stamped on the brow,
Nor sacred thread on neck. Who doth right
*   deed*
Is twice-born and who doeth ill deeds vile.
Give me to drink, my brother; when I come
Unto my quest it shall be good for thee"
Threat the peasant's heart was glad, and gave.

Speaking for myself, I am not a Buddhist nor am I a practitioner of Buddhism. I do not belong to the community of scholars of Buddhism. But the life of the Buddha has always interested and continues to captivate me.[9] The life of the Buddha is hardwired into the mind of every Indian. What we don't realize is how much the popular imagination of that life was moulded by *The Light of Asia*. That, more than anything else, has been the motivation for this book written in the form of a story. Alexander Pope had a wonderful epitaph for Isaac Newton:

Nature and nature's laws lay hid in night;
God said "Let Newton be and all was light.[10]

A similar epitaph for Arnold may well have been:

Buddha and Buddha's teachings lay hid in night;
God said "Let Edwin Arnold be" and all was light.

Ultimately, I believe that *The Light of Asia* became the cultural phenomenon it did because it focused on the Buddha's humanity, instead of his divinity.

Notes

1. In writing this biography I have been influenced by two books that have a similar objective: Sabyasachi Bhattacharya's *Vande Mataram: The Biography of a Song* (Penguin, 2003) and David Bello's *The Novel of the Century: The Extraordinary Adventure of Les Miserables* (Farar, Strauss and Giroux, 2017)
2. As late as 1902, Arnold was writing panegyrics to British Viceroys in India.
3. I thank Nayanjot Lahiri for pointing out that the pipal tree was sacred to the Harappans as well. There is also a verse on it in the *Rg Veda*.
4. The word was used first in 1869 by Thomas Huxley, who was described as Darwin's 'bulldog'.
5. The poem called *God's Funeral* was written sometime between 1908 and 1910 and forms the title of A.N. Wilson's fine book on the decline of faith in the Victorian world. It was also in 1882 that Friedrich Nietzsche, the German philosopher, famously declared: 'God is dead. God remains dead. And we have killed him.'
6. In 1850, one of the most famous poems in English, called *In Memoriam*, by Lord Tennyson, was published. This is usually seen as a requiem for the Poet Laureate's beloved friend, who had died earlier at the young age of twenty-two. But as A.N. Wilson has written in Wilson (1999): '*In Memoriam* is the great poem of bereavement, but it is also the work of which explores the agonizing processes of religious doubt, from the position of not nihilistic atheism but of a faith which is strong enough to hold on . . .'
7. In 1863, the French scholar Ernest Renan's *Vie de Jesus (The Life of Jesus)* had become a huge best-seller. Renan's Jesus, like Arnold's Buddha, was 'wholly human'. The miracles were there—but not necessarily to be believed.

8. The famous mantra from the *Rg Veda* which was traditionally chanted by Brahmin boys when adorning the sacred thread to signify that they were twice born. Gradually, other castes too adopted this practice. Dr Radhakrishnan's translation is thus: 'We meditate on the effulgent glory of the divine Light; may he inspire our understanding.'

9. Two decades I ago I had written on the paradox of Buddhism in Sri Lanka, a country romanticized by Arnold and racked by conflict in recent decades. Ramesh (2000).

10. There is an equally wonderful extension to this by another British poet, J.C. Squire:

> *It did not last: the Devil crying "Ho!*
> *Let Einstein be!" and restored the status quo.*

25

A Note of Thanks

I am privileged to have had His Holiness the Dalai Lama write the foreword to this book. He is a source of continuing admiration and inspiration.

Much of this book was researched and written during the Covid-19 lockdown period of the months of April–October 2020. A large community of scholars from across the globe have been generous with their time and knowledge.

Among those outside India, I deeply appreciate the assistance of Donald Lopez and Urs App; Toni Huber; Christopher Clausen and Jeffrey Franklin; Richard Jaffe, Michah Auerback and Judith Snodgrass; Tom-Eric Krijger; Alicia Turner, Lawrence Cox and Brian Bocking; Penny Edwards, Anne Hanson and Trent Walker; Patrick Jory and Nidhi Eeseewong; Yuri Takahashi and Soe Myint; Anne Blackburn, Elizabeth Harris and Asanga Tilakaratne; Arunabh Ghosh and Tansen Sen; Todd Lewis and David Waller; Colin Chambers, Rosalind O'Hanlon and Lawrence Normand; Mick Brown, Christopher Howse and Philip Waller; Harjot Oberoi, Douglas Ober and David Geary; Sumit Guha and Shivaji Mukherjee; Robert Pryor; Velcheru Narayana Rao and Sanjay Subrahmanyam; Erin Garrow; Anthony Goedhals; Marieke Bloembergen; Catherine Robinson, Lawrence Normand, Brian Murray and Alexander Bubb; Gajendran Ayyathurai; Jana Igunma and Annabel Gallop; Steven Kemper; George Michell; Robert Pamplun; G.W. Swicord; Tim Jeal; Hwansoo Kim; Robin Darwall-Smith and Rosie Llewellyn-Jones; Jorn Borup and Helena Capkova; Vasudha Dalmia, and Sita Anantha Raman; Dinyar Patel and John Edmond McLeod; the

Japan Society and the Buddhist Society in London; the Birmingham and Midland Institute.

In India, I thank Suvarna Nalapat and P. Vijay Kumar; V. Geetha, Stalin Rajangam and John Samuel; Lalit Mansingh and Aditya Panda; Urvish Kothari, Sanjay Parikh and Tridip Suhrid; Dr. Mukta; Menka Shivdasani; Sakti Roy; Sabuj Kali Sen; Probal Dasgupta; Hirdepal Singh, Poonam Singh, Amarjit Chandan and K.B.S. Sodhi; Aakash Singh Rathore and Ananya Vajpeyi; S.N. Pandita and Peter Heehs; Gopalkrishna Gandhi and A.R. Venkatachalapathy; Seetha Ravi, Lakshmi Ramachandran and Jayshree Menon; Rahul Noronha and Omar Ali; Pramoda Devi; Reba Som; Anurag Vishwanath, Ananth Krishnan and Debasish Chaudhuri; Sitanshu Yashaschandra Mehta; Tasneem Mehta; Rakshanda Jalil; Devapriya Roy; the Mahabodhi Society in Kolkata; and Jaya Ravindran of the National Archives, New Delhi.

Anuradha Kumar helped in accessing material from various archives in the USA. Shailaja Chandra not only read the entire manuscript but also educated me on the mathematical significance of the *Lalitavistara*.

I thank Alwyn Turner and Mohammed Michael ('Mikki') Arnold for extended conversations on their families.

I am grateful to Siddiq Wahid for his involvement in many ways.

Geetanjali Surendran read the full manuscript and made a number of very useful suggestions.

As always, Nayanjot Lahiri was a constant source of advice and a sounding board for various ideas.

Sources and Bibliography

I. Archives

USA
1. Massachusetts Historical Society, Boston
2. Houghton Library, Harvard University
3. Harry Ransom Centre, University of Texas, Austin
4. Smithsonian Institution
5. Valdosta University, Georgia
6. Yale University Library
7. Duke University, David M. Rubinstein Library
8. Dickinson College Special Collections

UK
1. Bodleian Library, Oxford University
2. University College Library, Oxford University
3. British Library
4. National Archives
5. King's College Archives

India
1. National Archives New Delhi

II. Doctoral Dissertations

Ayyathurai, Gajendran, Foundations of Anti-Caste Consciousness: Pandit Iyothee Thass, Tamil Buddhism, and the Marginalised in South India, Columbia University, 2010

Chaudhuri, Rosinka, Oriental Themes and English Verse in Nineteenth Century India, Oxford University, 1995

Clausen, Christopher, A Critical Edition of Edwin Arnold's Light of Asia, Queens University, Kingston, Ontario, Canada. May 1972

Di Ruocco, Adele, The Buddhist World in Modern Russian Culture 1873–1919 Literature and Fine Arts, University of Southern California, Los Angeles, May 2011

Eiben, Emily Rose, Representing Buddhism in British Media and Popular Culture 1875–1895, Ludwig Maxmillian Universitat Munich, 2016

Garrow, Erin, Flower Unfurling: Buddhist Modernism and the Early Writings of James Joyce, City University of New York, 2020

Geary, David, Destination Enlightenment: Buddhism and the Golden Bazaar in Bodh Gaya Bihar, University of British Columbia, Vancouver, December 2009

Murray, John Ralph, Sir Edwin Arnold's Buddhism, University of Florida, 1952

Ober, Douglas David, Reinventing Buddhism: Conversation and Encountering Buddhism in Modern India 1839-1956, University of British Columbia, Vancouver, December 2016

Paskins, Susan Karin, Imagining Enlightenment: Buddhism and Kipling's *Kim*, Birkbeck, University of London, January 2017

Powell, Michael, Cultural and Religious Themes in the Life of F.L. Woodward, University of Tasmania, 1999

Sastri, Hesaraghatta Narasimha Lakshminarasimha, Sir Edwin Arnold's Anglo-Indian Poetry, University of Toronto, October 1960

Surendran, Gitanjali, The Indian Discovery of Buddhism: Buddhist Revival in India 1890-1956, Harvard University, August 2013

Takahashi, Yuri, Shwe U Daung and the Burmese Sherlock Holmes: To be a modern Burmese citizen living in a nation-state 1889–1962, University of Sydney, April 2017

Tamizhselvi, S.T., A Comparative Study of The Light of Asia by Edwin Arnold and Asia Jyothi by Kavimani Desiga Vinayagam Pillai, University of Madras, 2012

III. Masters Dissertation

Van Stenis, The Lotus, The Lion and the Detective: An Exploration of Buddhism and its Theory of Karmic Causation in Arthur Conan Doyle's Sherlock Holmes Stories, Leiden University, Leiden June 2019

IV. Academic Monographs

Hundoo, Shiv Nath A Monograph of Announcement of Discovery of 47 newly-found Vakhs of Lal Ded and Sir Edwin Arnold's English translation, so far unpublished, of 120 Vakhs, embodied in the manuscript of PANDIT

AMAR NATH'S *'LALLESVARI-VAKYANI'*, Siddharth Publications, New Delhi, October 2002

Mitra, Dilip Kumar 'Preface in Remembering Rajendralala Mitra', The Asiatic Society, Kolkata, Reprinted January 2019 (first published 1978)

Palat, Madhavan K. The Spiritual in Nehru's Secular Imagination, The Jawaharlal Nehru Memorial Lecture, November 14 2019, Jawaharlal Nehru Memorial Fund, New Delhi.

V. Research papers in Books or Journals

Arjunwadkar, Leela, The Buddha and Belles Lettres, Annals of the Bhandarkar Oriental Research Institute, Vol 67, No 1/4 (1986) pp 99-108

Allen, Margaret, Henry Polak: The Cosmopolitan Life of a Jewish Theosophist, Friend of India and Anti-racist campaigner in J. Haggis, et al 'Cosmopolitan Lives on the Cusp of Empire', Palgrave Macmillan, 2017

App, Urs, St. Francis Xavier's Discovery of Japanese Buddhism: A Chapter in the European Discovery of Buddhism (Part I: Before the Arrival in Japan, 1547-1549), Eastern Buddhist, 30 (1), pp 53-78, 1997; and (Part 2: From Kagoshima to Yamaguchi, 1549-1551), Eastern Buddhist, 30 (2), pp 214-244 1997.

Blacker, Carmen, Sir Edwin Arnold 1832-1904: A Year in Japan, 1889-90 in Hugh Cortazzi (ed) Britain and Japan: Biographical Portraits, Vol IV, Routledge, London 2002

Bloembergen, Marieke, Borobudur in the Light of Asia: Scholar, Pilgrims and Knowledge in Michael Laffan (ed), Belonging Across the Bay of Bengal: Religious Rites, Colonial Migrations and National Rights, Bloomsbury, London 2017

Chambers, Colin, 'A Flute of Praise': Indian Theatre in Britain in the Early Twentieth Century in Susheila Nasta (ed) India in Britain: South Asian Networks and Connections, Palgrave Macmillan, Basingstoke 2013

Chaudhuri, Rosinka, History in Poetry: Nabinchandra Sen's *Palashir Yuddha* (Battle of Palashi) (1875) and the Question of Truth, in Raziuddin Aquil and Partha Chatterjee (eds), History in the Vernacular, Permanent Black, Ranikhet, 2008.

Doherty, Gerald, The Nirvana Dimension: D.H. Lawrence's Quarrel with Buddhism, The D.H. Lawrence Review, Vol 15 No.1/2 (spring-summer 1982) pp 51-67

Dubois, Martin, Edward Lear's India and the Colonial Production of Nonsense, Victorian Studies Vol 61, No.1 (Autumn 2018) pp 35-59

Geary, David, Rebuilding the Navel of the Earth: Buddhist pilgrimage and transnational religious networks, Modern Asian Studies, 48 (3), 645-692 2014

Greenberger, Evelyn Barish, Salsette and Elephanta: An Unpublished Poem by Clough, The Review of English Studies, Vol 20, No. 79 (August 1969), pp 284-305

Haider, Aziz, Influence of Buddhism on Urdu Literature in Narendra K. Dash (ed), Buddhism in Indian Literature, Aryan Books International, New Delhi 2007

Hansen Kathryn, The Birth of Hindi Drama in Banaras, 1868–1885 in Sandra B. Freitag (ed) Culture and Power in Banaras, University of California Press, Berkeley and Los Angeles, 1992

Hay, Stephen, The Making of late-Victorian Hindu: M.K. Gandhi in London, 1888-1891, Victorian Studies, Vol 33 No. 1 (Autumn 1989). pp 71-98

Henning, Joseph, M, 'Very Beautiful Heathenism': The Light of Asia in Gilded Age America, Journal of American- East Asian Relations, 26 (2019), pp 21-50

Hijiya, James A. The Gita of J. Robert Oppenheimer, Proceedings of the American Philosophical Society, Vol 14, No.2, June 2000

Jetley, M.K., 'Sindhi' in Buddhist Themes in Modern Indian Literature, Institute of Asian Studies, Chennai. 1992

Jory, Patrick, Thai and Western Buddhist Scholarship in the Age of Colonialism: King Chulalongkorn Redefines the Jatakas, The Journal of Asian Studies, Vol 61, No. 3, August 2002

Karpiel, Frank, Theosophy, Culture and Politics in Honolulu, 1890-1920, The Hawaiian Journal of History, Vol 30 (1996)

Keune, Jim, The Intra- and Inter-Religious Conversions of Nehemiah Nilakantha Goreh, Journal of Hindu-Christian Studies, Vol 17, Article 8, 2004

Killingley, Dermot, Edwin Arnold's translation of the Hitopadesa, Asian Literature and Translation, Cardiff University Press, Vol 5, No. 1 2018 pp 25-71

Kim, Hwansoo, A Buddhist Christmas: The Buddha's Birthday Festival in Colonial Korea (1928-1945), Journal of Korean Relations, Vol 2 No. 2 (October 2011) pp 47-82

Kosambi, Meera, Indian Response to Christianity, Church and Colonialism: case of Pandita Ramabai, Economic and Political Weekly, Vol 27, Issue No. 43–44, 24 October 1992

Lecourt, Sebastian, Idylls of the Buddh: Buddhist Modernism and Victorian Poetics in Colonial Ceylon, PMLA, 131.3 (2016), published by the Modern Language Association of America

Mirajkar, N.D., 'Marathi', in Buddhist Themes in Modern Indian Literature, Institute of Asian Studies, Chennai, 1992

Misra, B.P., Sir Edwin Arnold's Role in the Artistic Development of James Joyce, Indian Journal of English Studies, Vol 2, Issue 1, 1961

Misra, B.P., Indian Inspiration of James Joyce, Gaya Prasad and Sons, Agra, 1963

Murray, Brian, Ulysses in 'darkest Africa': Transporting Tennyson with H.M. Stanley and Edwin Arnold, in S. Chaudhuri et al (eds) Commodities and Culture in the Colonial World, Routledge, London 2017

Naravane, Vasant S., Edwin Arnold and The Light of Asia, Indian Horizons, Vol 29 no 1 (1980) published by the Indian Council of Cultural Relations, New Delhi

Pryor, C. Robert, Bodh Gaya in the 1950s: Jawaharlal Nehru, Mahant Giri and Anagarika Dharmapala, in David Geary et al (eds) Cross-Disciplinary Perspectives on a Contested Buddhist site: Bodh Gaya Jataka, Routledge, London 2012.

Rajangam, Stalin, Living Buddhism, Paper presented at a Conference on The Genealogies of Dalit Learning and Humanist Buddhism in 19th and 20th Century India, Centre for South Asian Studies University of Toronto, October 25 2018

Robinson, Catherine (2009), "O our India": towards a reassessment of Sir Edwin Arnold, Religions of South Asia, 3 (2): pp 203-219

Robinson, Catherine (2014), Interpreter of Hinduism to the West? Sir Edwin Arnold's (Re)Presentations of Hindu Texts and their Reception, Religions of South Asia 8 (2) pp 217-236

Roy, Rohan Deb, White Ants, Empire, and Entomo-Politics in South Asia, The Historical Journal, 63, 2 (2020), pp 411-436

Saha, Jonathan, Whiteness, Masculinity and the Ambivalent Embodiment of 'British Justice' in Colonial Burma, Cultural and Social History, 14:4, 2017, pp 527-542

Sigalow, Emily, Breaking Down the Barriers: The Encounter between Judaism and Buddhism in the Late Nineteenth Century, American Jewish History, Vol 102, No.4, October 2018

Sinha, Mishka, Corrigibility, Allegory, Universality: A History of the Gita's Translational Reception, 1785-1945, Modern Intellectual History; 7, 2 (2010); pp 297-317

Snodgrass, Judith, *Budda no fukuin*: The Deployment of Paul Carus's *Gospel of Buddha* in Meiji Japan, Japanese Journal of Religious Studies, 1998 24/3-4

Snodgrass, Judith, Performing Buddhist Modernity: The Lumbini Festival, Tokyo 1925, Journal of Religious History, Vol 33, No. 2 June 2009

Stenerson, Douglas C, Some Impressions of the Buddha: Dreiser and Sir Edwin Arnold's The Light of Asia, Canadian Journal of American Studies, Winter 1991, Vol 22 Issue 3

Whitlark, James, Matthew Arnold and Buddhism, The Arnoldian: A Review of Mid-Victorian Culture, Vol 9 No.1 Winter 1981, pp 5-16

VI. Articles in Magazines/Newspapers

Banerjee, Prathama, Bhagavad Gita wasn't always India's defining book. Another text was far more popular globally, www.theprint.in December 15 2019

Blavatsky, Madame, The Light of the World, Lucifer Vol VIII, No. 44, April 1891, pp 170-173

Brown, Mick, The Daily Telegraph Editor who brought Buddha to life, Daily Telegraph, November 20 2009

Cotes, Mrs Everard, The Ordination of Asoka, Harper's Monthly Magazine, 105 (October 1902), pp 753-751

Kumar, Anu, How a thousand-year Sanskrit love poem has travelled the world, www.scroll.in October 2 2016

Ramesh, Jairam, The Killing of Buddha, India Today, June 26 2000

Riskin, Jessica, Just You Thinking Pump!, New York Review of Books, July 2 2020

VII. Books

Ahir, D.C. The Pioneers of Buddhist Revival in India, Satguru Publications, New Delhi 1989

Allen, Charles, The Buddha and The Sahibs: The Men Who Discovered India's Lost Religion, John Murray London 2002

Allen Charles, Kipling Sahib: India and the Making of Kipling, Little, Brown, London. 2007

Allen, Charles, The Prisoner of Kathmandu: Brian Hodgson in Nepal: 1820-1843, Speaking Tiger, New Delhi 2016

Aloysius, G., Religion as Emancipatory Identity: A Buddhist Movement Among the Tamils under Colonialism, New Age International, New Delhi 1998

Almond, Philip, The British Discovery of Buddhism, Cambridge University Press 1988

Amunugama, Sarath The Lion's Roar: Anagarika Dharmapala and the Making of Modern Buddhism, Oxford University Press, New Delhi 2019

Anantha Raman, Sita. A Madhavaiah: A Biography, Oxford University Press, New Delhi 2005

App, Urs, The Birth of Orientalism, University of Pennsylvania Press, Philadelphia, 2010

App, Urs, The Cult of Emptiness: The Western Discovery of Buddhist Thought and the Invention of Oriental Philosophy, University Media, Wil (Switzerland), 2012 and 2014

Arnold, Edwin, A Letter From the Ex-Principal of an Indian Government College to his Appointed Successor, Bell and Daldy, London 1860

Arnold, Edwin India Revisited, Trubner & Co. London 1886

Arnold Edwin, East and West, Being Papers Reprinted From the "Daily Telegraph" And Other Sources; Longmans, Green & Co. London 1896.

Arnold, Julian, Palms and Temples: Notes of a Four Months' Voyage Upon the Nile, Tinsley Brothers, London, 1882

Arnold, Julian Giants in Dressing Gowns, Argus Books, Chicago 1942

Auerback, Micah L., Storied Sage: Canon ad Creation in the Making of a Japanese Buddha, University of Chicago Press, 2016

Austin, Alfred: The Autobiography of Alfred Austin Vol 2, Macmillan & Co London, 1911

Bakker, Freek L. The Challenge of the Silver Screen: An Analysis of the Cinematic Portraits of Jesus, Rama, Buddha and Mohammed, Brill, Leiden. 2009

Barnett, Andrew, Sibelius, Yale University Press, 2007

Barua, Dipak K., Buddha Gaya Temple: Its History, Buddha Gaya Temple Management Committee, Buddha Gaya, 1981 (2nd revised enlarged edition)

Basham A.L., The Wonder that was India, Sidgwick and Jackson, London, 1954

Beatty-Kingston, William, Music and Manners: Personal Reminiscences and Sketches of Character, Vol 1, Chapman and Hall, London, 1887

Bishop, Peter, The Myth of Shangri-La: Tibet, Travel Writing and the Western Creation of a Sacred Landscape, University of California Press, Berkeley, 1989

Blackburn, Anne, Locations of Buddhism: Colonialism and Modernity in Sri Lanka, University of Chicago Press, Chicago,2010

Bloembergen, Marieke and Martijn Eickhoff, The Politics of Heritage in Indonesia: A Cultural History, Cambridge University Press, 2020

Borges Jorge Luis and Osvaldo Ferrari, Conversations Vol. II, University of Chicago (translation 2014)

Bratlinger, Patrick, Rule of Darkness, Cornell University Press, Ithaca 1988

Bristow, John, The Cambridge Companion to Victorian Poetry, Cambridge University Press, 2000

Buell, Lawrence, Emerson, Harvard University Press, 2003

Buswell Jr, Robert E. and Donald S. Lopez Jr., The Princeton Dictionary of Buddhism, Princeton University Press, 2013

Butcher, Tim, Blood River: A Journey into Africa's Broken Heart, Vintage Books, London, 2008

Campbell, Joseph, The Hero's Journey: Joseph Campbell on his Life and Work, New World Library, California, Centennial Edition 2003

Carnegie, Andrew and John Van Dyke, Autobiography of Andrew Carnegie, Constable & Co. London, 1920

Ch'en, Kenneth K.S., Buddhism in China: A Historical Survey, Princeton University Press, 1964

Chetanananda, Swami, Girish Chandra Ghosh: A Bohemian Devotee of Sri Ramakrishna, Vedanta Society of St. Louis, 2009

Chudel, Alaka Atreya, A Freethinking Cultural Nationalist: A Life History of Rahul Sankrityayan, Oxford University Press, New Delhi 2016

Cranston, Sylvia, HPB: The Extraordinary Life and Influence of Helena Blavatsky, TarcherPerigee, New York, 1993

Dalmia, Vasudha, The Nationalization of Hindu Traditions: Bhartendu Harischandra and Nineteenth-Century Banaras, Oxford University Press, 1997

Dalmia, Vasudha, Poetics, Plays and Performances, Oxford University Press, New Delhi, 2006

Dandekar, Deepra, The Subhedar's Son, Oxford University Press, New York 2019

Das Gupta, Hemendra Nath, The Indian Stage: Volume III, Girish Centenary Edition, Metropolitan Printing and Publishing House, Calcutta, 1944

Das Sarat Chandra, Journey to Lhasa. Speaking Tiger, New Delhi 2017 (resissue)

Dentith, Simon, Epic and Empire in Nineteenth Century Britain, Cambridge University Press, 2006

Dillingham, William B. Melville and His Circle: The Last Years, University of Georgia Press 2008

Dong Weng, Longmen's Stone Buddhas and Cultural Heritage: When Antiquity met Modernity in China, Rowman and Littlefield, 2020

Eck, Diana, India: A Sacred Geography, Harmony Books, New York, 2012

Farrar, Reginald, The Life of Frederic William Farrar, sometime Dean of Canterbury, J. Nisbet, London 1904

Fields, Rick, How The Swans Came to The Lake: A Narrative History of Buddhism in America, Shambala, Boston 1981

Filipiuk, Marion, Michael Lewis and John Robson (eds), The Collected Works of John Stuart Mill, Vol XXXII, University of Toronto Press and Routledge, London, 1991

Franklin, J. Jeffrey, The Lotus and the Lion: Buddhism and the British Empire, Cornell University Press, Ithaca and New York 2008

French, Patrick, Younghusband: The Last Great Imperial Adventurer, HarperCollins, London, 1994

Fitze, Sir Kenneth, Twilight of the Maharajas, John Murray, London, 1956

Gandhi, Mahatma, The Collected Works of Mahatma Gandhi, Publications Division, Ministry of Information and Broadcasting, Government of India, 100 volumes.

Geetha V and S.V. Rajadurai, Towards a Non-Brahmin Millennium: From Iyothee Thass to Periyar, Samya, Kolkata 1998

Goedhals, Anthony, The Neo-Buddhist Writings of Lafcadio Hearn, Brill 2020

Gombrich, Richard F., How Buddhism Began: The Conditioned Genesis of the Early Teachings, Munshiram Manoharal Publishers, New Delhi 1997

Gopal, Sarvepalli, Radhakrishnan: A Biography, Oxford University Press, New Delhi 1989

Gordon Cumming, C.F., Two Happy Years in Ceylon, 2 Vols, William Backwood and Sons, London 1882

Graham, Colin, Ideology of Epic; nation, empire and Victorian epic poetry University of Manchester Press, Manchester 1998

Guha, Ramachandra, Gandhi: the years that changed the world 1914-1948, Penguin New Delhi. 2018

Guruge, Ananda, Return to Righteousness: A Collection of Speeches, Essays and Letters of Anagarika Dharmapala, Government Press Colombo September 1965

Hagerman, Christopher, Britain's Imperial Muse: The Classics, Imperialism and the Indian Empire, 1784-1914, Palgrave Macmillan 2013

Hanayama, Shinsho, Bibliography of Buddhism, Akshaya Prakashan, New Delhi 2005

Harris, Elizabeth, Theravada Buddhism and the British Encounter: Religious missionary and colonial experience in nineteenth century Sri Lanka, Routledge, London 2006

Hatton, Joseph, Journalistic London: Being a Series of Sketches of Famous Pens and Papers of the Day, Sampson Low, Marston, Searle and Rivington, London 1882

Hecker Hellmuth and Bhikku Nanatusita, The Life of Nyanatiloka Thera: The Biography of a Western Buddhist Pioneer, Buddhist Publication Society, Kandy 2008

Heffer, Simon, High Minds: The Victorians and the Birth of Modern Britain, Random House UK, 2013

Heffer, Simon, The Age of Decadence: Britain 1880 to 1914, Random House, UK 2017

Hendrick Burton and David Henderson, Louise Whitfield Carnegie: The Life of Mrs. Andrew Carnegie, Hastings House, New York 1950

Higham, Charles, The Civilisation of Angkor, The University of California Press, Berkeley and Los Angeles, 2001

Holcombe, C. John, Sextus Propertius Elegies, Ocasio Press, Santiago, Chile 2009

Howsam, Leslie, Kegan Paul: A Victorian Imprint, Kegan Paul, London 1998

Howse, Christopher, How We Saw It: 150 Years of the Daily Telegraph: 1855-2005, Equity Press, London 2004

Huber, Toni, The Holy Land Reborn: Pilgrimage and the Tibetan Reinvention of Buddhist India, University of Chicago Press, 2008

Humphreys, Christmas, A Buddhist Students' Manual, The Buddhist Society, London, 1956

Hunt, James D., Gandhi in London, Promilla & Co. 1978

Jackson, Carl T., The Oriental Religions and American Thought: Nineteenth Century Explorations, Greenwood Press Westport, 1981.

Jaffe, Richard, Seeking Sakyamuni: South Asia in the formation of modern Japanese Buddhism, University of Chicago Press, Chicago 2019

Jeal. Tim, Stanley: The Impossible Life of Africa's Greatest Explorer, Faber and Faber, London 2007

Jha, Hetukar, Amaranatha Jha, Makers of Indian Literature Series, Sahitya Akademi, New Delhi 1997

Kearns, Cleo McNelly, T.S. Eliot and Indic Traditions: A Study in Poetry and Belief, Cambridge University Press, 1987

Keer, Dhananjay, Mahatma Jotirao Phooley: Father of the Indian Social Revolution

Kemper, Steven, Rescued From the Nation: Anagarika Dharmapala and the Buddhist World, University of Chicago Press, 2015

Kennedy, Dane: The Highly Civilised Man: Richard Burton and the Victorian World, Harvard University Press, 2005

Kosambi, D.D., Myth and Reality: Studies in the Formation of Indian Culture, Popular Prakashan, Bombay, 1962

Kosambi, Meera, Dharmanand Kosambi: The Essential Writings Permanent Black, Ranikhet 2010

Lahiri, Nayanjot, Marshalling the Past, Permanent Black, Ranikhet 2012

Lahiri, Nayanjot, Ashoka in Ancient India, Permanent Black, Ranikhet, 2015

Lahiri Choudhury, Deep Kanta, Telegraphic Imperialism: Crisis and Panic in the Indian Empire c1830-1920, Palgrave Macmillan London, 2010

Lopez Jr., Donald S. and Peggy McCracken, In Search of the Christian Buddha: How and Asian Sage became a Medieval Saint, W.W. Norton & Co. New York 2014

Lopez Jr, Donald S., From Stone to Flesh: A Short History of the Buddha, University of Chicago Press, Chicago 2013

Lutyens, Mary, Krishnamurti: The Years of Awakening, John Murray, London, 1975

MacLaren, Roy (ed), African Exploits: The Diaries of William Stairs, 1887-1892, McGill Queen's University Press, Montreal 1998

Macy, Joanna Rogers and Eleanor Zelliot, Tradition and Innovation in Contemporary Indian Buddhism, in A.K. Narain (ed), Studies in History of Buddhism, B.R. Publishing Corporation, New Delhi 1980

Marshall, P.J. The British Discovery of Hinduism in the Eighteenth Century, Cambridge University Press,1970

Middleton, Ruth, Alexandra David Neel: Portrait of an Adventurer, Shambala, Boston and London, 2013

Miedama Virgil and Stephanie Spald Miedame, Mussoorie and Landour: Footprints of the Past, Rupa Publications, New Delhi 2014

Miller, Barbara Stoler, The Gitagovinda of Jayadeva, Motilal Banarasidass, New Delhi 1984

Mineka, Francis and Dwight N. Lindley (eds), Collected Works of John Stuart Mill, Vol XVII, The Later Letters of John Stuart Mill, 1849-1873, University of Toronto Press and Routledge & Kegan Paul, London, 1972

Mitchell, John Murray, In Western India: Recollections of My Early Missionary Life. David Douglas, Edinburgh 1899

Mitter, Partha, Art and Nationalism in Colonial India: 1850-1922, Cambridge University Press, 1994

Mitter, Partha, The Triumph of Modernism: Indian Artists and the Avant Garde, 1922-1947, Reakton Books, London 2007

Moon, Vasant (ed), Dr. Babasaheb Ambedkar Writings and Speeches, Volume 11-Supplement, Pali and Other Sources of The Buddha & His Dhamma With An Index, Preface, First Edition by Education Department, Government of Maharashtra, 1992

Mount, Ferdinand, The Tears of the Rajahs: Mutiny, Money and Marriage in India: 1805-1905, Simon & Schuster, London 2015

Mukherjee, Sushil Kumar, The Story of the Calcutta Theatres: 1753-1980, K.P. Bagchi & Company, Calcutta, 1982

Murray, Paul, T.S. Eliot and Mysticism: The Secret History of *Four Quartets*, Macmillan and Company, London 1991

Naidu, Sarojini, The Golden Threshold, William Heinemann, London, 1905

Nanda, B.R., The Nehrus: Motilal and Jawaharlal, The John Day Company, New York 1963 (first American edition)

Nasaw, David, Andrew Carnegie, Penguin, London, 2007

Nehru, Jawaharlal, The Discovery of India, Meridian Books, London, 1946 (first edition)

Nethercot, Arthur, The First Five Lives of Annie Besant, The University of Chicago Press, Chicago, 1960

Newman, James L., Imperial Footprints: Henry Morton Stanley's African Journeys, Brassey's Inc. Washington D.C., 2004

Nikhilananda, Swami (trans), The Gospel of Sri Ramakrishna, Ramakrishna-Vivekananda Center, New York, 1942 (first published)

Normand L. and A. Winch (eds), Encountering Buddhism in Twentieth Century British and American Literature, Bloomsbury Academic, 2013

Oaten, Edward Farley, A Sketch of Anglo-Indian Literature (The Le Bas Prize Essay for 1907), Kegan Paul, Trench, Trubner & Co. 1908

O'Hanlon, Rosalind, Caste, Conflict and Ideology: Mahatma Jotirao Phule and Low-Caste Protest in Nineteenth Century Western India, Cambridge University Press, 1985

Olcott, Henry S., Old Diary Leaves, Third Series 1883-1887, The Theosophical Publishing House, Chennai and Wheaton, 2002a

Olcott, Henry S., Old Diary Leaves, Fourth Series 1887-1892, The Theosophical Publishing House, Chennai and Wheaton, 2002b

Olivelle, Patrick, King, Governance and Law in Ancient India: Kautilya's *Arthasastra*, Oxford University Press, New Delhi 2013

Orr, N. Lee, Dudley Buck: A Popular Victorian Composer of organ and choral music, University of Illinois Press, 2008

Paranjape, Makarand, Sarojini Naidu: Selected Letters, Kali for Women, New Delhi, 1996

Patel, Dinyar, Naoroji: Pioneer of Indian Nationalism, Harvard University Press, Cambridge, 2020

Paulin, Roger, The Life of August Wilhelm Schlegel: Cosmopolitan of Art and Poetry, OpenBook Publishers, London 2016

Prothero, Steven, The White Buddhist: The Asian Odyssey of Henry Steel Olcott, Indian University Press, Bloomington 2011

Raghavan, Srinath (ed), Imperialists, Nationalists, Democrats: The Collected Essays of Sarvepalli Gopal, Permanent Black, Ranikhet 2013

Raman, Sir C.V., Books That Have Influenced Me, G.A. Natesan & Co, Madras, 1947

Rao, Velcheru Narayana, Text and Tradition in South India, Permanent Black, Ranikhet 2016

Rathore, Akshay Singh, Ambedkar's Preamble: A Secret History of the Constitution of India, Vintage Books, New York, 2020

Rose, Andrew, The Prince, the Princess and the Perfect Murder, Hodder and Stroughton, London 2013

Ray, Himanshu Prabha, The Return of the Buddha: Ancient Symbols for a New Nation, Routledge 2014

Rosen, Jerome, The Last Titan: A Life of Theodore Dreiser, University of California Press, 2005

Sachau, Dr. Edward C., Alberuni's India, Rupa & Co. New Delhi 2002

Sala, George Augustus, Things that I have Seen and People I have Known, Cassell and Company, London, 1891

Saliba, George, Islamic Science and the Making of the European Renaissance, MIT Press, Cambridge USA, 2007

Schueller, H.J., The German Verse Epic in the Nineteenth and Twentieth Centuries, Martinus Nijhoff, The Hague, 1967

Sedlar, Jean W., India and the Greek World: A Study in the Transmission of Culture, Rowman and Littlefield, Totowa, New Jersey, USA, 1980

Singh, Upinder, The Discovery of Ancient India: Early Archaeologists and the Beginnings of Archaeology, Permanent Black, Ranikhet 2004

Singh, Dr. Karan. Sri Aurobindo: The Prophet of Indian Nationalism, Bharatiya Vidya Bhavan 1963

Sivaramamurti, C., An Album of Indian Sculpture, National Book Trust, New Delhi, 1975

Siveshwarkar, Leela, Chaurapanchasika: A Sanskrit Love Lyric, National Museum, New Delhi 1967

Slate, Nico, Gandhi's search for the Perfect Diet, Orient BlackSwan, Hyderabad, 2019

Smith, Catherine Parsons, Making Music in Los Angeles: Transforming the Popular, University of California Press, 2007

Sternbach, Ludwik, The Hitopadesa and its Sources, American Oriental Series, Vol 44, American Oriental Society, 1960

Sultaan, Abida, Memoirs of A Rebel Princess, Oxford University Press, Karachi, 2004

Sweetman, Will, Mapping Hinduism: "Hinduism and the study of Indian religions, 1600-1786, Verlag Franckesche Stiftungen, Halle, 2003

Tartakov, Gary Michael, The Durga Temple at Aihole: A Historiographical Study, Oxford University Press, New Delhi, 1997

Thapar, Romila, Early India: From the Origins to AD 1300, Penguin Books, London, 2002

Thapar, Romila, The Past Before Us: Historical Traditions of Early North India, Permanent Black, Ranikhet, 2013

Torma, Minna, Enchanted by Lohans: Osvald Siren's Journey into Chinese Art, Hong Kong University Press, 2013

Trevithick, Alan, The Revival of Buddhist Pilgrimage at Bodh Gaya 1811-1949, Motilal Banarasidass, New Delhi 2006

Tucker, Herbert, Epic: Britain's Heroic Muse: 1790-1910, Oxford University Press 2008

Turner, Alicia, Lawrence Cox and Brian Bocking, The Irish Buddhist: The Forgotten Monk Who Faced Down the British Empire, Oxford University Press, New York 2020

Turner, Grace, Adventures and Testimonies, Woodfield Publishing, London 2020

Tweed, Thomas A. The American Encounter with Buddhism 1844-1912: Victorian Culture and the Limits of Dissent, University of North Carolina Press, Durham, 2000 (first published 1992)

Waller, David, The Magnificent Mrs.Tennant: The Adventurous Life of Gertrude Tennant, Victorian Grande Dame, Yale University Press, 2009

Walsh, Declan, The Nine Lives of Pakistan, Bloomsbury Publishing, London 2020

Whitlark, James, Illuminated Fantasy: From Blake's Visions to Recent Graphic Fiction, Farleigh Dickinson University Press, 1988

Wickremeratne, Ananda, The Genesis of an Orientalist: Thomas Rhys Davids and Buddhism in Sri Lanka, Motilal Banarasidass, New Delhi 1984

Wilson, A.N., God's Funeral, W.W. Norton & Company New York, 1999

Wolpert, Stanley, Tilak and Gokhale: Revolution and Reform in the Making of Modern India Oxford University Press, New Delhi 1990 (first published 1962)

Wright, Brooks, Interpreter of Buddhism to the West: Sir Edwin Arnold, Bookman Associates, New York 1957

Sir Edwin Arnold's Major Works

India-related

1. Education in India (1860)
2. The Book of Good Counsels (1861)
3. The Marquis of Dalhousie's Administration of British India (2 vols; 1862 and 1865)
4. The Indian Song of Songs with other Oriental Poems (1875)
5. The Light of Asia (1879)
6. Indian Poetry (1881)
7. Indian Idylls (1883)
8. The Song Celestial (1885)
9. The Secret of Death (1885)
10. India Revisited (1886)
11. Lotus and Jewel (1887)
12. The Chaurapanchasika: An Indian Love Lament (1896)
13. The Queen's Justice (1899)

Islam-related

1. Pearls of the Faith (1883)

Christianity-related

1. The Light of the World (1891)

Africa-related

1. The Voyages of Ithobal (1901)

Egypt-related

1. Palms and Temples (1882)
2. Potiphar's Wife and Other Poems (1892)

Japan-related

1. Adzuma, or The Japanese Wife (1893)
2. Seas and Lands (1890)
3. Japonica (1891)

Turkey-related

1. A Simple Transliteral Grammar of the Turkish Language (1877)

Persia-related

1. With Sa'di in the Garden (1888)
2. The Gulistan (1999)

Collection of *Daily Telegraph* and other Articles

1. Wandering Words (1894)
2. East and West (1896)

Others

1. The Feast of Belshazzar (1852)
2. Poems: Narrative and Lyrical (1853)
3. Griselda and Other Poems (1856)
4. The Poets of Greece (1869)
5. Death—And Afterwards (1887)
6. In My Lady's Praise (1889)
7. The Tenth Muse and Other Poems (1895) [includes translations of Hafiz]
8. Poems: National and Non-Oriental (1896)
9. Victoria, Queen and Empress (1896)

Index

note: Italicized page locaters indicate images.